t35.
Eoh

D1713455

THE CHARITABLE IMPERATIVE

THE WELLCOME INSTITUTE SERIES IN THE HISTORY OF MEDICINE
Edited by W. F. Bynum and Roy Porter, The Wellcome Institute

Medical Fringe and Medical Orthodoxy, 1750–1850
Edited by W. F. Bynum and Roy Porter

Florence Nightingale and the Nursing Legacy
Monica Baly

Social Hygiene in Twentieth-Century Britain
Greta Jones

Problems and Methods in the History of Medicine
Edited by Roy Porter and Andrew Wear

Vivisection in Historical Perspective
Edited by Nicolaas Rupke

Abortion in England
Barbara Brookes

Birth Control in Germany, 1871–1933
James Woycke

The Hospital in History
Edited by Roy Porter and Lindsay Granshaw

THE CHARITABLE IMPERATIVE

HOSPITALS AND NURSING IN ANCIEN REGIME AND REVOLUTIONARY FRANCE

Colin Jones

Routledge
London and New York

362.11
J76c

First published in 1989
by Routledge
11 New Fetter Lane, London EC4P 4EE

Simultaneously published in the USA and Canada
by Routledge
a division of Routledge, Chapman and Hall, Inc.
29 West 35th Street, New York, NY 10001

© 1989 Colin Jones

Word processed and laserprinted by Laserscript
Printed in Great Britain by Billing & Sons Ltd, Worcester

All rights reserved. No part of this book may be reprinted or reproduced or utilized in any form or by any electronic, mechanical, or other means, now known or hereafter invented, including photocopying and recording, or in any information storage or retrieval system, without permission in writing from the publishers.

British Library Cataloguing in Publication Data
Jones, Colin, *1947–*
The charitable imperative: hospitals and nursing in ancien régime and revolutionary France. – (Wellcome series in the history of medicine)
1. France medical services 1700 – 1900
I. Title II. Series
362.1'0944

Library of Congress Cataloging-in-Publication Data
Jones, Colin, *1947–*
The charitable imperative: hospitals and nursing in ancien régime and revolutionary France/Colin Jones.
p. cm. – (The Wellcome Institute series in the history of medicine)
Includes bibliographies and index.
1. Hospitals–France–History. 2. Nursing– France–History. 3. Asylums–France–History. 4. Charities–France–History.
I. Title. II. Series.
[DNLM: 1. Charities–history–France. 2. Health Services–history–France. 3. Hospitals–history–France. 4. Medical Indigency – history – France. 5. Nursing Services–history–France.
WX 11GF7 J7c]
RA989.F7J66 1989
362.1'1'094409–dc20
DNLM/DLC
for Library of Congress

ISBN 0–415–02133–2

Contents

UNIVERSITY LIBRARIES
CARNEGIE-MELLON UNIVERSITY
PITTSBURGH, PENNSYLVANIA 15213

List of Maps, Figures, and Tables

Maps

Figures

Tables

Acknowledgements

A number of the essays in this volume appeared in similar form as articles in learned journals, conference proceedings, and so on. I have revised and refashioned all of them and updated references. My thanks are none the less due to the publishers and editors involved in these earlier efforts:

- to Dr Christopher Smith, editor of *Seventeenth-Century French Studies*, as regards 'Hospitals in seventeenth-century France', which appeared in vol. vii, 1985;
- to the editors, *French Historical Studies*, as regards 'The social functions of the hospital in eighteenth-century France: the case of the Hôtel-Dieu of Nîmes', which appeared in volume xiii, 1983;
- to Father Luigi Mezzadri and the editors of *Annali della Missione*, for the 1984 volume (xci) devoted to the *VII Convegno di animazione vincenziana*, which included my article, 'Le Figlie della Carità nell'Hôtel-Dieu Saint-Eloi di Montpellier nei secoli diciasettesimo e diciottesimo'; and Father Mezzadri as regards 'The Filles de la Charité in hospitals, 1633–c. 1838' which appeared in *Vincent de Paul, Actes du colloque international d'études vincentiennes (Paris 1981)*, Rome 1983;
- to Prof. William Speck, editor of *History*, as regards 'The welfare of the French foot-soldier', which appeared in vol. lxv, 1980;
- to Associated Book Publishers (UK) Ltd and the editorial collective of *History Workshop. A Journal of Socialist and Feminist Historians*, as regards 'Prostitution and the ruling class in eighteenth-century Montpellier', which appeared in issue 6, 1978;
- to the editors, *Medical History*, as regards 'The treatment of

the insane in eighteenth- and early nineteenth-century Montpellier: contribution to the prehistory of the lunatic asylum in provincial France', which appeared in volume xxiv, 1980.

Michael Sonenscher co-authored the *French Historical Studies* article, and I gratefully acknowledge here his permission for me to use that article in this context, and also the help he has given me on many of the problems with which I have tried to get to grips in the present volume.

Thanks for help and suggestions at some stage along the way are also due to Jonathan Barry, Sandra Cavallo, Richard Cobb, Michael Duffy, Christopher Holdsworth, Olwen Hufton, Brian Kirby, Dr Louis Dulieu, Martyn Lyons, John MacManners, Father Luigi Mezzadri, Hazel Mills, Malyn Newitt, David Parrott, Frank Tallett, Derek Watts, Dora Weiner, Stuart Woolf, and the late John Wylie. Many of the papers have been presented as seminar papers in a wide variety of university contexts in Britain and the United States of America, and I thank those who attended these for help in thinking things through. I benefited enormously from a period in 1986 as Visiting Fellow at the Shelby Cullom Davis Center for Historical Studies, Princeton University. An earlier version of Chapter 3 was given there as a seminar. The comments on the seminar and invigorating conversations at other times with, in particular, Peter Brown, Natalie Davis, and Ellen Ross have helped to reshape my thinking about many of the topics here under consideration. I owe a particular debt of gratitude to Lawrence Stone, Director of the Davis Center, for his support and suggestions in regard to my work, and also for suggesting that I should write the present volume. My wife Nicole had the idea at about the same time. I thank them both, and hope they like the end-product.

Colin Jones

Abbreviations

A.D.	Archives départementales
A.D.G.	Archives départementales du Gard
A.D.H.	Archives départementales de l'Hérault
A.M.M.	Archives municipales de Montpellier
A.N.	Archives Nationales
Ann.E.S.C.	*Annales. Economies. Sociétés. Civilisations*
B.N.	Bibliothèque Nationale
BP	Bon Pasteur
I.S.	*Inventaire sommaire*
D.H.G.E.	*Dictionnaire d'histoire et de géographie historiques*
HD I	Hôtel-Dieu Saint-Eloi de Montpellier (archives antérieures à 1790)
HD II	Hôtel-Dieu Saint-Eloi de Montpellier (archives postérieures à 1790)
HG I	Hôpital Général de Montpellier (archives antérieures à 1790)
HG II	Hôpital Général de Montpellier (archives postérieures à 1790)
L	*Letters of Saint Louise de Marillac* (Emmitsburg, Maryland, 1972)
R.H.M.C.	*Revue d'histoire moderne et contemporaine*
VdeP	P. Coste (ed.), *Saint Vincent de Paul. Correspondance, Entretiens, Documents* (14 vols, 1920–5)

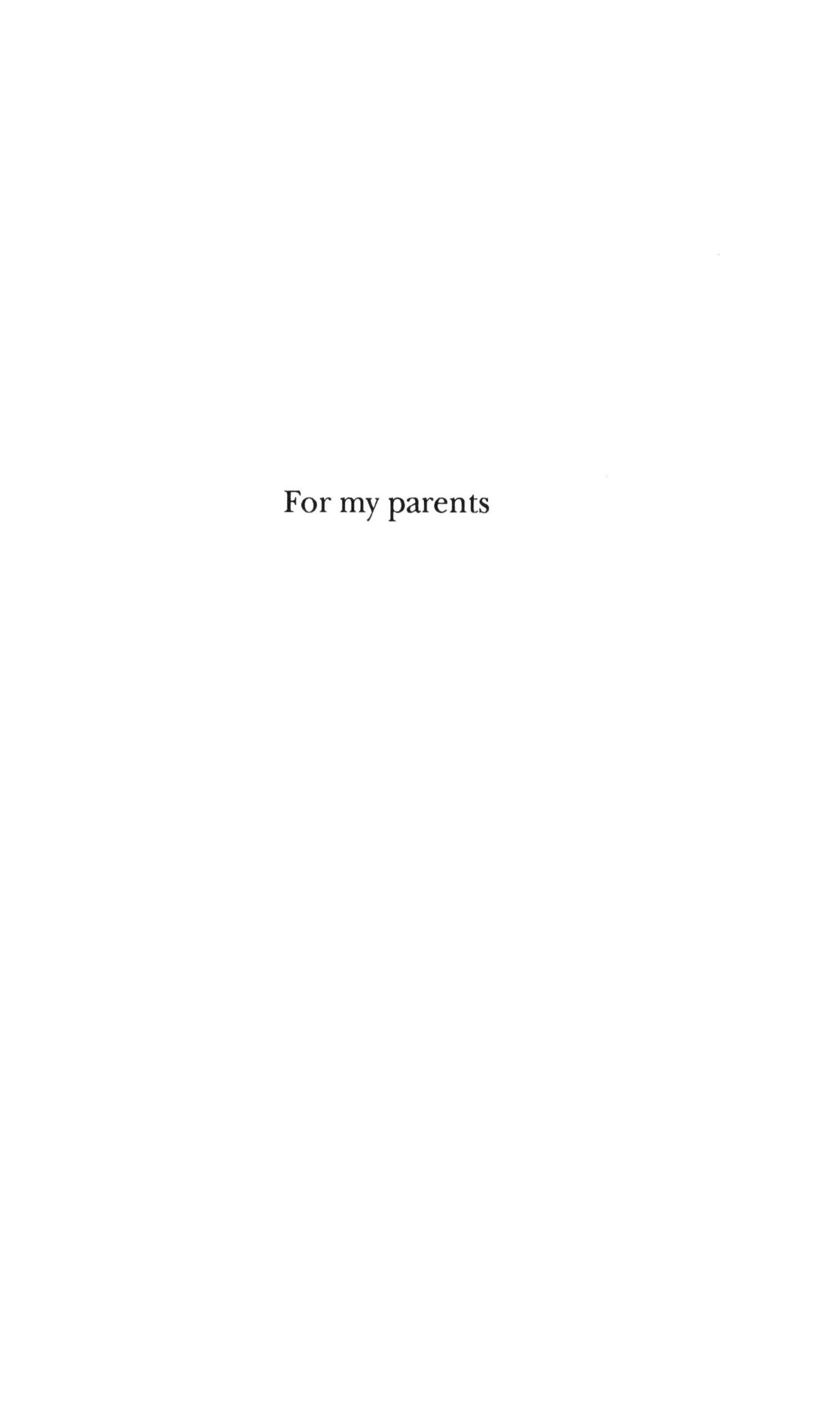

For my parents

Introduction: The Charitable Imperative

I

Since the development of welfare states over the last century, it has been common to view charity towards the poor and needy – voluntaristic, individually motivated, compassionate, freely given – as essentially opposed or contradictory to the principle of compulsion. The two concepts, however, had an associative rather than an antonymous relationship for most of the medieval and early modern period. The concept and the practices of charity were enmeshed within a matrix of moral obligation, religious dutifulness, and social exigency and expectation. Though the phrase sounds oxymoronic to twentieth-century ears, the idea of a 'charitable imperative' lay at the heart of medieval and early modern poor relief. Medieval devotional literature, for example, habitually exalted the moral obligation implicit in the virtue of giving to the poor and needy, viewing charity as consubstantial with God's love, and urged it unceasingly on the faithful. Medieval charity unfolded moreover within a wide circle of social and religious relationships. A single testament, for example, might include benefactions for the parish poor, paupers who attended the funeral, impoverished relatives of the deceased, churches and chapels, monastic houses, colleges, confraternities, and hospitals of all descriptions.[1] In that powerful metaphorical and affective figure deriving from Saint Matthew and so deeply embedded in medieval piety, the recipients of this charity were held to represent Christ himself, and indeed the whole movement of charitable giving was predicated upon the equation between Christ and the pauper.[2]

Although the category of 'Christ's poor', the *pauperes Christi,* was amorphous and wide-encompassing in the minds of medieval charitable donors, the hospital was a particularly privileged institutional target of testamentary generosity. Following a fertile period of foundations from about 1150 to 1300, medieval France – as indeed the whole of western Europe – had been covered with a dense network of hospitals.[3] The latter were primarily social rather than medical institutions. Although the medical component of hospital care has sometimes been underplayed by historians, it nevertheless remains true that the commitment of medieval hospitals – and their early modern successors – was to the suffering poor rather than the classifiably sick. They contained a variety of social types, whose common denominator was poverty and need, not disease: abandoned children, for example, the aged and infirm, the insane, pilgrims, as well as the sick. Even though some institutions were more specifically for the sick, they were aimed at *pauvres malades* (paupers who were sick) rather than to *malades pauvres* (sick individuals who, incidentally, were poor). The wealthy, when ill, were cared for in their homes, and would enter the portals of the hospital only as an exercise in asceticism or pious self-abasement.

Hospitals throughout Europe almost without exception were adversely affected by the social, economic, and political disruptions of the later Middle Ages, while the Reformation had the effect of breaking down institutional stability, and stimulating new attitudes towards the treatment of the poor. Popular rebellions in the later Middle Ages which cast the poor as 'dangerous classes' also somewhat tarnished the halo of 'holy poverty' and prepared the way for a new approach.[4] From Augsburg to Zurich, by way of London, Paris, Nuremberg, Ypres, Madrid, Toledo, Venice, and many places besides, major schemes for the reorganization and rationalization of the tottering structures of existing poor relief in the urban context were introduced from the 1520s onwards. Contrary to a hoary historiographical myth which contrasts the puritanical views of Protestants with the more indulgent, works-orientated attitudes of Catholics, it now seems clear that these new approaches to poor relief spanned the confessional divide.[5] The so-called Ypres programme, for example, expounded by the Catholic humanist J.L. Vives, and elaborated in his much republished, much translated work *De Subventione pauperum* (1526), was widely imitated in Catholic and in Protestant states. It exemplified a more rationalized and laicized form of assistance to the poor: city fathers now oversaw or replaced the clerics who had often dominated the older charitable institutions; hospitals were integrated into a centralized municipal system of relief; and those institutions adjudged socially useless were liable to be destroyed outright or else merged into more viable institutions. Moreover, though the movement of reform instituted a new compassion towards the deserving poor, for whom work-schemes and systematized home relief were now made available, the undeserving poor – most notably able-bodied beggars and vagrants who shunned work – were given short shrift. Indeed the whole movement of reform may broadly be characterized as an overarching movement of social discipline: setting the poor to work, instituting new levels of labour surveillance and control, establishing protocols for the assessment, education, and moralization of the poor, and greater severity of punishment to those judged undeserving.

Vives's text *De Subventione pauperum* was one of the most crucial texts in European attitudes towards poverty in the early modern period.[6] Its emphasis on discrimination in the distribution of relief, on the prohibition of manual almsgiving, on the condemnation of work-shyness, on the inculcation of discipline and on the imperative need to canalize charitable giving towards socially approved target groups were to remain enduring and perennial themes within the approach to poverty within all major European states well into the nineteenth century. Clearly these precepts were never universally observed. The prohibition of begging, for example, predicated a renunciation by the rest of society of manual almsgiving to the poor: yet everything that we can glean about the actual volume of charitable giving in Ancien Régime France suggests that this kind of charity was always predominant.[7] None the less, poverty had been to a large extent desacralized and throughout western Europe governments were henceforth inextricably involved in poor relief issues if only because the poor seemed to pose a problem of public order.

If the Ypres programme set much of the agenda for the institutionalized treatment of the poor for the remaining two centuries, the way in which it was interpreted and implemented depended much on local circumstance. The emergence of

Protestantism, for example, heightened regional diversity in the approach to poor relief: in England the Dissolution of the Monasteries in the 1530s and 1540s which followed on from Henry VIII's break from Rome effectively obliterated the network of English hospitals, which had been numbered in hundreds in the Middle Ages. The lack of political centralization on the Italian peninsula meant that most of its fertile experiments in this domain remained at the level of the city-state.[8] In France, in contrast, the precocious centralization of political authority allowed poor relief schemes to be implemented on a far larger canvas than anywhere else in Europe. Government attempts to encourage the municipalization of poor relief in the sixteenth and early seventeenth century were accompanied by major state involvement, particularly through the King's personal chaplain, the Grand Aumônier du Roi, in the review of hospital property and its redisposal within reformed structures of poor relief.[9]

In the event, however, the central government's activities in the seventeenth and eighteenth century tended to support the existence of diversity rather than to push as far down the road of centralized poor relief as once had seemed likely in the sixteenth century. For all the trappings and rhetoric of absolute monarchy, and the occasional ringing declaration of intent,[10] the French state during the Ancien Régime never achieved the kind of uniformity and community obligation in the relief of poverty that the English state achieved through the generalization of the parish-based rating system from the sixteenth century onwards. In this we can detect one of the principal socio-political strategies of the absolutist government in France, which tended to support diversity and bolster existing privilege, balancing its own centralizing instincts with the conservation of local and corporative liberties.[11]

Respect for autonomy and, in particular, for the sphere of activity of the Catholic church, subverted plans for a system of poor relief enforced uniformly and nationwide. French cities in the sixteenth century had flirted with a rating system levied on property-owners.[12] The late sixteenth and early seventeenth centuries, however, were to see voluntary charity triumph over community obligation, a triumph very much due to the resurgent and revitalized church. The alms and bequests of the faithful – and particularly testamentary dispositions – had been the first instance and the institutional lubrication of all medieval establishments. Under the social impact of the Counter Reformation in the seventeenth century, the plentifulness of charitable giving provided an argument – perhaps an alibi – for the continuing avoidance of the principle of obligation. The charitable imperative circumvented the need for local measures of compulsion. In addition, the charitably donated administrative services, freely given to hospitals by clerics and godly laymen (many of them members of the Robe nobility), had the effect of reducing municipal involvement in hospital management which was increasingly in the hands of local notables. Hospitals thus found their autonomy newly respected. Their central role in the relief of poverty in France was reaffirmed; existing hospitals were refurbished; new creations proliferated, notably the nationwide network of Hôpitaux Généraux established in the last decades of the seventeenth century to confine a wide variety of paupers and social deviants; and the central government undertook a massive movement of hospital reorganization, so as to make the existing hospitals more financially viable and more effective.

Hospitals remained the keystone of social policy towards the poor down to the nineteenth century. Their enduring orientation around charity was, however, something of an Achilles' heel. Dependence on religiously inspired charity made them highly vulnerable to the growth of religious indifference and the escalation of institutional running costs which occurred in the eighteenth century.[13] The type of poor relief which they represented came under increasing attack from Enlightenment thinkers. Critics attacked their charitable status as a cause of their ineffectiveness, pointing out that there were too many hospitals in areas where there was wealth, while many disinherited areas were totally bereft of charitable provision; they accused the Hôpitaux Généraux in particular of keeping would-be workers locked up away from the labour market; and they argued that their record of hygiene was such that, far from combatting disease and death, they actually engendered them. These arguments cut ice with central government. In the 1760s, as many of France's largest hospitals came close to bankruptcy, the government attempted to reformulate the nation's poor laws in ways which reduced the central role of hospitals. Nothing came of this, although the establishment in 1767 of state-run *dépôts de mendicité* which interned beggars and vagrants relieved pressure of numbers on the Hôpitaux Généraux.[14] More serious attempts to rationalize a system of relief which was on the point of disintegration were made during the Revolution. Unfortunately these attempts only caused the total collapse of the hospital system.[15] State-based pensions schemes which were supposed to take over the role of the hospitals crashed in the financial débâcle of the 1790s; private charity seemed to dry up altogether; and hospitals found their incomes shrinking as the number of the needy coming to their doors increased. Perhaps one-third of France's hospitals perished in this decade. From the Directory, however, the central government switched course towards an acceptance of the importance of large hospital institutions in the nation's system of relief, now buttressed by state-sponsored though charitably funded home relief agencies, the *bureaux de bienfaisance.*

The two-pronged attack on charity and hospitals, gestated in the Enlightenment and implemented in the Revolutionary decade, was thus a failure. The refurbished, slimmed-down hospital network remained the centre-piece, albeit a dilapidated one, of the nation's poor laws in the post-Revolutionary period. The Napoleonic regime and its successors also stimulated private charitable giving, seeing the latter as an important adjunct to the assistance which central and local government now accorded relief institutions.

If the long-lived vitality of the charitable impulse in French hospital financing was a distinctive feature of France's system of poor relief, so too was the importance of the caring services provided by religious communities of sisters of charity. Harassed and persecuted in the Revolutionary decade, they, like hospitals and charitable giving, were rehabilitated under Napoleon. An offshoot of post-Tridentine commitment to religious life in the world, and of the revitalized Catholic church's widened scope for female social mission, these sisters too may be portrayed as responding to a moral imperative: but whereas testamentary donors and alms-givers gave of their wealth, the sisters gave themselves. And with telling effect, moreover. Created and diffused throughout France from the seventeenth century onwards, they played a key role in poor relief. Partly perhaps because of the enormous influence on Catholic social reform of Vincent de Paul, the co-founder of the

Daughters of Charity, the most important community of nursing sisters, they achieved before 1789 a significance achieved nowhere else in Europe. Indeed, most countries had to await the age of Florence Nightingale before they enjoyed the managerial competence and levels of care of women of this commitment, vocation, and stamp of character.[16] The sisters also, as we shall see, had a role as the proponents of medical care, which was an important adjunct to (and sometimes substitute for) medical services offered within hospitals.

The hospital mould through which poor relief was mediated, the significance of nursing sisters in all charitable institutions, and the workings at all levels of a kind of charitable imperative were thus particularly striking features of French society's approach to poor relief, in the Ancien Régime period and even beyond. The essays which follow explore a number of themes within the overlapping fields of charity and social obligation. They do not pretend to comprehensive treatment of a subject in which – despite an enormous amount of recent work by historians – there still remains a great deal to be done. Nor do they attempt to chart the contours of poverty in the world outside hospital walls over the same period, an area of research which has been brilliantly illuminated by the work of Olwen Hufton, Jean-Pierre Gutton, Stuart Woolf, Alan Forrest, and many others. Rather than depict the raw realities of the lives of the poor, what I have tried to do here is to focus on the social construction of poverty, by analysing some of the diverse institutional settings in which rich interfaced with poor, through the medium of charity.

II

As Chapter 1 demonstrates, the term 'charity' in the seventeenth century encompassed both compassion and repression. Just as the charitable donor acted out of moral compunction, so the recipient of charity might have to be forced to play out the role of grateful pauper. The reform and reorganization of hospitals in the seventeenth century culminated in the creation, under the supervision of central government and stimulated by lay confraternities of Catholic militants, of new catch-all institutions, the Hôpitaux Généraux. These were to act as refuges for the helpless poor – homeless old people, disabled paupers, orphans, and foundlings – as well as those paupers adjudged dangerous or in need of correction into better ways, spiritual orthodoxy, or social deference. The *grand renfermement des pauvres* was thus true to the spirit of Vives in being as much an exercise in social discipline as in public assistance, though a far greater role was now accorded the institutional confinement of the poor. The scale of this movement should not be underestimated. Although we lack aggregate data for the Ancien Régime, an inquiry in 1791 undertaken by the Public Assistance Committee of the Legislative Assembly suggests that French hospitals, more than 2,000 in number, contained in excess of 120,000 individuals, over half of whom were located within Hôpitaux Généraux.[17] To these should be added the many thousands of abandoned children under the care of the Hôpitaux and farmed out to wet-nurses in rural areas.

The scale of this enterprise in social reclusion rank France as having the largest hospital population of any European state under the Ancien Régime: England, in contrast, could muster only 3,000 hospital inmates in 1800.[18] Whether even this, however, justifies the title *grand renfermement* is very much a moot point. France's population grew from 20 million to 28 million over the eighteenth century, and if we follow Olwen Hufton's estimation that between one-fifth and one-third of France's population could normally be classed as indigent,[19] then it is abundantly clear that the hospital population represents only a tiny proportion of the poor and needy in society as a whole.

Nor should we overestimate the judicial and repressive dimensions of the institutions, which have won them such a bad name among recent historians following the writings of Michel Foucault. The internal regime of these institutions was certainly a dour and punitive mix of enforced piety and labour. However, financial stringency, lack of local initiative, institutional priorities, and the structure of local demand for assistance combined to make most Hôpitaux Généraux devote less of their energies to repression than to relief. Apart from a number of brief state-sponsored anti-vagrancy campaigns scattered sporadically over the century – in 1700–1, 1720, 1724–30, 1748–50, and 1764–6 – most eighteenth-century Hôpitaux Généraux spent most of their time and money on the very young and the very old. The clientele of the Hôpitaux

Généraux in the Ancien Régime, while rarely curably sick, tended overwhelmingly to be ailing rather than able-bodied. In addition, Hôpitaux Généraux continued to make a major contribution to the poor in the form of bread doles and other forms of home relief. The Hôpital Général at Montpellier, for example, contained between 500 and 650 individuals in the 1740s; yet at the same time it was giving bread to 4,500 individuals in the town and maintaining hundreds of abandoned children with wet-nurses in the Cévennes. At Grenoble, to take another well-documented example, the hospital in the 1770s contained between 350 and 400 inmates and provided home relief for 3,500 individuals.[20]

Whatever their motivation and their original sources of inspiration, Hôpitaux Généraux thus made a considerable contribution to the needs of the local poor. Recent research is suggesting that far from being mere warehouses for the reclusion of social marginals as they have often been represented, the institutions constituted throughout the Ancien Régime a valued resource for local paupers, in particular at times of difficulty in the family life-cycle.[21] Rather than representing monolithic instruments of social control, their role could encompass meeting a demand for assistance 'from below'. The fact that most Hôpitaux Généraux provided aid for widows, one-parent households, the aged, and children under 15 does not signal that these groups were socially marginalized but rather that such groups had been engendered at vulnerable moments in the life-cycle of any poor or poorish family. Though the poor always preferred home relief to hospital confinement, and shuddered at the thought of institutionalization, they could nevertheless adapt their local Hôpital Général within a family subsistence strategy. In this perspective, the hospital represented a surrogate family for individuals whose biological family could not support them. Indeed, administrators seem to have been aware of this fact, which came out in their way of looking at their task. It was commonplace, for example, for them to refer to the whole hospital community – inmates, nurses, orderlies – as a 'family', and their public pronouncements always played up their roles as 'fathers of the poor'. By wielding the patronage and protection a hospital afforded, local notables could build up and cement a clientele among the local resident poor, and not simply among urban drop-outs. An Hôpital Général could thus be an integrative force within local society rather than a divisive or marginalizing institution.

These multi-faceted Hôpitaux Généraux thus geared their services around the requirements of need rather than of sickness. The same was true of the myriads of small hospitals which lay scattered throughout France. Even despite the very large-scale hospital reorganization and rationalization which occurred in the late seventeenth century as part of the government's campaign to find resources for its new Hôpitaux Généraux, the towns and villages of France still contained in excess of 2,000 hospitals in the eighteenth century. The 'snapshot' revealed by the 1791 hospital inquiry suggests that there were more than 1,500 small hospitals – often containing fewer than 10 beds – which had a bed capacity of some 40,000 to 50,000. As far as it is possible to judge, these institutions admitted individuals, from the local community in particular, with every variety of distress, sickness included.

In the early seventeenth century it would appear that much the same applied for the 400-odd institutions which were called Hôtels-Dieu and which were in theory destined for 'the sick poor' (*les pauvres malades*). In this period of disastrous subsistence crises and economic disruption, filling the stomachs of the poor was the major priority, and hospitals contained a good admixture of those with no curable illness or ailment.[22] Though the creation from the 1650s onwards of the big Hôpitaux Généraux helped to sift out from the inmate population of the Hôtels-Dieu many varieties of the more able-bodied inmates, the orientation around need rather than sickness may well have remained intact throughout the Ancien Régime, if the case of the Hôtel-Dieu at Nîmes (Chapter 2) is at all typical. Analysis of admissions to the latter hospital over the eighteenth century reveals the extent to which provincial Hôtels-Dieu – whose inmate population in 1792 was in excess of 20,000 – persisted in serving social rather than medical requirements. The local poor, who preferred to cluster around the local Hôpital Général, were not the principal clients of the institution; rather, the Hôtel-Dieu served as a staging post for itinerant and migrant workers, providing them with a roof over their head and solid food to buck them up and tide them over. One may legitimately wonder whether all of the individuals admitted to such institutions were genuinely ill. It was the opinion of hospital physician Jacques Razoux at Nîmes that many were not clinically sick but rather 'resting', and it may be that a present-day clinician would concur. We would, however, need to know more about the cases in question, and also to have a better understanding of cultural definitions of illness among the poor, to be able to pronounce with any sureness.

What is certain about provincial Hôtels-Dieu in the eighteenth century, however, is that – whether 'cured' or simply 'rested' – most individuals who entered, left alive. This point needs some iteration in that recent historiography has painted a kind of Black Legend of the Pre-Clinical Hospital in early modern France. Echoing the ideas of the *philosophes* and of medical reformers like Razoux and Tenon, historians as diverse as Jean Meuvret and Michel Foucault have portrayed the hospital as a death-trap. As the evidence expounded in Chapter 2 makes abundantly clear, it simply was not. With one or two appalling exceptions, not least the Paris Hôtel-Dieu, whose unhygienic state set the agenda for much public discussion of the role of hospitals in the Late Enlightenment, only about one in nine or ten of those admitted to an Hôtel-Dieu left it feet first. The population of these hospitals can be better characterized as being one of mobility and marginality rather than mortality and moribundity.

If the death-rate in other types of hospitals was higher, this was to a large extent because of the nature of their intake. Village hospitals and city Hôpitaux Généraux admitted a high proportion of biologically fragile individuals – abandoned children, whose life chances were small, and the aged, many of whom entered an Hôpital precisely to end their days there. It was not unknown for children admitted to an Hôpital to live to a ripe old age within its walls, while relatively few of the aged succumbed with undue celerity. Although clearly it would be silly to whitewash the Black Legend, or to underestimate the peril to life of prolonged stays within hospital walls, closer examination of the daily realities of hospital life rather than the rhetoric of hospital reformers shows a far less sombre reality than historians have been disposed to allow.

Although exact measurement is impossible, because of the changing nature of hospital populations, lack of reliable records and the transformation in the demographic regime, it seems probable that the hygienic state of hospitals improved considerably over the period from the early seventeenth to the early nineteenth century. Another widespread historiographical myth – that any such improvements were due to an alleged 'medicalization' of the hospital at the very end of the eighteenth century and the beginning of the nineteenth century, coincident with the 'birth of the clinic' – also needs to be knocked on the head.[23] Certainly medical men achieved a higher profile within hospitals at this time. Yet seen in the *longue durée* – a most important perspective to adopt when considering French hospitals – this was only the intensification of a process which had been going on for centuries.[24] To generalize outrageously from highly deficient materials, it does seem probable that only big hospitals in the bigger towns enjoyed the presence of medical men much before 1450 or 1500. The Paris Hôtel-Dieu – an institution founded in the seventh century – had to wait more than half a millenium for the first medical practitioner to be mentioned in its archives – physicians being called in from the early fourteenth century. The great surgeon Guy de Chauliac frequented the Lyon Hôtel-Dieu at about the same time; the Marseille hospital made a contract with local physicians in 1338; and medical men appear in the hospitals of Nantes, Narbonne, Angers, Chartres, and La Rochelle towards the middle and end of that century.[25] Most of these early figures were surgeons or barber-surgeons, however, and it is only really in the sixteenth century, often as part of the rationalization and reorganization of poor relief at municipal level, that we find all kinds of medical practitioners – physicians, surgeons, apothecaries, and quacks – establishing a presence in the major hospitals, a presence which would develop in intensity over the succeeding centuries.

In its simplest stages, the medical presence was consultative and *ad hoc*, practitioners being called in when and if an illness developed beyond the capabilities of hospital staff. A surgeon was called into the hospital at Mende in 1635, to take an example, 'to cut the big toes from the feet of an inmate because of the gangrene which had taken hold of him'; a wandering healer was called into the Grenoble hospital in 1648 to treat the children within it for an epidemic of *la rasche*; the Paris Hôtel-Dieu employed a dynasty of empirics up to the middle of the seventeenth century whenever it wanted someone to be cut for 'the stone'.[26] Sometimes a hospital whose administrators felt that they could not offer appropriate medical services would feel it incumbent upon them to do what they could to get a sick pauper aid: the hospital at Mende in 1602, to take an example, paid for a boy bitten by a mad dog to be transported to Montpellier to receive treatment.[27] Such was Montpellier's medical renown, moreover, that a great many small hospitals seem to have devoted much of their income in the Ancien Régime in simply ferrying sick paupers towards the city.

Consultations by physicians, who could often pretend to the status of local notable, often had something of the charitable gesture about them, and seemed to spring less from an eager desire for practical involvement than from a sense of moral dutifulness. Increasingly, however, they became monetary transactions similar to payments for the services of the more lowly surgeons and apothecaries. It became the custom for stated practitioners to be attached to a hospital, and to be paid for their availability. Payment might come from the coffers of the hospital itself, or it might (especially in the sixteenth century, when the practice, widespread in Germany and North Italy, of hiring a 'municipal physician' was in vogue) be paid for by the municipality.[28] It might be on an honorarium basis or alternatively by visit. Sometimes the local physicians or the guild of surgeons or apothecaries undertook to supply one of their members on a quarterly rota basis, an arrangement which rarely brought satisfaction.[29] Details we have concerning frequency of visits under any of these arrangements are tantalizingly few, especially as records often only state that a doctor or surgeon should visit 'when needed' or – as at Landerneau in 1689 – 'from time to time'.[30] Although this is again something which varied according to region, size of institutions, availability of medical personnel, and so on, it would appear generally to be the case that doctors' visits to Hôtels-Dieu tended to be on a fairly regular basis: once or even twice a day was quite common in the major hospitals by the late seventeenth century. In even some of the bigger Hôpitaux Généraux, in contrast, things were more lax, partly because inmates were not supposed to be curably sick: no physician was attached to the Hôpital Général in Issoire before 1749, in Nevers before 1761.[31]

The medical armature of the hospital was further elaborated as, from the mid- and late seventeenth century, many hospitals contracted with local master surgeons to maintain an apprentice-surgeon living in within the hospital. Some hospitals had similar arrangements with local apothecaries.

The medical role assigned such individuals was not always very great: one of their chief functions, for example, was to examine candidates for admission to check that they did not have contagious diseases, which were normally banned; while administrators expected their medical men to be particularly alert to the likelihood of the death of an inmate so that the chaplain could be informed and brought in to administer the last rites.[32] Many apprentice-surgeons seem to have spent much of their time shaving male inmates and cutting their hair. Nevertheless, the increased use of surgeons in hospitals was advantageous from the point of view of inmates – assuming that the apprentice showed some capacity, which was not always the case – in that it entailed a permanent medical presence within the hospital. It won the favour of the master surgeons, partly because it was a devolution of work on to their apprentices, partly because they were aware that hospital service could provide an apprentice with an excellent field of training and experiment (range of cases, chances for operations, cadavers, etc.).[33] Unlike wealthier patients, moreover, the poor didn't answer back if things went wrong. The central government appears to have accepted the desirability of surgical presence within hospitals. From late in the seventeenth century it accorded many of the larger hospitals the right to have their living-in apprentice-surgeon awarded his mastership after (usually) six years of satisfactory service. The post of *gagnant-maîtrise* came to be much sought after, especially in the larger hospitals which ran open competitions for the place.[34]

There was an awareness among many hospital administrators of the ethical problems involved in allowing medical men to train within hospitals. The hospital regulations at Dijon, for example, forbade physicians and surgeons from 'choosing the inmates to perform experiments on their persons'.[35] Yet it is clear that the pedagogic function of hospitals increased from the late seventeenth century onwards. The surgeon Félix, for example, experimented in anticipation for operating on Louis XIV's anal fistula on the back-sides of the unfortunate inmates of the Paris Hôtel-Dieu; master surgeons increasingly took apprentices on their hospital rounds; anatomical courses and instruction in surgical operations were laid on in some institutions. From the middle of the eighteenth century physicians too were showing more interest in the teaching value of the hospital.[36]

III

Any account of the developing 'medicalization' of hospitals in Ancien Régime France must not exclude, however, the role of nursing sisters, who are the subject of the second part of this book. Communities of hospital nurses had of course existed in the Middle Ages; but most had suffered badly in regard to morale, recruitment, and standing prior to the sixteenth century. Nursing sisters, on the model of the Daughters of Charity founded by Saints Vincent de Paul and Louise de Marillac, provided highly effective nursing services both within hospitals and 'in the world', in the form of home visits. As I point out in Chapter 3, such women came to take over the running of nearly all hospitals and charitable instructions in France by the end of the Ancien Régime, a process which must rank as one of the most remarkable achievements of working women in the early modern period. They contributed in no small measure not only to the better management of hospitals but also to their 'medicalization'.

The sisters had important medical functions. The Daughters of Charity ran the hospital pharmacy in every institution in which they served, and the same was true for many other communities. The advent of sisters of charity thus normally brought to an end contractual arrangements which had often been set up in the sixteenth century between the hospital administrators and the local guild of apothecaries. They had some basic surgical training too – Daughters of Charity going out to establish themselves in a new hospital always took with them a box of lancets and other surgical instruments. Although they were told to defer to trained physicians, the patchy attendance of doctors and master surgeons in the hospital gave them a pretty clear field, in the early days at least. They appear to have regarded themselves as the medical superior of apprentice-surgeons – perhaps they were. They were particularly protective of the women's wards, into which the (celibate) apprentice-surgeons found it difficult to penetrate, and where the basic surgical procedures (dressing wounds, applying poultices, etc.) were performed by the sisters. They were also sole arbiters of everything relating to the cooking and distribution of food: no small ingredient in staple hospital therapy.

The presence of different kinds of medical practitioners within the hospitals – physicians, surgeons, apprentice-surgeons, and nursing sisters – meant that boundary disputes and questions of precedence were a continual problem. The norm was that the physician supervised the activities of both surgeons and sisters – but deviations from the norm were frequent. In the last decades of the Ancien Régime, moreover, disputes reached serious proportions. As Chapters 4 and 5 show, there was a spate of quarrels in the late eighteenth century between doctors and nurses over the nature of hospital care.[37] This came about not because the nursing sisters altered their standards and levels of care, but rather because of a change in attitude on the part of physicians. Partly this was a consequence of the growing professionalization of the medical corps, and its tendency to view any medical practitioner who had not undergone proper university-based instruction as a 'charlatan' – a dustbin term which incorporated everything the physicians did not like, from presumptuous surgeons and apothecaries to itinerant mountebanks, and from nursing sisters to wizards and wise women.[38] In addition, Enlightenment medicine prized the idea of the clinic, and urged its practitioners to haunt the bedside. Partly, as with the surgeons before them, this was part of a realization that the presence of disease provided an excellent educational setting; but there was a research dimension to it too. Medicine would progress as a science not through the consultation of the writings of the Ancients but through the 'clinical gaze' on the body of the diseased. Attendance at a hospital thus passed from being a charitable gesture or a contractual undertaking to being a pedagogic strategy and a scientific desideratum.

When this new kind of physician attempted to get to the bedside of the hospital inmate, he found his way blocked by the formidable figure of the nursing sister. The latter saw inmates as *pauperes Christi*, not medical guinea-pigs. Enlightenment-trained physicians liked to represent the disputes which inevitably ensued as a clash between science and medicine on the one hand and religion and superstition on the other. Historians have often tended to accept these whiggish battle-lines. Yet only if we regard medicine as solely comprising 'What Doctors Do' can we view things in this way. For all the evidence is that sisters of charity had their own views of medicine and their own sets of practices and conventions.

Even by the lights of many physicians, moreover, the medical ideas of the sisters were far from obscurantist. The Hippocratic revival in medical schools in the eighteenth century placed great store by allowing Nature to run its course, and by minimizing medical ministrations. This was not so very far removed from the conceptions of the nursing communities. What was at issue then was a clash not between reason and mumbo-jumbo, but between competing systems of power, within a spectrum of medical opinion in which, on some issues at least, nurses' views on therapy might come quite close to those of a strand of established medical practitioners. The fact that nursing sisters felt that they had a greater commitment to the sensibilities of the poor within hospitals, and a better track record of humane care than medical men inflamed quarrels. So, probably, below the surface, did gender difference.

Contrary to frequently held assertions, the late eighteenth century did not see the end of this kind of dispute, or the unchallenged triumph of the medical men. By 1789 the physicians had won many battles, but not the war. The French Revolution, in many ways a watershed in the history of the French medical profession, may have temporarily swayed things their way.[39] Surgery and medicine were amalgamated into a unified profession for the first time in the 1790s; the education of doctors was rationalized, with clinical practice incorporated within it for the first time; and the emergence of the Paris Medical School, with its illustrious practitioners, Laennec, Bichat, *et al.* added to medical prestige. Government now gave medical men greater status and presence within hospitals which – consequent on the latter's financial débâcle in the 1790s – were more closely under state supervision than formerly. Even so, although the medical profession emerged from the Revolution with its standing enhanced, the same was true of the nursing sisters. Temporarily abolished at the height of the anti-clerical wave of the mid-1790s, many nursing sisters had shown exemplary courage and commitment to their charges by staying unofficially at their posts and helping to see hospitals through some of the darkest days in their history. The post-Revolutionary hospitals were therefore to continue to be the locus for disputes and micro-struggles for supremacy between what one recent author has called 'medical power' and 'clerical power', struggles which lasted well into the second half of the nineteenth century.[40]

IV

Competing views of the hospital inmate are the subject of the third section of this volume, which deals with a number of 'limiting cases': individuals who were neither *pauvres malades*, nor *malades pauvres*, but who were none the less subjected to charitable-cum-repressive institutionalization. By looking at these cases over the Ancien Régime and Revolutionary period, we can detect changing criteria in and attitudes towards their presence within the hospital population. We can also register the growing importance in some spheres of medical personnel.

Chapter 6 presents an overview of the group in whose treatment over the period there is the most marked continuity, namely sick and disabled soldiers. A commitment to maintaining the health and the welfare of the troops was a perennial concern of the French state from the time of the emergence of a large standing army, in the early seventeenth century onwards, and testifies to the extensive and elastic qualities of the parameters of charity under the Ancien Régime. Over that period, state welfare took a variety of forms, of which institutional care was probably the most dominant. The military counterpart to the Hôpital Général was the Hôtel des Invalides, and in it was embedded a similar mixture of compassion and repression: it was kind no doubt to offer military veterans a home – but it was politic and safe too, given their proclivity for crime and turbulence. The military hospital network which was established from the late seventeenth century onwards similarly testified to the ambiguity of the state's charitable impulses, for it was motivated as much by crude populationist considerations as by compassion. It should be stressed that this military hospital network, for all its failings (which were legion, especially in time of war) represented a signal effort of medicalization. In important respects, the sick soldier – and sailor, for there exists a parallel history of naval welfare policies not touched on here[41] – was the first hospital patient. For while the prime consideration in the care of civilians related to his or her poverty, the sole reason for the presence of the soldier within hospital walls was that he was sick. As a corollary of this, the medical dimension of care was more pronounced in military hospitals than in their civilian counterparts. Hospitals shorn of their charitable carapace, administered by state bureaucrats rather than benevolent notables and run by paid orderlies rather than by sisters of charity (the nursing communities were only spasmodically involved in military institutions) were more directly accessible to trained medical staff, doctors, surgeons, and apothecaries. If the civilian hospital inmate was the object of a charitable gesture, the sick soldier was the guinea-pig which clinically minded doctors in the eighteenth century were so keen to find. Clinical teaching methods were being tried out in military establishments half a century before clinical medicine was incorporated into the standard syllabus of French universities; records of observation were more fully maintained than elsewhere; and new medical approaches – not least as regards the soldier's perennial problem, venereal disease – were experimented with on ailing soldiers.

The sick or incapacitated soldier in the Ancien Régime was thus – as Isser Woloch has put it – 'the frontier of social welfare'.[42] This was particularly true, moreover, after 1789, and reflected changed social attitudes as regards the poor and needy. The populationist calculus of the Bourbon monarchy gave way to the enthusiastic social radicalism of the Terror – which in turn was replaced by Napoleon, whose health propaganda and charades of concern hid a basic cynicism about the expenditure and disablement of human life. Military welfare policies were thus a kind of litmus test for social and political values, and also for the changing contours of the charitable imperative.

If from the point of the charitable institution the soldier, like the poor, is always with us, the same was not true of the prostitute. The place of prostitution within the parameters of social concern in the seventeenth century was testimony, as Chapter 7 shows, to the moralizing dimension of social policy at that period. As Michel Foucault, for all his faults, has brilliantly illuminated, the *grand renfermement des pauvres* mixed up the 'deserving' and the 'undeserving' poor, the needy and the dangerous classes, and created thereby a world of confinement in which a motley array of moral and social deviants – not only prostitute and pauper, but also sexual misfits, homosexuals, religious and political dissidents, ethnic minorities (notably the gypsies) – were promiscuously mixed.[43] Medical practitioners had little or nothing to do with the prostitute's presence here initially, although some institutions did later offer treatment for venereal disease. Rather the creation of special facilities for prostitutes was part of the more general movement of reclusion: indeed although in Montpellier, as Chapter 7 demonstrates, the prostitute was imprisoned in tailor-made facilities in the Bon Pasteur reformatory, in many cities she was shut away within Hôpitaux Généraux.[44] As with other inmates within these institutions, her place was not seen in wholly negative terms. Her confinement was often motivated by the desire of her family to protect its respectability, it is true, but there was also some concern for her own honour. In a society in which sexual probity (preferably virginity) was an essential requirement in the curriculum vitae of any single woman seeking employment, institutions for the 'tutelage of honour', to use Sandra Cavallo's phrase, could help in the rehabilitation of the 'fallen woman' and prepare her for reinsertion into society by giving her space for working out her repentance, learning a trade, and assuming the deferential attitude expected of the deserving poor.[45]

The anti-hospital critique of the Enlightenment was, however, to prove as unsparingly critical of these institutions as of hospitals *tout court*. Like the Hôtels-Dieu, an institution such as the Bon Pasteur could be accused of being a sink of infection; like the Hôpitaux Généraux, it could be attacked for immobilizing labour and increasing social costs. The religious motivation behind the institutions was also less lively in the eighteenth century – and not only among intellectuals and *philosophes*, but also among the very kind of men and women from the social elite who had led the move for the policing of morals in the previous century, but who now viewed post-Tridentine moral policing as embarrassingly anachronistic. Yet although the Revolution was to see the end of such institutions, the policing of prostitution soon revived under the administrative aegis of the state, and the nineteenth century witnessed a regulation of prostitution – for reasons of public order and social hygiene – just as intrusive and as repressive as that which had been provided by the moralizing vigilantes of the Counter-Reformation.

Throughout the period under review, public security and the honour of respectable families were the underlying social exigencies behind measures aimed at prostitutes. Much the same was true in regard to the lunatic. Like the prostitute, facilities for their institutionalization developed from the late seventeenth century onwards – Montpellier, for example, the subject of Chapter 8, establishing special facilities from 1713.[46] The lunatic was every bit a part of the *renfermement des pauvres* as of the world of unreason. Yet the trajectory of the lunatic was to be very different from that of the prostitute. The latter was to be thrown into the meshes of the market economy in 1789. The former, in contrast, became in the 1790s the object of medical science. Though there had been signs during the Enlightenment of a developing medical sensitivity towards the insane, this had not always been very apparent within institutions which actually received lunatics. In the hospital at Lanmeur in Brittany which specialized in receiving the insane under the Ancien Régime, it was said by an administrator, that 'most of the persons reacquire their sanity through the intervention of the saints to whom the hospital inmates pray'.[47] The Revolution speeded up the medicalization of the treatment of the insane partly through the running down of many of the religious institutions which formerly catered for them, partly by shaking loose facilities for medical treatment. From the mid-1790s onwards, as is well known, Paris contained a number of institutions which were the showpiece and the seedplot of the 'New Treatment' of the insane: most notably the female poor-house of La Salpêtrière, where so legend (if not, it would appear, reality) has it, Philippe Pinel had famously inaugurated the humane treatment of the insane by releasing inmates from chains, and the *Maison Nationale de l'Aliénation mentale*, established by the Directorial government in Charenton. There were a number of curious and contradictory features about the medicalization of insanity which took place in such institutions: not least the fact that the 'moral treatment' preached by physicians like Pinel specifically rejected purely 'medical' means (drugs, bleedings, etc.) in favour of 'moral' and 'psychological' methods of care – methods in fact which resembled the religious and consolatory methods which religious communities such as the Brothers of Charity and the Daughters of Charity had utilized prior to 1789.[48] Yet the institutional treatment of the insane became one of the principal channels of the professionalization of the nascent psychiatric profession.

As Chapter 8 illustrates, social criteria usually continued to prevail over medical considerations in arrangements for the treatment of the insane. Towns, like post-Revolutionary Montpellier, and, from 1838, the central government (through the law instituting lunatic asylums throughout the departments of France) provided the resources for the institutionalization of the insane not because they wished the doctors well, but rather because they perceived in the insane a problem of social order and family dishonour. Even in the more medicalized world of the nineteenth century, charity continued to be conjugated along with repression.

In general terms too, it would appear that only the advent of the welfare state was to undermine the logic of the charitable imperative, which had characterized society's attitudes towards the poor over the *longue durée.* The Revolution of 1789 failed to do more than dent it. While the impact of the Revolution on poor relief was, it is true, immense, in many important ways there was greater continuity than transformation in hospital structures and the objectives of relief in the 1790s. The Revolution's greatest legacy in this sphere was in the realm of ideas, most notably in the principles of a kind of democratically based welfare state, then adumbrated for the first time and only to take shape a century or so later. Post-Revolutionary France was still a pre-industrial society – or at very best a slowly industrializing society – and its structures of relief inevitably reflected that fact. Those structures of relief moreover had a durability and resilience which made them difficult objects to transform, whether into state-orientated institutions or medical ones. Clerical power, the *esprit de clocher,* and the workings of the charitable imperative kept medical power in check within hospitals for much of the nineteenth century, despite the state's growing support for the medical profession.[49]

Notes

1. P. Ariès, *L'Homme devant la mort* (Paris, 1977) esp. pp. 164 ff.

2. For the theory behind almsgiving, see B. Tierney, *Medieval Poor Law: a Sketch of Canonical Theory and its Application in England* (Berkeley, Calif., 1959). Cf. too Matthew, ii, 35–45, and numerous contributions to M. Mollat (ed.) *Etudes sur l'histoire de la pauvreté au Moyen Age* (2 vols, Paris, 1974).

3. For the blossoming of institutional charity in medieval Europe, see M. Mollat, *The Poor in the Middle Ages: An Essay in Social History* (London, 1986); and Mollat (ed.) *Etudes.* Specifically for France, cf.

M. Candille, 'Pour un précis d'histoire des institutions charitables', *Bulletin de la Société d'histoire des hôpitaux* (1974); and J. Imbert, *Les Hôpitaux en droit canonique* (Paris, 1947).

4. M. Mollat and P. Wolff, *Ongles bleus, Jacques et Ciompis: les révolutions populaires en Europe aux XIVe. et XVe. siècles* (Paris, 1970); A. Vauchez, 'Le peuple au Moyen Age: du "populus christianus" aux classes dangereuses', in T. Riis (ed.) *Aspects of Poverty in Early Modern Europe* (Odense, Denmark, 1986). For disruption caused by war, see H. Denifle, *La Désolation des églises, monastères et hôpitaux en France pendant la Guerre de Cent Ans* (2 vols, Paris, 1897–9).

5. On Protestant–Catholic parallelism, see esp. B. Pullan, 'Catholics and the poor in early modern Europe', *Transactions of the Royal Historical Society* (1976). There is an overview of the poor-relief programme as a whole in R. Jütte, 'Poor relief and social discipline in sixteenth-century Europe', *European History Review* (1981). See too the broad brush strokes in J.P. Gutton, *La Société et les pauvres en Europe (XVIe.–XVIIIe. siècles)* (Paris, 1974) esp. pp. 93 ff.; C. Lis and H. Soly, *Poverty and Capitalism in Pre-Industrial Europe* (London, 1982) pp. 87 ff.; and E. Chill, 'Religion and mendicity in seventeenth-century France', *International Review of Social History* (1962). Two excellent studies of Lyon show the reforms in action: N.Z. Davis, 'Poor relief, humanism and heresy: the case of Lyon', in her *Society and Culture in Early Modern France* (London, 1975); and J.P. Gutton, *La Société et les pauvres: l'exemple de la généralité de Lyon (1534–1790)* (Paris, 1971).

6. The work appeared in Bruges in 1526. Further Latin editions appeared in Paris in 1530, and in Lyon in 1532. There was a German translation out of Strasbourg in 1533, an Italian one in 1545, and a French one in 1583. The work was also translated into English in the 1530s. For Vives, cf. M. Bataillon, 'J.L. Vives, réformateur de la bienfaisance', *Bibliothèque d'humanisme et Renaissance* (1952); and M. Fatica, 'Il "Subventione pauperum" di J.L. Vivès: suggestioni luterane o mutamento di una mentalità collettiva?', *Società e storia* (1982). Cf. too S.J. Woolf, *The Poor in Western Europe in the Eighteenth and Nineteenth Centuries* (London, 1986) p. 21; P. Slack, *Poverty and Policy in Tudor and Stuart England* (London, 1988) pp. 9, 23, 116.

7. See esp. Gutton, *La Société et les pauvres*, pp. 415 ff.; and Gutton, *La Société et les pauvres en Europe*, pp. 145 ff.

8. For England, Slack, *Poverty and Policy*, p. 13, and R.M. Clay, *The Medieval Hospitals of England* (London, 1909); and for Italy, see for example B. Pullan, *Rich and Poor in Renaissance Venice* (Oxford, 1971); and B. Pullan, 'Poveri, mendicanti e vagabondi (secoli XIV–XVII)', in *Storia d'Italia. I. Dal feudalismo al capitalismo* (Turin, 1978) pp. 981 ff.

9. F. Dissard, *La Réforme des hôpitaux et maladreries au XVIIe. siècle* (1938), passim; and M. Portal, 'Le Grand Aumônier de France (jusqu'à la fin du XVIIe. siècle)', *Revue de l'Assistance publique à Paris* (1954); L. Le Grand, 'Comment composer l'histoire d'un établissement hospitalier', *Revue d'histoire de l'Eglise de France* (1930) pp. 218–22.

10. For royal pronouncements appearing to institute community obligation towards the poor in 1650, 1693, and 1709, see C. Bloch,

L'Assistance et l'état en France à la veille de la Révolution (Paris, 1908) pp. 47, 134.

11. D. Parker, *The Making of French Absolutism* (London, 1983) pp. 139 ff.; D. Richet, *La France moderne: l'esprit des institutions* (Paris, 1973) esp. pp. 37 ff.; G. Durand, *Etats et institutions (XVIe.–XVIIIe. siècles)* (Paris, 1969); R. Bonney, 'Absolutism: what's in a name?', *French History* (1987).

12. For sixteenth-century attempts to institute municipal obligation, see M. Fosseyeux, 'Les premiers budgets municipaux d'assistance. La taxe des pauvres au XVIe. siècle', *Revue d'histoire de l'Eglise de France* (1934).

13. See, for example, C. Fairchilds, *Poverty and Charity in Aix-en-Provence, 1640–1789* (Baltimore, 1976) pp. 131 ff.; K. Norberg, *Rich and Poor in Grenoble, 1600–1815* (Berkeley, Calif., 1985) pp. 241 ff.; C. Jones, *Charity and 'Bienfaisance': The Treatment of the Poor in the Montpellier Region, 1740–1815* (Cambridge, 1982) pp. 60 ff., 73 ff.; and O. Hufton, *The Poor of Eighteenth-Century France, 1750–89* (Oxford, 1974) pp. 139 ff. The best analysis of the debate over charity and hospitals in the Enlightenment is still to be found in Bloch, *L'Assistance et l'état*, esp. pp. 179 ff., 211 ff., 365 ff. See too Gutton, *La Société et les pauvres*, pp. 431 ff.; and the influential writings of M. Foucault, notably his *Folie et déraison: histoire de la folie à l'âge classique* (Paris, 1961) pp. 492 ff.; and *The Birth of the Clinic: The Archaeology of Medical Perception* (London, 1974) pp. 18 ff.; 39 ff.

14. For the 1760s see Bibliothèque Nationale, Manuscrits français 8129–30, plus the commentaries based essentially on that source in Paultre, *De la Répression de la mendicité et du vagabondage en France sous l'Ancien Régime* (Paris, 1906) pp. 381 ff.; Bloch, *L'Assistance et l'état*, pp. 157 ff.; and Jones, *Charity and 'Bienfaisance'*, pp. 137 ff. For the *dépôts de mendicité*, see Hufton, *The Poor*, pp. 219 ff.; Norberg, *Rich and Poor* esp. p. 222; and T.S. Adams, *An Approach to the problem of beggary in eighteenth-century France: the 'dépôts de mendicité'* (University microfilms edn, 1979, of University of Wisconsin PhD thesis, 1977).

15. For the impact of the Revolution, see A. Forrest, *The French Revolution and the Poor* (Oxford, 1981); M.C.R. Gillett, *Hospital Reform in the French Revolution* (University microfilms edn, 1980, of The American University PhD thesis, 1979); J. Imbert, *Le Droit hospitalier de la Révolution et de l'Empire* (Paris, 1954); Jones, *Charity and 'Bienfaisance'*; and C. Jones, 'The politics and personnel of social welfare from the Convention to the Consulate', in G. Lewis and C. Lucas (eds) *Beyond the Terror: Essays in French Regional and Social History, 1794–1815* (Cambridge, 1983) pp. 86 ff.

16. O. Hufton and F. Tallett, 'Communities of women, the religious life and public service in seventeenth-century France', in M.J. Boxer and J. Quataert (eds) *Connecting Spheres: Women in the Western World, 1500 to the Present* (Oxford, 1987) offers a good recent overview. For the range of communities, see C. Molette, *Guide des sources de l'histoire des congrégations féminines françaises de vie active* (Paris, 1974), and the still highly useful L. Hélyot, *Histoire des ordres monastiques, religieux et militaires et des congrégations séculières de l'un et de l'autre sexe* (8 vols,

Paris, 1721). Specifically on the Revolution, see D.B. Weiner, 'The French Revolution, Napoleon and the nursing profession', *Bulletin of the History of Medicine* (1972); Jones, 'The politics and the personnel', pp. 73 ff. A reaction against 'Florentiocentric' histories of nursing has set in in recent years in England, led by Ann Summers, Christopher Maggs, and others. Though clearly Florence Nightingale was not the *fons et origo* of all western nursing, most moves towards professionalized lay nursing occurred in the latter half of the nineteenth century.

17. M. Jeorger, 'La structure hospitalière de la France sous l'Ancien Régime', *Annales E.S.C.* (1977) pp. 1,026, 1,031–2.

18. B. Abel-Smith, *The Hospitals, 1800–1948* (London, 1964) p. 1. Of course it might be argued that the comparison is unfair and that one should either include on the English side inmates in workhouses or exclude on the French side all but inmates from Hôtels-Dieu. Yet the latter in France contained between 20,000 and 25,000 inmates, which still represents a pretty staggering difference.

19. J. Dupâcquier, *La Population française aux XVIIe. et XVIIIe. siècles* (Paris, 1979) pp. 34, 81; Hufton, *The Poor*, pp. 23 f.

20. Jones, *Charity and 'Bienfaisance'*, pp. 61–2; Norberg, *Rich and Poor*, p. 177.

21. This paragraph borrows very heavily from the arguments expounded in Woolf, *The Poor in Western Europe*, esp. the Introduction. See too S. Cavallo, 'Conceptions of poverty and poor relief in the second half of the eighteenth century', unpublished paper, 1986.

22. See esp. F. Dinges, 'L'hôpital Saint-André de Bordeaux au XVIIe. siècle', *Annales du Midi* (1987) pp. 303, 323; and cf. M.J. Villemon, 'A partir des sources hospitalières: l'alimentation des pauvres de l'Hôpital Général de Caen au début du XVIIIe. siècle', *Annales de Normandie* (1971); Y. Pottier, 'La population de l'Hôpital Saint-Yves de Rennes dans la première moitié du XVIIIe. siècle (1710–50)', *mémoire de maîtrise*, Université de Haute-Bretagne (1974).

23. Foucault, *Birth of the Clinic*; Foucault *et al.*, *Les Machines à guérir. (Aux origines de l'hôpital moderne)* (Paris, 1979); and Foucault, *Discipline and Punish: The Birth of the Prison* (London, 1979).

24. See the article by J.P. Gutton, 'La mise en place du personnel soignant dans les hôpitaux français (XVIe. – XVIIIe. siècles)', *Bulletin de la Société d'histoire des hôpitaux* (1987). For the sixteenth century the rather dated C.A. Wickersheimer, *La Médecine et les médecins en France à l'époque de la Renaissance* (Paris, 1906), is still useful, esp. pp. 324 ff. I hope it is not thought too whiggish to argue that the improved hygienic record of hospitals may have had something to do with better provision of trained medical care. There is, however, quite a debate on this very point in the historiography concerning English hospitals. For an 'optimistic' recent contribution, see S. Szreter, 'The importance of social intervention in Britain's mortality decline, c. 1850–1914', *Social History of Medicine* (1988).

25. M. Mollat, *The Poor in the Middle Ages*, p. 289; P. Amarguier, 'La situation hospitalière à Marseille', in *Assistance et charité. Cahiers de Fanjeaux. XIII* (Toulouse, 1978) p. 245; J. Caille, *Hôpitaux et charité*

publique à Narbonne au Moyen Age (Toulouse, 1978) p. 99; C. Port, *Inventaire sommaire* (henceforth – *I.S.*) *des archives hospitalières d'Angers* (Angers, 1870) p. xiii.

26. L. Costecalde, 'Notice sur l'hôpital de la ville de Mende et l'Oeuvre de Miséricorde', *Archives gévaudannaises* (1915) p. 341; A. Prudhomme, *I.S. des archives hospitalières de Grenoble* (Grenoble, 1892) p. xiii and E 5; T. Gelfand, *Professionalizing Modern Medicine: Paris Surgeons and Medical Science and Institutions in the Eighteenth Century* (Westport, Conn., 1980) p. 26.

27. Archives départementales (henceforth – A.D.) de la Lozère H 949.

28. See the articles in A.W. Russell (ed.) *The Town and State Physician in Europe from the Middle Ages to the Enlightenment* (Wolffenbuttel, 1981). My own impression in France is that the employment of municipal physicians was linked to the containment of plague, and that when plague started to disappear – in the late seventeenth century – so did municipalized physicians.

29. For a quarterly rota of service, and the objections it raised see, for example, from a list which could be much extended: A.D. Ille-et-Vilaine, Fonds Hardouin, F22381; A.D. Haute-Vienne: archives hospitalières de Limoges E 1; A.D. Lozère E dépôt Marvéjols E 10; A.D. Pyrénées-Atlantiques: archives hospitalières de Bayonne E 17; A.D. Puy-de-Dôme L 1043 (Riom), and Archives hospitalières de Montferrand H II (unclassified).

30. A.D. Finistère. Archives hospitalières de Landerneau E 2.

31. B. Bellande, *L'Ancien Hôpital Général d'Issoire: histoire institutionnelle et sociale de 1684 à la Révolution* (Montpellier, 1966) ; abbé Bouthillier, *I.S. des archives hospitalières de Nevers* (Nevers, 1877) p. 23.

32. A. Bénet, *I.S. des archives départementales du Calvados. Archives hospitalières de Honfleur* (Caen, 1900) p. 167; J.H. Libéral, *Les Hôpitaux de Quimper* (Paris, 1941) p. 73; A.D. Côte-d'Or: archives hospitalières de Dijon E 1, E 2; A.D. Aisne: archives hospitalières de Laon 12 E 11.

33. Cf. Gelfand, *Professionalising Modern Medicine*, pp. 51–5, 101 ff.

34. See the Letters Patent of every major Hôpital Général. These are normally located in the A series of the hospital archives. The registers of the deliberations of the Montpellier hospitals in the eighteenth century contain extensive documentation on the competitions for the post of the *gagnant-maîtrise.*

35. Lallemand, *Histoire de la charité. Les temps modernes (XVIe.–XIXe. siècles)* (Paris, 1912) p. 553.

36. Gelfand, *Professionalising Modern Medicine*, p. 34 for the fistula. For surgical training, ibid. passim for the Parisian hospitals; and for elsewhere, P.L. Thillaud, *Les Maladies et la médecine en pays basque nord à la fin de l'Ancien Régime (1690–1789)* (Paris, 1983) pp. 87–8 (Bayonne, 1733); L. Accarias, *L'Assistance publique sous la Révolution dans le département du Puy-de-Dôme* (Savenay, 1933) p. 43; A.D. Isère: archives hospitalières de Grenoble II G 1. I hope to write an article on the very extensive surgical training available in the Montpellier Hôtel-Dieu Saint-Eloi in the eighteenth century.

37. Besides the cases discussed on pp. 153–4 and 196–7, it is instructive to consider the long-running dispute between the Parisian surgeons and the Brothers of Charity, over the latter's practice of surgery without formal surgical qualification. See e.g. Gelfand, *Professionalising Modern Medicine*, p. 106; and for provincial ramifications, A.D. Moselle, Archives hospitalières de Metz F 20; J. Gardère, *I.S. des archives hospitalières de Condom* (Auch, 1883) p. 26; A.D. Isère: archives hospitalières de Grenoble II G 1.

38. For the anti-charlatanism campaign, see M. Ramsey, *Professional and Popular Medicine in France, 1770–1830: The Social World of Medical Practice* (Cambridge, 1988); T. Gelfand, 'Medical professionals and charlatans: the *Comité de salubrité enquête*, 1790–1', *Histoire sociale/Social History* (1978); and J.P. Goubert, 'L'art de guérir: médecine savante et médecine populaire dans la France de 1790', *Ann. E.S.C.* (1977).

39. P. Huard, *Sciences, médecine, pharmacie de la Révolution à l'Empire* (Paris, 1970); D.M. Vess, *Medical Revolution in France, 1789–96* (Gainesville, Fla, 1975); E.H. Ackerknecht, *Medicine in the Paris Hospital, 1794–1848* (Baltimore, Md, 1967); and D.B. Weiner, 'French doctors face the war, 1792–1815', in C.K. Warner (ed.) *From the Ancien Régime to the Popular Front: Essays in the History of Modern France in Honor of S.B. Clough* (London and New York, 1969).

40. See the interesting perspectives opened up in J. Goldstein, *Console and Classify: The Birth of the Psychiatric Profession in Nineteenth-Century France* (Cambridge, 1988) esp. pp. 216 ff.

41. See, for example, P. Huard and P. Niaussat, 'Les hôpitaux de la marine française au XVIIIe. siècle', *La Médecine hospitalière au XVIIIe. siècle* (Strasbourg, 1980); and J.C. White, 'Un exemple des réformes humanitaires dans la marine française: l'hôpital maritime de Toulon (1782–7)', *Annales du Midi* (1971).

42. I. Woloch, *The French Veteran from the Revolution to the Restoration* (Chapel Hill, NC, 1980) pp. xvi, 316 ff.

43. Foucault, *Histoire de la folie*, esp. pp. 97 ff.

44. Most classically this was true at La Salpêtrière in Paris: L. Boucher, *La Salpêtrière: son histoire de 1656 à 1790* (Paris, 1883). For other provincial cases, see A. Soucaille, 'Notice sur la Maison du Refuge ou du Bon Pasteur de Béziers', *Mémoires de la Société archéologique de Béziers* (1885) (the institution was founded in 1686 and run by the Hôpital Général); Norberg, *Rich and Poor*, p. 84 (the Bon Pasteur, founded 1724, within the grounds of the Hôpital Général); A. Péghoux, *Recherches sur les hôpitaux de Clermont-Ferrand* (Clermont-Ferrand, 1845) and Archives hospitalières de Clermont-Ferrand. Fonds Bon Pasteur, unclassified (foundation in 1666); Gutton, *La Société et les pauvres*, p. 391–3 (institutions at Lyon and Saint-Etienne, founded in the 1670s and 1680s).

45. S. Cavallo, 'Assistenza femminile e tutela dell'onore nella Torino del XVIII secolo', *Annali della Fondazione L. Einaudi*, 1980. Cf. Woolf, *The Poor in Western Europe*, p. 24.

46. Other provincial examples include: Carcassone (1651), J.C. Héliès, 'Aperçu sur les hôpitaux de Carcassonne à la fin du XIXe. siècle',Toulouse, thesis, 1977; Aix-en-Provence, 1691, J. Alliez *et al.*,

'L'hospice des insensés de la Trinité à Aix-en-Provence', *Histoire des Sciences médicales* (1977); Marseille, 1699, J.B. Lautard, *La Maison des fous de Marseille. Essai historique et statistique sur cet établissement depuis sa fondation en 1699 jusqu'en 1837* (Marseille, 1840); Clermont-Ferrand (facilities inside the Hôpital Général from 1707), A.D. Puy-de-Dôme C 7552; Saint-Malo (facilities within the Hôpital Général), A.D. Ille-et-Vilaine: archives hospitalières de Saint-Malo 2 E 1; Albi, 1763, B. Pailhas, 'Enfermerie diocésaine ou primitif asile d'aliénés d'Albi?', *Bulletin de l'histoire de la médecine,* 1902.

47. A.D. Finistère: archives hospitalières de Lanmeur H dépôt 4.

48. Cf. on this point Goldstein, *Console and Classify*, esp. pp. 197 ff. and 217.

49. For later in the nineteenth century, the works of Jacques Léonard are essential reading. See in particular his *Les Médecins de l'Ouest au XIXe. siècle* (Paris-Lille, 1978); *La Vie quotidienne du médecin au XIXe. siècle* (1977); *La France médicale au XIXe. siècle: médecine et malades au XIXe. siècle* (1978); and *La Médecine entre les savoirs et les pouvoirs* (1981). For the advent of social security, see too H. Hatzfeld, *Du Paupérisme à la sécurité sociale: essai sur les origines de la sécurité sociale en France, 1850–1940* (1971).

I

The Social Role of Hospitals

1
Hospitals in Seventeenth-Century France

'A place to which retire those poor who do not have the means to live, and where a particular care is taken of their salvation': Richelet's 1680 dictionary definition of 'hospital' is a useful place to start an overview of seventeenth-century hospitals.[1] Revealingly the definition accentuates two crucial aspects of such institutions – poverty, religion – yet totally ignores the notion of medical attention with which we tend today to associate hospitals. Two eye-witness reports on seventeenth-century hospitals take the process of defamiliarization one stage further. One visitor to a Norman hospital noted

> a little room in which there are two beds laid in a line for the guardians and door-keepers who care for the poor sick. From there, we entered a big room with a chimney in the middle and on two sides five beds in rows, each furnished with good mattresses, good white sheets and curtains of grey material, all very clean and very convenient for the sick . . . . Above the room is a chapel dedicated to Our Lady in which there is an altar where divine service is performed assiduously for the convenience of the sick poor.[2]

Lest this should appear unduly idyllic, here is another account of a different hospital:

> The room was so dark that we could not see without a candle, and it was so full of muck that our feet sank in . . . . On both sides were set closed-in beds which, for sole furnishing, had some straw whose stench [we] bore with only great difficulty.[3]

There were perhaps – no one has ever tried to count – between 2,000 and 3,500 institutions which were called hospital in seventeenth-century France, whose date of origin was situated somewhere along a temporal line which led back to the sixth century of the Christian era.[4] Most were situated in villages. Most were small – even in towns, probably the majority had dimensions no more grand than the institutions described above. Inmates might, as in a present-day hospital, be suffering from some illness. The common denominator between inmates was, however, not sickness, but poverty. This was usually made explicit in hospital regulations, and indeed the statistical analyses of inmates which historians have been carrying out in recent years all underline the extent to which hospitals drew their clientele from among the poorer classes. These analyses also suggest that only a relatively small proportion of inmates were classifiably sick.[5]

Whether urban or rural, most hospitals appear to have performed functions closer to the medieval *xenodochium* than to the 'health-factory' of the future.[6] That is to say, they offered hospitality – it is banal to point out the etymological and semantic linkages between *hospitalité* and the main terms used to describe hospital (*hôpital, hôtel-dieu, maison-dieu*) – to a wide variety of social types: short-stay entrants such as pilgrims, travelling clerics, itinerant workers, travellers and migrants, and longer-term cases such as resident paupers – the chronically infirm, the aged, abandoned or orphaned children, for example – who either had no homes to go to, or else who had for some reason fallen between the meshes of the normally supportive networks of family and kinship. This wide variety of inmates was normally crowded together pell-mell into the single multi-purpose chamber (or *grande salle*) which was the most prominent architectural feature of hospitals since the Middle Ages.[7] Some hospitals, it is true, did manifest a degree of specialization: in cities, for example, it was quite common to have a gamut of institutions, with individual institutions serving as, for example, refuges for the blind, almshouse-type dwellings for the old and infirm, asylums for ageing repentant prostitutes, ailing members of guilds and confraternities, and so on. Similarly most towns had an *hôtel-dieu* which in theory was destined for the 'sick poor' (*les pauvres malades*) (though in practice most were very catholic in their admission policies). Specialization and differentiation were not medical criteria. It seems clear, moreover, that the only real spatial differentiation within hospital institutions was the accommodation of the sacred alongside the profane. Even small hospitals like the first example cited above had their chapel. In that case it is situated in the rafters, but more normally it would be at one end of the *grande salle*, with the altar so placed that all the eyes of the bed-ridden could be trained upon it.[8] (The altar-cross thus represented the medieval functional equivalent of the television in present-day hospitals.)

Given the character of these institutions, their hygienic record was hardly outstanding. Undoubtedly a great deal of nonsense has been written about such institutions as 'death-traps' and 'dying-places', for it seems evident that a clear majority of those who entered such institutions walked out rather than were carried out feet first.[9] Nevertheless, though some efforts might be made towards maintaining cleanliness, conditions were pretty grim. The sights and the sounds of suffering, the stench of decaying and unwashed bodies, the promiscuous tactility of the shared, multi-place beds which were the rule in all hospitals, the anonymity and strangeness of an alien world – these experiences were powerful enough to deter many from entry. It was widely felt that individuals had to divest themselves of some portion of their self-respect to enter such portals. The very fact that it was a signal mark of devotion for a charitable soul from the social elite to seek out admission or (more frequently) burial in a hospital only proved the point:[10] for them, the experiences of hospital life were the stigmata of sanctification, a passport to humility; while for the majority of entrants, they were the avatars of humiliation.

Much of the picture presented thus far stayed intact throughout the seventeenth century. Indeed, even in 1789, a quarter of France's hospitals contained fewer than ten beds;[11] and there are some surprising similarities and rapprochements to be made between the reports of seventeenth-century hospital visitors and those who recorded hospital life in provincial France in the middle of the nineteenth century.[12] Similarly the studies of architectural historians should not blind us to the fact that, although there was a great deal of construction of new hospitals in the seventeenth century, by 1700 most hospitals were still housed in the same premises as in 1600, hedged and bodged, built-on and extended perhaps, but still very much the same. Yet for all the forces of inertia at work, there were also operative important new elements of dynamism in the circumstances of French hospitals in this century.

I

Virtually all hospitals owed their establishment and continued existence to private charity, often in the form of testamentary donations. The religious motivation behind giving to hospital – 'the path of hospitals', opined Madame de Miramion, 'is the path of heaven'[13] – continued and even, as we shall see, intensified over the course of the seventeenth century. Yet in 1600, to survey the hospital scene, it seemed clear that charity was no longer enough. The Wars of Religion in the sixteenth century had caused a great deal of damage to all poor-relief institutions. The decay of religious fervour in the late Middle Ages had also had deleterious effects on institutions heavily dependent on religiously motivated charity. The situation was particularly bad at village level. In very large numbers of cases, hospitality was no longer being provided. Although in some cases in these circumstances hospital revenues were still being collected to be distributed in the form of home relief, in many cases this income simply lined the pockets of private individuals, or else hospital property was left to stagnate and decay, or was put to some other use (the Madeleine hospital at Lyon, for example, had become a brothel in the late sixteenth century).[14]

The most glaring example of institutional functions unfulfilled was the nationwide network of leper-houses. The reasons for the decline of leprosy in the late Middle Ages are obscure, but the fact of decline was unequivocal as early as 1350.[15] The number of leper-houses in a given area – there had been as many as 250 in Normandy, for example[16] – came far, far to exceed the number of lepers who could be found to fill them. From the fifteenth and sixteenth centuries, many leper-houses which still admitted inmates were peopled with individuals of dubious status – dynasties of pseudo-lepers in many cases (leprosy was accounted to be hereditary), sufferers from chronic skin complaints and syphilis and other usurpers – 'riff-raff', as a royal declaration unkindly put it in 1612, 'who to stay out of the hands of the judge and hangman arm themselves with lepers' clappers'.[17] Even before the crown became interested in this problem, municipal officials and village assemblies throughout France had cast avaricious eyes upon the empty buildings and run-down farmland which was all that was left of many former leper-houses, and had begun to take over such property for their own uses or else to reallocate it to some other charitable destination (schools, plague-hospitals, etc.)

The sixteenth century had been the century of municipalization of poor relief. Historians for long maintained that moves to rationalize assistance at the municipal level in that period were a distinguishing mark of Protestantism. (The good Catholic humanist Juan-Luis Vives, for example, was time without number made a crypto-Protestant without a shred of supporting evidence save for his authorship of one of the best-known systems of poor-relief reorganization.)[18] It is now clear, however, that what have been seen as distinctively Protestant features of charitable reform in the sixteenth century were shared by poor-relief schemes introduced by Catholic municipalities.[19] The emphasis on system and rationalization; the funding of new schemes by expropriating existing foundations (leper-houses, disaffected hospitals, etc.); the moral apartheid separating 'deserving' from 'undeserving' poor; the emphasis on setting the poor to work: all these features ignored the confessional divide. So too – though this seems less well-known – did the acceptance of obligatory collective self-taxing as a means of financing the relief of poverty. England's famous poor rate had its equivalents in the municipalities of Catholic France, upheld by the city fathers.[20]

The striking parallelism between the responses to the problem of poverty by Catholic and Protestant, English and French, changed drastically in the decades around 1600. For reasons which have never been satisfactorily elucidated, the poor-rate system of French cities fell into abeyance, and a return was made towards a more voluntaristic method. The material destruction visited upon many cities by civil war in the sixteenth and early seventeenth centuries may well have contributed to this. The growth of the French state – a process unmatched on this side of the Channel, for example – seems also to have counted. The state came to challenge municipalities for control over disaffected or available hospital property and revenue. It was also, after 1620, making financial demands on the population which made it arguably less willing to countenance ambitious poor-relief schemes at local level which might damage the ability to pay state taxes.[21]

Even in the sixteenth century, the crown had involved itself in the fate of disaffected leper-houses and hospitals. Acting particularly through the office of the *Grand Aumônier du Roi*, governments had stamped out maladministration, restored hospitality where this was feasible, or else diverted uncommitted revenues to large institutions. This activity redoubled from the decades around 1600. In 1612, in particular, the crown established a reforming committee of magistrates and bureaucrats, the *Chambre de la Générale Réformation des Hospitaux et Maladeries de France*, which was to reform numerous hospitals in the period down to 1672.[22]

An added reason for governmental intervention in this domain was the concern to provide for retired and disabled veterans from the army. Even before the quantum leap in army size during the Thirty Years War, customary mechanisms for providing for these individuals had been proving unworkable.[23] The revenues of disaffected hospitals and leper-houses seemed a convenient and appropriate fund to be tapped. From the 1620s and 1630s as state commitment towards the welfare of its soldiers became increasingly pronounced, major reform in this sphere through the extensive reorganization of hospitals seemed to be on the governmental agenda. The political difficulties of mid-century, not least the Fronde, delayed reform in this area down to the 1670s. In 1670 the Hôtel des Invalides was created as a retirement-home for common foot-soldiers. Minister of War Louvois devised an alternative arrangement for officers by using as a kind of front the virtually defunct international nursing order, the Order of Saint-Lazare. The Order was to be taken over by the state and ingeniously fitted out as an organization for rewarding military veterans.[24] Meritorious retired officers were offered commands within the Order, with jurisdiction over part of France. Within that jurisdiction, the officers could lay claim to the revenue of leper-houses as well as to the property of all hospitals in which hospitality was no longer being properly observed. The property reverted to the Order, the revenue was enjoyed by the officer. This scheme – which did not, however, as we shall see, last until the end of the century – produced a great deal of state-sponsored hospital reorganization.

II

If increased government intervention represented a distinctive area of dynamism in the field of hospital provision within France in the seventeenth century, so too did the revival of Catholicism in French society in the wake of the Council of Trent.[25] Charitable institutions have always done well in an age of faith. The post-Tridentine religious revival in France produced a larger number of foundations of hospitals, home-relief institutions, charity schools, refuges for fallen women, charity pawnshops, and so on than in any previous period, and the treasurers of every kind of existing institution found a bountiful flow of private donations clinking into their coffers. The financial viability of institutions which had been threatened by social and economic dislocation, confessional strife, the municipalization of poor relief and government attempts at reform now brightened dramatically. An excellent indication of the new spirit of confidence in the charitable sphere was the rash of hospital construction and rebuilding that took place, with a commanding use of space and florid baroque decoration soon inviting the grumble from traditionalists that the 'houses of the poor' were coming to resemble palaces.[26]

As important in improving hospital fortunes as the influx of cash, moreover, was the remarkable input of energy into the administration and support of charitable institutions which France's social and ecclesiastical elites now made. Encouraged by policy laid down at Trent, bishops began to take seriously again their time-honoured role as 'fathers of the poor' (*pères des pauvres*), a role they had tended to neglect in the sixteenth century.[27] At grassroots level the reformed and increasingly zealous and committed parish clergy were often crucial in the revival of hospital fortunes. The Counter-Reformation also denoted a greater involvement in church affairs by the laity, notably in confraternities.[28] Either attached as tertiaries to the houses of established religious orders or else (increasingly in the course of the seventeenth century) operating at parish level, confraternities served the dual function of promoting the spiritual edification of members and encouraging good works. A key development in this was the emergence of charitable confraternities of women along lines derived from Italian precedent and popularized by the work of Saint Vincent de Paul, who in 1617 had established the first 'confraternity of charity' or 'confraternity of Ladies of Charity' at Châtillon-les-Dombes in the Lyonnais.[29] By the 1620s and 1630s this type of female confraternity was spreading like wildfire in the parishes of Paris, and its progress in the towns and villages of provincial France continued throughout the remainder of the century.[30]

Another charitable offshoot of the post-Tridentine religious revival in France was the reform of hospital nursing.[31] The great international nursing orders which had provided care in numerous hospitals in the Middle Ages had fallen prey to religious decadence and social, economic, and political strife in the later Middle Ages, and had declined into virtual non-existence by 1600. The revival of the vocation of hospital nursing owed much, as we shall see, to Vincent de Paul. From 1633, in response to the proven need of charitable administrators (Ladies of Charity, hospital boards, municipal officials, etc.) for a devoted and devout labour force to implement their charitable initiatives, he helped Louise de Marillac organize the community of nurses which came to be known as the Daughters of Charity (*Filles de la Charité*). Drawn from poorer social groups than usually had access to life as females religious, the Daughters of Charity formed an open, flexible community which, organizationally speaking, owed as much to the confraternity as to the regular order (previous hospital nurses had been cloistered nuns, drawn largely from the middle and upper classes). The Daughters of Charity proved themselves able to perform, without fuss or neurosis, those unglamorous and humdrum jobs of book-keeping, staff supervision, charring and basic medical care which any well-run hospital required. The new model of hospital nurse created by Vincent de Paul and Louise de Marillac caught the imagination of clergy and laity alike. The community was soon operating on a nationwide basis and from the 1630s onwards helped to inspire a host of similar communities of active life – in schooling, home relief, and every form of charitable commitment as well as hospital nursing – whose regulations exuded a similar commitment to the discreet and pragmatic service of the poor. Given the psychologically demanding and physically unpleasant character of hospital life which we have already evoked, it probably required the heightened sense of religious vocation of these charitable professionals – under whose ardent gaze the scars and the stench of material hardship and debility were transformed into the stigmata of holy poverty – for hospital inmates to be treated with decency and respect.

At a more elevated and ambitious level, another type of confraternity to emerge as a powerful force in the domain of hospital organization and poor relief was the Company of the Holy Sacrament (*Compagnie du Saint-Sacrement*), the so-called *cabale des dévots*.[32] A clandestine organization of religious activists including militant clerics as well as influential laymen from the highest reaches of the social elite, the Company acted from its foundation in the late 1620s down to the 1660s to reform all aspects of poor relief in the capital (hospital care, home relief, prison visits, etc.). Working through over fifty daughter branches, it stimulated similar initiatives throughout France. The Company was particularly solidly based in the upper reaches of the Robe nobility, and the religious fervour of its members (which extended to onslaughts on Protestantism and religious dissent) was mixed with a keen awareness of the threat to social order which seemed to be posed by popular disorder in a period of massively widespread rebellion and revolt.[33] Where nursing communities were often motivated by a compassionate concern with the fate of *nos frères crestiens* ('our Christian brothers'),[34] the Company of the Holy Sacrament was more authoritarian and hierarchical in its approach, and looked for a recasting of the nation's poor laws which would restore social and religious harmony through the inculcation of discipline and orthodoxy. From the 1630s the Company was convinced that it had found the answer to the nation's problems in the wholesale confinement of the poor, both 'deserving' and 'undeserving'. Religious motivation thus merged with the more mundane desire to keep the poor off the streets. Under the influence of the idea of the 'general confinement of the poor' (*renfermement des pauvres*), a new type of hospital-cum-workhouse, the Hôpital Général, would be established, on one hand to submit the undeserving poor (beggars, vagrants, prostitutes, and so on) to a draconian regime of short, sharp shocks, and on the other to provide the deserving poor (the aged, infirm, abandoned children, and so on) with shelter and refuge. The streets could thereupon become as free of beggars and undesirables as the consciences of the social elite would be free of moral reproaches. Moreover

– and this point struck a special chord with government officials, who were increasingly receptive to mercantilistic arguments – the confined poor could be set to work within the institutions in textiles and other consumer industries, and they would thus help to improve the nation's balance of trade at the same time that they contributed to the financial solvency of the Hôpitaux.

The image of an institution which could transform social marginals into both orthodox Catholics and productive workers explains the popularity and compelling power of the concept of an Hôpital Général.[35] It was an image which exercised its fascination over the social elite as well as the central government. The Company of the Holy Sacrament was instrumental in the establishment of the prototype Hôpital Général in Paris in 1656–7; some eleven of the twenty-eight members of the administrative board of the institution established by royal letters patent are known to have been members of the Company.[36] The Company's provincial adherents showed great enthusiasm too for the generalization of the model throughout France, and they helped secure a royal edict in 1662 which instructed every city and *bourg* within France to establish such an institution. The Company's dissolution in the early 1660s by Louis XIV and Mazarin – who feared the political threat the Company might come to represent – retarded the spread of the new institutions. From the mid-1670s, however, the movement to generalize them throughout France got under way again.[37] In a campaign that showed a remarkable unanimity among France's social, ecclesiastical, and administrative elites, well in excess of a hundred such institutions were created in the years down to the turn of the century, and all were run on lines similar to the distinctive regimen of religious austerity and forced labour which characterized the Paris Hôpital Général.

Despite the successful grafting together of governmental will and local elite support augured well for the new network of Hôpitaux Généraux, it seems with hindsight ridiculously over-ambitious to hope to shut away a good proportion of the nation's population in these institutions. All the more was this the case, moreover, in that the government did not shrink from utilizing the Hôpitaux Généraux in repressive campaigns against a wide range of marginals and dissidents: Protestants even before the Revocation of the Edict of Nantes in 1685, prostitutes, gypsies, recipients of *lettres de cachet*, and others.[38] It is not surprising, therefore, that the difficulties in establishing and financing such institutions were soon apparent at local level – especially in economically difficult times like the 1680s and 1690s. As the 1680s wore on, the message came in to Paris from the provinces – in petitions, Intendants' reports, bishops' supplications, and so on – that the financial base of the new Hôpitaux Généraux was insufficient. In response, the crown expropriated the charitable resources of the Protestant community and reallocated them to the nearest Hôpital. As even this proved insufficient, the government came to cast its eyes on the charitable property which had come into the hands of the Order of Saint-Lazare.

Louvois's ingenious scheme for rewarding retired military officers through commanderships in the Order had not worked out as well as might have been hoped. The officers of the Order were given every form of state encouragement in their systematic search for revenue from leper-houses and disused hospitals. But in spite of this, and in spite of the well-attested vigour of Louvois himself (who became vicar-general of the Order in 1673), officers soon found themselves entangled within a veritable maquis of legal documentation, as seigneurs, municipalities, bishops, monastic houses – and even the Pope! – resisted their claims and fought against them tooth-and-nail in the law courts.[39] By the time of the death of Louvois in 1691, the whole scheme was looking decidedly shaky. It was made to appear more or less redundant, moreover, after 1693 when the government introduced the Order of Saint-Louis as a pensions scheme for retired officers.[40] Nevertheless, a great deal of property had changed hands, and the government had now to decide what to do with it.

As one of the worst mortality crises of the last century of the Ancien Régime unleashed itself,[41] as the cruel winter of 1692 passed into the hungry spring of 1693, with the Hôpitaux Généraux still unable to provide much help, and with queues for hastily improvised bread-doles building up across the length and breadth of France, the royal council acted. By a decree of March 1693 all property which had passed into the hands of the Order of Saint-Lazare was removed from its control, and it was decreed that such property should be diverted to succour the local poor and needy. In August of the same year a further decree stated that if such property could not be used to establish or re-establish a viable hospital in a locality, then it should pass into the possession of the nearest large hospital (which in most cases was an Hôpital Général). The Order of Saint-Lazare, which had been used as a means of rewarding deserving veterans, thus from 1693 became a major factor in the improved endowment of the network of Hôpitaux Généraux which was being established throughout France.

The value of this new source of endowment and the pattern of its distribution have never been satisfactorily assessed, though it seems clear that many hundreds of institutions were destroyed in the mergers performed between 1672 and the end of the century.[42] One effect of this was a tendency towards the urbanization of hospital care, as numerous country areas lost their hospital facilities and the charitable resources which underpinned them. In the diocese of Montpellier, to take a single example, rural areas were virtually denuded of hospital facilities, which went to help put the city of Montpellier's big Hôpital Général (founded in 1678) on its feet.[43] Here, as in a great many other regions in France, the last half century of the seventeenth century witnessed the most extensive reorganization of hospitals and hospital property in their history (with the possible exception of the French Revolution).

Many small village hospitals managed to ride out the reforms and to subsist well into the eighteenth and even nineteenth centuries. But the late seventeenth century had also seen the creation of what was to remain down to the French Revolution the main cornerstone of France's poor-laws and an enduring, often sinister (vide *Manon Lescaut*) reality of eighteenth-century urban life: the big Hôpital Général containing hundreds, even thousands of individuals in a motley inmate population ranging from the vagrant to the abandoned child, the orphan to the aged, the lunatic to the prostitute, the gypsy to the political prisoner. There was, moreover, a new element of drab austerity, cold uniformity of piety and unbending discipline about these institutions which made them in their way no doubt a fitting monument to Louis XIV's social and religious policies.[44]

One further point about the hospital reorganization and rationalization which took place deserves notice. In this chapter I have presented seventeenth-century hospitals as institutions whose clinical future was as yet unperceived and which were emphatically part of a system of poor relief rather than agencies for disease-prevention and cure. However, by the creation of a network of Hôpitaux Généraux to which all categories of able-bodied or chronically infirm individuals had potential access, the way was made slightly clearer for the emergence of hospitals which were more closely designated for individuals suffering from curable disease (individuals *à cure de médecin* was the frequently used phrase). This was particularly the case with urban Hôtels-Dieu. Not all illnesses were accepted within these institutions – they normally debarred individuals suffering from contagious diseases, skin and venereal complaints as well as pregnant women – and to a considerable extent they continued to serve as refuges for the travelling poor.[45] Nevertheless, the traditional inmate population of 'sick poor' probably contained more of the sick than hitherto. Alongside this development, one notes a definite long-term trend towards improvements in the medical services on offer. Doctors visited most Hôpitaux Généraux on a weekly, even fortnightly basis; but by 1700 most Hôtels-Dieu of substance were being visited by their stipendiary physician once or even twice daily, and institutions were better equipped with surgical staff, including living-in apprentice-surgeons. It was in the Hôtels-Dieu furthermore that the nursing communities which had sprung up in the seventeenth century did much of their best work. Indeed their advent often had the effect of improving a hospital's supply of drugs and medicines and leading up to the construction of apothecary premises under their control.[46] It was still far too early to talk in terms of a 'medicalization' of hospitals, or even of Hôtels-Dieu, for to do so would be to ignore the preponderantly social and religious tasks which hospitals were assigned in the seventeenth century. Nevertheless one can detect by 1700 – after more than a millenium in their history – a few glimmers of the medical future of French hospitals.

Notes

1. P. Richelet, *Dictionnaire français* (Geneva, 1680).
2. Cited in J.P. Dissard, *La Réforme des hôpitaux et maladreries au XVIIe. siècle* (Paris, 1938) pp. 34 f.
3. Cited in R. Piacentini, *Origines et évolution de l'hospitalisation. Les chanoînesses Augustines de la Miséricorde de Jésus* (Paris, 1957) p. 114.
4. Apart from the by now rather outdated monograph by Dissard

(cited in note 2), most of the best work on seventeenth-century hospitals has been regional in scope. The most impressive recent studies combine the angles of vision of historical demography with those of religious sociology: see esp. A. Croix, *La Bretagne aux XVIe. et XVIIe. siècles: la vie, la mort, la foi* (Paris, 1981); and F. Lebrun, *Les Hommes et la mort en Anjou aux XVIIe. et XVIIIe. siècles. Essai de démographie et de psychologie historiques* (Paris, 1971). Other fine studies include J.P. Gutton, *La Société et les pauvres: l'exemple de la généralité de Lyon, 1534–1789* (Paris, 1971); C. Fairchilds, *Poverty and Charity in Aix-en-Provence, 1640–1789* (Baltimore, Md, 1976); and K. Norberg, *Rich and Poor in Grenoble, 1600–1914* (London and Berkeley, Calif., 1985). The *Société d'histoire des hôpitaux* has also contributed to the revival of interest in the theme in recent years. For a good representative sample of the type of work it has inspired, see P. Cugnetti, *L'Hôpital de Grenoble des origines à la fin du Second Empire (XIe. – 1870)* (Grenoble, 1980).

5. See Chapter 2. For supporting evidence for the hypothesis there presented, especially for the seventeenth century, see Croix, *La Bretagne*, pp. 652, 663; M.C. Dinet-Lecomte, 'Recherches sur la clientèle hospitalière aux XVIIe. et XVIIIe. siècles: l'exemple de Blois', *R.H.M.C.* (1986); J.P. Bériac, 'Le Parlement, la Jurade et l'hôpital Saint-André de Bordeaux face à "l'effrénée multitude des pauvres" au XVIe. et au début du XVIIe. siècle', *Revue historique de Bordeaux* (1973) pp. 41 ff.; and M. Dinges, 'L'Hôpital Saint-André de Bordeaux au XVIIe. siècle', *Annales du Midi* (1987).

6. For an overview on medieval hospitals, see M. Mollat, *The Poor in the Middle Ages: An Essay in Social History* (London, 1986); and M. Mollat (ed.) *Etudes sur l'histoire de la pauvreté au Moyen Age* (2 vols, Paris, 1974).

7. For the general evolution of hospital architecture, see D. Leistikow, *Ten Centuries of European Hospital Architecture* (Ingolheim, 1967), and J.D. Thompson and G. Goldin, *The Hospital: A Social and Architectural History* (New Haven, Conn., 1975).

8. See, for example C. Jones, 'The Hôtel-Dieu at Beaune', *History Today* (1983).

9. See Chapter 2 and the references in note 5.

10. For the evidence of wills, M. Vovelle, *Piété baroque et déchristianisation en Provence au XVIIIe. siècle* (Paris, 1973); P. Chaunu, *La Mort à Paris (XVIe., XVIIe., XVIIIe. siècles)* (Paris, 1978); P. Ariès, *L'Homme devant la mort* (Paris, 1977); and P. Hoffman, *Church and Community in the Diocese of Lyon, 1500–1789* (New Haven, Conn., 1984).

11. M. Jeorger, 'La structure hospitalière de la France sous l'Ancien Régime', *Annales E.S.C.* (1977) pp. 1,025 ff.

12. For the seventeenth century see the evidence in Croix, *La Bretagne*; Dissard, *La Réforme des hôpitaux*; Lebrun, *Les Hommes et la mort*, passim, plus C. Guérin, 'Une tentative de réforme militaire et hospitalière, 1672–93: son application en Normandie', unpublished thesis, Ecole des Chartes, 1968. For the nineteenth century A. de Watteville, *Statistique des établissements de bienfaisance. Rapport à M. le Ministre de l'Intérieur sur l'administration des hôpitaux et hospices* (Paris, 1851).

13. Cited in M. Fosseyeux, *Une Administration parisienne sous l'Ancien Régime: l'Hôtel-Dieu aux XVIIe. et XVIIIe. siècles* (Paris, 1912) p. 57.

14. A. Steyard and F. Rolle, *Inventaire sommaire des archives hospitalières antérieures à 1790. Ville de Lyon* (5 vols, Lyon, 1874–1908) ii, p. 21; and N.Z. Davis, 'Scandale à l'Hôtel-Dieu de Lyon (1537–43)', *Etudes réunies en l'honneur de Pierre Goubert* (2 vols, Paris, 1984, i).

15. Besides the work of Dissard and Guérin cited above, see too L. Le Grand, 'Comment composer l'histoire d'un établissement hospitalier', *Revue d'histoire de l'Eglise de France* (1930) pp. 163 ff.; L. Le Grand, 'Les Maisons-Dieu et léproseries du diocèse de Paris au milieu du XIVe. siècle', *Mémoires de la Société de l'histoire de Paris* (1899); P. Hildenfinger, 'La léproserie de Reims du XIIe. au XVIIe. siècle', *Travaux de l'Académie de Reims* (1903–4); E. Le Roy Ladurie, *Les Paysans de Languedoc* (Paris, 1966) pp. 195–6. For some recent (if unconvincing) speculations on the decline of leprosy in Europe generally, see W.H. McNeill, *Plagues and Peoples* (Oxford, 1977) pp. 175–7.

16. Guérin, 'Une tentative', p. 240.

17. Cited in Dissard, *La Réforme des hôpitaux*, p. 20.

18. J.L. Vives, *De Subventione pauperum* (Bruges, 1526).

19. B. Pullan, 'Catholics and the poor in early modern Europe', *Transactions of the Royal Historical Society* (1976); and two case studies by W.J. Pugh, 'Social welfare and the edict of Nantes: Lyon and Nîmes', *French Historical Studies* (1974), and 'Protestant and Catholic testamentary charity in the seventeenth century', *French Historical Studies* (1980).

20. M. Fosseyeux, 'Les premiers budgets municipaux d'assistance. La taxe des pauvres au XVIe. siècle', *Revue d'histoire de l'Eglise de France* (1934); and P. Slack, *Poverty and Policy in Tudor and Stuart England* (1988), esp. pp. 8–14 for a European overview. More comparative Anglo-French work on this topic would be welcome.

21. For an overview of the impact of state taxation and its social effects, see R. Briggs, *Early Modern France, 1560–1715* (Oxford, 1977) pp. 65–8, 114–24, 216–17.

22. Dissard, *La Réforme des Hôpitaux*, and Guérin, 'Une tentative', provide the best guide to this episode.

23. See Chapter 6.

24. Guérin, 'Une tentative', pp. 224 ff.

25. The diffusion of the precepts of the Council of Trent into France were rather slow, and not fully accepted until well into the seventeenth century. See J. Imbert, 'Les prescriptions hospitalières du Concile de Trente et leur diffusion en France', *Revue d'histoire de l'Eglise de France* (1956); and also the regional monographs of the French school of religious historical sociology: L. Pérouas, *Le Diocèse de La Rochelle de 1648 à 1724* (Paris, 1964); T.J. Schmitt, *L'Assistance dans l'archidiaconé d'Autun aux XVIIe. et XVIIIe. siècles* (Autun, 1957); J.F. Soulet, *Traditions et réformes religieuses dans les Pyrénées centrales au XVIIe. siècle* (Paris, 1974).

26. For examples, see Leistikow, *Ten Centuries*, and Thompson and Goldin, *The Hospital*.

27. Cf. Imbert, 'Les prescriptions'.

28. Hoffman, *Church and Community*; and R. Harding, 'The mobilisation of confraternities against the Reformation in France', *Sixteenth-Century Journal* (1980).

29. See pp.92–4

30. K. Norberg, *Rich and Poor*, includes an analysis of the activities of such women in a single provincial town (Grenoble). There is a lot of room for further studies on this fascinating topic.

31. For the revival of nursing in the seventeenth century, see Chapter 3.

32. An excellent introduction to this organization is E. Chill, 'Religion and mendicity in seventeenth-century France', *International Review of Social History* (1962). Useful too are R. Elmore, *The Origins of the Hôpital-Général of Paris* (University microfilms edn, Michigan, 1975); R. Allier, *La Cabale des dévots* (Paris, 1902); and the unpublished London University thesis of E. Archer, 'The assistance of the poor in Paris and in the north-eastern provinces of France, 1641–1660' (1936). For good examples of regional branches in action, see Gutton, *La Société et les pauvres*, pp. 337 ff.; Norberg, *Rich and Poor*, esp. pp. 27–64; and R. Allier, *La Compagnie du Saint-Sacrement à Marseille* (Paris, 1909).

33. For contrasting views of rebellion in early-seventeenth-century France, see B. Porschnev, *Les Soulèvements populaires en France de 1623 à 1648* (Paris, 1963) and R. Mousnier, 'Recherches sur les soulèvements populaires en France avant la Fronde', *R.H.M.C.* (1958). For a recent overview, Y.M. Bercé, *Revolt and Revolution in Early Modern Europe* (Manchester, 1987).

34. Croix, *La Bretagne*, p. 672n for this quotation which in fact comes from the sixteenth century, but which seems to sum up an important aspect of reformed nursing in the seventeenth.

35. For an overview of the *renfermement des pauvres*, see C. Paultre, *De la Répression de la mendicité et du vagabondage en France sous l'Ancien Régime* (Paris, 1906). The penetrating, if sometimes wrong-headed views of M. Foucault, *Folie et déraison. Histoire de la folie à l'âge classique* (Paris, 1961), are still worth reading on this whole problem.

36. Elmore, *Origins*, p. 158.

37. Paultre, *De la Répression*, pp. 221 ff.; Guérin, 'Une tentative', p. 504; Gutton, *La Société et les pauvres*, p. 327 ff.

38. See pp.217–8.

39. Guérin, 'Une tentative', pp. 318 ff.

40. ibid., pp. 524 ff.

41. The severity of the crisis of 1692–4 is brought out in all the main demographic works. See, for example, J. Dupâcquier, *La Population française aux XVIIe. et XVIIIe. siècles* (Paris, 1979) p. 43.

42. *Etat général des unions faits des biens et revenus des maladreries, leproseries, aumôneries et autres lieux pieux aux Hôpitaux et des pauvres malades* (1705) for a list of mergers.

43. Archives départementales de l'Hérault. Hôpital Général de Montpellier (archives antérieures à 1790) A 1.

44. According to Jeorger, 'La structure hospitalière', there were 177 Hôpitaux Généraux in France at the end of the Ancien Régime, and they contained over 50 per cent of France's total hospital capacity.

45. See Chapter 2.

46. See pp.193–5.

2

The Social Functions of the Hospital in Eighteenth-Century France: The Case of the Hôtel-Dieu of Nîmes*

I

The history of French medicine in the early nineteenth and, in particular, the late eighteenth century has attracted a great deal of attention in recent decades. E.H. Ackerknecht's *Medicine in the Paris Hospital, 1794–1848*, published in 1967, is only an early example of an interest which has been especially marked among scholars in North America (Rosen, Greenbaum, Weiner, Gelfand, Staum, Ramsey, and so on)[1] and among writers in France, where the influence of Michel Foucault has helped to elicit a notable response, particularly among historians working within the tradition of the *Annales* school.[2] The basis of all this interest, of course, is the emergence in these years of what Ackerknecht characterized as 'hospital medicine' (in contrast to the 'laboratory' or 'library medicine' which had preceded it) and which Foucault has labelled the 'birth of the clinic'.

The veritable explosion of research on this period and this problem has, however, added surprisingly little to our stock of knowledge of how French hospitals in the 'pre-clinical' age operated. We know quite a lot about what the ideologists of the new medicine thought a hospital *should* be; we know far less about what it actually was. Two factors seem to have contributed to this lacuna in the research. First, despite often profound differences of opinion, historians have tended to focus their attentions on the formation of the medical profession or on changes in medical ideology and practice. Consequently hospitals tend to enter the picture mainly as presumptive locations for the practice of the new medicine.

**Written in collaboration with Michael Sonenscher*

Second, there has been an almost total concentration by medical historians on the hospitals of Paris, and in particular on the city's main institution, the Hôtel-Dieu, whose gutting by fire in 1772 led to a famous debate on the values and forms of hospital care.[3]

Not only have historians concentrated their attentions on the Paris Hôtel-Dieu, but also they have implied that the institution embodied the essential traits of all preclinical hospitals. Levels of hygiene within the Parisian hospital were appalling: one in four of those who entered it died there, quite probably from diseases contracted within it.[4] If this had been the case within the kingdom's greatest hospital, in which Desault was practising towards the end of the Ancien Régime, how much worse would the situation have been in other hospitals denied the enlightened theory and practice of such an eminent practitioner? This kind of 'tip-of-the-iceberg' argument was current in the late eighteenth century. When Diderot penned the article 'Hôtel-Dieu' in the *Encylopédie*, for example, he wrote solely about the Parisian institution, as if it typified all other hospitals.[5] And the view seems to have general currency among twentieth-century historians of hospitals, who, using particular evidence of conditions in the Paris Hôtel-Dieu,[6] are only too ready to dismiss the eighteenth-century hospital as a 'gateway to death', an 'antechamber to the mortuary', even as a 'septic tank'(!)[7]

It seems hardly fair to visit the sins of the Paris Hôtel-Dieu on all French hospitals. French hospitals numbered in excess of 2,000 and had a capacity of well over 100,000 persons.[8] Sheer weight of numbers argues more for complexity and

Table 2.1: Death-rates in a Number of French Hospitals at the End of the Ancien Régime, according to Tenon

Location/Hospital	*Death-rate*
Paris Hôtel-Dieu	1 death per 4 1/2 entrants
Paris Charité	1 death per 7 1/2 entrants
Paris Saint-Sulpice	1 death per 6 1/2 entrants
Saint-Denis	1 death per 15 1/8 entrants
Lyon	1 death per 11 2/5 or 13 2/3 entrants
Versailles	1 death per 8 2/5 entrants

Source: see note 9.

variety than for uniformity. Furthermore, despite the Black Legend which has grown up around French hospitals, the high death-rate of the Paris Hôtel-Dieu, which is usually taken as a defining characteristic of all institutions, is simply not found in other hospitals. Jacques Tenon, surgeon and hospital reformer at the end of the Ancien Régime, produced death-rate figures – which historians have largely ignored – that underline this fact (see Table 2.1).[9] Research on hospitals in the Montpellier region at the end of the Ancien Régime supports the relatively favourable picture of provincial hospitals which emerges here (see Table 2.2).[10]

Table 2.2: Death-rates in a Number of Hospitals in the Future Department of the Hérault at the End of the Ancien Régime

Location/Hospital	*Death-rate (%)*
Montpellier Hôtel-Dieu Saint-Eloi	Between 9.4 and 10.9
Béziers Hôpital Mage	6.9
Cazouls-les-Béziers	11.9
Pézenas	Between 9.4 and 14.0
Marseillan	Between 6.0 and 14.0
Saint-Pons	7.3
Saint-Chinian	4.8

Sources: see note 10.

Evidence from other quarters is similarly emphatic: provincial hospitals in the late eighteenth century had death-rates which generally varied from 6 or 7 per cent to 14 or 15 per cent – in other words, between a quarter and just over a half the death-rate of the Paris Hôtel-Dieu. The latter institution, from the point of view of mortality at least, seems less the tip of an iceberg than a sore thumb.

The majority of the hospitals cited in Tables 2.1 and 2.2 were either Hôtels-Dieu – that is institutions which were located in towns and which provided mainly for the sick poor or else *hôpitaux*, often village or parish institutions which catered for most local varieties of need, from the sick to the aged. Many of the largest hospitals in France were, however, of the Hôpital Général type.[11] As we have seen in earlier chapters, in the Hôpitaux Généraux, both the 'deserving' and the 'undeserving' (particularly the able-bodied) poor were to be confined and, in theory at least, moralized into good work habits and religious orthodoxy.[12] In practice, by the early eighteenth century the more repressive aspect of the institutions had been attenuated, and they served first as orphanages-cum-foundlings' homes for unwanted children and second as old people's homes for the aged and infirm. It is of course true that a large, often very large, proportion of individuals admitted to these institutions died there: the children because of the horrifying system of baby-farming and because of poor wet-nursing;[13] the aged simply because they were aged. Because of this, death-rates in the Hôpitaux Généraux are a pretty meaningless index of institutional levels of care and hygiene.

Although critics of hospitals in the late eighteenth century waxed indignant about the excesses perpetrated by the Hôpitaux Généraux,[14] it is on the Hôtels-Dieu that the present chapter will focus. It was into the latter – rather than into the Hôpitaux Généraux with their motley collections of stunted and decrepit individuals – that the medical profession was keenest to make incursions, for they alone offered the requisite number and range of sick individuals for bedside observation and instruction. For the most part, moreover, it was the Hôtels-Dieu which, over the course of the nineteenth century, were to become clinical institutions. It is they, therefore, which manifest the clearest signs of ancestry to modern hospitals, and therefore have most relevance to the 'birth of the clinic'.

In order to gauge how an eighteenth-century hospital operated, I will take as a case study the Hôtel-Dieu at Nîmes. This institution deserves study for reasons other than the fact that it is not located in Paris. It possesses exceptionally fine admissions registers for the eighteenth century, which record, besides the names of entrants, their sex, their marital status (for females), their parish and diocese of origin, their age, their occupation (for males – for females the occupation of their husband or father), their date of entry and of exit (or death).[15] These documents, which allow the social composition of entrants to be judged with some minuteness, are, moreover, complemented by other valuable material: in particular, documents relating to the service of inmates performed by the congregation of nursing sisters, whose pivotal position in the running of the hospital we will discuss later;[16] and the *Tables nosologiques* – a kind of clinical record – kept by Jacques Razoux, one of the Hôtel-Dieu's doctors, between 1757 and 1761, which allow the patterns of institutional morbidity and mortality to be assessed.[17]

The hospital under review is representative of Hôtels-Dieu

of the large provincial towns. Nîmes, *chef-lieu* of the present-day department of the Gard, was one of the crescent of important urban centres fanning out across the Bas-Languedoc from Beaucaire on the Rhône through Montpellier, Sète, Agde, Béziers, and Narbonne to Carcassonne, Castelnadaury, and Toulouse in the Haut-Languedoc. Its population grew over the course of the eighteenth century from some 20,000 to over 40,000 inhabitants. This increase owed much to the startling development of the local silk industry, which, in one way or another, provided employment for over half of the city's adult population on the eve of the Revolution. By then Nîmes had become the second largest city in Languedoc and one of the largest score or so of French cities.[18] In earlier times it had been a predominantly Protestant city, but by 1789 the combination of government repression on the one hand, and immigration from the traditionally Catholic regions in the hinterland on the other, had substantially altered the confessional balance. By the late eighteenth century Catholics made up two-thirds of the population of Nîmes, and it was for them that the city's poor-relief institutions operated. There was a Miséricorde, a pious confraternity of lay-women specializing in good works, and four parish *bureaux de charité*, which together provided home relief for the needy poor. The Hôpital Général, founded in 1686, admitted the aged, infirm, foundlings, orphans and illegitimate children, and the like. And there was the Hôtel-Dieu, which dated back to 1343, and which saw its mission as the care of the sick poor (*pauvres malades*).[19] This complement of institutions was kept closely under the influence of the ecclesiastical establishment, and though recipients of relief might be Protestant, they would often have to put up with a barrage of proselytizing from zealous Catholics – administrators, chaplains, nursing sisters, and even fellow inmates. Significantly hospitals' death registers also recorded abjurations of their faith by Protestants.

The Hôtel-Dieu of Nîmes was fairly representative too in its mode of administration and financing. Under the provisions of letters patent awarded by the central government – similar to those which all hospitals of any substance possessed – the affairs of the hospital were directed by an administrative board headed by the local bishop and on which sat a mixture of lay and ecclesiastical, ex officio and rotating members chosen from the city's most important corporate bodies (the chapter, the municipality, the local Sénéchaussée court, etc.). These local dignitaries offered the Hôtel-Dieu not only charitable service but also charitable donations. Although the letters patent granted the institution a range of financial privileges (the most important of which was a share of municipal tolls), almsgiving, donations, and deathbed bequests comprised the lifeblood of the institution. By far the most important item of income, for example, derived from the returns on the investments the administrative board had been able to make with sizeable bequests.[20]

The hospital contained some eighty beds at the end of the Ancien Régime, a figure which a royal hospital inspector who visited the hospital in the 1780s found risibly low for a city of Nîmes' importance. The insufficiency was all the more acute in that a quarter of the beds were occupied not by the poor and needy but by soldiers. This was mainly because the hospital had not only the financial structure but also the financial problems of most eighteenth-century French hospitals. The inflationary pressures of the period pushed up institutional overheads at the same time as they swelled the ranks of the poor and needy. Yet a fall in the flow of charities – connected perhaps to a decline in religious fervour – nibbled at the financial basis of the institution. In these circumstances, the administrative board tried to cover its deficits by admitting large numbers of soldiers in order to collect the fixed sum which the Ministry of War was required to pay for each man's daily care. In so far as the somewhat incomplete admissions registers allow us to judge,[21] the Hôtel-Dieu admitted about 150,000 individuals in the 90 years preceding the Revolution. About a third of these were soldiers.

That the Ministry of War was willing to place so many troops at the disposal of the hospital suggests that the institution can hardly have been seen solely as a death-trap. This is borne out by statistics relating to mortality. The death-rate of soldiers was consistently far lower than that of civilians and registered a pronounced fall over the course of the eighteenth century (that of civilians was far less determinate) (see Figure 2.1). For all categories, the hospital registered death-rates only a fraction of those of the Paris Hôtel-Dieu. The proportion of deaths to admissions in three sample periods which were subjected to close analysis was, for civilians, 10.4 per cent in the period 1740–4, 11.3 per cent in 1757–61, and 14.3 per cent in 1777–84. For soldiers the figures were 4.8, 5.1, and 1.7 per cent.[22] The overall proportion of civilian deaths was 11.7 per cent – a figure which underlines again how relatively

Figure 2.1: Variations in Mortality Rates of Entrants to the Nîmes Hôtel-Dieu.

representative of other provincial Hôtels-Dieu the Nîmes hospital was. Certainly the indiscriminate application of the label 'gateway to death' to a hospital in which only one entrant in nine or ten actually succumbed seems inappropriate.

If, in the light of these mortality levels, the old paradigm of the eighteenth-century hospital will clearly not do, how best can we characterize the social functions of the institution? A careful study of the clientele of the hospital and the care which it offered suggests a quite different idea of what these functions were.

II

Analysis of the registers of admissions to the Nîmes Hôtel-Dieu suggests that the hospital served a variety of functions, and that one of the most important was that of staging post or hostel for the young travelling worker. Two out of every three civilian entrants were men. An obvious reason for the male predominance (66.9 per cent) was that the institution had less available capacity for women. This is a tautology, however, rather than an explanation. It may be that other local charitable institutions – notably the Miséricorde, which offered home relief and which always counted aged widows and the like among their most numerous clients – enabled many local women to avoid entering the hospital.[25] It may also have been that women felt greater repugnance for the idea of entering hospitals, which had something of a popular notoriety for the dissecting aspirations and lewd humour of medical students and apprentice-surgeons. The most plausible explanation, however, is that men were more likely than women to have been long-distance travellers, and the admissions registers show that the majority of entrants were, in fact, outsiders to the city.

Only 16.4 per cent of the men and 25.7 per cent of the women admitted to the Nîmes Hôtel-Dieu were from Nîmes itself; over three out of four civilian entrants were outsiders to the city (as virtually all soldiers were, of course). The vast majority were natives of France; only 5.4 per cent – mostly men – were foreigners. Most of these were from the Mediterranean countries, notably Italy, Savoy, and Piedmont; with a much smaller representation from Spain, the Swiss cantons, and the German states; and a very tiny number of exotic cases – a Greek, two Hungarians, and a couple of Englishmen.

The pattern of immigration reveals remarkable geographical breadth (see Map 2.1). With the single exception of the (eastern) diocese of Saint-Dié, every one of the 121 dioceses of metropolitan France was represented among those

Map 2.1: Geographical Origins (by Dioceses) of Strangers to Nîmes Admitted to the Nîmes Hôtel-Dieu in the Eighteenth Century.

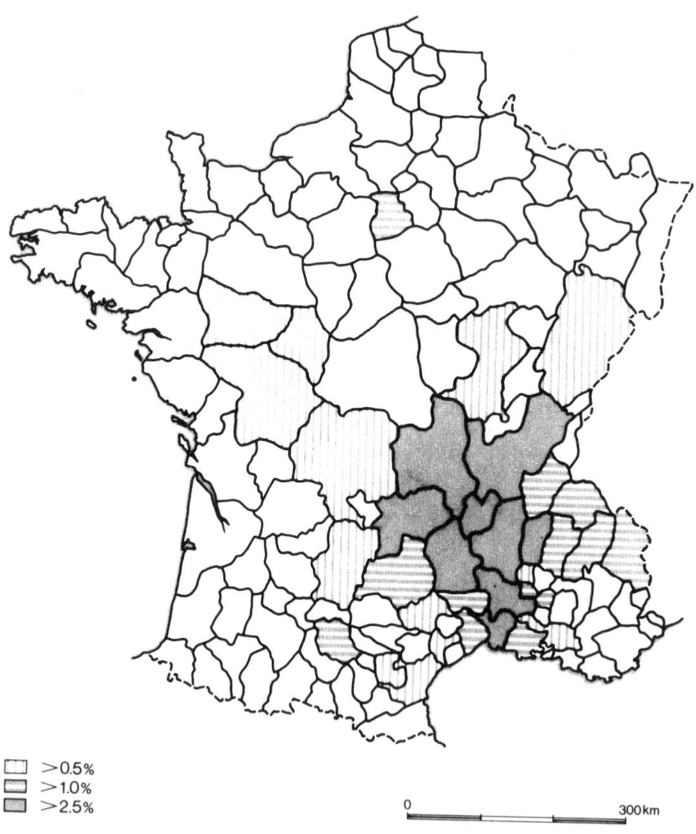

individuals who entered the hospital in the 18 sample years. Many of the regions were, however, represented by only a small handful of cases.

By far the largest proportion of long-distance entrants was drawn from two zones. The first ran down the Rhône from Lyon, extending eastwards into the dioceses of Embrun, Die, Grenoble, and Gap and running down through Orange, Carpentras, Avignon, and Arles towards Marseille. The second followed the route down the other bank of the Rhône, from Le Puy through the Vivarais, to merge with the major channels of migration towards the city to the west of the Rhône. Beyond these two main axes there were a certain number of centres with which Nîmes had long-standing commercial and, more importantly, manufacturing links, notably Paris and Tours, both centres of silk production. Most of western France, in contrast, remained seemingly immune to the attraction of Nîmes, distanced as it was from the Rhône corridor and characterized in any case by short-term migrations. As for the north-west, virtually unrepresented in the hospital, there were more than enough big cities – Paris not least – to capture the migrant population well before it reached Lyon and the south. The small numbers of entrants from Bas-Provence and the southern Alps is probably indicative of another circuit of migration centred upon Avignon, Aix, and Marseille.[24]

If the breadth of immigration which emerges from the hospital's admissions is remarkable, so too is the predominance of what was clearly the city's main recruiting area: extending from the diocese of Uzès northward and westward into the Massif Central. The dioceses of the central and eastern parts of the Massif – Viviers, Mende, Rodez, Saint-Flour, and Le Puy – together with the two more adjacent dioceses of Nîmes and Uzès, accounted for about a third of non-Nîmois males admitted to the hospital, a reminder of the close and complex social, economic, and cultural ties binding together mountain and plain in the Mediterranean of the *longue durée*.[25] The dioceses of the southern fringe of the Massif also provided the majority of women from outside Nîmes who entered the hospital. Women moved over smaller distances than did men, and the areas of traditional migration from the city's hinterland therefore predominate.[26]

Most of these travellers and migrants from far and near brought with them few skills. The occupational breakdown of men admitted to the hospital shows very few representatives of the propertied or professional classes, with traders and merchants – including many pedlars – and those with paramilitary occupations or past military careers making up small contingents (see Table 2.3). A tiny handful of pilgrims testified to the durability of the hospital's function as a haven for those bound for Rome or for Compostella.[27] Most entrants were unequivocally from the lower orders. Nearly a third worked the land, the vast majority as agricultural labourers (*travailleurs de terre*). They comprised the largest single category of entrants to the Hôtel-Dieu. Some 10 per cent were unskilled labourers, employed in transport or as domestic servants.

Table 2.3: Occupations of Male Entrants to the Nîmes Hôtel-Dieu

Occupation	*1740–4*		*1757–61*		*1777–84*	
1. Military	2.38		1.60		0.65	
2. Clergy	0.24		0.32		0.15	
3. Pilgrims	1.32		1.60		0.41	
4. Middle classes and professions	1.94		1.63		0.38	
5. Commerce	1.92		2.13		3.21	
6. Skilled and semi-skilled artisans						
i) Wood/building	4.20		4.20		8.29	
ii) Leather/shoes	4.30		3.44		4.42	
iii) Metal	3.94	35.88	3.35	35.64	4.60	46.17
iv) Textiles/clothing	22.10		23.83		27.29	
v) Miscellaneous	1.34		0.82		1.57	
7. Maritime trades and fishing	0.72		0.85		0.6	
8. Unskilled						
i) Domestic service	2.57		2.48		3.34	
ii) Urban labouring	5.66	9.84	6.38	10.35	6.49	11.15
iii) Transport	1.61		1.49		1.32	
9. Agriculture						
i) Farmers	3.50		4.08		2.7	
ii) Day-labourers	22.65		24.05		23.27	
iii) Herders	1.82	28.02	1.78	30.06	0.72	26.7
iv) Miners	0.05		0.15		0.01	
10. Institutionalized	2.33		3.38		2.87	
11. Beggars	6.62		5.98		1.62	
12. No profession	1.32		0.87		0.72	
13. Children	5.78		4.14		3.49	
14. Miscellaneous	1.22		1.05			
Total = 13,615						

Sources: see Table 2.5.

There were fairly considerable contingents of beggars, of the institutionalized poor (from either the Hôpital Général or the local prison), a smattering of those with no occupation, and a number of children too young to be associated with any regular occupation and entering with ailing parents.

The women admitted to the hospital were drawn from very similar social origins. Their own occupations were usually not recorded and the majority of those that were, were employed as seamstresses or domestic servants. Since most women's paid work was probably more seasonal than men's (linked either to the reeling of silk in the summer months or the preparation and sale of agricultural products on an irregular basis), this absence of information was predictable. The occupations of their husbands and fathers, moreover, mirrored those of the men admitted to the hospital.

If the majority of the entrants to the hospital were thus drawn from the poorer elements of society and included more than a fair admixture of down-and-outs, they were not, however, about to die. The age structure of those admitted to the hospital reinforces the impression conveyed by the death-rate statistics and suggests a relatively 'healthy' clientele (see Figure 2.2). In principle, the Hôtel-Dieu did not admit children, except those who were accompanying their parents. Most entrants were still, however, in the prime of life. This was certainly true of the high proportion of entrants who were soldiers, and was equally the case for the majority of civilians. Thus 49.4 per cent of men were between 15 and 35 years of age. Most of the women who entered the hospital were unmarried, hardly surprising in a France in which the age at marriage was still late. There was, it is true, a substantial minority of middle-aged and aged entrants, more so among the women than among the men, but the mass of those admitted to the Hôtel-Dieu were drawn from a population which can be characterized biologically in terms of youth and vigour rather than decrepitude, senility, or moribundity.

The type of individual for whom the Nîmes Hôtel-Dieu seemed especially to cater in the eighteenth century was thus the solitary individual, often unmarried, usually a long way from home, and doubtless in a great many cases lacking the supportive structures of kin and community upon which native Nîmois could rely. There is a certain amount of evidence that the institution was also increasingly serving as port of call for

Figure 2.2: Ages of Entrants to the Nîmes Hôtel-Dieu.

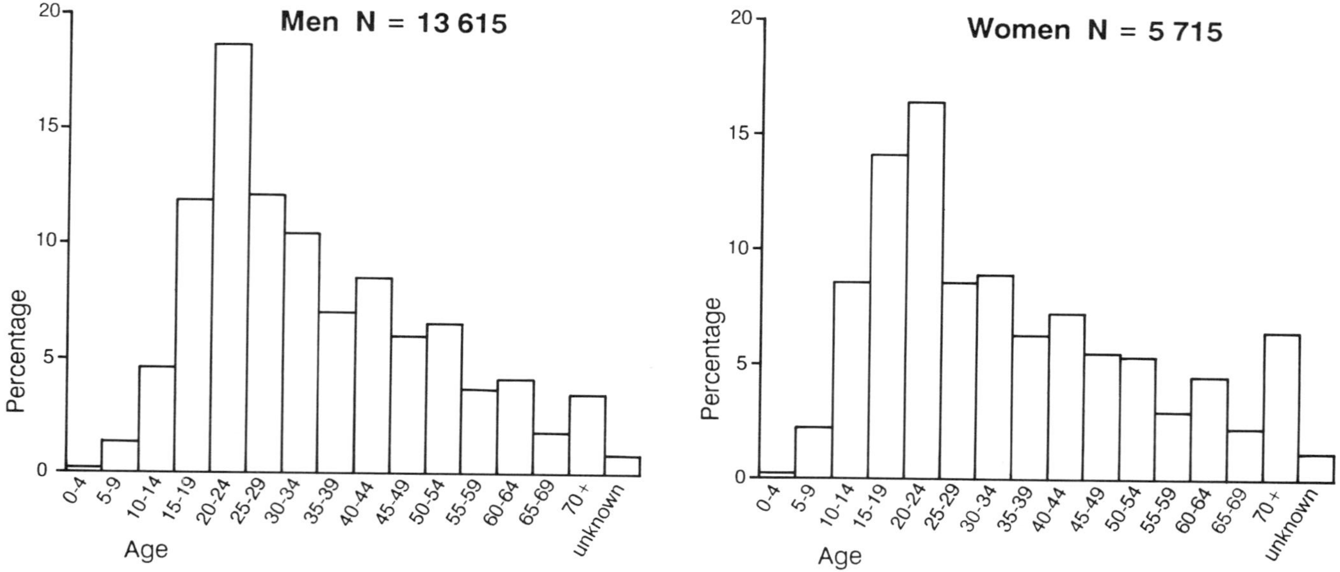

uprooted proletarians who had expended their lives in Nîmes's growing manufacturing sector. The proportion of skilled and unskilled urban workers, notably from the building and textile industries, rose from 35.9 to 46.1 per cent between the first and the third sample periods; the proportion of male entrants who were natives of Nîmes also grew over the same period from under 17 per cent to over 20 per cent; while there was also a growth in the proportion of aged and middle-aged entrants, with the percentage of males over 45 years old rising from 20.7 to 27.7, and females from 24.9 to 27.7 per cent. Yet if those who entered the hospital towards the end of the eighteenth century were marginally less youthful, less itinerant, and more dependent than hitherto on waged work in urban industries, the large majority still conformed to the traditional pattern. Although the slow evolution in the social composition of entrants may have helped to sensitize hospital reformers to the potential of such institutions, the prevailing image was still not so much the *machine à guérir*,[28] dear to the hearts of Enlightenment social theorists, but rather of the medieval *xenodochium*, orientated around the needs of the homeless and the far from home.[29]

With certain nuances, the traditional picture holds true when we consider the structure and incidence of mortality within the hospital. Since only about one entrant in ten died there, the vast majority evidently left never to return. Yet the incidence of mortality was most uneven. It could oscillate according to 'good' or 'bad' harvest years, for example (see Figure 2.3). It did so less, however, than admissions into the hospital.

In 1740–1, for example, the price of rye rose sharply, and markedly buoyed up the number of civilians admitted to the hospital, yet the death-rate stood at only 9.7 per cent – well below the secular average. A similar picture is observable in the period of high rye prices between 1758 and 1761. The irregularity of the relationship between admissions and mortality is evident too in the fact that the highest incidence of mortality among male civilians occurred in 1710–11 (16.8 per cent), 1721–2 (16.6 per cent), 1747–8 (15.9 per cent), and 1779–80 (15.4 per cent) – all years in which the number of entrants was less than in preceding years. If the rhythm of admissions does indicate – as Jean Meuvret was among the first to suspect – that in years of high prices the hospital could

Figure 2.3: Rye Prices in Nîmes (Monthly Average, September–September).

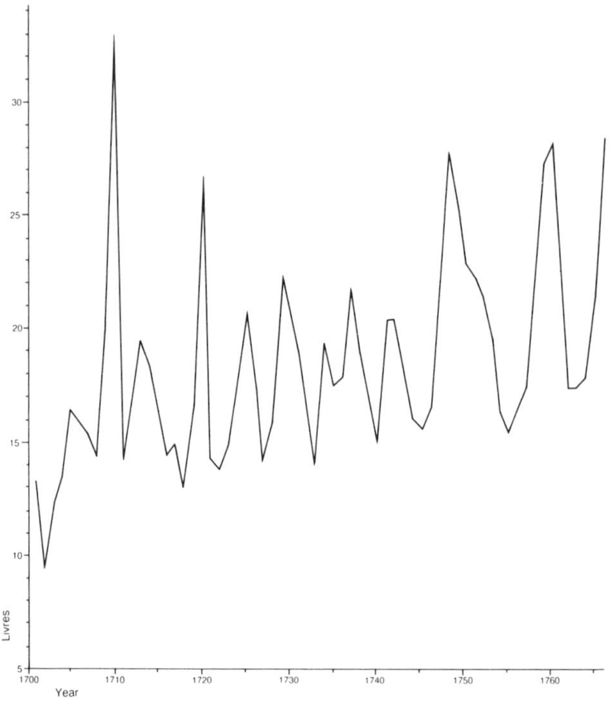

become an important refuge for the distressed, the contrapuntal rhythm of institutional mortality points rather to epidemic disease or some alternative factor to dearth as the main killer of hospital inmates.[30]

Death-rates within the Nîmes Hôtel-Dieu could vary also, as we have seen, according to the type of entrant. The death-rate of soldiers, for example, was only 4.5 per cent; that of civilians 11.7 per cent. The death-rates of the two sexes differed too, with the incidence of mortality among women consistently and increasingly out-distancing that of the male civilians. Female mortality averaged 13.2 per cent over the century as against the 10.2 per cent for civilian males, who were, it will be remembered, a more mobile group than their female counterparts. Similarly the death-rate varied according to occupation: and again the most numerous and most plebeian of the categories were far from having the highest mortality.[31]

Death's reaping was uneven in respect to age too. The very young suffered disproportionately. The survival chances of the few children under the age of 5 who entered the hospital (most of them alongside an ailing relative) were three times lower than the average (see Figure 2.4). The 5- to 9-year-old age group also suffered disproportionately. Such statistics comprised a saddening comment on the inability of hospital authorities to provide an environment appropriate to proper child care.

Figure 2.4: Percentage of Deaths in Age Categories of those to the Admitted Nîmes Hôtel-Dieu.

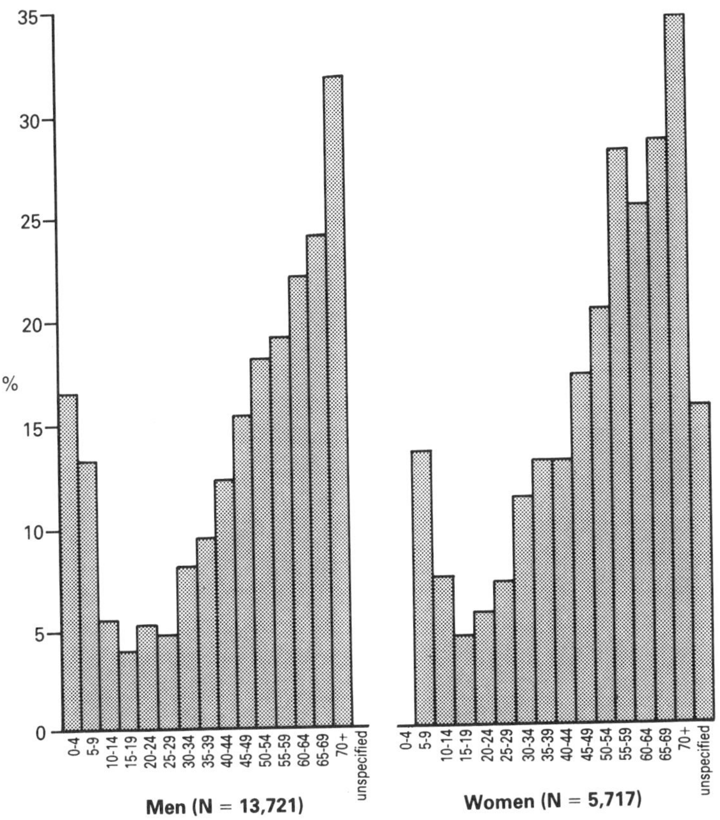

At the other end of the age-scale, too, the incidence of death was troubling (see Figure 2.4). Adults over the age of 70 were as prone to death within the hospital as the under-5s. Yet the converse of this situation – and perhaps the most remarkable feature of age-specific mortality within the Hôtel-Dieu – was that adults in the prime of life stood a chance of survival far better than the one to nine or ten chance which was the institutional mean. Entrants between 15 and 30 stood approximately a one in twenty chance of succumbing within the institution. Those between 10 and 14 and men between 30 and 40 also stood proportionately good chances of survival. These age-specific levels of mortality are very similar to that of soldiers.

Set within the overall context of low mortality levels and notwithstanding the fortunes of the very young and very old within the institution, the general picture emerges of a hospital clientele which was young and restless, a set of individuals very much 'on the move' – and whose mobility was only rarely ended by entering the hospital.

Figure 2.5: Average Length of Stay of Entrants to the Nîmes Hôtel-Dieu.

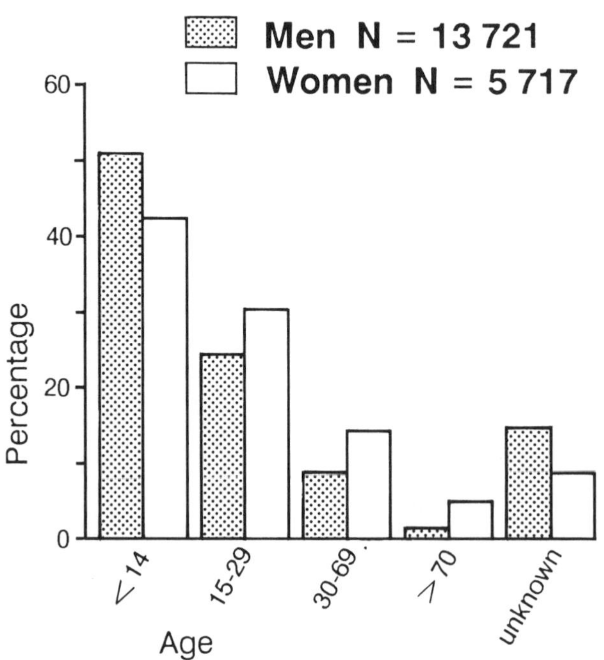

Statistics relating to average length of stay within the hospital further bolster this view (see Figure 2.5). There were, admittedly, a handful of long-term inmates – individuals who lasted months, even years, within the Hôtel-Dieu, doubtless wasting away to a quiet death. Most entrants were, in contrast, short-termers, individuals who stayed in the hospital for a fortnight or less. This was especially true of the men. Furthermore, the proportion of short-term inmates would have been even greater had it not evidently been hospital practice to keep inmates well beyond their putative 'date of recovery' and release them in batches on the first day of the month or at some other signal occasion.

With the evidence at hand relating to mortality and length of stay, it would be tempting to accord the Nîmes Hôtel-Dieu a pretty clean bill of health. If one stopped at this point, one might proceed by inference and suggestion to ascribe the hospital a position in the vanguard of the demographic revolution of the eighteenth century. Although, it might be argued, its record was somewhat blemished in the cases of the very young and very old – demographically vulnerable groups in any context – the hospital nevertheless provided for the vigorous sections of the population who were its main clients, an environment in which life was – *pace* the Black Legend – rarely at risk and where therefore (presumably) cure rates were high. This suggestion might match the conclusions being reached by recent historians of certain English provincial hospitals,[32] and it would be quite consonant with the picture that has recently been presented of the 'gestation of the clinic' originating in the slow and relatively unremarked growth in the involvement of surgeons in Parisian hospital practice over the course of the eighteenth century.[33]

This scenario, however rosy and attractive at first sight, seems to err considerably on the side of medical optimism. Concentration on the 'inputs' and 'outputs' of the eighteenth-century hospital – though important in itself – should not blind us to the content of hospital care and the nature of hospital therapy. Evidence relating to the internal functioning, the medical services, and the general ethos of the Nîmes Hôtel-Dieu suggests a far greater degree of scepticism about its therapeutic record and – in consequence – its medical status.

III

The person who kept the admissions registers at the Nîmes Hôtel-Dieu in sprawling and phonetic hand was a member of the congregation of nursing sisters known as the soeurs hospitalières de Saint-Joseph. This congregation of nursing sisters – which in common with others like it provided home relief for worthy paupers and elementary school classes for the daughters of the poor as well as hospital care – had been founded in La Flèche in Anjou in 1636.[34] It took over the internal running of the Nîmes Hôtel-Dieu, under the guidance of the administrative board, in the late seventeenth century, and by the end of the Ancien Régime had sprouted branches throughout France and even in Canada. In the second half of this chapter I will argue that nursing sisters – who were to be found in a majority of major hospitals as well as in a good number of minor ones – were crucial in establishing the atmosphere and values of the traditional hospital, and that any account of the 'medicalization' of the hospital should accord them an important place.

Some of these congregations had originated in the Middle Ages – such as the body of nurses who ran the great Hôtel-Dieu in Paris, who claimed to have been founded in the ninth century.[35] Most however had been created, and all had been reformed, at the height of the religious revival in France which followed the Council of Trent. Particularly important at that time in the rehabilitation of the vocation of hospital nurse, which, after flourishing in the twelfth and thirteenth centuries, had fallen into the doldrums in the late Middle Ages, was the work of Saint Vincent de Paul. The Daughters of Charity which the latter founded in 1633 were in many ways the archetype of these new female communities of active life, as well as the most widely spread such community throughout France by the late seventeenth century.[36] The Daughters of Charity formed a highly centralized and effective body, the elements of whose organization and the spirit of whose regulations were immensely influential on similar bodies being created or reformed at about the same time: the Soeurs de Saint-Charles de Nancy (est. 1652), for example, the Soeurs de Saint-Thomas de Villeneuve (est. 1661), the Filles de la Sagesse (est. 1703), and many often smaller ones. Their influence is patent too in the regulations of the soeurs hospitalières de Saint-Joseph – who ran the Nîmes Hôtel-Dieu – which were drawn up in 1686.[37]

These regulations proudly reaffirmed the medieval vocation of the hospital servant: their daily routine was to be an uncompromising combination of religious duties, hard manual labour, and self-abnegating devotion to the *pauperes Christi* – the sisters were theologically rather than sociologically minded – who made up the clientele of their hospital. The order's regulations made it clear for the would-be novice that, in regard to the hospital entrant,

> the hospitaller will extend him a charitable welcome, and will gently caution him to put himself in good state so that God will give His blessing to the food and remedies which he needs.[38]

The ensuing ritual of confession, preparation of a bed, the washing of feet, and the like might all have been – and probably were – cribbed wholesale from the regulations of the medieval nursing orders and hospitals.[39] As was the case with the medieval hospital, moreover, post-Tridentine spirituality accorded spiritual and moral edification of inmates equal if not prior status over bodily care:

> As the salvation of the soul is incomparably more important than the health of the body, the sisters must keep it in their minds in all the services which they render to the sick poor, working affectionately for their instruction so that they are led to serve and honour God by the good use of their illnesses, and that those leaving the hospital carry off with them health of the soul as well as that of the body, and that those who die there may go to Heaven.[40]

The preparation of hospital entrants for their putative passage into the next world was thus one of the main preoccupations of the nurses who ran the Hôtel-Dieu in Nîmes.The hospital was certainly not untypical in having a goodly number of individuals arrive on their doorstep in the final stages of their life. The admissions registers occasionally record such cases in typically cryptic fashion: 'a man was brought in who stayed only an hour or so. He received Extreme Unction. We don't know his name. He was about 30 years old'.[41] For such individuals – a small but significant proportion of entrants as the death statistics show – there was little the nursing sisters could hope to do except to procure them a 'good death'.[42] For these entrants, at least, the Nîmes Hôtel-Dieu lived up to the time-honoured reputation of the traditional hospital as 'la porte du ciel' ('the gateway to death').[43]

The desperate individual requiring spiritual consolation on his passage to the afterlife was only one of the different categories of entrants to whom the Christian hospital had always proferred its aid. For the medieval nurse, the practice of *hospitalité* had been indiscriminate. The eighteenth-century nursing sister, despite her general attachment to the precepts of her medieval forebear, showed a shade more discrimination in her admissions policy. The rules of the soeurs hospitalières de Saint-Joseph prohibited the order from treating the insane (including epileptics) or those suffering from diseases regarded as incurable, humiliating (*infâme*), or contagious.[44] The traditions of the Nîmes Hôtel-Dieu also restricted entries in certain ways. The chronically and incurably sick and infirm, along with the disabled and various types of abandoned child, were referred to the city's Hôpital Général, which offered a long-term refuge to the locality's *invalides* ('impotent' poor); or else they were redirected to their home parishes. The hospital's charter also forbade the nursing sisters from taking in individuals suffering from contagious diseases, including syphilis.[45]

These limitations on the sort of indiscriminating welcome which the medieval hospital had offered the poor were largely pragmatic in motivation. There was obviously a good deal of sense, for example, in wishing to exclude individuals with contagious diseases which placed the whole hospital community – sisters and inmates – at risk. The exclusion of persons suffering from venereal disease, as well as pregnant women and nursing mothers, seems to have sprung from a desire to uphold both the moral and the physical integrity of the little community. To admit the syphilitic, or the mother without a decent home to go to, was to open the door to vice and, in the eyes of the sisters, thereby to place a shadow over the institution's good name. Such a slur could occasion unpopularity with potential entrants and would-be benefactors.

In addition, the provision of facilities for such special cases would place a financial and organizational strain on the hospital which it would find difficult to bear – especially in the eighteenth century, when hospital finances were under great stress. However pragmatic and understandable these limitations were, however, it should be noted that they seriously affected any claims the hospital might have had to be in the forefront of the struggle against disease. How could an institution which either specifically excluded or else restricted entry to many of the most biologically vulnerable categories of the poor – children, mothers in childbirth, those suffering from contagious diseases – possibly be in the vanguard of the 'demographic revolution'?

According to a time-honoured formula, the hospital received the *pauvre malade:* but the admissions procedure indicates that the medical response to *illness* was not to prevail over the respect and assistance due to *poverty*. The careful examination of entrants by no means resembled a medical examination in the strict sense: it was a liturgical rather than narrowly medical procedure. It was the nursing sister who kept the registers of entries and who supervised admission. Her religious cast of mind and traditions of her vocation made her receptive and responsive to all manner of need, except those cases specifically excluded entry to the hospital. Her preoccupation was more likely to be with the observance of her religious duties toward the *pauper Christi* than with a scrupulous definition of ailments. Her lack of formal medical training and her semi-literacy were further limitations on her diagnostic insight. Furthermore, the doctors of the Hôtel-Dieu were not – the point deserves emphasis – consulted over admissions. The clinical record which the hospital doctor Jacques Razoux kept makes it clear that the doctor's job was to treat those who were in the hospital without concerning himself with how they got there.

Although hospital doctors were not involved in the examination of entrants, the apprentice-surgeons who lived within the hospital might be called in to give their opinion. Their task was essentially a negative one, however: less to ascertain and describe the specific ailment of entrants than to act as a safety net for the sisters in ensuring that no one afflicted with a medical condition which the hospital traditionally excluded slipped into the hospital unawares. This was probably a role they were called on to perform most frequently in cases of suspected venereal disease and with males, towards whose bodily ailments the sisters, mindful of their vows of chastity, were enjoined to manifest a strict and proper distance. Furthermore, the medical prowess of the apprentice-surgeons was hardly, if at all, more inspiring than that of the sisters. They had no formal surgical training and were often left to their own devices by the stipendiary surgeon attached to the hospital. Razoux, who presents a picture of medical care within the hospital in a deliberately favourable light, is nevertheless forced to record a number of instances of bad gaffes by apprentice-surgeons in which loss of life resulted.[46]

The deficiencies of medical inspection at the door of the hospital – the limitations of the apprentice-surgeons, the open-handed generosity of the nursing sisters supervising admission – are reflected in the list of illnesses which Razoux compiled from individuals within the hospital under his care between 1757 and 1761.[47] Passing tentatively beyond the nosological terminology which Razoux employed, it is possible to ascertain something of the range of conditions which a hospital doctor would encounter (see Table 2.4). Malarial illness (*fièvres intermittentes quotidiennes, tierces et quartes*) was among the most frequently found – testimony to the harmful influence of the swampy littoral of the Bas-Languedoc. Treated with cinchona, deaths from malaria were not, however, frequent – although given the shortage of diagnostic insight, it may be that some of the other cases recorded (*vomissements* – twelve cases cited, for example), were presenting undetected symptoms of terminal malaria. More deadly than malaria, however, were a number of relatively common ailments, notably typhoid fever (*typhus*), dysentery (*dysenterie*), possibly some cases of *diarrhée*, and tubercular illness (*phtisie*). With such diseases present in such numbers, it should be noted that the Hôtel-Dieu's ban on contagious diseases was not fully observed – proof again of the perfunctoriness of medical examination on entry. Furthermore, of other supposedly prohibited 'maladies', epilepsy (4 cases) was also present, while cited cases of *vérole* (syphilis? – 10 cases), *dysurie* (dysuria – 5 cases), and *inflammation des testicules* (3 cases) were more than likely to have been venereal in origin. A number of the typical afflictions of the aged were there in force too: *rhumatismes* (225 cases),

Table 2.4: Razoux's Categories of the Diseases Afflicting Entrants to the Nîmes Hôtel-Dieu (1757–62).

Disease	*Per cent admitted*	*Per cent deaths of category admitted*
Synochus	22.0	1
Fièvres intermittentes	13.2	0.1
Fièvres éphémères	9.2	4.5
Fièvres putrido-malignes	9.6	7.5
Dysenterie	5.6	8.3
Diarrhée	4.0	3.3
Catarres	4.0	7.8
Rhumatismes	3.8	–
Phtisie	3.5	35.3
Pleuropneumonies	3.2	19.2
Hydropisies	2.7	27.1
Typhus	2.2	32.1
Erysipèles	2.2	0.8
Plaies avec ulcère	2.1	–
Opthalmies	1.4	–
Angines	1.2	–
Others	10.0	–
Total = 6.380		

Source: J. C. Vincens and J.B. Baumès, *Topographie de la Ville de Nîmes.*
Note: The low overall mortality rate – some 6 per cent – reflects the inclusion of soldiers among Razoux's cases.

angines (74 cases), *paralisie* (10 cases), and *ankylose* (1 case). Skin disorders were also well represented: *érysipèles* (134 cases), *plaies* (with or without *ulcères*) (115 cases), tinea (*dartres* – 10 cases), scurvy (*scorbut*, falsely accounted as a contagious disease, incidentally – 10 cases), malignant abscesses (*charbon* – 7 cases), scabies (*gale* – 4 cases). The respiratory system seemed especially at risk, as was witnessed by the large number of *catarres* (241 cases), *pleuropneumonies* (170 cases), *asthme* (28 cases), and the like.

The most prevalent illness of all was the *synochus*, or *fièvres continues simples*, of which Razoux recorded no fewer than 1,406 out of 6,380 identified. The primacy of this ailment is all the more striking when it is grouped together with the *fièvres éphémères prolongées*, which a twentieth-century diagnostician would be unable to distinguish from the basic symptom of *synochus*. These were seasonal ailments: together they accounted for 42.1 per cent of entrants in the month of July and 33.6 per cent of all entrants between July and November.

The febrile symptom makes classification difficult, although doubtless there might have been rheumatic fever, tubercular glands, and bronchitis present under this general heading. Were all the ailments covered by these catch-all terms so serious, however? Razoux seems to have classified under these rubrics the numerous cases he encountered of day-labourers admitted to the Hôtel-Dieu suffering from what were popularly known as *coups de soleil* or *efforts* which were little more than the consequences of over-exertion on the road or in the fields in the Mediterranean sun.[48] Similarly hospital care seemingly boiled down to little more than a rest from travelling for a good number of the soldiers admitted. It was common practice, for example, for soldiers returning to their regiments after treatment for venereal disease or skin ailments at the Hôpital Saint-Louis, the Bas-Languedoc's main military hospital, located in Montpellier, to stop off at the Nîmes Hôtel-Dieu 'to rest a while'.[49] In addition, many of the other medical conditions encountered by Razoux could be accounted for by the rigours of the labouring or migratory life: dropsy, for example (*hydropisie*, 143 cases), *vomissements* (12 cases), marasmus (*marasme*, 4 cases), *hernie* (2 cases).

The calendar of entries into the hospital and deaths within it is also instructive in this respect (see Figure 2.6). The sultry summer and autumn months, in the context of the poor levels of hygiene and the unhealthy malarial atmosphere of the littoral, caused high levels of morbidity in the population as a whole – especially among infants who were, however, excluded from the Hôtel-Dieu. These months were also, significantly however, the period of the great migratory movements from the Massif Central, when huge numbers of workers poured south out of the mountains for the annual grain-, wine-, and hay-harvests.[50] Were those from this annual flood of migrants who entered the Nîmes Hôtel-Dieu really 'diseased', or merely displaying the symptoms of that over-exertion and vulnerability to the environment which were the daily lot of the labouring, and especially the migratory, classes? If it were the former, then one would expect the hospital's death-rate to remain stable or even to rise somewhat in the hyper-migratory summer months. Yet this was clearly not the case. To explain this apparent discrepancy it might be argued that the care offered inmates was better in the summer months than at other times of the year. In fact, the opposite was true: the number of inmates

Figure 2.6: Monthly Incidence of Mortality as a Proportion of those Admitted to the Nîmes Hôtel-Dieu.

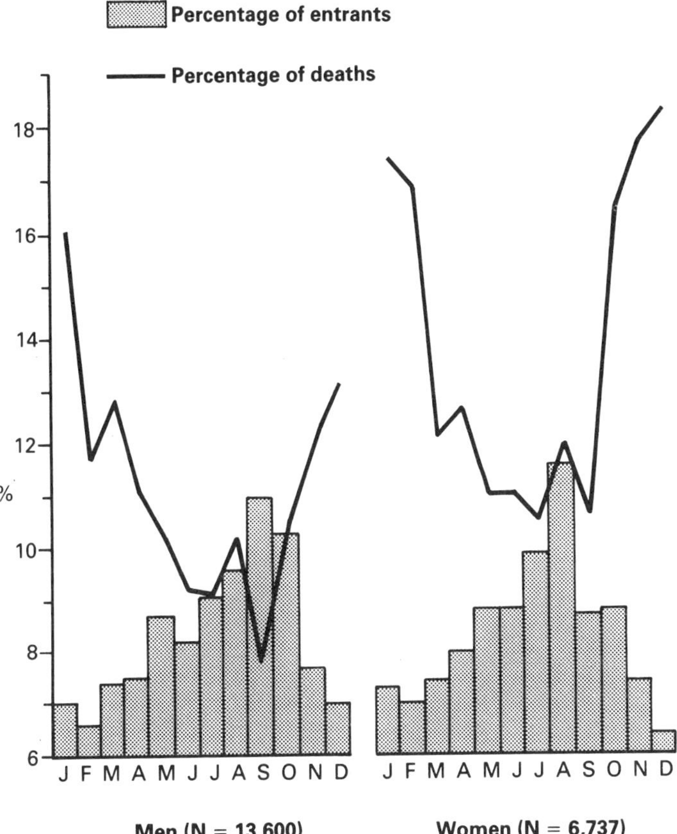

always exceeded the number of beds and, in palliation, recourse was had to the practice of doubling (even tripling!) inmates together in the same bed, or supplementing normal accommodation with camp beds and straw pallets on the floors of already over-crowded halls. Given the unavoidable seasonal unhealthiness of hospital conditions in the summer and autumn, moreover – the heat in the halls was often intense and humidity levels high – the proportional drop in the death-rate at that time suggests an alternative explanation: not improvements in levels of care, but rather that a very large proportion of entrants in this hyper-migratory period were merely itinerant workers seeking out employment and eagerly availing themselves of the care which a hospital like the Nîmes Hôtel-Dieu traditionally provided for the needy-looking individual who turned up hungry and homeless on their doorstep.

The calendar of entries and deaths, institutional morbidity, and materials relating to the nature of hospital care thus generally support the hypothesis, originally suggested by the analysis of the social composition of entrants, that the Nîmes Hôtel-Dieu acted as a staging post for the needy and in particular for the rootless and the traveller. Razoux's remarks in particular are instructive in this respect. Yet it would be erroneous to suppose that it was Razoux's purpose to underline the traditional role of the hospital. The opposite was the case: he was one of the legion of medical writers and social critics towards the end of the Ancien Régime who sought to 'medicalize' the hospital, to transform it into a *machine à guérir.* In keeping a daily record of the state and progress of the illness of every hospital inmate, a doctor such as Razoux saw himself as pioneer and trail-blazer in a great medical crusade.[51] This particular medical prophet was not, however, much appreciated in his own country.

Razoux was isolated even among the staff at the hospital. For reasons which are not clear but which may well have had something to do with hostility to his clinical intentions, Razoux's appointment as hospital doctor in succession to his father, Jean Razoux, had been blocked for a number of years before 1757.[52] Even when finally appointed, moreover, Razoux shared his medical duties with another doctor who did not show the same enthusiasm for bedside observation. As a result of lack of co-operation from his colleague, Razoux was able to provide in his *Tables* detailed medical information for only half the months between 1757 and 1761. This evidently detracts from the putatively scientific and statistical value of the information provided.

Razoux was also not fully at ease with other members of the hospital staff. He evidently resented the Hôtel-Dieu's principal surgeon who, he noted acerbicly, 'is despotic master in this institution of all surgical illnesses'.[53] Razoux's criticisms of the inexperience of the apprentice-surgeons is probably designed to throw a critical light on their master too. At all accounts, as Razoux himself recounts, he met with great suspicion and distrust from his hospital colleagues as soon as he embarked on his ambitious clinical project from the middle of 1757:

> People were unaccustomed to see such behaviour in this institution. My first visit far exceeded the usual limits. There was not a little murmuring as they waited for me to finish. They consoled themselves with the hope that following visits would not be the same. They said so quite openly. However, in spite of these daily rumours, in spite of the opposition I had to sustain, in spite of the mockery that I attracted, the trouble that they laid on for me, and all the efforts of those who opposed me, I have continued up to this day and will continue in the same way as long as my strength and my health permit.[54]

The authentically paranoid tone of this passage captures the lonely isolation of the medical researcher in the traditional hospital. It was doubtless for diplomatic reasons, in the light of his continued holding of the post of hospital doctor, that Razoux did not state in his *Tables* exactly from which quarter the keenest opposition to his intervention in the life of the hospital emanated. His interference would almost certainly not be keenly appreciated by the inmates, for the poor traditionally had a low estimation of the medical profession.[55] In particular, they feared the scalpel being used on their mortal remains in the post-mortems which the academically minded doctor prized highly. Fear of post-mortem was sufficient to drive at least one dying inmate out of the hospital, a case which Razoux records with detached humour, but which was doubtless not unrepresentative.[56] He complains too on several occasions that he was denied permission to perform autopsies on the bodies of particularly interesting medical cases.[57] The refusal of the hospital's administrators reflected the opposition which nursing sisters normally put up against something which was viewed as a sort of sacrilege. Although it is necessary to proceed by inference in this field, it seems likely, in fact, that the most vigorous opposition to the medical intervention of Razoux came from the nursing sisters.

The late eighteenth century was a troubled period in the history of relations between doctors and nurses in France.[58] The new clinical interests of the medical profession brought them into closer contact with the traditional custodians of hospital life than ever before. For a doctor to abandon the benevolent torpor which had seemingly characterized the behaviour of those of the profession formerly attached to the hospitals, and to adopt a more interventionist attitude towards therapy, was to threaten traditional patterns of territoriality within the hospital. It was the nurses who had long since ruled the roost; the new interest of doctors in the condition and treatment of inmates would make deep inroads into a sphere of responsibility which they had long since regarded as their own, would upset a subtly and finely tuned equilibrium within the hospital establishment. Elsewhere in France, this potential point of conflict between doctors and nurses was particularly explosive where the growing influence of hospital doctors led to demands to upgrade the status of ancillary medical personnel: for example, to reverse the traditional pecking order between nurses and apprentice-surgeons so that the latter rather than the former were entrusted with carrying out the medical prescriptions of the doctors – a course of action which any self-respecting nurse regarded as humiliating, derogatory, and ultimately against the interest of the inmates.

The conflict of interests did not take this precise form in the Nîmes Hôtel-Dieu. Here the most contentious matter seems to have been the question of the diet of the hospital inmates. Like other doctors at the time who, increasingly aware of the role of a poor diet in occasioning disease, were moving towards an appreciation of the importance of a healthy diet as a therapeutic weapon, Razoux was convinced that the food ration with which the hospital inmate was served was as important as the drugs he was prescribed or the surgical treatment he received.[59] He therefore complained most bitterly against the excesses of the inmates' diet, which was evidently the norm in the hospital. It was wrong, he felt, that inmates in the midst of a violent illness were permitted up to seven helpings of *bouillon* a day: a much lighter diet, based on water and on *tisanes,* would be much more beneficial. Inmates convalescing from illness or suffering from chronic illness were also, according to Razoux, 'similarly fed too much'.[60] 'There is always a fear in this institution that the poor might die of hunger', he stated, 'they never tire of feeding them';[61] and then again 'It is a fault that cannot be corrected in our hospital. The sick are given too much to eat'.[62]

In the matter of hospital diet was embodied the conviction of Enlightenment doctors that in a well-regulated hospital everything down to the smallest minutiae of institutional life should serve a therapeutic purpose and all obstacles to health and hygiene should be eradicated. This conception of the role of hospital diet clashed with the traditional view espoused by the nursing sisters. For them a copious, even over-copious, provision of the basic needs of hospital inmates was a source of pride and honour. Just as the spiritual hunger of entrants should be continually replenished and nourished by consolation, edification, and prayer, so too should their bodies be coddled and restored by a ferment of charitable effort. This attitude had its roots in the clause found in many hospital charters in the Middle Ages to the effect that the needs of the poor should be met with a bountiful generosity,[63] and it had been strengthened by the reaffirmation of the religious aspect of nursing in the post-Tridentine Catholic reform movement. It should also be borne in mind that the seventeenth century, which saw the foundation or reform of most nursing orders, was also a period in which the most glaring social problems sprang from the terrible crises of subsistence which periodically decimated whole populations. At such times, the main objective of any charitable institution was somehow to feed the starving poor and needy. As we have shown, there is evidence to suggest that many entrants into the eighteenth-century hospital continued to fall into this category. To provide inmates with a good square meal thus would seem to the eighteenth-century nursing sister not only a point of religious duty but also one of time-honoured pragmatism. To go against this basic precept, as the medical profession was trying to do in the name of scientific dietetics, was anathema to the nurses. That the medical profession campaigned against the sisters in the putative interests of the inmate – whose welfare had always been the prime concern of any conscientious nursing sister – only rubbed salt into the wounds and made clashes more likely and more vehement.

Numerous horror stories recounting how the medical recovery of hospital inmates had been impeded by over-indulgent eating and drinking made the attitude of the nursing sisters seem nothing short of obscurantist and self-willed. A protracted and extraordinarily acrimonious dispute at the Paris Hôtel-Dieu towards the end of the Ancien Régime brought forward much evidence of over-bountiful rations causing relapses and dangerous digestive problems. Even prior to that,

Pierre Fournier, doctor at the Hôtel-Dieu in neighbouring Montpellier in the 1760s, had cited chapter and verse how over-feeding tolerated and even encouraged by the sisters led to premature deaths from digestive disorder. He and others like him also pointed to the danger of wounds being inflamed and made more dangerous by an over-rich diet. Indeed, reading Fournier's clinical records, one gains the impression that over-eating was one of the major causes of hospital mortality![64]

Jacques Razoux was aware of these points. He gave another example of how the sisters' generosity could harm their patients. They had, he stated, a regrettable tendency to allow inmates to remain beyond their time of recovery:

> It very often happens that civilians, being cured of the illness which obliged them to present themselves at the hospital, do not leave as so as they ought: either because bad weather prevents them returning to their employment; or because the lack of strength that they feel deprives them of the courage to go and resume their work; or else because a kind of idleness makes them wish to stay in an institution where, without doing anything, they are well fed and well accommodated. Then indubitably they contract a very dangerous illness which spares few of those it gets in its grip. This is what is commonly called hospital fever (*fièvre d'hôpital*).[65]

The extended convalescence which nursing sisters tolerated and even encouraged thus exposed inmates to diseases subsumed under the catch-all title, *fièvre d'hôpital* (typhus, typhoid fever, dysentery, etc.). The good Razoux was, for all his clinical aspirations, totally ignorant, of course, of the nature of infection. His nosological system exhibited the most promiscuous confusion of contagious and non-contagious diseases; and there is no evidence from his clinical record that within the hospital he endeavoured to separate dangerously infectious cases (even supposing he had been able to recognize them) from others. His apparent conviction that the *fièvre d'hôpital* was a natural consequence of a lengthy stay in the hospital revealed an acquired pessimism about the nature of hospital care. In much the same way that, half a century later, Napoleon's great surgeon-general Larrey was to be a perfervid amputationist on the grounds that the expeditious removal of damaged limbs was less dangerous to life than a protracted stay in the hospital, so Jacques Razoux favoured speedy discharges in order to avoid the effects of incidental disease.[66] It was not so much, therefore, that eighteenth-century hospitals were 'death-traps' in the sense that the likelihood of death for all entrants was high: as we have seen, this was certainly not the case. Given the nature and ethos of the traditional hospital, however, and given the inability of the medical profession to dominate the institution and insist on organizational steps which minimized illness and ill health, the threatening presence of death and disease hovered capriciously over hospital halls. Hospitals were symbols of death as well as of the destitution and misfortune which characterized most of their clients; but it was above all arbitrary and unexpected death which caused most fear, not its near certainty, as proponents of the Black Legend would have us believe.

The Enlightenment critique of hospitals pointed forward towards the conception of the social role of the hospital as a kind of 'health-factory', which has since prevailed in the contemporary world. It is possible, as we have suggested, that this critique was bound up with slow but dimly perceptible changes in the nature of hospitals' clientèle: notably the formation of an older, rather more settled and occupationally more homogeneous 'patient' population, whose existence emphasized the limitations of traditional hospital care. None the less, what is most striking about the performance of the Nîmes Hôtel-Dieu over the course of the eighteenth century – and in this the hospital is probably not untypical[67] – is the extent to which it continued to perform the variety of functions which had always characterized it. Some entrants were evidently looking for nothing more than a place to die in Christian surroundings. Others were almost literally scraped off the streets to be prepared for death or coddled back to good health. A great many others seem to have seen the institution as something like the medieval *xenodochium*: as a refuge for the poor, the needy, the traveller, and the rootless, where care was orientated around restoring strength rather than anything more medically ambitious. For such people, it should be noted, the growing intervention of the medical profession in hospital life was not an unqualified blessing. Inmates can hardly have relished the moralizing and stern disciplinarianism of the nursing sisters. Yet in general their sympathies are more likely to have lain with the 'obscurantist' sisters than with the doctors. They expected preparation for death as Christians – or rather Catholics – restorative care, warm beds, and the opportunity to cram themselves with food to the point of bursting; certainly not medical examinations, operations, post-mortems, and medically approved diets. Moreover, in what was still a pre-antiseptic, pre-anaesthetic age, in which medical learning was still very primitive in many spheres, there was undoubtedly a great deal to be said for restricting access to doctors. Given the gap between the professional pretensions of the latter and their positive achievements, it is hardly surprising that hospital inmates as well as nursing sisters – supported on occasion by hospital administrators – should be unashamedly 'archaic' in their attitudes towards the content of hospital care. If 'the birth of the clinic' was predicated upon the submission of the patient to the scrutiny of doctors, it was also closely related to the elimination of opposition to that intruding scrutiny. Here the redefinition of the functions and duties implied by the phrase 'nursing sister' was of particular importance. The example of the Hôtel-Dieu of Nîmes indicates that there is a need to give greater consideration to the ways in which mistrust of the medical profession was negotiated and eventually transcended.

Table 2.5: Exant Admission Registers of the Nîmes Hôtel-Dieu in the Eighteenth Century

Type of entrant	*Years for which registers survive*	*Years with no figures*	*Sources*
Men	1706–9	1709–10	Registers with the
	1710–17	1717–18	following provisional
	1718–32	1732–3	numbers: F7, F12,
	1733–85	1785–6	F14, F17, F20bis,
	1786–92		F23, F26, F29 and F35.
Women	1697–1706	1706–7	As above: F5, F13,
	1707–52	1752–3	F18, no *cote*, F27bis,
	1753–93		F33.
Soldiers	1705–9	1709–10	As above: F7, F11,
	1710–11	1711–12	F15, F16, F19, F21,
	1712–14	1714–15	F22, F24, F27, F31,
	1715–38	1738–9	F34, F36.
	1739–54	1754–8	
	1759–75	1775–82	
	1782–91		

Note: The years expressed from September 4 to the same date the following year.

Notes

1. Relevant works are far too numerous to list here. Note in particular however G. Rosen, 'Hospitals, medical care and social policy in the French Revolution', in his *From Medical Police to Social Medicine: Essays on the History of Health Care* (New York, 1974); essays by L.S. Greenbaum, notably 'J.S. Bailly, the Baron de Breteuil and the "four new hospitals" of Paris', *Clio Medica* (1973); '"Tempest in the Academy": J.B. Le Roy, the Paris Academy of Sciences and the project of a new Hôtel-Dieu', *Archives internationales d'histoire des sciences* (1974); and '"Mesure of civilization": the hospital thought of Jacques Tenon on the eve of the French Revolution', *Bulletin of the History of Medicine* (1975); D.B. Weiner, 'Le Droit de l'homme à la santé: une belle idée devant l'Assemblée Constituante, 1790–1', *Clio Medica* (1970); and her 'French doctors face the war, 1792–1815', in C.K. Warner (ed.) *From the Ancien Régime to the Popular Front: Essays in the History of Modern France in Honour of S.B. Clough* (New York, 1969); T. Gelfand, *Professionalizing Modern Medicine: Paris Surgeons and Medical Science and Institutions in the Eighteenth Century* (Westport, Conn., 1981); M. Staum, *Cabanis: Enlightenment and Medical Philosophy in the French Revolution* (Princeton, NJ, 1980); M. Ramsey, *Professional and Popular Medicine in France, 1770–1830: The Social World of Medical Practice* (Cambridge, 1988). See also H. Mitchell, 'Politics in the service of knowledge: the debate over the administration of medicine and welfare in the late eighteenth century', *Social History* (1981).

2. Among a list which could be considerably extended, note in particular M. Foucault, *The Birth of the Clinic* (English translation, London, 1974); M. Foucault *et al.*, *Les Machines à guérir: aux origines de l'hôpital moderne* (Paris, 1979); J.P. Desaive *et al.*, *Médecins, climat et épidémies à la fin du XVIIIe. siècle* (Paris and The Hague, 1972); and J.P. Goubert, *Malades et médecins en Bretagne, 1770–90* (Rennes, 1974) – the latter particularly valuable for being less Paris-orientated than most.

3. For a good example from an impeccable secondary source of the way that the fate of the great Parisian hospital seems to monopolize discussion of late eighteenth-century hospitals, see C.C. Gillispie, *Science and Polity in France at the End of the Old Régime* (Princeton, NJ, 1980) pp. 251 ff. Social historians of poverty in the Ancien Régime have devoted more attention to non-Parisian institutions than medical historians. See in particular O. Hufton, *The Poor of Eighteenth-Century France, 1750–89* (Oxford, 1974); C.C. Fairchilds, *Poverty and Charity in Aix-en-Provence, 1640–1789* (Baltimore, Md, 1976); K. Norberg, *Rich and Poor in Grenoble, 1600–1815* (Berkeley, Calif., 1983); A. Forrest, *The French Revolution and the Poor* (Oxford, 1981); J.P. Gutton, *La Société et les pauvres: l'exemple de la généralité de Lyon, 1534–1789* (Paris, 1970). Of older works, see too the erudite Camille Bloch, *L'Assistance et l'Etat en France à la veille de la Révolution, 1764–90* (Paris, 1908).

4. For a brief introduction, P.A. Richmond, 'The Hôtel-Dieu of Paris on the eve of the Revolution', *Journal of the History of Medicine and Allied Sciences* (1961).

5. *Encyclopédie, ou Dictionnaire raisonné des sciences, arts et métiers* (VIII,

Neufchatel, 1765) pp. 319 f.

6. Other significant sources of evidence frequently adduced include the partial writings of the hospital reformers and anti-clerical writers of the Enlightenment; and the registers of deaths within hospitals. Deaths were especially numerous in bad harvest years: cf. J. Meuvret, 'Les crises de subsistances et la démographie de la France d'Ancien Régime', in his *Etudes d'histoire économique* (Paris, 1971). However dramatic fluctuations in mortality may have been, it makes little sense to use registers of deaths without setting the results against figures of admissions. The relative rarity of registers recording admissions has, regrettably, encouraged this methodological *faux pas.*

7. Examples of historical pessimism on the role of hospitals abound. For a general statement from an influential source, see K. Helleiner, 'The population of Europe from the Black Death to the eve of the vital revolution', *Cambridge Economic History of Europe: IV* (Cambridge, 1967) p. 91. For more specific examples, see F. Lebrun, *Les Hommes et la mort en Anjou aux XVIIe. et XVIIIe. siècles, Essai de démographie et psychologie historiques* (Paris, 1972) esp. pp. 536–60; J. Kaplow, *The Names of Kings: The Parisian Labouring Poor in the Eighteenth Century* (New York, 1972) p. 95; J.C. Perrot, *Genèse d'une ville moderne: Caen au XVIIIe. siècle* (Paris, 1975) pp. 939–40 – where the Caen Hôtel-Dieu is described as 'une antichambre mortuaire' and 'un étrange puisard'. Even Olwen Hufton, normally so sensitive to social realities, states unequivocally that Hôtels-Dieu were 'concerned with the sick, or more precisely, the dying sick': *The Poor of Eighteenth-Century France,* p. 144, n. 1.

8. The inquiry of the Constituent Assembly's Comité de Mendicité in 1790–1 suggested a total of 2,188 hospitals, though this was certainly an underestimate. C. Bloch and A. Tuetey (eds) *Procès-verbaux et rapports du comité de mendicité de la Constituante, 1790–1* (Paris, 1911), seventh report. In the Fonds Tenon in the Bibliothèque Nationale, M. Jeorger has discovered a further statistical inquiry conducted in 1792 by the Comité de secours publics which has information on 1,961 institutions. See her 'La structure hospitalière de la France sous l'Ancien Régime', *Annales. E.S.C.* (1977).

9. J. Tenon, *Mémoires sur les hôpitaux de Paris* (1788). The details are conveniently reproduced in Gillispie, *Science and Polity,* p. 254.

10. Fuller details are provided in C. Jones, *Charity and 'Bienfaisance': The Treatment of the Poor in the Montpellier Region, 1740–1815* (Cambridge, 1982) pp. 102 f. For supporting examples, see F. Martin and F. Perrot, 'L'Hôtel-Dieu de Provins et la population des "pauvres malades" à la fin du XVIIe. siècle (1673–1708)', *Provins et sa région* (Provins, 1976): death-rate of 16.4 per cent through some of the most demographically traumatic years of the last century of the Ancien Régime; P. Loupès, 'L'Hôpital Saint-André de Bordeaux au XVIIIe. siècle', *Revue historique de Bordeaux* (1972): death-rate hovering between 10 and 13 per cent in the 1760s; and the important article of M. Dinet-Lecomte, 'Recherches sur la clientèle hospitalière aux XVIIe. et XVIIIe. siècles: l'exemple de Blois', *R.H.M.C.* (1986): death-rate at 12.6 per cent for 1720–37.

11. According to Jeorger ('La structure hospitalière'), the Hôpitaux Généraux numbered only 177 (9.02 per cent of the total number of hospitals), yet contained 53.28 per cent of hospital beds. The Hôtels-Dieu, in contrast, represented about one-fifth of all hospitals and represented about the same proportion of total hospital capacity.

12. See pp.8–10,39–40..

13. A particularly sensitive distillation of recent research on foundlings is to be found in Hufton, *The Poor of Eighteenth-Century France,* pp. 318 ff. It should also be borne in mind that most of the horrifyingly high infant mortality associated with hospitals in fact occurred outside hospital premises, in the homes of the mercenary wet-nurses to whom the children were dispatched. Their deaths tell us little, therefore, about the hygienic record of the hospitals. (This point was made to me by Maurice Garden.)

14. Although critics were keen to point out the abysmal record of hospitals in child care, insanitary conditions were not the prime target. The main theme of criticism was that Hôpitaux Généraux allegedly incarcerated large numbers of potentially productive workers, kept much effective human capital frozen, and distorted market forces. Cf. M. Foucault, *Folie et déraison. Histoire de la folie à l'âge classique* (Paris, 1961) pp. 486 ff. Significantly the article 'Hôpital' in the *Encyclopédie,* in contrast to that on 'Hôtel-Dieu' (see note 5), concentrated almost exclusively on the economic and social arguments against hospitals: *Encyclopédie,* VIII, 293 ff.

15. Unclassified series of registers and bundles of documents in the sub-series H-supplément of the Archives départementales du Gard (henceforth = A.D.G.), series F. See Table 2.5.

16. See in particular the *Règles et constitutions pour les Religieuses hospitalières de Saint-Joseph* (Autun, 1686).

17. J. Razoux, *Tables nosologiques et météorologiques très-étendues dressées à l'Hôtel-Dieu de Nismes depuis le premier juin 1757 jusques au premier janvier 1762* (Basle, 1767).

18. Population figures are conveniently summarized in D. Roche, *Le Siècle des lumières en province, 1680–1789* (Paris and The Hague, 1978) ii, pp. 359–61. For the economy and society of the region in the eighteenth century, see M. Sonenscher, 'Royalists and Patriots: Nîmes and its hinterland in the late eighteenth century' (Ph.D. thesis, Warwick University, 1978).

19. For a brief account of these institutions, see C.S. Bernard de Ballainvilliers, 'Mémoires sur les hôpitaux', Bibliothèque municipale de Montpellier, MS. 48 bis (1788).

20. ibid. for the Hôtel-Dieu's finances. See too the Archives départementales de l'Hérault (henceforth = A.D.H.), C 552, and Archives Nationales (henceforth = A.N.) F 15 226.

21. A.N., F 15 226; and A.D.H., C 554, for accounts of the presence of soldiers in the hospital.

22. The sample was taken in order to make the huge number of admissions more manageable. The periods in the 1740s, 1770s, and 1780s were chosen so as to facilitate comparisons (to appear elsewhere) with admissions in the same periods to the Hôtel-Dieu of

the neighbouring city of Montpellier. The period from 1757 to 1761 was specifically chosen to overlap with the years for which hospital physician Jacques Razoux kept his clinical records (see note 17). The selection of the three sample periods reduced the number of admissions to be studied to 32,680 (12,451 soldiers, 13,579 male civilians, and 6,650 females) out of a total of perhaps some 150,000 entrants over the course of the century. Other than aggregate numbers of admissions and deaths, information about military entrants was not analysed. Detailed analysis was thus confined to the 20,229 civilian entrants of the sample years. In what follows, estimates of percentages and proportions are based on these sample groupings unless otherwise stated.

23. A.D.G., H 780.

24. For Marseille, see M. Vovelle, 'Le Prolétariat flottant à Marseille sous la Révolution française', in his *De la cave au grenier* (Quebec, 1980). For the use of hospital records (normally deaths as opposed to admissions registers) for tracing migratory patterns, see in particular J.P. Poussou, 'Les mouvements migratoires en France et à partir de la France de la fin du XVe. siècle au début du XIXe. siècle', *Annales de démographie historique* (1970); Hufton, *The Poor of Eighteenth-Century France*; and E. Le Roy Ladurie, *Les Paysans de Languedoc* (Paris, 1966) pp. 93 ff.

25. 37.3 per cent from the dioceses stated. On the interdependence of mountain and plain, see the classic remarks of Fernand Braudel, *La Méditerranée et le monde méditerranéen à l'époque de Philippe II* (Paris, 1966) pp. 26 ff.

26. 25.7 per cent of the women admitted to the Nîmes Hôtel-Dieu were natives of the city. Over half of the remainder were from the dioceses of Nîmes, Uzès, Viviers, and Mende.

27. Cf. J. Imbert, *Les Hôpitaux en droit canonique (du décret de Gratien à la sécularisation de l'Hôtel-Dieu de Paris* (1505) (Paris, 1947) pp. 120 ff.

28. Foucault *et al.*, *Les Machines à guérir*, passim.

29. Imbert, *Les Hôpitaux en droit canonique*, pp. 120 ff.

30. Meuvret, 'Crises de subsistances' (see note 6). On the role of epidemics see the reflections of E. Le Roy Ladurie in his contribution to G. Duby and A. Wallon (eds) *Histoire de la France rurale.II* (1975) pp. 366 ff.

31. The incidence of mortality in the three most numerous categories of males admitted (agricultural labourers, textile workers, and urban labourers) was 9.5, 7.9, and 7.8 per cent respectively: all figures well below the overall rate.

32. Cf. E.M. Sigsworth, 'Gateways to death? Medicine, hospitals and mortality, 1700–1850', in P. Mathias (ed.) *Science and Society, 1600–1900* (Cambridge, 1972); J.H. Woodward, *To Do the Sick No Harm* (London, 1974) esp. pp. 374 ff.; S. Cherry, 'The role of a provincial hospital: the Norfolk and Norwich hospital', *Population Studies* (1972); and S. Cherry, 'The hospitals and population growth: the voluntary general hospitals, mortality and local populations in the English provinces in the eighteenth and nineteenth centuries', *Population Studies* (1980).

33. Gelfand, *Professionalizing Modern Medicine.*

34. P. Azais, 'La Charité à Nîmes', *Mémoires de l'Académie du Gard (année 1874)* (Nîmes, 1875) pp. 69 ff.; and cf. Lebrun, *Les Hommes et la mort*, pp. 250 ff.

35. C. Molette, *Guide des sources de l'histoire des congrégations féminines françaises de vie active* (Paris, 1974) for an admirable introductory survey on these religious orders.

36. No adequate biography of Vincent de Paul exists. P. Coste, *Le Grand Saint du Grand Siècle, Monsieur Vincent* (1932) is the standard work although, as the title suggests, the author is a little dazzled by his subject's sanctity. L. Mezzadri (1985) *Vincent de Paul* (1581–1660) is an excellent recent work of popularization, but extremely well-informed on recent scholarship.

37. Compare the *Règles et constitutions* with the copy of the rule of the Daughters of Charity in A.N., L 1665.

38. *Règles et constitutions*, p. 149.

39. Cf. L. Le Grand, 'Les Maisons-Dieu: leurs statuts au XIIIe. siècle', *Revue des questions historiques*, 1896.

40. *Règles et constitutions*, p. 149.

41. Entry in December 1741. ('on nous a porté un homme qui na demeuré qune heure ou environ. ila receu lextreme onction. ont na pas scu comment il sappelle il avez environ trente ans'.) Cf. Razoux, Tables, p. 42; and J.C. Vincens and J. Baumès, *Topographie de la ville de Nîmes*, Year X/1802) p. 46.

42. For the theme of the 'good death' in religious literature in this period, see D. Roche, '"La Mémoire de la Mort": recherches sur la place des arts de mourir dans la librairie et la lecture en France aux XVIIe. et XVIIIe. siècles', *Annales. E.S.C.* (1976).

43. See p.49 and note 7.

44. *Règles et constitutions*, p. 148.

45. A.D.H., C 8243; Ballainvilliers, Mémoires'.

46. Razoux, *Tables*, pp. 122, 176.

47. A convenient summary of Razoux's findings is in Vincens and Baumès, *Topographie*, pp. 456–61. I would like here to record my thanks to the late Dr John Wylie, for his advice and medical insights, provided with his customary erudition and good humour, into Razoux's classification of diseases.

48. Razoux, *Tables*, p. 28. Cf. ibid., pp. 81, 177, 238, 244.

49. ibid., p. 232. Cf. ibid., pp. 86, 176, 239, and, for women, Vincens and Baumès, *Topographie*, p. 510n.

50. Le Roy Ladurie, *Paysans de Languedoc*, pp. 93 ff.

51. Razoux, *Tables*, pp. 4 ff. ('Préface').

52. ibid., p. 9.

53. ibid., p. 177. Cf. ibid., p. 82.

54. ibid., p. 10.

55. For a discussion of popular attitudes towards healing and the medical profession in the Bas-Languedoc, see Jones, *Charity and 'Bienfaisance'*, pp. 113 ff.

56. Razoux, *Tables*, p. 254.

57. ibid., p. 172 (two cases).

58. Cf. p. 16. For cases of conflict see: a) Paris: Greenbaum, 'Nurses

and doctors'; R. Mandrou, 'Un problème de diététique à l'Hôtel-Dieu de Paris à la veille de la Révolution', *93e. Congrès National des Sociétés savantes* (1971); R. Massy, 'A l'Apothicairerie de l'Hôtel Royal des Invalides. Le conflit de 1772 entre l'administration de l'Hôtel et les Filles de la Charité, *Revue d'histoire de la pharmacie* (1954); T. Gelfand, 'A confrontation over clinical instruction at the Hôtel-Dieu of Paris during the French Revolution', *Journal of the History of Medicine* (1973); L.S. Greenbaum, 'Nurses and doctors in conflict: piety and medicine in the Paris Hôtel-Dieu on the eve of the French Revolution', *Clio medica* (1979); and A.N., S 6160. b) Provinces: Bloch, *L'Assistance et l'Etat*, pp. 69 ff (Pont-sur-Seine, Mézières, Etampes, Provins, Orléans); C. Port, *Inventaire des archives anciennes de l'Hôpital Saint-Jean d'Angers* (Paris and Angers, 1870); and, among archival sources, A.N., Series S (Filles de la Charité) 6161 (Béthune), 6163 (Caen), 6170 (Marly), 6172 (Nesle), 6180 (Yeres); A.D.H., Archives de l'Hôtel-Dieu Saint-Eloi de Montpellier (antérieures à 1790) E 11, 12, 13, 25 (together with A.N. F 15 226), A.D. Côte-d'Or C 374 (Auxonne) and A.D. Finistère: archives hospitalières de Landerneau E 7.

59. Razoux, *Tables*, pp. 42, 141, 163, 197.

60. ibid., p. 44.

61. ibid.

62. ibid., pp. 162 f.

63. L. Le Grand, 'Les Maisons-Dieu: leur régime intérieur au Moyen Age', *Revue des questions historiques* (1898) p. 142. It should be noted that even in the early thirteenth century there was some awareness that this attitude could lead to over-indulgence on the part of inmates which might be ultimately damaging to their health; ibid., p. 143.

64. P. Fournier, 'Observations sur les maladies qui ont regné dans l'Hôtel-Dieu de Montpellier pendant l'année 1763, suivi d'observations sur plusieurs maladies particulières', *Recueil d'observations de médecine des hôpitaux militaires* (i, 1766). Cf. A.D.H., Archives de l'Hôtel-Dieu de Montpellier (antérieures à 1790) E 25.

65. Razoux, *Tables*, p. 42.

66. Cf. P. Huard, *Sciences, médecine, pharmacie de la Révolution à l'Empire* (1970) p. 59.

67. As regards typicality, see the references cited in note 10, especially the article by Mlle Dinet-Lecomte, whose conclusions are convergent with those presented here. Note too the impressive study by Olivier Faure, *Genèse de l'hôpital moderne: les hospices civils de Lyon de 1802 à 1845* (Lyon, 1982): until 1830, and in many respects far beyond. Much the same kind of picture emerges – hospitals whose role was more that of 'refuges' than strictly medical institutions and whose administrative carapace the medical profession found difficult to penetrate.

II

Hospital Nursing

3

Vincent de Paul, Louise de Marillac, and the Revival of Nursing in the Seventeenth Century

To evoke a sister of charity in France in 1700 was to designate a vocation generally known and widely esteemed, a cultural archetype distinctly perceived. A sister of charity was patient, saintly, laborious, discreet, committed – and tough.[1] Her background was probably humble. She belonged to a religious community of active life which operated 'in the world' rather than, as with contemplative orders, from within the cloister. The theatre of her charitable activities might be the hospital, but could equally well be the homes of the poor or the schoolroom. The very ubiquity of her presence made her – as it makes her still – so banal a reality as to be overlooked, so apparently a timeless phenomenon as to make her specifically seventeenth-century origins easily forgotten. For while in 1700 everyone knew about such women, in 1600 they had not existed.

At the beginning of the seventeenth century the great nursing communities of the Middle Ages were in a state of numerical decline and moral rout. The few remaining with any vitality tended to canalize their energies into contemplative fervour rather than the good works which were to be the speciality of the new style of sisters of active life.[2] The latter developed in a way which made a powerful contribution to the organization of charity in Ancien Régime France and which also marked a major development in the history of women's work. At a time when women's wages were pitifully low and when the professions were male monopolies, membership of one of the new style of female communities of active life offered women from menial backgrounds material and spiritual rewards as well as the possibility of positions of responsibility and influence far beyond the reach of most women. They also achieved what amounts to an effective take-over of poor-relief institutions in France in the last century and a half of the Ancien Régime, and one which profoundly marked the emergence of institutions of assistance in the nineteenth and twentieth centuries. By 1789 just about every charitable institution of any size or substance was staffed by such women and even Protestants felt that they could entrust their hospitals to the expertise such women embodied.[3] If this represents a remarkable transformation in the fabric of poor relief in France, it is also, however, a largely unremarked one. True, there are the usual hagiographies; and no history of the Counter-Reformation in France fails to give such women a benignly approving nod. It usually stops there. The sister of charity needs rescuing from what, in a quite different context, E.P. Thompson called 'the enormous condescension of posterity'.[4]

The present chapter will explore only the roots of this phenomenon. My focus will be upon a single nursing community, the Daughters of Charity (*Filles de la Charité*), often in the early days referred to as the 'servants of the sick poor' (*servantes des pauvres malades*).[5] One among a myriad such communities in 1700, as we shall see, the Daughters of Charity were certainly the most important. Founded in 1633 by Saint Vincent de Paul and Saint Louise de Marillac, the Daughters of Charity could claim to be the first new-style nursing community. They were the largest of all such communities throughout the Ancien Régime. They had the most genuinely nationwide organization of all such communities: even on the deaths of the founders in 1660, the 60 or 70 institutions in which the sisters served were scattered far and wide throughout France, and by 1700, their 200-odd institutions had achieved an even broader coverage. The Daughters of Charity were in addition the most influential community of this new kind – so influential indeed that throughout the seventeenth and eighteenth century, contemporaries often conflated the more generic terms 'sister of charity' or sometimes (because of their uniforms) 'grey sisters', with members of this particular community. By concentrating on this single community, therefore, one is getting close to the heart of the more general phenomenon.

I

The pre-eminence that the Daughters of Charity enjoyed from the very earliest days owed a great deal to the personality and the charisma of their co-founder, Vincent de Paul.[6] The historiographical stock of the latter has risen sharply in recent years, as Counter-Reformation scholars have shifted the focus of their interests from doctrinal to pastoral concerns, from cultural ideals to religious comportment, from *âmes d'élite* to wider *mentalités.* A retrospective religious sociology, grounded in the *Annales* tradition but owing much too to the pioneering work of Gabriel Le Bras, has trained historians' eyes firmly on to the religious beliefs and behaviour of the 'people of Christian Europe', and in particular on how the latter were systematically brought into patterns of orthodox observance and belief for the first time.[7] In the perspective of this 'Christianization' of the masses – to borrow from recent literature a loaded term which does however have compelling heuristic power – Vincent de Paul emerges as 'one of the great makers of Western Civilisation in the first half of the seventeenth century'.[8]

The foundation of the Daughters of Charity in 1633 was only one offshoot of a life remarkably fertile in charitable initiatives and committed overall to the improved education of the secular clergy and to the evangelization of the rural masses. While the cities of early seventeenth-century France brimmed with an intense spiritual life, Saint Vincent observed in a famous perception, people in country areas were either unprovided for or else in the hands of immoral, crude, or semi-literate priests who failed to ensure salvation. This inspired in him a lifetime of missionary endeavour, most notably through his Congregation of the Mission (or Lazarists) which he founded in 1625. The whole of rural France was within the scope of his activities, as were more marginal groups remote from the pastoral mainstream both geographically (he organized missions, for example in Corsica, the Hebrides, and Madagascar) and socially (prisoners, galley-slaves, beggars, soldiers, war-refugees, and so on).[9]

Contrary to the popular mythology which sees him as a sunnily disposed humanitarian, Vincent de Paul was in fact a rather pessimistic individual – he seriously entertained the view, for example, that the life-span of the Catholic church in Europe might be ending and that its transfer to the New World might be imminent – and he had to work hard on himself to achieve his famed gentleness and sympathy.[10] Cautious and prudent in all things – he was, after all, the son of a Gascon peasant – he worked to no long-term set of goals, preferring to be guided by what we would probably call force of circumstance but which he called God. The origins and early history of the Daughters of Charity bear witness to this disposition of mind.

From 1617 Saint Vincent had developed the organization of confraternities of charity (*confréries de charité,* or *charités*), in which women within a parish banded together for mutual spiritual edification and for the practice of good works, most notably by attending to the spiritual and corporal well-being of the local sick poor through a system of home relief. *Charités* were instituted wherever he worked as a missionary and after 1625 his Lazarists were instructed to establish them in all villages where they held missions, as a means of prolonging the effects of their labours.[11] The institution became fashionable, and from 1630 *charités* were being established in many of the parishes of Paris under the patronage of women drawn even from the court aristocracy. It was soon found, however, that whereas farmers' wives and daughters in rural *charités* did not flinch at visiting, cleaning, cooking for, and caring for the sick poor in the latter's homes, the same was not true of the middle- and upper-class women of the Parisian establishments. Quite apart from the intrinsic unpleasantness of the task, fathers and husbands recoiled at the thought of their women-folk wandering around the poorer areas of the city clutching soup-ladles and herbal medicines; while the prevalence of the plague – there were outbreaks in the capital each year between 1622 and 1631[12] – made such sorties perilous in the extreme. The ladies took to sending their female servants in their place – an arrangement which suited no one.

From the late 1620s Saint Vincent had been supervising *charités* in Paris and the surrounding diocese in collaboration with a pious widow, Louise de Marillac, to whom since 1625 he had acted as spiritual director. Illegitimate daughter[13] of a member of the mighty but ill-starred Marillac clan, the widow since 1625 of Antoine Le Gras, erstwhile secretary to Marie de Médici, Saint Louise had, like her mentor, pledged her life to the service of the poor. She, probably more than he, grasped the solution to the dilemma of the Ladies of the Paris *charités*: capable serving girls under careful supervision would be hired out to provide assistance in the heavier and more repulsive tasks. From about 1630 she was taking into her home a number of young country women and hiring them out as needed (*VdeP*, I, 76, 99, 132, 196, 206, 268, . . .). In 1633, in order to give this association more consistency, and also so as to ensure a better quality product, Saint Vincent authorized Saint Louise to offer such women spiritual instruction as well as practical training in the work of the *charités*. This was the origin of the Daughters of Charity.[14]

An early opportunity for the little group to develop came in 1634, when Saint Vincent organized an elite of women from the Paris parishional *charités* into a confraternity, the Ladies (*sic*) of Charity (*Dames de la Charité*).[15] Initially the aim of these women was to help the Augustinian nuns who ran Paris's main hospital, the Hôtel-Dieu. In particular, they came in every afternoon, spoon in hand, to serve the inmates an afternoon collation of jellies, preserves, fruit, white bread, and biscuits, and to take the opportunity afforded by the general allegresse to catechize them and urge them gently into better ways. The social distance separating the down-and-outs who composed most of the hospital's population and the Ladies involved – the confraternity included a future queen, a princess, three duchesses, two baronesses, two countesses, four marquises, and a host of other women from the best robe and sword families[16] – was frightening. The Daughters of Charity were called in to help fill the gap.

In keeping with the instrumentalist character of their initial function, much of the initial activity of the Daughters of Charity was conducted under the aegis of either the Ladies of Charity or the Congregation of the Mission. Despite initial suspicion and hostility even from among the poor, their establishments soon snowballed (the metaphor is Saint Vincent's; *VdeP*, X, 100). As representatives of the Parisian *charités*, for example, sisters went where Ladies feared to tread, or else accompanied the latter on sometimes rather ritualized sorties among the flotsam and jetsam of metropolitan society. Towards the end of the 1630s they began to be attached to the rural seigneuries of Ladies of Charity. These were mainly, though not entirely, in the Paris region: in 1638, for example, two sisters were attached to the seigneurie of Richelieu's beloved niece, the Duchesse d'Aiguillon at Richelieu in the Touraine, and there offered aid to the sick and primary teaching for the daughters of the poor.[17]

When one of the Ladies, Marie-Louise de Gonzague, married the king of Poland, she took east with her a handful of Daughters of Charity as well as a group of Lazarists.[18] When the Congregation of the Mission organized spiritual and material aid to the war-torn province of Lorraine from the late 1630s, the sisters were drafted in to help them. They performed similar war- and famine-relief functions for Champagne and Picardy in the 1640s and for the Ile-de-France, devastated by rebel and royal armies alike during the Fronde.[19] Again, when the Lazarists performed missions in the Parisian hospitals of the Quinze-Vingts (1633) and the Petites-Maisons (1655), the sisters followed in their wake and were soon running both institutions.

Yet if the early activities of the Daughters of Charity were conditioned by their close 'family' relationship with the Lazarists and the Ladies of Charity, the Daughters did come to develop their own autonomy. Saint Louise's willingness to send sisters wherever they were called meant that inevitably they came to be established in localities outside the support system of the Lazarists and the Ladies of Charity. She seems in fact to have welcomed greater independence from the Ladies, whose social susceptibilities were easily ruffled and who lacked her own sound pragmatism and common sense (*VdeP*, III, 175, 211, 309, 518, 596; IV, 185; VII, 227–8; etc.). An important stage in the development of the sisters' identity was reached in 1640 when they entered service at the big Hôtel-Dieu at Angers after negotiating direct with the hospital's administrators and the city officials.[20] In 1645 they petitioned the archbishop of Paris for approval for their institute and regulations. By 1655 Saint Vincent determined that the superior of the Daughters of Charity on the death of Saint Louise should not be a member of the Ladies of Charity but an elected member of the Daughters (*VdeP*, V, 228; cf. IX, 327). Corporate autonomy had now been effectively achieved.

II

It is perhaps only with hindsight that this new creation seems to fit comfortably within the perspective of 'Christianization' with which religious historians have recently familiarized us. In fact, the creation of such an institute was intensely problematic, for reasons not only of precedent but also of gender. The Counter-Reformation had witnessed the emergence of new male religious orders (Jesuits, Oratorians, Barnabites, etc.) turned outwards towards the world beyond the cloister more emphatically than had been the norm prior to the Council of Trent; and there is much evidence to suggest that devout women too were increasingly attracted to a reforming church which placed more emphasis on social apostolacy towards the sick, the ailing, and the young.[21] Yet while the church was flexible and innovative towards male form of religious life, in regard to women religious it appeared to regard the old certainties as best. A papal bull of 11 August 1566 had formally enjoined all religious communities of women to observe the cloister, and had dissolved organizations which did not live up to this exacting requirement. Strict female observance of enclosure seemed to popes and prelates alike in the late sixteenth and early seventeenth centuries the best means of avoiding those scandals and moral back-slidings which had disfigured the record of female religious communities before the Council of Trent, and ensuring that the religious life was lived conscientiously and well. Such a view dovetailed very neatly, moreover, with the attitude of those well-heeled families which placed their pious or unwanted daughters in convents and for whom family honour required that the life and morals of female members should be above reproach.

The Daughters of Charity were thus established against a background of strong ecclesiastical and social pressures in favour of cloistering females religious. There were, it is true, dotted around the cities of northern France and Flanders so-called 'grey sisters' and 'black sisters' – small communities of women established in the late Middle Ages which observed the rule of Saint Francis and cared for the sick poor not only within hospital walls like other hospital communities but also sometimes, apparently, in the homes of the poor. These cases, shielded by diocesan indulgence, were few and little-known.[22] Just about everywhere else down to the 1620s and 1630s, the cloister was triumphant. Two years before the foundation of the Daughters of Charity, for example – in 1631 – the Pope had dissolved the most ambitious of new female communities, the 'English Ladies', the teaching community modelled on the

Jesuits which had been founded by the English émigrée Mary Ward in northern France at the turn of the century.[23] Vincent de Paul doubtless knew of this case, and would certainly have been aware of two other precedents, the Ursulines and Visitandines. The Ursulines[24] were a teaching order of women founded by Saint Angela Merici in Brescia in 1535 and whose branches fanned across Mediterranean Europe. In 1592 the order entered Provence, and communities soon started appearing elsewhere in France. The Ursulines were in the practice of giving classes to poor children outside the cloister, as well as of receiving well-off young women as private fee-paying students. In 1612, however, the Paris community requested that its rule be changed so as to accommodate the principle of enclosure. The classes for the poor stopped, and other Ursulines in France (with the exception of the sisters organized in still-Spanish Franche-Comté by Anne de Xaintonge)[25] followed suit directly. The case of the Order of the Visitation was an even more notorious example.[26] Founded in 1610 in Annécy by Saint Vincent's mentor, Saint François de Sales and by Saint Jeanne de Chantal, the Visitandines were to be a contemplative order which, however, was to express its love of God in visits to the sick poor. The Bishop of Lyon, however, frowned at this stipulation when the Order was introduced into his diocese in 1616. By 1618 Saint François ceded to pressure, withdrew the idea of visits throughout the order, and established the principle of enclosure. Saint Vincent was himself director of the Paris Visitandines.

A host of other, less well-publicized cases testify to the strength of pressures towards conformity over the matter of the cloister. The Order of Notre-Dame, which Saint Jeanne de Lestonnac had founded in Bordeaux in 1605–16 and which was to be in the forefront of the conversion of Protestant children later in the century, had to be instituted as a subsidiary of the Benedictines (1608) rather than as a new order, and thereby accept enclosure.[27] Another educational order, the Filles de la Présentation de Marie, established in Senlis in 1626 by Bishop Nicolas Sauguin, were cloistered by 1627, while the Augustinian canonesses of the Miséricorde de Jésus, who had run the Hôtel-Dieu at Dieppe since 1285, accepted new regulations in 1630 which imposed enclosure for the first time.[28] Nor did the foundation of the Daughters of Charity instantly turn the tide. The Soeurs de Saint-Charles at Nancy, for example, first recognized in 1652, were cloistered by 1663;

the Filles de Notre-Dame, founded in Flanders at the turn of the century, by 1670; the Augustinian Soeurs de Saint-Joseph at Poitiers (1644), in 1688. In some cases, enclosure was imposed despite vigorous opposition from the women themselves: the hospital sisters of Saint-Joseph of La Flèche, founded in 1634 without the principle of enclosure, for example, were driven into accepting it in 1659 on the advent of the Jansenistic Henri Arnauld as Bishop of Le Mans.[29]

Significantly, however, Saint Vincent de Paul was at the heart of moves to widen the sphere of action of devout women living under a rule. He fostered the development, for example, of the so-called Madelonnettes, which had been founded in Paris in 1617 for women of disordered sexual life, and from 1629 this institution for the sexually repentant was run by the Paris Visitandines, whose spiritual director he was.[30] He also interested himself closely in the activities of the Filles de la Providence de Dieu, an institution started up by Madame de Polaillion, an enthusiastic member of Saint Vincent's Ladies of Charity. This establishment, whose rule he is said to have composed in 1656, concerned itself with penitents and also with the education of Protestant children. He also offered his protection to the Filles de Saint-Joseph (also known as the Filles de la Providence) who were engaged in primary schooling activity, and a number of communities with a similar destination.[31] Poor relief was the subject of his concern as well as education. Besides popularizing confraternities of charity and founding the Daughters of Charity, he also helped to revitalize the Augustinian community which ran the Paris Hôtel-Dieu; he supported the Augustines de la Charité de Notre-Dame which was founded in 1628; and from 1636 offered his protection to the Soeurs de Saint-Agnès of Arras.[32]

Saint Vincent was thus something of a specialist in forms of female social apostolacy, and the breadth of his experience in this sphere evidently helped him set the institution of the Daughters of Charity on solid foundations. Equally important in smoothing the path before the new community were the prestige he enjoyed and his connections. Following the deaths in 1622 of François de Sales (whose Visitandines had signally failed to develop a social role beyond the cloister) and in 1628 of Pierre de Bérulle (whose attitude towards women and women's communities was far more conservative than Saint Vincent's), Saint Vincent became the most politically influential of the great saintly figures of the Counter-Reformation in France. Despite his humble background, he became exceptionally well connected at the highest levels of church and state. From 1613 to 1625 he had served as family chaplain to Philippe-Emmanuel de Gondi, general of the Mediterranean Galley Fleet and a member of the Gondi clan, which from 1569 to 1660 held the see of Paris almost as a fief (and also the father of the future Cardinal de Retz, himself coadjutor to the Archbishop of Paris from 1643 to 1654, and archbishop from 1654 to 1660).[33] Direction of the Ladies of Charity also brought Saint Vincent into close co-operation with women from the highest families in the land, especially those pious widows and spinsters – women such as Madame de Miramion, Madame Villeneuve, Madame Goussault, Madame Foucquet, and the fabulously wealthy Duchesse d'Aiguillon – who were the financial 'angels' behind many of the great religious and charitable enterprises of the Counter-Reformation in France. In the late 1630s he advised Richelieu on ecclesiastical appointments, and from 1643 to 1652 served as a member – the key member, according to some sources – of the Conseil de Conscience which decided episcopal and other major preferments.[34] Although ultimately Richelieu's affection for him seems to have cooled, while Mazarin came to distrust him, Louis XIII, Anne of Austria, and the young Louis XIV all respected him – and patronized his Daughters of Charity.

The experience and prestige of Vincent de Paul were essential ingredients in the difficult task of obtaining formal authorization for the Daughters of Charity. Seemingly realizing that it was foolhardy to try to take the church head-on over its unwillingness to countenance innovatory forms of female religious commitment, he acted cannily to circumvent direct opposition. When in 1645, for example, he approached the Archbishop of Paris for diocesan authorization, he could already point to the sterling services performed by the Daughters of Charity in the city and in the archdiocese of Paris over the previous dozen years. The fact that the suit went before his former pupil, Jean-François-Paul de Gondi, the archbishop's coadjutor (and the future Retz) also helped his cause. In such circumstances, Saint Vincent always made a point of playing down the innovatory aspect of the community: the Daughters of Charity were represented as merely a 'confraternity', and were to pass under the general supervision of the Archbishop of Paris on the death of Saint Vincent. This latter clause later worried Saint Vincent, for it seemed to make a diocesan organization out of a community which already had a nation-wide dimension and whose autonomy he cherished. By 1647 Queen Anne of Austria, no less, was petitioning the Pope on the community's behalf, and specifically requesting that on Saint Vincent's death direction of the Daughters of Charity should remain with the Superior of the Congregation of the Mission.[35] When in the early 1650s the document of 1645 containing archepiscopal approval was mysteriously lost – a loss in which there seems to have been a certain legerdemain[36] – Saint Vincent approached the archbishop a second time, this time in the person of the Cardinal de Retz, stipulating continued Lazarist direction for the community. Quite apart from the closeness of the relationship with Retz, the latter was also in the embarrassing position of being in political exile from France and doing his utmost to maintain support amongst his diocesan clergy. The fact that Saint Vincent had resisted strong diplomatic pressure from the French court to instruct the Lazarist house at Rome to offer hospitality to the vagabond Retz also put the latter in the saint's debt.[37] On 18 January 1655 Retz gave the Daughters of Charity his blessing, and the Lazarist succession was confirmed. Perhaps only a figure as prominent, as disinterested, and as respected as Vincent de Paul could have overcome the affront to Mazarin of offering Retz hospitality, yet still go on to get formal state authorization for the Daughters. Royal Letters Patent were issued in their favour in November 1657, and these were registered by the Parlement of Paris in December 1658.[38]

By his consistent support for innovatory forms of female religious life and by securing, in this tortuous fashion, authorization for the Daughters of Charity, Vincent de Paul helped turn the tide decisively in favour of the emergence of female communities of active life. What was already, by 1660, a considerable number of such communities swelled considerably over the remainder of the century, as large numbers of communities engaged in teaching, care of the sick, and other forms of social apostolacy grew up. Many of these were unequivocally modelled on the Daughters of Charity: this was certainly the case, for example, with the hospital sisters of Saint-Joseph (1630–43), the Soeurs de la Charité de Notre-Dame (1682), and the Soeurs de la Charité de la Présentation

(1696).[39] Even in other cases in which direct influence is uncertain – the Soeurs de Saint-Charles at Nancy (1652), the Soeurs de Saint-Thomas de Villeneuve (1661), the Soeurs de Saint-Maur (1666), the Soeurs de Nevers (1698), or the Filles de Sagesse (1703), for example[40] – the precedent which the Daughters of Charity had established by getting their existence formally ratified was of paramount importance. The cloister had proved a tough nut; by mid-century it had been unequivocally cracked.

III

It would be foolish to follow some of Saint Vincent's hagiographers and deduce that the success of the Daughters of Charity was essentially a personal achievement of the saint. To do so would be considerably to underestimate a number of other factors implicit in the new organization. Not least among these, moreover, was the contribution of Saint Louise de Marillac. The historiographical tradition that Saint Louise was merely Saint Vincent's robot, acting unthinkingly on his orders, has been effectively challenged.[41] It now seems clear that Saint Vincent's role in the day-to-day running of the Daughters of Charity was always patchy, usually small and, from the mid-1650s especially, often minimal. Although Saint Louise constantly turned to him for advice on worrying questions and on matters which required a policy decision, the bulk of the business of the expanding community was handled by her alone, assisted in the later years by a small number of trusted advisers from within the community. It was she who supervised the selection and the training of sisters in the mother-house, and she also oversaw the running of all the community's charitable enterprises in Paris. She dealt with personnel matters: the scale of her correspondence with sisters attached to far-off institutions, for example, appears to have been prodigious. She was also responsible for the healthy state of the community's accounts at a time when, with the state adopting all manner of stratagems to finance its wars, most other religious communities were experiencing great difficulties with their investment portfolios (*VdeP*, I, 568; II, 275, 445, 465; IV, 13, 370–1; VI, 401). Finally Saint Louise was herself a Lady of Charity and as such – and as a Marillac – she had entrée at court and among the highest aristocracy: a fact which benefited the community by attracting its patronage from the social elite.

Vincent de Paul and Louise de Marillac must also be credited jointly with devising a recruitment and training strategy for the community which proved a major asset in its fortunes. The founders were under no illusions regarding the difficulties of life as a Daughter of Charity: it was, Saint Vincent opined, 'impossible to persevere for long in this very distressing vocation, and to overcome our natural repugnance for it, if one does not have a great store of virtue'.[42] The mortality crisis was alive and well in early-seventeenth-century France: famine, plague, contagious disease, and wars both foreign and domestic punctuated the lives of the labouring poor at a hectic tempo. Even at the best of times, moreover, the homes of the poor were the perennial locus of dirt and disease, fetidity and fevers; while the stench of a hospital made even the able-bodied retch. There were psychological deprivations too which worsened the lot of the Daughter of Charity. No sister was allowed to serve in her native region, for example; 'to belong entirely to God', Saint Vincent reasoned, 'you must be estranged from your native-land' (*'il faut se dépayser'*: *VdeP*, X, 579), so all had to come to terms with a life of risk and estrangement.

A certain kind of mental fortitude and physical toughness were thus the *sine qua non* of Daughters of Charity, and the founders looked to a strong, disaster-proof sense of religious vocation as the best guarantee of commitment. Vocation also offset a tendency in some sisters towards materialism and cynicism. After all, though life as a Daughter of Charity was hard, so too was life as a single woman: and at least members of the community could enjoy, as we shall see,[43] a steady wage, free accommodation, clothing, security, a modicum of comfort in illness or old age, a decent burial, and also the sense of social promotion that membership of such an esteemed community entailed. The community needed 'workers' (*ouvrières*), not 'shirkers' or 'chatterboxes' or women who travelled up to the mother-house to see the bright lights of the city or to seek alternative employment (*L*, 47, 323a, 577b). The community was fortunate in having, in the Lazarists, a group of potential recruiting agents who knew at first hand what religious vocation was about. Saint Vincent was forever urging his

Lazarists to be on the *qui-vive* for likely recruits for the Daughters of Charity: what was needed were 'healthy and robust girls, disposed to enter the community, of irreproachable life, resolved to self-humiliation and to serve the poor for the love of God' (*VdeP*, VI, 189; cf. V, 635). Saint Louise used the Daughters and the Ladies of Charity to similar effect. In all cases strong-armed country girls were given preference, partly for health reasons but partly too because Saint Vincent thought that the morals of most city girls would almost certainly not be pure enough for the community's requirements (*VdeP*, IX, 80–6). All recruiting agents were expected to provide a thorough moral screening – 'from the cradle', Saint Louise insisted (*L*, 105) – on women who came to them (*L*, 105, 140, 427; cf. *VdeP*, X, 413). Without the moral sureties offered by the cloister, the Daughters of Charity had to be ironclads of chastity before being released on to the stormy waters of street sociability.

Potential recruits were usually tested for a period of months in a provincial house of the community near their homes. Those who survived this were sent to the mother-house in Paris, where the bulk of their training was carried out. Strong central control over the whole recruitment and training process was a distinctive characteristic of the Daughters of Charity, and one which contributed powerfully to the organization's development. Female religious orders in the past had often developed fissiparious tendencies, which could gnaw away at morale and cohesion.[44] Strong central authority could keep such centrifugal forces in check. It was also the best guarantee of uniformity of training of high quality. Just as soldiers were drilled and equipped before being sent out to battle, so the Daughters of Charity should see their mother-house as their training ground before they were sent out to join the 'Christian militia' (*VdeP*, IX, 511, 520; III, 125). The mother-house offered experience in every aspect of the operations of the community. Sisters there could visit the poor in their homes within the parish of Saint-Laurent. They could teach girls from poor families from within the parish in the community's school. There was an infirmary where sisters who were aged or whose health had broken down were looked after, and this reproduced the character of hospital care. There was an apothecary's shop attached to the mother-house where abler sisters could be offered training in preparation of remedies and in elementary (not to say hit-and-miss!) (*L*, 352) blood-letting. And the community's garden, with its herbs, vegetables, bee-hives, and pigs offered training in household domesticity (*L*, 259, 261, 343, . . .).

In addition the mother-house provided a far more intense spiritual life and testing-ground for recruits than any provincial house could offer. From the 1630s new recruits were organized in a 'seminary' under the supervision of a senior sister. Weekly conferences were held by Louise de Marillac which often had the character of consciousness-raising sessions. When he was not tied up with other work, Vincent de Paul would come each week to give instruction. New sisters would also come into contact with sisters from institutions outside Paris who returned to the mother-house on a regular visit for retreats which were aimed at recharging spiritual batteries. All in all, the mother-house offered a very intense training in all aspects, spiritual and physical, of the work of the Daughters of Charity. Centralization was thus a crucial aspect of the production of a string of highly motivated sisters who could be farmed out to charitable institutions throughout France on a contractual basis. Only when their vocation was set could sisters proceed to the taking of vows.

The question of vows was a key issue in canon law, for the pronouncement of perpetual vows by a female had always implied, *ipso facto*, a commitment to the cloister. True to his strategy of circumventing legal problems, Saint Vincent got round this difficulty by forbidding the sisters from taking solemn perpetual vows and insisting that their vows should be reassumed annually.[45] Simple vows, as they were called, thus circumvented canonical difficulties. But they were also an ingredient in the training and commitment of Daughters of Charity. Whereas many monastic orders had found that the taking of perpetual vows often degenerated into a rather formalistic act devoid of emotion or spiritual commitment, the taking of annual vows could be a solemn and psychologically challenging act. Peer pressure within the community acted to raise morale at the annual taking of vows and the act itself provided an excellent litmus test of continuing fervour.

By taking only simple vows, moreover, the Daughters of Charity effectively distanced themselves from nuns. Saint Vincent thought it was altogether inappropriate for Daughters of Charity to aspire to the status of regulars. He made something of a fetish, for example, of avoiding vocabulary which recalled the female orders: the Daughters of Charity were to be a 'confraternity', a 'company', a 'society', rather than an 'order'; their establishments were 'houses', not 'convents'; the local director of each was to be 'sister servant' (*soeur servante*) rather than 'superior'; and training was done in a 'seminary' rather than a 'noviciate'.[46] There was more to this than merely the placating of canon lawyers, or an acknowledgement that the social background of most Daughters of Charity was inferior to that of most regulars. In particular, he seems to have felt that with her ceaseless round of liturgical and spiritual exercises, the contemplative nun sought perfection in a way unsuited for a Daughter of Charity. The latter was to strike a balance between contemplation and service to the poor. She was to sail between the Scylla of 'contemplative ecstacies' divorced from charity to one's neighbour and the Charybdis of soulless giving, a spiritually empty rehearsal of the charitable act.

It was this balance between spiritual concerns and material commitment to service in the world which the training of the Daughters of Charity sought to inculcate. The programmatic vision of Saint Vincent in this respect was predicated on the assumption, first, that the pauper was Christ's earthly surrogate. Replicating views concerning the *pauper Christi* which had a long pedigree within the church, but which he now restated with a particularly strong affective force, Saint Vincent urged sisters to see the recipient of their charity as Christ himself: 'the poorest and the most abandoned are our Lords and Masters . . . and we are unworthy of rendering them our little services' (*VdeP*, X, 393; cf. X, 610). Every poor man at the gate was to be for the sisters an epiphany; every foundling or orphan cared for, the Christ-child incarnate; every sick man immobilized in his bed the human representation of the Crucifixion. Liturgical acts to foster a sister's sanctity should thus take second place to the primordial duty of service to her neighbour. This amounted to a reprioritization of the traditional views of religious communities which tended to view service to the poor as an ancillary act in their search for perfection, Even if the Daughter of Charity, in contrast, was in the middle of a mass or a prayer when the poor called out for help, she was to leave her devotions at once, for to do this was merely, in Saint Vincent's classic phrase, 'to leave God for God' (*VdeP*, X, 667).

The patient came first, therefore, not because he was more important than God, but because he was God. This view was, in Vincentian pedagogy, buttressed by a second view – logically in contradiction with the first, though that mattered little – that the life of the Daughter of Charity was to be a deliberate mimicry of the life of Christ, an *imitatio Christi*. 'You must go and find the sick poor,' Saint Vincent urged. 'You do in that what Our Lord did. . . . He went from town to town, from village to village and cured all he met' (*VdeP*, IX, 583). Whilst at their labours, sisters should recall that 'the trade of the carpenter was His. . . . He carried the hod and worked as a labourer and builder's mate' (*VdeP*, IX, 490; cf. IX, 493–5). This revalorization of manual work strove to make nursing drudgery divine.[47] Following the example of Christ himself, sisters were ceaselessly to strive to bring into a state of grace those they encountered in their work. The methods of love and gentleness, because they were Christ's own, were the best proven methods. And if the liturgical washing of feet often took precedence over the hygienic washing of hands, this was only because the caring for the bodies of the poor, to which sisters had pledged their lives and engaged their salvation, was part of a wider, more ambitious evangelizing exercise aimed at the saving of souls, the spiritual colonization of social marginals. Thus, as their Rule enjoined, they were to serve the sick poor not only 'corporally, in administering food and medicines', but also

> spiritually, by instructing the sick of the things necessary for salvation, in ensuring that they make a general confession of their past lives, so that by this means those who die leave this world in good estate and that those who get well resolve never more to offend God.

Christianization was thus the obverse of charity.

The principle of *imitatio Christi* had in earlier periods of the church's history been the occasion for a veritable holocaust of austerity and self-mutilation. Vincent de Paul, in contrast, put clear limits on the bodily mortifications to which Daughters of Charity were to subject themselves. He did not rule out the use of austerity and discipline, but he contrasted the lightness of such practices for Daughters of Charity with other communities – with the Carmelites, for example, whose collective self-whipping was a weekly event and whose diet seemed to consist almost entirely of rotten hard-boiled eggs.[48] By sparing themselves from excessive bodily mortification, and maintaining a *juste milieu* between self-sacrifice and self-preservation, the sisters could be better prepared to serve the sick poor in all their needs. If the life of a Daughter of Charity was thus less heroically wedded to Christ-like suffering than, say, a Carmelite, the spiritual and material benefits which resulted from their commitment were none the less widely disseminated within society. In their different ways, both kinds of life, active and contemplative, were exemplary for the rest of the church. The conduct of the Daughter of Charity was to be a kind of visual sermon, not just to the poor but to society in general and in particular to those with a superfluity of worldly goods. The sisters' behaviour, Saint Louise remarked, 'should attract benefactors by their open-handedness' (*L*, 390; cf. 284b). They owed respect 'to the poor because they are members of Jesus Christ and our masters; and to the rich so that they may give us their riches to help the poor' (*L*, 424). In their way, then, the Daughters of Charity pointed in the direction of a more Christian and a more compassionate society.

With neither the bodily mortification, intense liturgical prescription, nor the observance of the cloister which had formerly kept members of female communities within the observance of their rule, the Daughters of Charity were required to internalize their rules and regulations through a variety of spiritual exercises. This kind of strategy in the quest for spiritual perfection had been widely adopted by the new male orders in the sixteenth century (most classically, the Jesuits); but its adoption by female communities was relatively novel. It was important also to adapt spiritual instruction to the fact that most Daughters of Charity came from humble peasant backgrounds and had either little or no formal education. Saint Vincent's preaching style was deliberately simple, and was designed to be as comprehensible to the rude peasant or farmer's girl as was the Sermon on the Mount.[49] This precept influenced the way he – and, following his example, Saint Louise and their successors as superiors of the community – conducted sessions with the sisters many of whom (perhaps one-third in the early days)[50] were illiterate. The favoured form of instruction was the *conférence*, a dialectical method pioneered by Saint François de Sales and pitched midway between the sermon and the catechism. In the records of sessions which have come down to us,[51] we can see

Saint Vincent patiently teasing religious opinions and statements from women quite unhabituated to the articulation of abstract thought, and instructing them in an everyday, plain, and occasionally colourful manner in the mysteries of the faith and in the importance of their vocation.

Great emphasis throughout the *conférences* was placed on dissecting, repeating, and paraphrasing the rules of the community. Only the internalization of spiritual values learned thereby could foster a sense of vocation for women whose convent, as Saint Vincent classically put it, was to be the home of the sick poor, whose cloister was the street and for whom obedience was to serve as enclosure, fear of God as grille and modesty as veil (*VdeP*, X, 661). He set great store by the practice of internal prayer – oraison – which the Rule stated should be performed twice daily. Again, the way in which oraison was taught in the mother-house minimized the importance of formal education. Sisters could perform it not just (as was the usual practice) by reading scripture, but by the mere act of remembering Christ's passion or by concentrating on a religious statue or picture (*VdeP*, IV, 390; X, 574–5). Properly practised, oraison – 'the centre-piece of devotion' (*VdeP*, IX, 2) – formed an essential part of sisters' spiritual hygiene. According to Saint Vincent, 'a Daughter of Charity won't last unless she can say oraison' (*VdeP*, X, 416). It constituted 'a mystical arsenal which provides all kinds of weapons not only for our defence but also to drive off the enemies of the glory of God and the salvation of souls' (*VdeP*, XI, 84). Just as Seneca every day 'would review his day to see if he had lived like a philosopher' (*VdeP*, X, 606), so the oraison provided sisters with a practical guide to Christian living, and allowed them to keep in tune with Vincentian currents of spirituality learnt in the mother-house.

By orientating their teaching around the intellectual abilities of the Daughters of Charity and in particular by constructing an appropriate set of spiritual exercises, Saint Vincent and Saint Louise laboured to build up a sense of collective dedication in the fledgling community which served to bolster sisters' individual commitment. They also encouraged the emergence of a sense of purposive and uncompetitive sisterhood among recruits and older sisters. Hierarchy and authority were kept to what was regarded as a minimum; uniformity was regarded as the rule; and sisters were urged to view themselves as 'daughters of the same Father' (*VdeP*, X, 464). The officers of the community in Paris were elected for fixed-term periods; local *soeurs servantes* could be changed and alternated; older sisters were allowed no special privileges; anyone in a position of authority was to exercise that authority without imperiousness, and to see in themselves the 'packmules' of the community (*L*, 290b; 125b, 376). Sisters were enjoined to live harmoniously together in cheerful and forgiving manner, so that community life became a 'fore-taste of paradise'. [52] From the 1640s onwards, obituaries for deceased sisters, sometimes drawn up collectively during *conférences*, became a staple ingredient in the promotion of collective self-dedication. Such obituary notices illustrated and concretized the ideal, and enrolled sisters in the apprenticeship of sanctity. They came to be a standard part of the annual newsletters despatched every January to each of the community's establishments, and which also included news and encouragement, a message from superiors and a collection of pictures of saints to whom the coming year was dedicated and which were to adorn sisters' rooms, hospital wards, and schoolrooms. [53]

In an imaginative variety of ways, therefore, the founders of the Daughters of Charity offered to semi-literate peasant women – a group normally at best on the margins of seventeenth-century religious life – an intense and rigorously internalized piety, and give the lie to the traditional view that only cloistered women could aspire to a life of piety. The proof of the pudding, moreover, was in the eating. The success of the founders' recruitment and training programmes was emphatically borne out by the fact that the community not only

Table 3.1: Creation of Permanent Establishments of the Daughters of Charity outside Paris, 1633–99*

Date	*No*	*Date*	*No.*
1633–40	2	1670–4	12
1640–4	5	1675–9	13
1645–9	5	1680–4	14
1650–4	6	1685–9	24
1655–9	7	1690–4	27
1660–4	5	1695–9	35
1665–9	8		
		Total 163 institutions	

Sources: A.N., S 6160–80; and the printed correspondence of Vincent de Paul and Louise de Marillac.

Note: * Parisian institutions excluded.

survived the death of the founders in 1660 intact, but also entered into a phase of continued expansion (Table 3.1). The community's officers, most of whom down to at least 1700 had been personally trained by the founders, and who continued to operate under the overall guidance of the Congregation of the Mission, handled the necessary adaptation with considerable aplomb and in ways which – in spite of an inevitable increase in the bureaucratic nature of the organization – did not desiccate the original inspirational sources. The community's Rule, of which Saint Vincent had been negligent in establishing a final version, was formally agreed and then diffused within the community in the 1670s.[54] At about the same time, the officers developed a standard legal contract which they used as the basis for entering into any new undertaking.[55] In the late seventeenth century too, the community adopted a more systematic approach to visitations to outlying establishments – a development which, along with the continued emphasis on administrative centralization, further promoted the emergence of a nationwide network of institutions.[56]

An organizational framework staffed by a cadre of capable administrators drawn from their own ranks and acting under the overall spiritual direction of the Congregation of the Mission; a strict admissions policy; a rigorous and highly centralized training in which the spiritual and the material were amalgamated into a potent critical mass: these factors, originated by the founders and carried forward by their successors, produced a corps of Daughters of Charity who were highly trained as well as physically and mentally tough and were able to ensure the highest levels of patient care and institutional control. These intrinsic factors go a long way towards explaining the success of the Daughters of Charity in the seventeenth century. Supply also required demand, however, and it is worth considering the extent to which the character of French society in the seventeenth century favoured the establishment and diffusion of female communities of this sort.

IV

We should not ignore – any more than we should exaggerate – the importance of certain demographic features of seventeenth-century France which favoured the revival of nursing communities like the Daughters of Charity. One of the defining characteristics of the 'demographic Ancien Régime' in France was a high incidence – perhaps 7 per cent – of celibacy. A sizeable pool of labour, comprising women who in the main could well be attracted to life in a community which acted as surrogate kin – feeding, clothing, caring for and looking after a woman in illness and old age – might well be considered a prerequisite of the expansion of the Daughters of Charity. [57] Another significant demographic factor was the decline of bubonic plague. It is perhaps more than mere accident that the decline of the great medieval nursing communities coincided with the arrival of the Black Death in 1348.[58]

The reduced life chances of individuals with close propinquity to the poor and the diseased subverted the foundations of community. The early history of the Daughters of Charity bears witness to the kind of disruption plague could have. The former milkmaid Marguerite Naseau, whom Saint Vincent regarded as the prototypical Daughter of Charity and who had been attached to parishional *charités* in Paris even before 1633, had died in the arms of a plague victim she had been nursing.[59] The dedication of women of her sort was simply suicidal in a period of high plague incidence, even if their community took precautions against contagion.[60] Their demographic chances of surviving and prospering were much reduced, whatever their dedication to their tasks. Yet although plague had been particularly severe in the early years of the seventeenth century – it appeared in Paris in eighteen years until 1633 – it went into precipitous decline from the 1630s, the only outbreaks occurring thereafter in 1636, 1638, 1652, and 1668.[61] What was true of Paris became, *grosso modo*, true of France. Even though other contagious diseases continued to make life as a sister of charity a risky one, the decline of plague had let nursing communities breathe again.

It is with a greater degree of certainty that we can say that the success of nursing communities like the Daughters of Charity in the seventeenth century also owed an enormous amount to the socio-religious demands within society to which it was a response. The mission of the Daughters of Charity clearly dovetailed with the Christianizing concerns of the post-Tridentine Catholic church. Despite the initial problems over their status 'in the world', in general terms the sisters were swimming with the stream. The fact that they were seculars, under parishional and diocesan authority (though under Lazarist guidance) may have facilitated their ability to work productively with other dynamic elements within the revitalized Catholic church. Of the new male orders, the Lazarists, for example, worked hand in glove with them; bishops were often instrumental in their introduction into particular localities; and advanced *dévot* groups such as the Company of the Holy Sacrament (of which Vincent de Paul was a member)[62] and the Ladies of Charity (whom he directed) also sponsored their activities.

Jewel in the crown of the post-Tridentine church, the Daughters of Charity shone all the brighter moreover for being utterly unthreatening to the established ecclesiastical hierarchy. Saint Vincent placed great stress on avoiding law-suits and disputes – he did not want to be accounted a person 'of intrigues and interests' (*VdeP*, IV, 7) – and vaunted the virtues of corporate self-renunciation and obedience to superiors. 'The malady of all religious communities', he argued, 'is emulation, and its remedy is humility' (*VdeP*, V, 582). The humility which was a crucial ingredient in the sisters' vocation and which, if only because of their lowly social status, it was only seemly for them to embrace, should make them accept their place at the bottom of every pecking order. The uniformity of the treatment which all sisters had to accept – uniformity in food, in dress, in accommodation, and so on – highlighted this shirking from the world of rank and display: the Daughters of Charity were to be so many charitable clones, undistinguished in the eyes of the world and indistinguishable in the eyes of God save by their virtues.[63] By willingly opting out of the kind of jockeying for precedence and place which characterized much of church politics – as indeed politics *tout court* under the Ancien Régime – as well as by steering clear of the Jansenist controversy,[64] the community freed itself from the conventional round of rancours and resentments and this left them with their energies uncommitted and with their hands free to get on with the job. No ecclesiastical incumbent could possibly feel at risk from a body as genuinely disinterested as the Daughters of Charity – a fact which goes a long way towards explaining the almost total lack of major conflict which accompanied the expansion of the community.

The remarkably conflict-free character of the expansion of the community owed something too to the fact that its work fitted neatly within emergent patterns of involvement in poor relief. The sixteenth-century reform movement in poor relief had been spearheaded by the secular authorities, both local and national, which were increasingly dissatisfied with the church's stewardship over charitable institutions.[65] Secularization had gone off half-cock, however: in the civil strife occasioned by the Wars of Religion, government both central and local had other priorities besides poor relief. The revitalized church after Trent also bid fair to beat back secular involvement within limits less extensive than had at one stage seemed likely. A greater emphasis was now placed – even from the late sixteenth century – on voluntary commitment by religious activists. And it was increasingly accepted that this latter group might include women as well as men. The work of the Company of the Holy Sacrament showed that male charitable activism could still be important; while men gave as generously in their wills as women did.[66] Yet if the gender line was still a fuzzy one, it was increasingly clear that while men continued to dominate the public realm of authority and legislation, women were being offered a new scope for action – on condition that they renounce any participation in the exercise of power – in the more private sphere of gratuity and compassion. A gendered division of labour was emerging. The comments of Louise de Marillac in the 1650s, when the project for a Hôpital Général in Paris was being mooted are significant in this regard: 'if this work is regarded as political,' she wrote, 'it seems that men must undertake it; but if it is considered a work of charity, women can undertake it in the manner that they have undertaken other great exercises that God has approved'.[67] The Paris institution would in the end be established through the collusion of religious militants and central government – an excellent illustration of how harmoniously the division of labour between the public and private spheres could work.[68] The fact that both the Ladies of Charity and the Daughters of Charity were involved in its inception highlights too the endorsement of female charitable commitment. In a vast number of cases of hospital reorganization throughout France in the seventeenth century, moreover, it became almost a knee-jerk reflex to call in sisters of charity to take over the running of institutions. Primacy of female involvement in the sphere of home relief – as witnessed by the activities of confraternities on the lines of the Ladies of

Charity as well as by the Daughters of Charity themselves – in no way contested this emerging sexual economy of welfare.[69] In contrast to the Middle Ages, when nursing orders were of either sex, none of the nursing communities established in the wake of the Daughters of Charity in 1633 was male.[70] Nursing had become feminized, and the vocation now implied the kind of privacy, discretion, and self-effacement which marked it out as women's work.

The quality of the work which sisters did prevented self-effacement resulting in corporate oblivion. Shunning the corridors of power, the community found an instant and enduring popularity with the great. The fruitful connections of Saint Vincent with the social elite helped in this. But a government which especially at mid-century was experiencing real political difficulties was probably extra alert to the propaganda capital to be gained from supporting a group as clearly worthy as the Daughters of Charity. Bringing in the sisters to care for the poor at the 'palace-village' at Saint-Germain-en-Laye (Anne of Austria, 1638); making a grant for the care of Parisian foundlings (Louis XIII, 1642); introducing Daughters of Charity into military hospitals to care for wounded soldiers (Anne of Austria and Louis XIV, mid- and late 1650s): these were the kinds of gesture of grace and gratuity which could win public approval and remind society at large that the ruler was the fount of justice and mercy as well as a coercive and extractive agency.[71] The crude medical lore of the sisters – they ran hospital pharmacies, often organized dispensaries, and were adept at minor surgical operations – seemed an aid to health, especially in out-of-the-way rural areas where there were no doctors and where populations coped with disease as best they could with the help of the cult of saints, travelling bone-setters and wise women. From the 1680s, with frankly populationist aims in view, the government began to dispatch through its Intendant large chests of staple remedies, composed by physicians of the Royal Household, to the branches of the Daughters of Charity.[72] Even if the medicine which the latter practised looks from the present vantage-point very like folk medicine, in fact it constituted an adulterated and diluted form of orthodox medical culture.

Although the ideological capital which successive rulers extracted from their relationship with the Daughters of Charity was considerable, the number of establishments created by the royal family is relatively small in proportional terms (Table 3.2). Nearly half of known charitable founders were seigneurs and their wives, seeking to provide elementary medical and

Table 3.2: Charitable Donors: Individuals or Bodies Contracting for the Services of the Daughters of Charity, 1633–99[1]

	No.	%
Royal family	8	6.2
Seigneur or Seigneuresse[2]	60	46.2
Hospital administration, municipal officials, or similar	42	32.3
Other[3]	20	15.3
Total	130	known cases

Sources: A.N., S 6160–80; and the printed correspondence of Vincent de Paul and Louise de Marillac.

Notes: 1 Parisian institutions excluded.
2 Seigneuresses involved in 36 cases (27.7%).
3 Of whom 13 (10.0%) clerics.

nursing care for their peasants, and some primary education for the daughters of the poor. Charity towards vassals was of course an immemorial seigneurial duty, but it would appear that it was being progressively refurbished from the middle decades of the seventeenth century. In 1658, for example, the duc de Luynes published his *Instruction pour apprendre à ceux qui ont des terres dont ils sont seigneurs ce qu'ils peuvent faire pour la gloire de Dieu et le soulagement du prochain,* which restated the responsibilities of the seigneur in a way which merged archaism with the softer language of post-Tridentine piety.[73]

The resonance which de Luynes's work and others like it achieved in the late seventeenth century may reflect changes which were taking place in the social attitudes of land-holding elites. This was a key period in the crystallization of court ideology, as the work of Norbert Elias has demonstrated, [74] and it may well be that one motive behind the establishment of Daughters of Charity was a heightened sense of aristocratic emulation of royal policies. One notes among founders prominent court names such as Madame de Montespan and Madame de Maintenon as well as high-placed servants of the crown such as Le Tellier, Louvois, Colbert, Pontchartrain, and Lamoignon de Basville.[75] Another possibility is that the failure of the Fronde at mid-century drove formerly turbulent nobles towards piety and good works. Just as Conti spent his last years organizing charity in Pézenas, and just as in 1679 the ageing roué-rebel Retz was 're-establishing' in the lands of the abbey of Saint-Denis, 'a confraternity of charity instituted by the servant of God Vincent de Paul', so Mademoiselle de Montpensier, who at one memorable moment during the Fronde had trained the cannons of the Faubourg Saint-Antoine on the person of the young Louis XIV, was by the 1680s establishing branches of the Daughters of Charity all over her estates (Eu, Blangy, Trévoux, Saint-Fargeau. . . .).[76]

If guilt and political failure bred a concern with penitence and charity, so too did fear. The social and political tensions of the first half of the century[77] must have produced anxiety among ruling groups at the loosening of traditional social bonds. If the great tax revolts were dying out by the late 1660s and 1670s,[78] there was still a great deal of raw tension in the countryside, not least because many areas saw a bout of revision of land-registers which provoked one of the severest intensifications of the feudal and seigneurial burden before the French Revolution. The more intensive pastoral concerns of the post-Tridentine clergy could damp down social unrest – and Saint Vincent knew this because seigneurs wrote to him to thank him for the stabilizing role played by the Lazarists. The ideological and emollient virtues of seigneurial charity must have been particularly appealing; and no one bridged a gap more effectively than a Daughter of Charity.

In many ways the whole essence of the work of the Daughters of Charity and others like them in the seventeenth century was precisely the bridging of gaps: effectively, compassionately, discreetly, always without *éclat*. 'Cultural mediators' they certainly were. These offspring of two social *métèques* – one a Gascon peasant who advised the crown on the highest ecclesiastical preferments, the other a member of one of the mightiest dynasties of early modern France, yet who bore the stigma of bastardy – the Daughters of Charity excelled at crossing frontiers, at switching elements. Sexually these degendered beings offered aid to male and female alike without loss of reputation or male harassment. Walking in the poorest neighbourhoods to help the needy, they comprised an embodiment of the sacred in a world of profanity. The recipients of an intense spiritual training, they spent most of their time occupied with the drudgery of housework. Socially of the people, drawn largely from the peasantry, they were welcome in the homes of the great. Provincial women for the most part, they received their training in Paris and imbibed therein the values of urban religious elites. Hardly literate themselves, they taught. Medically untrained save for the routines of apprenticeship, they offered an alternative to folk medicine in rural areas bereft of trained physicians. Bridges mark effective distance between two sides, and it is tempting to conclude that the popularity of the community reflected the growing gap separating France's social elite from their inferiors, and insulating 'elite culture' from 'popular culture'. But bridges also connect; on balance for the seventeenth century at least it is fitting to view the Daughters of Charity and their ilk not simply as social insulators, doing the dirty work of the social elite and allowing the latter to keep their hands as clean as their consciences. Rather, in the light of the multiform activity of sisters of charity in bringing spiritual and material aid to those outside the set parameters of compassion of the social elite – to the poor, to hospital inmates, to foundlings, and so on – they should more correctly be seen as a force of integration and community and an element, if only a small one, in the making of a new moral and social consensus.

Notes

1. A good overview is provided by O. Hufton and F. Tallett, 'Communities of women, the religious life and public service in seventeenth-century France', in M.J. Boxer and J. Quataert (eds) *Connecting Spheres: Women in the Western World since 1500* (Oxford, 1987).

2. The best general starting-point for medieval communities is still the work of L. Le Grand, in particular his 'Les Maisons-Dieu. Leur régime intérieur au Moyen Age', *Revue des questions historiques* (1898), and his *Statuts d'Hôtels-Dieu et de léproseries. Recueil de textes du XIIe. au XIVe. siècle* (Paris, 1901). For a recent overview, cf. M. Mollat, *The Poor in the Middle Ages: An Essay in Social History* (London, 1986). For colourful details on the decline of morale among these communities, see E. Coyèque, *L'Hôtel-Dieu de Paris au Moyen-Age* (2 vols, Paris, 1891) esp. i, 175–7, 343–5, 353–64; M. Fosseyeux, *Une Administration parisienne sous l'Ancien Régime. L'Hôtel-Dieu de Paris aux XVIIe. et XVIIIe. siècles* (Paris, 1912); and N.Z. Davis, 'Scandale à l'Hôtel-Dieu de Lyon', in *La France d'Ancien Régime. Etudes réunies en l'honneur de Pierre Goubert* (Paris, 1985).

3. See for example, Madame Necker's use of the Daughters of Charity in the Hôpital Necker in Paris in the 1780s, and her advocacy

of their use in the Protestant Hospital of Montpellier in 1785 (Archives of the Montpellier Consistory, now housed in the Archives départementales de l'Hérault).

4. E.P. Thompson, *The Making of the English Working Class* (London, 1980 edn) p. 12. Thompson was talking about handloom weavers, 'the deluded followers of Joanna Southcott et al.'

5. The scholarly literature on the Daughters of Charity is uninspiring. L. Celier, *Les Filles de la Charité* (Paris, 1930) and P. Coste *et al.*, *Les Filles de la Charité. Trois siècles d'histoire religieuse* (Paris, 1933?) contain little for the seventeenth century not to be found in P. Coste's massive biography of Vincent de Paul, *Le Grand Saint du grand siècle. Monsieur Vincent* (3 vols, Paris, 1934). The best historical sketch of the community is A. Dodin's entry on 'Filles de la Charité' in the *Dictionnaire d'histoire et de géographie ecclésiastiques* (henceforth = *D.H.G.E.*), xvii, cols 6–13. See also a number of chapters in *Vincent de Paul. Actes du colloque international d'études vincentiennes* (Rome, 1983). See also notes 6 and 13.

6. Standard and indispensable for the life of the saint is Coste's *Monsieur Vincent.* Essential too are L. Abelly, *La Vie du vénérable serviteur de Dieu, Vincent de Paul* (Paris, 1664, re-edition 1843); and P. Coste (ed.) *Saint Vincent de Paul. Correspondance. Entretiens. Documents* (14 vols, Paris, 1920–5) (henceforth = *VdeP*). A popular but scholarly biography, L. Mezzadri, *Saint Vincent de Paul (1581–1660)* (Paris, 1985) contains the findings of much recent research.

7. For excellent syntheses of the new style of religious history, see J. Delumeau, *Le Catholicisme entre Voltaire et Luther* (Paris, 1971) and J. Bossy, *Christianity in the West, 1400–1700* (London, 1986). See too R. Taveneaux, *Le Catholicisme dans la France classique, 1610–1715* (2 vols, Paris, 1980). A great deal of the best work in the field has taken the form of local studies. See in particular J. Ferté, *La Vie religieuse dans les campagnes parisiennes, 1622–95* (Paris, 1963); L. Pérouas, *Le Diocèse de La Rochelle de 1648 à 1724* (Paris, 1964); T.J. Schmitt, *L'Organisation ecclésiastique et la pratique religieuse dans l'archidiaconé d'Autun de 1650 à 1750* (Autun, 1957); R. Sauzet, *Contre-Réforme et Réforme catholique en Bas-Languedoc au XVIIe. siècle* (Paris, 1979); J.F. Soulet, *Traditions et réformes religieuses dans les Pyrénées centrales: le diocèse de Tarbes de 1602 à 1716* (Pau, 1974); and P.T. Hoffman, *Church and Community in the Diocese of Lyon, 1500–1789* (London and New Haven, Conn., 1984). Cf. too the broad and critical perspectives opened up in J. van Engen, 'The Christian Middle Ages as a historiographical problem', *American Historical Review* (1986).

8. Taveneaux, *Le Catholicisme,* i, p. 225.

9. J. Delumeau, 'Missioni al popolo nel XVII secolo', in *San Vincenzo de' Paoli tra storia e profezia. IVe. Convegno di animazione vincenziana* (Rome, 1984), for a good introduction to a subject which is burgeoning. See too the special numbers of the journals *Dix-septième siècle* (1958) on 'Missionaires catholiques à l'intérieur de la France pendant le XVIIe. siècle', and *Annales de Bretagne* (1974), on 'Prédication et théologie populaires au temps de Grignion de Montfort'.

10. Abelly, *Vie*, ii, p. 318; *VdeP*, III, pp. 35–6, 53; V, pp. 417–18, and VI, pp. 353–4; plus J. Seguy, 'Monsieur Vincent, la Congrégation de la Mission et les derniers temps', in *Vincent de Paul. Actes*, pp. 217 ff.

11. *VdeP*, I, p. 59. In order to keep footnote reference within reasonable proportions, I will give references to the works of Vincent de Paul and Louise de Marillac in the text.

12. J.N. Biraben, *Les Hommes et la peste en France et dans les pays méditerranéens* (Paris, 1975) p. 386.

13. A fact unknown, glossed over or ignored in every biography until very recent times. But see now J. Dirven, *Saint Louise de Marillac* (New York, 1970), probably the best biography of the saint. For social aspects of her work, see Sister M. Flinton, *Sainte Louise de Marillac. L'aspect social de son oeuvre* (no place or date of publication: 1957?), and for the spiritual side, J. Calvet, *Sainte Louise de Marillac par elle-même* (1958). The basis of all biographies is N. Gobillon, *La Vie de la vénérable Louise de Marillac, veuve de M. Le Gras* (Paris, 1676). Of Saint Louise's own writings, see the very handy American edition of her correspondence, *Letters of Saint Louise de Marillac* (Emmitsburg, Md, 1972) (henceforth = *L*).

14. For the inception of the community, see esp. Abelly, *Vie*, i, pp. 99–100; Gobillon, *Vie*, pp. 50–1, 269; and Coste, *M. Vincent*, i, pp. 265–6.

15. P. Coste, *Monsieur Vincent et les Dames de la Charité* (1917) contains little for the period which is not contained in his *M. Vincent*, esp. i, pp. 323–84.

16. Coste, *M. Vincent*, i, pp. 337–8 for the list.

17. ibid., pp. 461 ff; and Archives Nationales (henceforth = A.N.) S 6174. Cf. similar foundations at Liancourt, for the Duchesse de Liancourt (*M. Vincent*, i, pp. 467–8, and A.N., S 6169); and at Nanteuil-le-Hardoin, for Madame de Maignelaye (*M. Vincent*, i, pp. 474–6). For the Duchesse d'Aiguillon, see A. Bonneau-Avenant, *La Duchesse d'Aiguillon* (1879).

18. Coste, *M. Vincent*, i, pp. 504 ff. The community flourished in Poland, but details are so sketchy that I have excluded it from discussion here.

19. A. Feillet, *La Misère au temps de la Fronde et Saint Vincent de Paul* (Paris, 1886) is good on these relief operations, as is the unpublished London University PhD thesis (1934) of E. Archer, 'The assistance of the poor in Paris and the north-eastern provinces of France, 1641–60'. See too J. Jacquart, *La Crise rurale en Ile-de-France, 1560–1660* (Paris, 1974), and his more tightly focused article, 'La Fronde des Princes dans la région parisienne et ses conséquences matérielles', *R.H.M.C.* (1960); and Mezzadri, *Vincent de Paul*, pp. 91 ff.

20. A.N., S 6161A. See too *VdeP* and *L*, passim, and C. Port, *Inventaire des archives anciennes de l'Hôpital Saint-Jean d'Angers* (Paris and Angers, 1870) Introduction.

21. Besides the works cited in note 7, see also K. Norberg, *Rich and Poor in Grenoble, 1600–1815* (Berkeley, Calif., 1986) passim.

22. L. Helyot, *Histoire des ordres monastiques, religieux et militaires et des congrégations séculières de l'un et de l'autre sexe* (8 vols, 1721) vii, pp. 301

ff. There is no evidence in his papers that Saint Vincent had any inkling of the existence of these groups.

23. M. Marcocchi, 'Esperienze di vita consacrata femminile nel mondo tra '500 e '600 (Italia e Francia)', *Vincent de Paul. Actes*, pp. 27 ff. For these female religious groupings, see in general Helyot, *Histoire des ordres monastiques*, and the excellent C. Molette, *Guide des sources de l'histoire des congrégations féminines françaises de vie active* (Paris, 1974). There is much to be gleaned too in the *D.H.G.E.*

24. M.C. Guesdré, *Histoire de l'Ordre des Ursulines en France* (3 vols, 1957–64); M.A. Jégou, *Les Ursulines du Faubourg Saint-Jacques à Paris (1607–62)* (Paris, 1981); Marcocchi, 'Esperienze'. pp. 27 ff; and Molette, *Guide*, pp. 30 ff.

25. Marcocchi, 'Esperienze', p. 28; Molette, *Guide*, p. 32.

26. Marcocchi, 'Esperienze', pp. 35 ff; Molette, *Guide*, pp. 33 ff.; R. Devos, *Vie religieuse féminine et société. L'origine sociale des Visitandines d'Annécy aux XVIIe. et XVIIIe. siècles* (Annécy, 1973).

27. Marcocchi, 'Esperienze'; p. 31; Molette, *Guide*, p. 51.

28. *D.H.G.E.*, xvii, cols 87 f.; Molette, *Guide*, p. 49.

29. See pp. 66ff.; Molette, *Guide*, pp. 34 ff., 49; Helyot, *Histoire des ordres monastiques*, viii, pp. 405 ff.

30. *D.H.G.E.*, xiii, cols 93 ff.

31. ibid., xvii, cols 54 f.

32. Molette, *Guide*, v, pp. 639 f.; Helyot, *Histoire des ordres monastiques*, iv, pp. 361 f.

33. R. Chantelauze, *Vincent de Paul et les Gondi* (Paris, 1882), passim.

34. P. Blet, 'Vincent de Paul et l'épiscopat de France', in *Vincent de Paul. Actes*, pp. 81 ff, for a good recent discussion.

35. *VdeP*, XIII, pp. 566–7.

36. Mezzadri, *Vincent de Paul*, p. 88.

37. J.H.M. Salmon, *Cardinal de Retz: Anatomy of a Conspirator* (London, 1969) p. 271.

38. *VdeP*, XIII, pp. 585 ff.

39. See Molette and Helyot, passim.

40. Molette, *Guide*, pp. 55, 313 f., 342 ff.; *D.H.G.E.*, v, col. 646.

41. Notably in Dirven's 1970 biography.

42. Abelly, *Vie*, i, pp. 99–100.

43. See Chapter 5.

44. This was a perennial worry, for example, as regards the Paris Visitandines, whom Saint Vincent directed. Cf. Coste, *M. Vincent*, i, p. 361.

45. In the earliest days, Saint Vincent allowed the most senior sisters to pronounce perpetual vows, but this practice died out in the 1640s and 1650s. Coste, *M. Vincent*, pp. 398 ff.

46. ibid., i, pp. 396 ff.; *VdeP*, VIII, p. 237; X, pp. 661 ff.

47. Compare

A servant with this clause
Makes drudgerie divine:
Who sweeps a room, as for thy laws,
Makes that and th'action fine.

It is worth bearing in mind that George Herbert's famous verse from his poem 'The Elixir' was written in the 1630s and early 1640s.

48. *VdeP*, X, p.59.

49. On preaching, see V. Kapp, 'Prêcher selon la "petite méthode": Vincent de Paul et l'éloquence de la chaire au XVIIe. siècle', in *Vincent de Paul. Actes*, pp. 206 ff.

50. The act of foundation in 1655 was signed by all sisters then inhabiting the mother-house. Ten out of thirty-six sisters were unable to sign their names. A.N., L 1054.

51. *VdeP*, vols IX to XIII.

52. Coste, *M. Vincent*, i, p. 361.

53. Potted versions of the newsletters are printed in the *Circulaires des supérieurs généraux et des soeurs supérieures des Filles de la Charité* (1865).

54. Sister B. Delort, 'Du "Règlement" de Châtillon aux "Règles" des Filles de la Charité', in *Vincent de Paul. Actes*, pp. 81 ff.

55. See pp. 165-7.

56. See A.N. LL 1663.

57. J. Dupâcquier, *La population française aux XVIIe. et XVIIIe. siècles* (Paris, 1979) p. 60.

58. Biraben, *Les Hommes et la peste*, pp. 174 ff, for a discussion of ecclesiastical mortality generally.

59. Cf. Coste, *M. Vincent*, i, pp. 260 ff.

60. For caution and precaution on the part of Saint Vincent and Saint Louise as regards plague, see *VdeP*, I, pp. 132 f., 323, 484, 503, 600, 605 f., . . .

61. Biraben, *Les Hommes et la peste*, pp. 485 ff.

62. For the Company of the Holy Sacrament, see E. Chill, 'Religion and mendicity in seventeenth-century France', *International Review of Social History* (1962); R. Allier, *La Cabale des dévotes* (Paris, 1902).

63. For the heavy emphasis on uniformity, see for example *VdeP*, VI, pp. 113 ff.

64. For Jansenism, see the magisterial study of L. Mezzadri, *Fra Giansenisti e antigiansenisti: Vincent de Paul e la Congregazione della Missione (1624–1737)* (Florence, 1977).

65. See pp. 2–5.

66. Cf. Hoffman, *Church and Community*, p. 127; K. Norberg, *Rich and Poor in Grenoble, 1600–1815* (Berkeley, Calif., 1986) p. 250; M. Vovelle, *Piété baroque et déchristianisation en Provence au XVIIIe. siècle* (Paris, 1974) p. 133.

67. Cited in Flinton, *Sainte Louise*, p. 268.

68. For the role of the saints in the foundation of the Hôpital Général, see R. Elmore, *The Origins of the Paris Hôpital Général* (University microfilms edn, University of Michigan, 1975).

69. More than three-fifths of the establishments served by the Daughters of Charity in the Ancien Régime concerned the distribution of home relief.

70. There was a single – and important – exception to the 'female' rule: the Brothers of Charity, or Brothers of Saint John of God, who were founded in Spain in the sixteenth century, introduced into France in 1602 – that is *before* the creation of the Daughters of Charity – and ran several dozen hospitals by the end of the Ancien Régime.

71. For Saint-Germain, *VdeP*, I, pp. 421 f., 447; for the foundlings, Coste, *M. Vincent*, ii, pp. 453 ff; and for military hospitals, *VdeP*, V, pp. 55 f. (Calais), VII, p. 185 (Châlons) and *L* 399 (Sainte-Menehould), etc., etc.

72. Biblothèque Nationale. Manuscrits français 6801. For how the medical care offered by the sisters fitted into the network of provision under the Ancien Régime, see F. Lebrun, *Se soigner autrefois. Médecins, saints et sorciers aux XVIIe. et XVIIIe. siècles* (Paris, 1983).

73. P. Berger, 'Rural charity in late seventeenth-century France: the Pontchartrain case', *French Historical Studies* (1978), provides an illuminating discussion of the under-researched topic of seigneurial charity.

74. N. Elias, *The Court Society* (London, 1983).

75. A.N. S 6172 (Madame de Montespan, at Oiron), S 6150 (Madame de Maintenon, at Maintenon), S 6164 and 6169 (Le Tellier, at Châville and Lézines), S 6161 and 6169 (Louvois, at Bessé and Louvois), S 6175 (widow Colbert, at Sceaux), and S 6173 (Pontchartrain, at Pontchartrain).

76. Ferté, *La Vie religieuse*, p. 218; A.N., S 6157 (Eu), S 6161 (Blangy), S 6166 (Saint-Fargeau), S 6177 (Trévoux), . . .

77. B. Porchnev, *Les Soulèvements populaires en France de 1623 à 1648* (Paris, 1963); R. Mousnier, *Peasant Revolts* (London, 1971).

78. E. Le Roy Ladurie, 'Peasant revolts and protest movements, 1675–1788', *The Local Historian* (1974).

4

The Daughters of Charity in the Hôtel-Dieu Saint-Eloi in Montpellier before the French Revolution

> The religious institutes devoted to succouring the poor and serving the sick are among those most worthy of respect. There is perhaps nothing greater on this earth than the sacrifice that the delicate sex makes of its beauty and its youth in caring within hospitals for the collection of every sort of human wretchedness, the very sight of which is so humiliating for mankind's pride, and so revolting for our niceties.

That Voltaire was willing sufficiently to suspend his habitual anti-clericalism to find words of praise for nursing communities is well-known. Just as he looked benevolently on the good curé as a civilizing agent in the countryside ensuring parishioners' physical and economic well-being, as well as their obedience, so the touchstone of social utility led him to spare a kind word for sisters of charity, who performed physically repellent, but socially advantageous, tasks.[1] Yet if it is fairly clear what Voltaire and other *philosophes* saw – and valued – in such women, it remains far more uncertain just what the latter in the Ancien Régime represented at the grassroots: in the towns and villages where they worked, in the institutions in which they served, to the poor that they assisted. This kind of question can be satisfactorily answered only by detailed locally based analyses, and it is such a case study that I wish to attempt in this chapter. Using a wide variety of local as well as institutional and national sources,[2] I shall explore the service that the Daughters of Charity – the largest and the best-known of Ancien Régime France's legion of communities of nursing sisters – performed in a single institution, namely Montpellier's major hospital, the Hôtel-Dieu Saint-Eloi. They first entered the institution in 1667, only a few years after the death (in 1660) of their founders Vincent de Paul and Louise de Marillac. Although they were to serve this institution well into the present century, it is only the period down to the Revolution – the period covering the personal reign of Louis XIV and the Age of Enlightenment – which will here be considered.

The Hôtel-Dieu Saint-Eloi changed considerably in the period under review. In the 1660s the first sisters had found a hospital which was tiny, comprising only a couple of dozen beds into which were crammed pell-mell, three or more to a bed, not only the sick poor but also a wide range of other social types, including abandoned children and orphans, the infirm, the chronically disabled, and the aged.[3] Moreover, the hospital was then acknowledged to be poorly administered; it had acquired notoriety as the home of vice and immorality; and it was something of a death-trap (one entrant in five seems to have succumbed within its walls). By the end of the Ancien Régime, in contrast, the refuge of poverty and distress had moved a good way towards becoming a hospital in the medical sense of the word: trained medical personnel closely supervised the treatment of inmates, admission was more carefully restricted to the curably sick, the death-rate had been brought down to about 10 per cent, and the institution had become one of the most reputed centres for care and cure in the whole of southern France. This was an impressive transformation. It is worth considering, then, what contribution the Daughters of Charity made to it, what their services entailed, and in what ways they adapted to the changing face of the hospital.

I

By the middle of the seventeenth century responsibility for the management of Montpellier's hospitals had devolved upon the city's municipal officials, or consuls. In particular, financial responsibility for the Hôtel-Dieu Saint-Eloi – which was at that time by far the most substantial of the city's charitable institutions – lay in the hands of the fourth consul, who was selected from the ranks of the city's artisans. From the 1620s, the fourth consul's role was complemented by a number of Intendants drawn from the city's wealthier classes, who regularly superintended most public business, such as the passing of contracts, the upkeep of property, the provisioning of the hospital, and so on.[4] At a more humble level, care of hospital inmates and day-to-day control of the institution was maintained by a lay individual, normally called a 'hospitaller' (*hospitalier*) and sometimes a 'steward' (*économe*). This person was aided by a fluctuating number of domestics and often by his wife.[5]

These administrative arrangements had signally failed to secure able and disinterested care of hospital inmates. Acrimony in public life between Protestants and Catholics doubtless had a part in this. There were complaints about corruption in hospital management and, significantly, a high turnover of *hospitaliers*. In 1605 the inmates were allegedly dying of hunger, and in 1630 a full-scale hunger riot broke out within the hospital, with angry inmates alleging that 'bread and meat were lacking for them'. Pressure on space within the hospital caused by overcrowding only worsened matters. Inmates were three to a bed in 1660, and with young boys and girls sharing the same living quarters, scandals of promiscuity were a regular occurrence.

In 1663 positive measures were at last taken to remedy matters. Aware of what they called a 'shortage of good subjects' in the locality for the post of *hospitalier*, the city's consuls appealed to the recently appointed Governor of Languedoc, the Prince de Conti, and to the Governor of the town and citadel of Montpellier, the Marquis de Castries, to procure more capable hospital servants in Paris. Negotiations were aided by the hospital's Intendant, *Trésorier-général* Jean-Paul Girard de Coulondres, who was dispatched to Paris for this purpose. The choice was initially fixed upon two widows attached to the service of La Salpêtrière, the women's section of the Paris Hôpital Général. The women were not, it was explained, nuns: however, according to Coulondres, 'they live in a condition of great regularity and with much gentleness, [and] they obey hospital administrators and distribute the food they are given for the poor'. In the event, one of these women dropped out, and her place was taken by two women who served in the Paris Hôtel-Dieu, and who were also adjudged 'capable and well-tried in the service of the poor'. On 30 October 1663 Anne Henault (from La Salpêtrière), widow of Claude Cabin, *bourgeois* of Paris, together with Louise Cornet and Anne Gaynier formally entered the Hôtel-Dieu Saint-Eloi.

They were to work strictly under the orders of the hospital's administrators, who would provide them with their food and lodgings, and who would pay them 80 *livres* each per annum.[6]

The service of these women – which seems to have improved standards within the hospital – was not however to last long. In 1665 Anne Gaynier requested permission to return to Paris and although she was seemingly replaced, when in 1667 widow Cabin died, her two companions also sought to return to Paris.[7] The hospital's administrators were not keen to appoint in their place a lay *hospitalier*, feeling as they did that

> the services which are rendered in hospitals by pure zeal and by the sole motive of the love of God differ and are much more beneficial than those services which are rendered by stewards who act most often by no other motive than that of self-interest.[8]

Following advice from the Bishop of Montpellier and the Marquis de Castries, the eye of the administrators alighted on the Daughters of Charity. A couple of these were now attached to the hospital, where they acquitted themselves in exemplary fashion. After six months, the Superior of the house of the Congregation of the Mission at nearby Agde, acting on behalf of the officials of the community in Paris, offered to pass a contract with the hospital which would ensure the institution service by the Daughters of Charity in perpetuity. The hospital administrators would have preferred, it seems, a more limited commitment, but eventually agreed to the proposal. On 9 February 1668 a contract was solemnly drawn up which formally and in perpetuity entrusted service of the hospital to the Daughters of Charity. There were initially to be three sisters based here – the first were to be Françoise Menage, Anne de Noal, and Catherine Alnot – and among their conditions of service it was stated that each was to be paid 40 *livres* per annum, and was to receive food and lodgings within the hospital.[9]

II

There were two factors in the new establishment which, from the point of view of the young community of the Daughters of

Charity, were as yet relatively novel. First, the new foundation was in a hospital. The vast majority of the community's foundations during the lives of Vincent de Paul and Louise de Marillac and after had been with parish *charités*, normally run by middle- and upper-class women organized in *confréries* (confraternities) of Ladies (*sic*) of Charity (*Dames de la Charité*). The first major provincial hospital which welcomed the sisters had been the Hôtel-Dieu of Angers in 1640. It is clear that Vincent de Paul regarded this foundation only as an 'experiment' (*essai*).[10] Both he and Louise de Marillac seem to have been aware of difficulties inherent in the sisters' attachment to hospitals, which were administratively more complex than parish charities, less susceptible to influence by Ladies of Charity or by members of the Congregation of the Mission, and more clearly within the orbit of the public authorities. At Angers, for example, Louise de Marillac had negotiated and entered into contract with the city's municipal officials – and this kind of link was to prove necessary in the case of most hospitals to which the sisters were to become attached. In the long term of course, in spite of the hesitancy which had marked its beginnings, the foundation at Angers was to turn out remarkably well, and in 1789 the sisters would be found in 175 hospitals throughout France. Yet even so, in the early days, there were teething troubles concerning the settlement of the sisters in the hospitals at Angers and in other localities (at Saint-Denis after 1645, for example, at Nantes after 1646, and at Montreuil-sur-Mer after 1647).[11] And even in 1668, the community's superiors were probably wary about committing themselves to the service of major hospitals.

The second unusual feature of the establishment of the community in Montpellier in 1668 was the distance of the city from Paris. In 1789 the Daughters of Charity's hundreds of institutions covering the whole of French national territory were to contrast with the far more limited geographical diffusion of most similar communities (the Filles de Sagesse, for example, were heavily concentrated in the west, the Soeurs de Saint-Charles de Nancy in the east, and so on). Yet in the early days of its history, the Daughters of Charity too were a regional rather than national body: the vast majority of the early foundations were in the north of France, and in particular in Paris and its environs – an area about a day or so's walking distance from the mother-house (Map 4.1).[12] The

Map 4.1: Foundations of the Daughters of Charity, 1633–60.

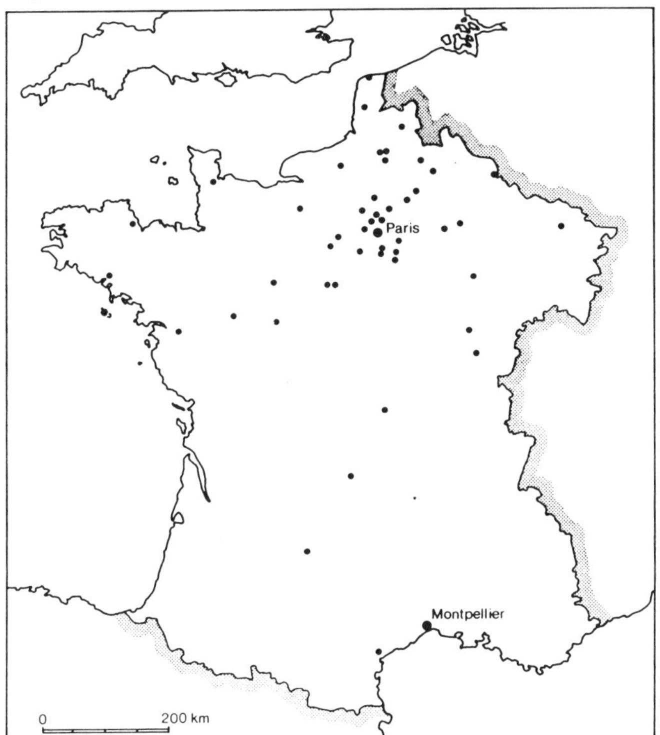

creation of branches at Angers (1640), Nantes (1645), Montreuil-sur-Mer (1647), Arras (1656), Calais (1658), Belle-Isle (1658), Alise Sainte-Reine (1666?), and Montluçon (1667)[13] showed that the community was capable of spreading its wings, but it also posed the question of how best these outlying foundations could be controlled from the centre. There was to be no foundation south of a line between Bordeaux and Geneva before the late 1650s. At that time, the community assumed responsibility (in 1658) for the orphans of Cahors and (in 1659) for the poor of the parishes of Narbonne. The remarks of Vincent de Paul in the *Conférence* he delivered as he sent off sisters to these far-distant locations clearly reveals the extent to which these establishments represented, for the community, a venture into the unknown.[14] There was to be no other foundation south of the Bordeaux-Geneva line before the Montpellier foundation in 1668.

Map 4.2: Foundations of the Daughters of Charity in the Montpellier Region in the Ancien Régime.

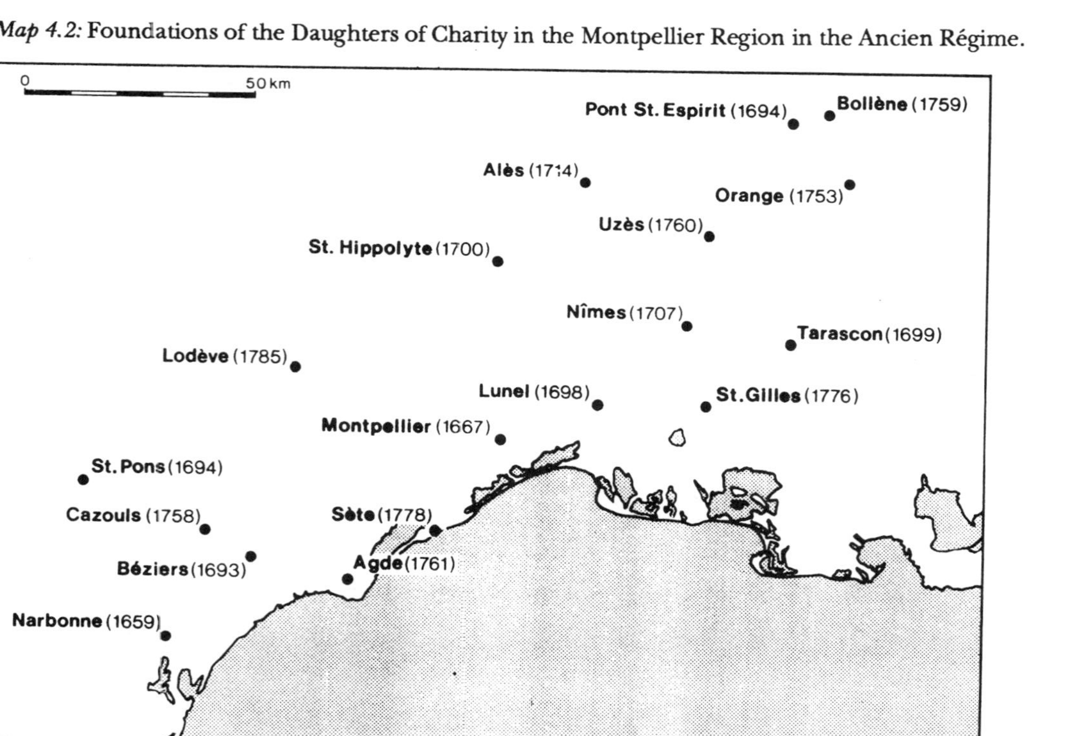

These three pioneering establishments at Cahors, Narbonne, and Montpellier were not without their difficulties in the early days – a fact partly no doubt explained by the distance factor. Yet the accelerating pace of establishment of new foundations in far-distant locations – Verviers in 1672, Autun, Rennes, and Luçon in 1673, Lyon in 1679, and so on – showed that the community was confident that it was developing means of control and co-ordination at a distance. By the eighteenth century Montpellier had become the hub of a dense network of outposts of the community throughout Bas-Languedoc and western Provence (Map 4.2). Of prime importance in this was the formalization in the 1660s, by René Alméras, Superior of the Congregation of the Mission, of the Rule of the community, no completely satisfactory version of which was in existence, and which was imperfectly diffused among the branches of the community. From the early 1670s Edme Jolly, Alméras' successor, was to circulate the definitive version of the Rule to all branches, thus according them a basic yardstick of uniformity in their everyday life. Also of major importance in establishing and maintaining control over the community's proliferating branches and in promoting a spirit of uniformity was the development of a standard notarial foundation contract which, with minor retouches and reformulations appropriate to the different kinds of institutions to which the sisters were attached, stipulated the nature of the service the sisters were permitted to perform and defined their recompenses and rewards.[15]

The contract which established the sisters in the Hôtel-Dieu Saint-Eloi in 1668 contained most but not all the provisions that were later to become routine items in the community's standard contract. It was not until 1693, when negotiations reached fruition for the placement of an additional three sisters within the hospital, that the full set of standard clauses and conditions was found.[16] It seems that the Montpellier sisters came to regard the 1693 contract, rather than that of 1668, as embodying the fullest expression of their rights and responsibilities.

III

The introduction of the Daughters of Charity into Montpellier in 1668 was part of a wider process of 'recatholicization' of a city which in the sixteenth and early seventeenth century had been a major centre of Protestantism and in which Protestants and Catholics had vied for local power down to 1628.[17] Long before the more draconian approach signalized by the Revocation of the Edict of Nantes in 1685, ecclesiastical authorities in the diocese had conducted vigorous campaigns of conversion and instruction. In a veritable 'invasion des religieux' (X. Azéma), for example, religious orders came en masse to establish themselves within the walls of the city. Houses of the Frères Prêcheurs (1623), the Capucins (1624), the Jesuits (1629), the Visitandines (1636), the Ursulines (1657), and the Récollets (1666) were created, while among those who re-established themselves in the city following the destruction caused by the Wars of Religion were the Trinitaires (1623), the Augustins (1624), the Observantins (1631), the Carmes (1639), and the Pères de la Merci (1663). The episcopacies of François Bosquet (1656–76) and Charles de Pradel (1676–96) were important in concerting the new spirit of missionary endeavour and in stimulating a number of new initiatives. Rebuilding and reconsecration of churches proceeded apace, following the iconoclasm of the Wars of Religion. Confraternities – notably those of the Saint-Sacrement (from the 1640s), of Saint-Roch (1661), the Propagation de la Foi (1679), and various Pénitents – were revitalized and popularized, as were the *tiers-ordres* attached to a number of religious houses. Bosquet attempted to regenerate the University, while his successor was particularly noted for the stimulus he gave to the creation of *petites écoles* (primary schools).

Very much part of the Catholic Revival was a growing concern for poor relief.[18] In 1646, for example, a Maison de Charité had opened in the city to care for orphans and foundlings. In 1672 the institution's administrators, aware that children and adolescents within the establishment needed to be brought up devoutly and industriously, called in three Daughters of Charity to supervise the children.[19] In this age of the *renfermement des pauvres,* concern for social welfare shaded imperceptibly into a desire for social control. By the 1670s Montpellier's consuls were expressing great alarm about the proliferation of beggars and vagrants in the city, and in 1678, aided both by the central government and the Bishop of

Montpellier, they took steps to transform the Maison de Charité into a Hôpital Général on the lines of the Parisian prototype which had been created in 1657. The new institution was to endeavour to confine both the needy as well as the dangerous and feckless poor, and to regiment them into better morals and work habits. (This function in regard to young women was to be complemented by the creation in 1676 of the Refuge and in 1691 of the Bon Pasteur which confined women of dubious morals.) For several years the Daughters of Charity continued to operate within the old Maison de Charité, which maintained a degree of autonomy from the new Hôpital Général establishment, which came to be run by a small community of women drawn from within Montpellier. The full merger of the two institutions in 1682, however, caused the Daughters of Charity to withdraw. Their contract in 1672 – like that of the sisters attached to the Hôtel-Dieu Saint-Eloi in 1668 – had stipulated that they were to enjoy a monopoly of service within the institution they served. Working alongside the little community of Montpellier-born women recently attached to the Hôpital thus presented insuperable problems.[20] In addition, the superiors of the Daughters of Charity in Paris may well have been cautious about committing their members to the service of fully fledged Hôpitaux Généraux, whose disciplinarian and repressive character was at this period still very pronounced.[21]

More orientated around the relief rather than the repression of the poor, Montpellier's *Dames de la Miséricorde* ('Ladies of Mercy') were to enjoy the services of the Daughters of Charity on a more permanent and more constructive basis.[22] The *confrérie* had originated in the Middle Ages, but was extensively remodelled during the Catholic Revival of the seventeenth century, most notably in 1658, when it was organized on lines very similar to those of Vincent de Paul's Ladies of Charity. The wives and daughters of the city's social and political elite composed the membership of the body which, meeting together for mutual spiritual edification, practised a wide variety of good works largely towards the poor in their homes (distribution of food, linen, and medicines, supervision of the Bon Pasteur, training in sewing for young girls) and also in the form of prison visiting. The Daughters of Charity were called in to help run the institution in 1669 and a contract was drawn up similar to the one passed the previous year with the Hôtel-Dieu. This was to be the origin of a link which outlasted the Ancien Régime and which still survives today.

Following the Wars of Religion, during which religious buildings of all sorts had been extensively damaged, the Hôtel-Dieu Saint-Eloi had become virtually Montpellier's sole hospital. It was inevitable therefore that the regeneration of poor-relief provision in the city during the seventeenth century should be marked by thorough-going reform in the institution. The appalling state of disrepair into which the small and cramped hospital had fallen by mid-century cried out for action. From the 1650s[23] it was allowed to expand as a result of mergers of adjacent houses, buildings, and gardens. This did not prevent chronic overcrowding, however, and the hospital came under intense pressure in the late 1680s and 1690s, partly as a result of poverty caused by bad harvests, partly because an influx of 'Nouveau Converti' paupers who prior to the Revocation of the Edict of Nantes had been cared for by Protestant charities, partly too as a result of the huge numbers of sick soldiers from the Piedmontese and Spanish fronts who were evacuated on the hospital. From the 1690s a fresh round of rebuilding and enlargements began. Whereas the hospital in the middle of the seventeenth century had housed a population of forty or fifty, by the 1690s there were often over two hundred inmates crowded within the institution.[24] Furthermore, such individuals would be more likely to be classifiably sick than their predecessors a generation or two earlier. Able-bodied paupers were now referred to the Hôpital Général, and in 1695 the Hôtel-Dieu's administrators declared it was their policy to refuse entry to all individuals suffering from any 'longlasting and languishing illness', and only to admit individuals susceptible to cure. Significantly too, in 1697 an agreement with the Hôpital Général transferred all care for abandoned children and orphans to the Hôpital – prior to this, all such children aged between 4 and 7 had been kept in the Hôtel-Dieu. Thus, from the last years of the seventeenth century, the Hôtel-Dieu was much more exclusively the home of the *pauvres malades* ('sick poor') who were the prime object of the care of the Daughters of Charity.

These changes went hand in hand with improvements in medical provision within the hospital. In the early part of the seventeenth century the institution's doctors had tended to be young physicians anxious to perfect their knowledge by the kind of practical experience a hospital provided, and they were changed annually.[25] The Hôtel-Dieu's administration seems to have become aware of the deficiencies of this system and from 1672 to 1679 annually renewed their contract with Raymond Vieussens, a Montpellier graduate soon to be internationally renowned for his physiological studies. In 1679 he was made doctor for life (he was to die only in 1714). Prior to the 1640s the provisioning of the hospital in drugs and medicines had been done on an informal and *ad hoc* basis; but from then onwards, standardized contracts were drawn up with cartels of the city's apothecaries, so as to put this part of the medical services on a more systematic basis. A similar arrangement came into being with the hospital's surgeons, and from 1657, the master surgeon who held the contract was obliged to keep one of his apprentices (*garçons chirurgiens*) permanently lodged within the hospital. By the late seventeenth century this system had slowly evolved into the kind of contractual arrangement for life under which the hospital's doctors served. Regulations in 1693 insisted that the hospital's doctor and surgeon were to visit the institution twice daily at fixed hours. These staffing improvements were accompanied by closer attention to the needs of inmates. In particular the enlargement of the hospital allowed some rudimentary forms of segregation to be introduced. From 1663 special provision was made to keep convalescents separate from the main wards. Similar concern was shown to segregate children and incurables (though both groups would be transferred *en bloc* to the Hôpital Général in the 1690s) and also the insane. Greater care was taken too to exclude individuals suffering from contagious diseases which put both inmates and staff at risk: in 1673 scrofular cases were specifically debarred and in the 1680s this measure was extended to individuals suffering from scurvy (erroneously accounted a contagious disease).[26]

These improvements were testimony to the capacity for reform of the hospital's administrators. The Intendants were of crucial importance here, lending the weight of their practical experience in business and in administration and often placing their wealth too at the disposal of the hospital. In addition the Bishop of Montpellier tended to take more interest in the hospital: from 1626 he was permitted to attend all major meetings concerning the hospital's affairs, and from the 1670s he seems to have availed himself of this right more thoroughly. The powerful Intendant of Languedoc concerned himself with the hospital too, notably from the 1680s. The weak link in the administrative chain remained, however, the fourth consul who was in overall financial control of the hospital. A number of scandals compromised holders of this post, most notably in 1687 when fourth consul André Coustol got himself so hopelessly in debt that he fled the city, leaving his poor wife to fight a legal battle with the hospital's administrators over lost income. Finally in 1694, seemingly on the initiative of Lamoignon de Basville, the dynamic Intendant of Languedoc, a royal decree (*arrêt du Conseil*) put the hospital's administration on an entirely new footing.[27] The management of the institution was removed from the custody of the fourth consul, and placed in the hands of an administrative board (*bureau d'administration*) headed *ex officio* by the Bishop of Montpellier and on which the consuls could sit, albeit with only one vote between them. The rest of the board was composed of four *syndics* and four intendants, who were to be drawn from the notable corporative bodies of the city and who were to serve for fixed intervals. In addition, the decree stated that the city could tax its inhabitants to the tune of 6,000 *livres* a year, which sum was to be paid into the hospital's coffers – a provision which put the institution on a much stabler financial keel following the mismanagement of successive fourth consuls.

The Daughters of Charity played a key role in the administrative overhaul of the Hôtel-Dieu Saint-Eloi in the second half of the seventeenth century. Their presence seems to have improved the moral tone of the establishment at a stroke: talk of scandal and immorality dried up as soon as they arrived. Their foundation contract referred to the sisters as 'servants of the poor' (*servantes des pauvres*), and it is doubtless true that care of the sick – including washing, cleaning, cooking, and heating – would have been a major preoccupation. Yet the foundation document also made it clear that there was to be an administrative aspect to their work: they were employed 'to serve the sick poor of the said hospital and to take care of the stewardship of the latter'. With the population of the hospital mushrooming in size, and with the hospital's administrators (down to 1694 at least) showing considerable incapacity, the sisters' administrative role seems to have grown disproportionately, even at the expense of their caring duties. In 1685, for example, it was reported that one of the three sisters was in charge of the hospital's children while the two others shared responsibility for the stewardship of the institution, as well as doing the cooking and washing. Of care of the sick there is no mention, and it seems likely that a great deal of strictly nursing activity within the hospital was performed by paid servants and domestics operating under the sisters' orders.[28]

IV

The combination, in the sisters' duties, of administration and care of the sick endured throughout the Ancien Régime, though probably the balance between them was more evenly redressed than at the end of the seventeenth century. As the hospital grew in size and complexity and as its medical functions became more refined, there were trends, in the service of the sisters, in three main directions: towards an increase in their number; towards a widening of their responsibilities; and towards a more precise definition of specific roles.

Table 4.1: Number of Daughters of Charity Attached to the Hôtel-Dieu Saint-Eloi of Montpellier under the Ancien Régime.

Date	*Number of New Sisters*	*Total Community Size*
1668	3	3
1693	3	6
1699	2	8
1717	1	9
1719	1	10
1734	1	11
1737	1	12
1745	1	13
1747	1	14
1757	1	15
1779	1	16

Sources: A.N., S 6171; and registers of deliberations, HD 1 E 1-13. Note that from 1763 the hospital did have a sixteenth sister, though she was classed as a *soeur surnuméraire*. It was only agreed that a sixteenth sister was part of the regular establishment in 1779.

There were attempts to supplement the three original sisters in 1685, when it was hoped to procure an additional three members of the community.[29] This plan came to nothing, however, and it was not to be until 1693 – a quarter of a century after their foundation in Montpellier – that an additional three sisters were added to the hospital staff. By the turn of the century the little community here numbered eight, by 1719, ten, and by 1779, sixteen, a number that was to remain stable until the Revolution (Table 4.1). By that time, they constituted one of the Daughters of Charity's larger establishments in France – for most foundations had only two, three, or four members attached to them.[30]

Normally the hospital's administrative board acceded to increases in numbers in response to representations from the local superior, or *soeur servante*, to the effect that increased pressure of work required extra hands. The increases in numbers in the 1690s, for example, were directly linked to the vast influx of paupers, Protestants, and soldiers from the late 1680s. Sometimes the hospital's administrators granted an increase in numbers only on the assumption that staff savings could be made among the paid domestics.[31] On a number of occasions, moreover, an increase in the number of sisters resulted from charitable donations to the hospital made conditional on the employment of additional sisters. In 1699, for example, Jeanne de Gévaudan, Comtesse de Ganges, donated an annual annuity of 150 *livres* to the Hôtel-Dieu, providing that it took on an additional sister to help in the hospital pharmacy, with which the sisters had been entrusted in 1694.[32]

The latter case exemplifies another trend in the sisters' running of the hospital, namely the tendency to widen their range of responsibilities. There had proved to be problems in the practice of the city's apothecaries supplying the hospital in drugs and medicines. In 1693 on the advice of the hospital physician, Vieussens, a pharmacy was created actually within hospital walls, to supply the needs of both the hospital and the Miséricorde. In 1694 this new establishment received a boost when the royal decree which reformed the hospital's administration placed care of it in the hands of the Daughters of Charity. Almost ever since their foundation, the community had possessed a reputation for pharmaceutical skill, and it did not prove difficult to find a sister capable of running the pharmacy. From 1699 as a result of the benefaction of the Comtesse de Ganges, two sisters were permanently attached to it. Another example of the breadth of the sisters' concerns was the establishment in 1718 of an additional sister (the ninth) to care for the insane, special cells for whom had recently been constructed within the hospital. The new contract stipulated that the sister in question was to divide her time between attending to the insane, assisted in dangerous cases by a male domestic, and also looking after the hospital's wine-cellar![33]

Supervision of the hospital pharmacy, care of the insane – these developments highlight the important fact that in the pre-clinical hospital, the Daughters of Charity could be regarded as independent medical practitioners in their own right. They were it is true subservient to the salaried medical personnel of the hospitals, to whom both Rule and contract enjoined them to show a proper respect.[34] Ward-sisters, for example, accompanied the hospital doctor and the surgeon on their twice-daily rounds, and were jointly responsible for the execution of medical prescriptions along with the apprentice-surgeons attached to the institution. In practice, these arrangements left the sisters a considerable amount of leeway. The doctor's visits seemingly lasted about an hour or an hour and a half – yet with at very least 200 inmates to see in that time (an average of about half a minute to each inmate) the medical staff inevitably left a great deal to the discretion of the sisters. The sisters also, of course, ruled the pharmacy, and brooked no interference from doctor, surgeon, or apothecary in this domain. They seem to have kept a close eye too on the behaviour of apprentice surgeons, especially in all that regarded the women's wards, where the behaviour of male staff was closely vetted. Furthermore, while the administration of drugs and medicines was seen as the concern of doctors, the provision of food and drink was very largely seen as the domain of the sisters. One seems, in sum, to detect a kind of medical division of labour between the medical men and the sisters which was more complex and less one-sided than the type of relationship between 'doctors' and 'nurses' in hospitals after the 'birth of the clinic'. Although as we shall see by the end of the eighteenth century several altercations between the medical staff and the sisters reflected a growing interest by medical men in the workings of the hospital, in general the even very distinguished doctors and surgeons who served the hospital over the period under review found very little cause for dissatisfaction with the services rendered by the Daughters of Charity.

Besides the Daughters of Charity's flexible and pragmatic approach towards assuming new responsibilities, including those of a medical kind, there was also a growing differentiation in the various tasks assigned individual sisters within the hospital. In 1694 *soeur servante* Marie Espingoula explained to the administrative board how she would be disposing the five sisters now under her authority: one would be attached to the main men's ward, where her job would be to

> serve and to supervise the service by the hospital's servants of the sick poor, to give them bouillons, to distribute bread and wine following the prescriptions of the physician, [and] to provide them with linen and other objects necessary to them.

A second sister would perform the same tasks within the women's ward, and a third the same for the room in which were kept convalescents and those suffering from wounds, though she would also have responsibility for the wine-cellar. A fourth sister was designated to look after the children still within the hospital and would be in charge of the hospital's laundry. The fifth would supervise the kitchen and the wood-store. The sixth sister, the *soeur servante* herself, was responsible for the spiritual cohesion of the little community and, under the direct orders of the administrative board, for overall management.[35] One of the most important features of the latter task was the keeping of registers and account-books. There were registers for weekly expenditure on current necessities, supplies of heating and lighting materials, and for the admission of inmates. By the eighteenth century the *soeur servante* was responsible as well for registers which recorded the property of inmates, which listed sales of bran extracted from hospital flour, and which recorded sales of the effects of deceased paupers.[36] From 1734, moreover, when the administrative board acknowledged that the supply of grain and making of bread was an area of concern which required close and careful attention, there were special registers in this field kept by a sister specially brought in for this purpose.[37] By the end of the Ancien Régime, the division of labour among the sisters was even more advanced: besides the *soeur servante*, there were two sisters attached full-time to the pharmacy, three to the kitchens, one to the hospital bakery, two to the laundry, one to the care of the insane, while the six others headed each of the six main sick-rooms which composed the hospital.[38]

V

The first contract between the hospital and the Daughters of Charity in 1668 fixed the latter's wages at 40 *livres* a year. As their food and lodgings were provided gratis by the hospital, the bulk of this sum seems to have been destined for the upkeep of their clothes: the 1668 contract in fact stipulated that the sisters were scrupulously to keep to the community's manner of dress, 'without their being able to change either the colour or the form of the material'. This wage level of 40 *livres* – considerably less it should be noted than that of their immediate predecessors – was maintained well into the eighteenth century for three of the sisters. However, the additional sisters who joined the establishment in the 1690s were paid 60 *livres*. This two-tiered wage-structure became even more complicated in 1721 when the administrative board decided that, because the *rente* which secured the wages of two of the sisters had been reduced in the financial farrago of the John Law 'System', those sisters should henceforward be paid only 36 *livres* a year.[39] From 1742 the administrative board was making annual *ex gratia* payments to the sisters rather than agree to the principle of a wage-rise. It was not until 1745, during negotiations between the hospital and the mother-house over the foundation of a thirteenth sister within the hospital, that the administrative board at last agreed to raise the wages of *all* sisters to 60 *livres*. The middle and later decades of the eighteenth century were a period of marked inflation, and it was not long before the little community's *soeur servante* was petitioning the administrators for a further raise. In 1777 the board did agree to raise the wages to 72 *livres*. They were dismayed to find the sisters coming back for more in the 1780s. They pointed out that the Daughters of Charity attached to hospitals in nearby cities received far less than the 100 *livres* which the sisters of Montpellier were now requesting: at Toulouse and Narbonne, for example, they received 60 *livres* each, and at Béziers 80 *livres.* The mother-house, however, countered by arguing that these wage-levels had been fixed in the distant past and were no longer realistic, and that in the 1780s the community's policy was only to accept new foundations in which each sister could be assured a wage-level of 100 (and even 120) *livres.* The new *soeur servante* who had arrived in Montpellier in 1784 also pointed out that on her arrival she had found her predecessor 600 *livres* in debt, as a result of the insufficiency of the sisters' wages in a city where price levels were high. In the end a compromise was struck, and in 1786 the wage of the Montpellier sisters was raised to 84 *livres.*

In the absence of exact details on what contribution the Montpellier sisters were expected to make to their own régime (food, lighting, heating, and so on) it is impossible to say whether these figures were generous or ungenerous. Because of the way in which wage levels were originally fixed, it seems likely that wages always tended to lag behind prices in a period of inflation. The Daughter of Charity was undoubtedly an increasingly precious commodity. But even in purely economic terms she still represented good value. Her wages were well ahead of the hospital's other servants and domestics for most of the century. Yet by the end of the Ancien Régime, the female servants' wages had caught up, and those of the male domestics had surpassed her annual income (Figure 4.1).[40] Moreover, in so far as it is possible to judge, it would appear that the cost of living rose faster than the wages of the sisters over the eighteenth century. The fact that by the 1780s the community's mother-house was claiming that each sister required a guaranteed sum of at least 100 *livres* if the community was not to be out of pocket does not, when set against this background, seem so very unreasonable.[41]

Of the other material prerequisites of service in the Montpellier Hôtel-Dieu, we know little. The sisters' regime seems for the most part to have been the same as that of other inmates who were fit and well. Documents in 1736 state, for example, that while the sick were to receive each day three-quarters of a *livre* of meat (half in beef, half in mutton) with their bouillon, the sisters, together with the hospital's domestics, chaplains, apprentice-surgeons, and any able-bodied inmates were to receive one *livre,* together with 'le petit

Figure 4.1: Salaries of Daughters of Charity and other Domestics in the Hôtel-Dieu Saint-Eloi of Montpellier.

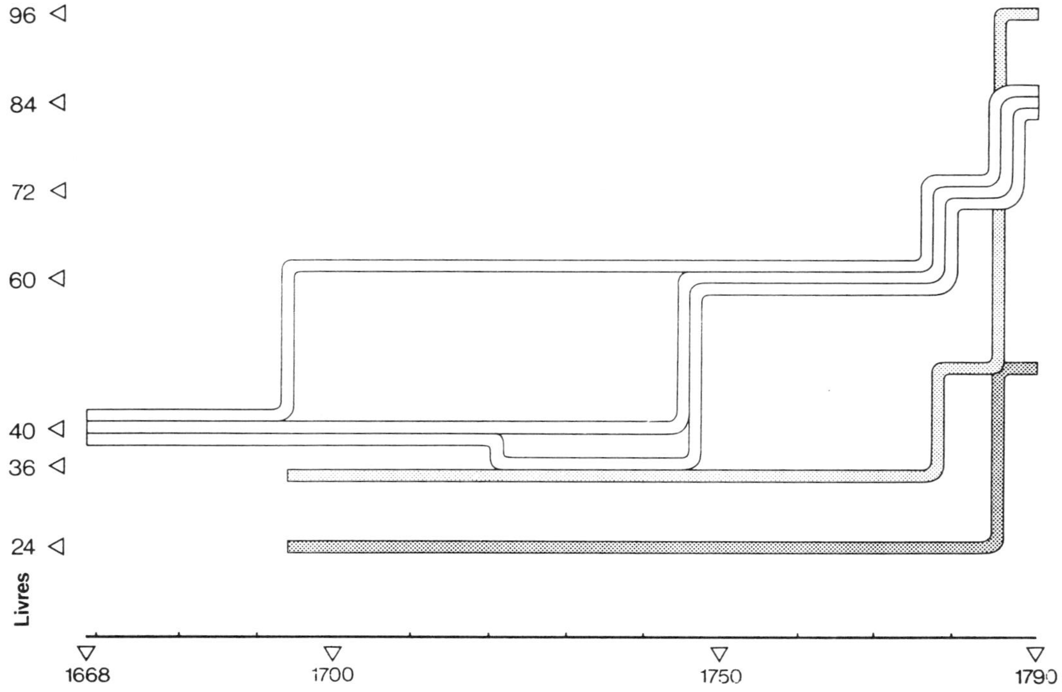

salé' and 'other provisions' – whatever they may have been.[42] Among other material 'fringe benefits', one might note the provision of free medical and nursing care for any sister who fell ill within the hospital. From 1693 it was also agreed – in a clause which was becoming standard in all the contracts of the Daughters of Charity – that if a sister were to become permanently invalided in the service of the hospital, she would be cared for until death if necessary at the hospital's expense. This did in fact happen in the 1760s when sister Marianne became an invalid and the hospital had grudgingly to agree to accepting at their own expense a *soeur surnuméraire* (supernumerary).[43] After 1693 it was accepted too that if a sister had performed six years service within the hospital, the hospital authorities would pay her travelling costs either to her next appointment or back to Paris. This is a provision which seems to have been utilized fairly frequently, and which could allow elderly sisters to return to Paris to end their days in retirement. In 1784, for example, sister Blondel, after a quarter of a century as the hospital's *soeur servante*, was pensioned off at her own request to the Paris mother-house. Finally, if a sister died within the hospital, then the administrators would lay on the kind of funeral adjudged appropriate for a Daughter of Charity.

The latter kind of provision is an apt reminder that the benefits and rewards of hospital service for the Daughter of Charity were more than just material. Foremost among the spiritual aspects of the sisters' life was their obligation to live according to the Rule of the community. Every contract the community passed made it clear that this was an essential prerequisite of their service. The material surroundings of the hospital were not always ideal for the demands of the spiritual life: only in the 1770s, for example, did building plans allow the creation of a separate meeting-place and chapel for the sisters, a facility which the administrators confessed was long overdue.[44] Although in matters temporal the sisters were duty-bound to respect and obey the hospital administrators, in spiritual matters they were subject to their superiors: the Superior of the Daughters of Charity, and ultimately to the Superior of the Congregation of the Mission. The 1668 contract stated that the latter, or a person deputed by him, was to be allowed to visit the sisters to ensure that they were properly observing their rule. The Superior of the

Congregation of the Mission was also entitled to appoint the sisters' confessor. Normally, this was not the hospital chaplain. Indeed, in 1735, there was even an incident when the hospital's administrators attempted to stop the curé of the parish officiating at the funeral of a deceased sister.[45] The hospital administrators, long habituated to the docility of the sisters, recorded in astonishment the 'commotion, sedition and revolt' this occasioned among the sisters, one or two of whom, it was alleged, even behaved like 'furies'. With this single exception, relations with the religious establishment in the city and diocese seem to have been tranquil and harmonious. Immediately on their arrival in 1668, the Bishop of Montpellier, François Bosquet, had drawn up a notarized act, to which the hospital administrators assented, stating that the sisters were not to be considered to be establishing a regular community, that they were not to recruit without his permission, that their confessor should be a priest who was approved within the diocese, and that the sisters should accept the general supervision of the bishop. This document – which bespeaks a certain lack of acquaintance with the way in which the Daughters of Charity worked, since most of the points were quite uncontentious – does not seem to have served any further purpose.[46] Relations between the sisters and successive bishops of Montpellier seem to have been cordial and indeed, on a number of occasions, as we shall see, the bishop took the part of the sisters in disputes they had with the hospital's administrators.

VI

However substantial the rewards of service for the Daughters of Charity in the Montpellier Hôtel-Dieu, there was no escaping the fact that life in a hospital before the coming of antisepsis was grim, exacting, and dangerous, as well as emotionally afflicting.[47] It may have been partly to set some kind of limits to the sisters' exposure to distress that – here as elsewhere – they were specifically prohibited from the treatment of *femmes de mauvaise vie,* and of individuals suffering from venereal disease. In 1730 the sisters' steadfastness on this point was instrumental in causing the failure of the central government's attempts to set up within the hospital facilities for the treatment of soldiers affected by syphilis.[48] The 1668 contract also – and again, this was typical of other contracts – debarred the sisters from treating women in childbirth: perhaps it was felt that the kind of women who preferred hospitalization to home delivery would inevitably include women of ill-repute, possibly venereally infected. The Hôtel-Dieu's regulations also excluded – especially from the 1690s – individuals suffering from skin afflictions and from contagious diseases. Such individuals undoubtedly did, however, find their way into the hospital: the very concept of contagion was imperfectly understood of course; the diagnostic skills of the sisters and apprentice surgeons who presided over the admissions of paupers were doubtless not always sufficient to weed out all contagious cases; and there is even a strong possibility that the surgeons connived in the admittance of such cases so that they could improve their knowledge of such illnesses.[49] Risks of cross-infection, then, between inmates and staff must have been high.

Material conditions within the hospital were poor and added to the aura of disease which hung over the institution. The maxim of the famous surgeon and hospital reformer, Jacques Tenon, at the end of the eighteenth century, to the effect that the principles of health and hygiene had never presided over the building and disposition of French hospitals[50] found a particularly apt illustration in the case of the Hôtel-Dieu of Montpellier. As in the seventeenth century the hospital grew in size merely by adding surrounding buildings as they became available. Attempts in the late eighteenth century to give the hospital a classical façade and to rearrange space internally on more geometrical lines could not disguise the fact that the hospital throughout the Ancien Régime was essentially a ramshackle collection of hastily adapted private dwellings. As late as 1737, the hospital's administrative board described it as 'a muddled pile of ruined buildings and a filthy uninhabitable cesspool'.[51] Considerable efforts were made thereafter, it is true, to improve the material shell of the hospital. The hospital endured severe financial problems in the last century of the Ancien Régime, however, and although it just staved off the bankruptcy which disrupted the city's Hôpital Général in the 1760s, its financial predicament left only limited leeway for fundamental reform. As early as 1715, for example, the administrative board had decreed that inmates should sleep one to a bed. Yet growing pressure of admissions in the eighteenth century, combined with the financial limitations of the hospital, made this policy chimerical. Putting two (sometimes three) to a bed was standard practice in all but the slackest times. The administrators were aware of the physical and psychological dangers of such a practice: but in the circumstances, only refusing entry to the needy – a practice they would not countenance – would have precluded its necessity. In 1759 pressure on places was so intense that, with the beds overflowing, a third rank of mattresses was improvised in the main corridors of the wards. The sanitary consequences of such practices was grim. From the 1770s the administrative board had to strive ceaselessly to counter rumours that the hospital was intrinsically unhealthy, and a generator of disease. Try as they might, however, they could not rid the hospital of the unpleasant stench that ran throughout the institution, which made soldiers from the city garrison shudder at the thought of being taken there. 'Wounds no longer cure there', it was disarmingly admitted in 1786. 'The slightest scratch often degenerates into a gangrenous ulcer', reported the celebrated physician and *Encyclopédiste* Henri Fouquet in the same year, and he went on to evoke the 'thick and gothic masonry' of an institution 'as poorly situated as it is poorly constructed'.[52]

Although it is true that the hospital death-rate fell over the course of the eighteenth century from over 20 to 10 per cent,[53] conditions were unhygienic and perilous to life and limb throughout the period under review, and this inevitably took its toll of hospital staff and nursing sisters. In 1693 the hospital administrators had noted how the staff 'have pallid faces and often fall ill', and made of this a reason for the elementary segregation of some categories of the sick.[54] It is possible that some process of immunization came to protect some sisters against the diseases prevalent within the hospital. And there are cases of sisters who lived to a ripe old age: one sister in the early eighteenth century died aged 95, while in 1788[55] sister Reyne, the hospital pharmacist, died after thirty-four continuous years of service in the institution.[56] One probably needed an iron constitution and a strong stomach to last this long. There are cases of sisters who were permanently invalided in the service of the sick, while the hospital's death registers reveal that the bulk of the sisters who actually died within the institution did so long before their appointed span – in middle age, or even in youth.

Table 4.2: Personal Details about Daughters of Charity Attached to the Hôtel-Dieu Saint-Eloi of Montpellier in the Seventeenth and Eighteenth Centuries, Drawn from the Hospital's Deaths Registers

Date	*Name*	*Place of origin*	*Age*	*'dans l'hôpital'*	*Other*
9/6/1693	Jeanne Barale	Clermont (dioc. Lodève)	95		
5/11/1706	Marie Blancanne	Montmirail (d. Meaux)	38		
29/12/1730	Marie Françoise Beurier	Paris	50	'12 ans'	
14/2/1733	Anne Amelin	Marsan (d. Saint-Malo)	74	'12 ans'	*Soeur servante*
10/5/1735	Louise Marcelot	Migicour (d. Laon)	?	'six mois'	
27/12/1754	Geneviève Legrand	Blangy (d. ?)	22		'longue maladie'
21/8/1759	Marie Coufard	La Réolle (d. Bazas)	33		
9/3/1764	Françoise Clément	Provenchère (d. Saint-Dié)	60		sacristaine'
1/7/1765	Françoise Marie Bernard	Gitay en Bretagne (?)	30		'maladie de quinze mois'
14/4/1770	Catherine Morel	Pont-à-Mousson (d. Toul)	27		
14/3/1778	Magdelaine Leblanc	Gien (d. Orléans)	41		
11/8/1778	Marie-Anne Lecler	Choisy-le-Roi (d. Paris)	72		
7/5/1779	Luce Legris	Bar-le-Duc (d. Toul)	78		
19/8/1781	Louise Roger	Aumetre (?) (d. Amiens)	67		'arrivée le 2 septembre 1742'
30/8/1788	Marie Agnès Cornet	–	55		
20/4/1792	Etienette Marguerite Philibert	–	52		'économie'

Source: A.M.M., CG 44–56.

Another element in the hardness of life in hospitals for the Daughters of Charity was moral rather than physical, namely the feeling of being in a strange and alien environment. Travel was still slow and fraught with difficulties in this period: merchants setting out from Montpellier to Paris, for example, would have their wills drawn up before doing so![57] It was a period too in which doctors regarded homesickness as a classifiable medical complaint, especially frequently found among individuals like soldiers and sailors who worked far away from their homes.[58] The vast majority of sisters who worked in the Montpellier Hôtel-Dieu in this period were themselves very much in this position: of the dozen or so about whom this information is available, only one originated less than 350 kilometres away from Montpellier (Table 4.2).[59] The hospital's sisters were predominantly from the north and north-east, with small contingents from the east and west, but with the centre and south almost totally unrepresented. Initially at least, then, they would not even be able to speak or understand the occitanian language which was the first, and sometimes the only tongue of most inmates. Vincent de Paul had frequently stressed the need for sisters, as a test of their vocation, to be completely cut off from their previous life and normal environment, and he, Louise de Marillac, and their successors were well aware of the nerve-wracking misery which could engulf a sister feeling lonely and far from home, though they insisted that the feeling should if possible be transcended. 'Nobody is happy in foreign lands,' Vincent de Paul told an unhappy sister in the 1650s, 'and yet people go there and stay there'.[60] Though the Superiors did show sympathy for sisters who failed to take root in a given community, and allowed transfers to other institutions, they were also conscious that a strong element of 'estrangement' (*dépaysement*) was intrinsic to the very vocation of being a Daughter of Charity.[61]

VII

Crucial in maintaining the morale of the little community of sisters attached to the Montpellier Hôtel-Dieu was the sister appointed by her superiors in Paris as the local superior or *soeur servante*. Foremost among her assigned tasks was the maintenance of communal cohesion, grounded in adherence to the rule of the Daughters of Charity. The task called for special leadership qualities. All the more was this the case, moreover, in that – with the exception of sisters who were *soeurs servantes* and possibly those with skilled occupations such as the pharmacists – most sisters did not stay long in the hospital. Evidence from the late seventeenth and the first two decades of the eighteenth century suggests that most remained for less than five years.[62] Sisters who failed to settle down here and requested a transfer accounted for some of this high turnover; so too did institutional mortality; and so did the practice of detaching sisters from the institution to set up new foundations elsewhere. In addition, there was also the fact that the community's superiors in Paris were always keen to promote sisters who showed talent and aptitude. Promotion nearly always meant transfer elsewhere – much to the chagrin of the hospital's administrators. An illustration of the kind of career pattern which might occur is sister Antoinette Deleau, who served in Montpellier before being dispatched as *soeur servante* to the military hospital at Saint-Hippolyte (in the present-day department of the Gard); after a couple of decades here, she was promoted into the national hierarchy, and was to be Superior General of the community during the turbulent revolutionary decade.[63] One can understand administrators being upset at losing individuals of such capacity. In the 1730s the administrative board even formally protested to Paris over the proposed displacement of two of their more experienced sisters to Narbonne. It was only with the persuasion of the Bishop of Montpellier that the administrators reluctantly accepted the point that, for the community as a whole to exist and to continue to service its myriad institutions, this kind of mobility was indispensable.[64]

Yet if the tasks of ensuring communal cohesion and maintaining morale were made difficult by the high turnover of sisters within the hospital, they were eased by the fact that most *soeurs servantes* served rather lengthy periods (Table 4.3). The first about whom full details are known was Marie Espingoula, who served from 1685 to 1703 – a period during which the size of the community expanded from three to eight. Her immediate successor, Germaine Rousseau, stayed ten years. A later successor, Marie Blondel, lasted a quarter of a century, from 1759 to 1784. This tendency of long service partially offset the problem of high staff turnover, and helped ensure a sense of stability and continuity in the internal management of the hospital which was doubtless much appreciated by the administrative board.

Table 4.3: *Soeurs Servantes* of the Community of Daughters of Charity Attached to the Hôtel-Dieu Saint-Eloi of Montpellier in the Seventeenth and Eighteenth Centuries

Dates	*Name*	*Length of service (in years)*
1668–?*	Anne Menage	?
1685–1703	Marie Espingoula	18
1703–13	Germaine Rousseau	10
1713–18	Martine De La Marre	5
1718–21	Anne Godefroy	3
1721–33	Anne Amelin	12
1733–6	Antoinette d'Anteny	3
1736–43	Marguerite Boussard	7
1743–?	*soeur* Roglin	?
?–1759	*soeur* Mauguin	?
1759–84	*soeur* Blondel	25
1785–7	*soeur* Favier	2
1788–92	Etienette Marguerite Philibert	4
1792–?	*soeur* Dergueulh	?

Sources: Registers of deliberations, HD I E 1–13; and annual account-books (also series E).
Note: *Anne Menage was still *soeur servante* in 1674.

Given that the maintenance of hospital discipline and morale was essentially in their hands, these long-serving *soeurs servantes* had often to be long-suffering. They supervised the behaviour of inmates, domestics, and sisters alike, and in all spheres their margin of authority was great. Few issues of internal discipline were thought important enough to involve the administrative board of the hospital. If clashes of personality developed, if disputes and disagreements occurred, if old sisters, weighed down by their responsibilities, became negligent, embittered, or burnt out, if new sisters fell prey to moping, homesickness, and depression, then there were channels of advice which the *soeur servante* could utilize; but none substantially detracted from her autonomy of action. She might consult with the mother-house in Paris, for example: but Paris was far, and communication slow. In the early years of the eighteenth century, partly to offset problems caused by the distance factor, a nation-wide system of provincial inspections was organized: but the influence of regional inspectors was inevitably sporadic rather than continuous. The sisters' confessor could monitor internal problems, it is true, and the Superior of the house of the Congregation of the Mission at nearby Agde might be referred to at times for specific problems: yet it seems unlikely that they were much referred to. To a large extent and for most of the time, the *soeur servante* was on her own. Besides her qualities of character, this situation placed a heavy onus on the community's Rule, which partly by strongly emphasizing on the principle of obedience within communal life, must have been a major standby of the *soeur servante* in maintaining the morale of her community. The Rule implicitly recognized its status as source of inspiration and regularity: in the section entitled 'Advice for the *soeur servante* of a hôtel-dieu or hospital', it stipulated that 'the *soeur servante* will always have the Rule before her eyes, to serve as example to her sisters'.[65]

VIII

Of prime importance in maintaining morale and in ensuring the effectiveness of her community within the hospital, the *soeur servante* was also crucial in determining the quality and the intensity of the sisters' relationship with the administrators of the hospital. This aspect of her work too was tough and unrelenting: the post of *soeur servante* in the Montpellier Hôtel-Dieu, noted Bourgeat, spiritual director of the Daughters of Charity in the 1780s, was one in which 'they have to be nearly always on their feet and find difficulty in performing all their various functions'.[66]

Just as the Rule of the Daughters of Charity was the touchstone in everything relating to the internal community life of the sisters, the contract of service was the document which regulated most matters regarding the relationship between sisters and administrators. It is abundantly clear, from the hospital board's deliberations, that the contract was constantly referred to on matters of detail. The 1693 contract, for example, had stipulated that if a sister who was being transferred elsewhere had served in the hospital for more than six years, then her travelling costs, and those of her replacement, should be borne by the hospital. This clause also obtained if a sister died in the service of the hospital. For one reason or the other, it was invoked for the replacement of sisters at very least in 1703, in 1718, in 1731, in 1733, in 1734, in 1736, in 1740, in 1741, in 1743, in 1753 and in 1784.[67] The administrative board of the Montpellier Hôtel-Dieu, moreover, seems to have won something of a reputation as sticklers for their legal rights. In 1721 they cut the wages of two sisters, payment of whom had been covered by a *rente* whose value had been reduced by government decree, and, in similar circumstances later in the century, the Superior General of the Daughters of Charity expressed surprise and dismay at how pernickety the administrators were in ensuring their rights.[68] In 1738 the administrative board complained that the *soeur servante* was acting unreasonably, and beyond the letter of her contract, in serving as inspector to other communities of the Daughters of Charity in the region, and thereby depriving the hospital of time and energy which should have been expended there. The administrators made a similar complaint about sister Blondel in 1765, and seem to have been successful in restricting her extra-mural activities. Similarly in 1736, they kicked up a fuss on discovering that potential novices to the Daughters of Charity were being admitted for a trial period in their hospital: arguing that the contract did not allow for this kind of arrangement, they scotched this development and insisted that the community pay standard hospitality rates for the young women involved.[69]

Matters were occasionally complicated by the fact that the content of the different contracts which regulated the service of the sisters varied in certain particulars. The 1668 contract, for example, dated from a period before the Daughters of Charity had fully devised the standard contract which was used as the basis of their service in all foundations from the 1670s and 1680s. The Montpellier sisters and the community's superiors in Paris thus tended to regard the 1693 contract as constituting the fullest expression of their duties and rights. A number of clashes arose from this ambiguity, particularly in regard to the right which the 1668 contract seemed to establish that the hospital administrators had the right to dismiss a sister if she proved unsatisfactory, and that all travelling costs incurred by her and by her replacement should be borne not by the hospital but by the community.

The question of right of dismissal was one issue at stake in an acrimonious dispute which developed in 1718 between the hospital's administrators (notably the *syndic* Combelle) and the *soeur servante* Anne Godefroy.[70] The board had accepted the latter only with bad grace as *soeur servante*: she had worked for a number of years as *soeur servante* of the Montpellier Miséricorde, where she had acquired a reputation for bad health. Hearing that she was to be destined for the Hôtel-Dieu, the board did all it could to prevent this transfer. After grudgingly agreeing to give her a few months trial, they made up their mind in December 1718 to dismiss her under the provisions of the 1668 contract, provisionally appointed a ecclesiastic as *économe*, and wrote to Paris for a replacement. Within three months, their action had been totally overturned. On 11 March 1719 the Bishop of Montpellier read the board a letter from Jean Bonnet, Superior of the Congregation of the Mission, in which he informed them that it was the expressed wish of the Regent, the Duke of Orléans (who had heard of the affair through the bishop) that Anne Godefroy be reinstated in full. It was a request to which the administrators could only agree. Yet the decision rankled, particularly, it would seem, with Combelle. In 1720 a new dispute broke out when the latter accused Anne Godefroy of illicitly selling meat during Lent within the hospital. Despite being hauled over the coals over this issue by the Intendant of Languedoc, Combelle persisted in the dispute, instituted a full-scale search of hospital premises, and even brought a case against sister Godefroy in the local Présidial court. The other members of the administrative board seem to have become embarrassed by the zeal of their colleague, and when he died in 1723 they ordered that proceedings against the Daughters of Charity be dropped.[71] Soon afterwards, the Intendant of Languedoc received a royal *lettre de cachet* which, on the request of the superiors of the Daughters of Charity, ordered that all documents relating to the case in the archives of the Présidial be destroyed. The community wished to keep the reputation of the community unblemished - and they had friends in high places to help them do so.

Another chastening example of misjudgement on the part of the administrators lay behind a further important dispute between the administrative board and the sisters.[72] In 1733 *soeur sevante* Anne Amelin died, after an illness which had incapacitated her for a number of years. Rather than have an unknown sister from outside replace her, the hospital's administrators requested permission from the community's mother-house that they be allowed to promote to the post one of the young sisters already in the hospital. The sister in question was Antoinette d'Anteny, who had often deputized for sister Amelin during her illness. Perhaps it was foolish for the hospital's administrators to assume that they were better judges of character and capacity than the community's superiors. At all events, by 1736 one of the syndics, Bosc, was writing to Paris bewailing the 'poor behaviour and lack of discernment' displayed by their protégée, whom Bosc now characterized as 'a small-minded individual whom everything annoys and embarrasses and who ceaselessly gives us troubles and harassment which are most undesirable in a charitable institution'. In both of the essential functions of the *soeur servante* she had revealed her total incapacity. First, morale among the sisters had been lowered: 'far from establishing union and peace', it was reported, 'she causes disturbances and consternation'; the other sisters seemed actively to dislike her, and were beginning to write to Paris to request transfers elsewhere. Second, she had failed to establish a satisfactory *modus vivendi* with the administrators. As Bosc put it, she was

> a reed much agitated by the slightest wind. Everything we decide on has the misfortune to displease her. It all ends in fits of unhappiness, machinations and ideas so far from the mark that we can no longer bear them.

While not unaware of the irony of the situation, the community's superiors agreed to provide a replacement for d'Anteny who would be moved to a parish *charité* in Toulouse where, according to the Superior General, 'the occupations will be more confined and more in proportion to the spirit that God has given her'.

Even more contentious than this affair was a dispute that developed in 1785 over the implementation of certain reforms within the hospital.[73] The Royal Inspector of Hospitals and Prisons, Jean Colombier, had visited the city's hospitals in December 1785, and there followed a demand from the king's minister Chaumont de la Millière that a number of reforms be introduced into the Hôtel-Dieu. The administrative board of the hospital, which cherished its independence of action, and resented the innovative practice of government inspections, replied at first rather negatively to this demand. Under pressure from Paris, however, they had to give ground and endeavour to introduce certain of the reforms. Two particular innovations, however, raised the ire of the *soeur servante*: namely that the contents of the hospital pharmacy should be annually inventoried by an independent source; and that in executing the prescriptions of the doctors towards hospital inmates, the sisters should work in very close conjunction with the apprentice-surgeons.

In both of these cases, the hostility of the Montpellier sisters was not singular. The growing interest of doctors and surgeons in the internal workings of hospitals in this period in which the stirrings of clinical medicine were becoming increasingly apparent, inevitably caused demarcation disputes with hospital sisters. There were numerous cases of quarrels between the latter and medical men in the last decades of the Ancien Régime in hospitals scattered throughout France.[74] There seems to have been an increase in tension over this period too in the relations between the sisters and medical personnel in the Montpellier Hôtel-Dieu. In 1756 a medical report stated that the sick within the hospital were being fed too copiously by the Daughters of Charity and that this was impeding their recovery, particularly in the case of inmates suffering from inflamed wounds. The charge was repeated on a number of occasions thereafter. Quarrels over other issues too – dissections, for example, or the presence within the hospital of medical students – further exemplified the development of bad feeling between the two sides.[75]

There is much evidence to suggest that the Hôtel-Dieu's administrators in 1785 would have been perfectly happy to maintain the status quo rather than to implement the government-inspired reforms. Pressure from the central government forced their hand, however, with a major dispute with the sisters emerging as a consequence. The sisters even threatened to withdraw from the hospital *en bloc* if the reforms were implemented. They called for moral support upon their superiors in Paris, who argued that the reforms in question would have compromised the very status of the Daughters of Charity. There may well have been some crossed wires and mutual misunderstanding on the question, however, for the minister noted that the sisters were only being asked to do what members of their community already did in a great many other hospitals. Their intransigence in regard to the Montpellier Hôtel-Dieu, however, only made it seem to the administrators that they wished to become 'absolute masters of the administration'. Increasingly irate, the board now requested that the mother-house withdraw the offending *soeur servante* from the hospital at its own expense under the provisions of the 1668 contract. The Superior General claimed that no copy of the 1668 contract existed in her archives, and that in any case the community was not legally bound by contracts entered into before the community had evolved a standard, model contract. Eventually the conciliatory intervention of Antoine Jacquier from the mother-house of the Congregation of the Mission in Paris smoothed things over. Not before, however, pressure had built up so much on the *soeur servante* at the centre of the case that she resigned and was transferred elsewhere. A new, more conciliatory successor was chosen – and as the Revolution approached, the whole question of the reforms was quietly forgotten.

Disputes, then, did occur between the sisters and the administrators of the hospital, and could become bitter and acrimonious. Yet it would be foolish to pretend that, in general, for most of the time, relations were not good. The division of labour between the two sides enshrined by the contract – the sisters attending to most matters of internal management inside the hospital under the general authority of the administrative board, while the latter were left free to concentrate on more general administrative issues such as the keeping of accounts, the passing of contracts, and so on – worked extremely well. Extensive areas of the running of the hospital could be left almost entirely to the sisters' care: internal discipline, day-to-day purchases, the pharmacy, admissions, and so on. Moreover, the administrators seem to have valued the advice of the *soeur servante* on many more general issues: over the composition of the hospital bouillon, for example, over staffing matters, over the maintenance of decency and order within the wards, and so on. When asked their opinion on the service of the Daughters of Charity, the administrators mingled speechless admiration with a matter-of-fact acceptance of the excellence of their sisters: 'the general reputation' of the sisters, they commented in 1775 'leaves nothing that may be added to the eulogies devoted to them'.[76]

IX

The services of the Daughters of Charity in the Montpellier Hôtel-Dieu were therefore highly valued by the hospital's administrators. There are other indications too of the quality of the service which they provided here. The fall in the death-rate over the course of the eighteenth century from one-fifth to one-tenth, and the growing reputation of the hospital as a medical centre owed much to the quality of the medical care provided in an unpromising material environment. Yet if this is in part a compliment to the physicians and surgeons of the hospital over this period, it is also one to the Daughters of Charity, for they were, as we have seen, medical practitioners in their own right, and a crucial link in the chain of medical provision within the institution. A further indication of their popularity and effectiveness was the establishment of numerous further branches on the community in the Montpellier region over the last century of the Ancien Régime (Map 4.2). Nor was this expansion the result of advertising! The power of example and word-of-mouth seemingly sufficed in spurring charitable administrators to seek to procure Daughters of Charity for their own institutions. A final test of their popularity – not just within the hospital itself, but within the local urban community – was to come during the Revolution. Whereas in many other localities the Daughters of Charity and other nursing communities like them were driven out, in Montpellier the sisters attached both to the Hôtel-Dieu and to the Miséricorde were allowed, even encouraged, to remain. In particular, oaths of allegiance to the Revolution were demanded of them in so anodine a form as in no way to compromise their religious beliefs.[77] Although they were obliged by revolutionary legislation to put aside their ecclesiastical costumes, the sisters remained at their posts throughout the turbulent Revolutionary decade. Some historians of the Daughters of Charity have seen in such behaviour an example of quintessential fidelity to the precepts of Vincent de Paul and Louise de Marillac. In a way this is true. Yet it is also true that their behaviour in the revolutionary decade, just as earlier under the Ancien Régime, also exhibited critical qualities of discretion, pragmatism, and a matter-of-fact capacity to accept and assimilate change.

Notes

1. Voltaire, *Oeuvres complètes* (52 vols, Paris, 1877–85) xii, p. 344.

2. The archives of the Hôtel-Dieu Saint-Eloi are located in the Archives départementales de l'Hérault (henceforth = A.D.H.). Research for the present article is based particularly on the archives prior to 1790 (henceforth = HD I), and most notably on the registers of the administrative board of the hospital: HD I E 1 (1693–1700), E 2 (1700–9), E 3 (1710–16), E 4 (1716–23), E 5 (1724–38), E 6 (1739–47), E 7 (1748–54), E 8 (1754–60), E 9 (1761–5), E 10 (1765–79), E 11 (1770–81), E 12 (1781–6), and E 13 (1786–9).

The archives of the municipality of Montpellier (henceforth = A.M.M.) were especially useful for the seventeenth century: notably the registers of the deliberations of the municipal council (henceforth = BB Reg.); the registers of the so-called 'notaires du Consulat', who handled a great deal of municipal business (henceforth = BB Consulat); unclassified bundles of materials in series GG relating to hospitals, public assistance and so on (henceforth = GG unclassified); and the registers of *état civil* relating to the hospital (GG 44–56).

Other series in the departmental, hospital, and municipal archives of Montpellier were also utilized. In the Archives Nationales (henceforth = A.N.), there is an important dossier on Montpellier in the archives of the Daughters of Charity, S 6171.

3. For conditions in the hospital in the seventeenth century, see L. Dulieu, *Essai historique sur l'hôpital Saint-Eloi de Montpellier, 1183–1950* (Montpellier, 1953) esp. pp. 23 ff. This valuable work also contains much of interest on the workings of the institution throughout the period under review, though only passing references to the Daughters of Charity. For conditions in the hospital in the eighteenth century, cf. C. Jones, *Charity and 'Bienfaisance': The Treatment of the Poor in the Montpellier Region, 1740–1815* (Cambridge, 1982), passim.

4. Dulieu, *Essai*, pp. 275–6 for lists of Intendants.

5. For conditions up to and including 1663, A.M.M., BB Reg., GG unclassified, and BB Consulat, passim.

6. Copy of the contract in HD I B 2, and BB Consulat (1663).

7. HD I B 2.

8. BB Reg., 19 July 1663.

9. Copies of the contract, with some related materials in HD I E 1; HD I B 2; BB Consulat (1668); and A.N., S 6171.

10. P. Coste (ed.) *Saint Vincent de Paul. Correspondance. Entretiens. Documents* (14 vols, Paris, 1920–5), (henceforth = *VdeP*), II, p. 196. Cf. A.N., S 6160.

11. Cf. *VdeP*, XIII, pp. 430–2, 629, 637, etc.

12. Sources of the map: the commemorative volume, *1660–1960. Monsieur Vincent vit encore . . .* (1959); A.N., S 6160–80; *VdeP*.

13. Besides material in *VdeP*, cf. A.N., S 6160–80.

14. *VdeP*, X, pp. 578–9. And cf. (for Arras), ibid., IX, p. 225. For Cahors and Narbonne, A.N., S 6163 and 6172. There was an institution established at Ussel in the present-day department of the Corrèze in 1658 (*VdeP*, VII, p. 232).

15. See pp. 165–8.

16. A.N., S 6171. It appears that the 1693 contract was closely based on that agreed with the hospital of Montauban in 1685 (ibid).

17. For the religious history of Montpellier in the seventeenth century, see the chapters by M. Laget and X. Azéma in G. Cholvy (ed.) *Le Diocèse de Montpellier* (Montpellier, 1976). L. Guiraud, 'La Réforme à Montpellier', *Mémoires de la Société archéologique de Montpellier* (1918), also contains a great deal of interest. For accounts of the establishment of religious houses within the city, see too the chronologies in *Mémoire de ce qui s'est passé de plus remarquable dans cette ville de Montpellier . . . depuis l'année 1621 jusques à présent [1690],* (A.D.H., 10 F 90); and [P. Serres], *Annales et mémoires de la ville de Montpellier* (A.D.H., 10 F 23).

18. The works cited in the preceding note contain much of relevance to this theme. See too P. Béral, *Histoire de l'Hôpital de la Charité de Montpellier, 1646–82* (Montpellier, 1899).

19. Besides material in Béral, see too A.D.H. Archives de l'hôpital général de Montpellier (antérieures à 1790) F 19.

20. The refusal to share service with any other group of persons was inscribed in both the Rule and the standard contract. For the community's caution in regard to hôpitaux généraux, see pp.174–6.

21. For the so-called *grand renfermement,* see esp. E. Chill, 'Religion and mendicity in seventeenth-century France', *International Review of Social History* (1962); J.P. Gutton, *La Société et les pauvres. L'exemple de la généralité de Lyon, 1534–1789* (Paris, 1971) pp. 303–49; and M. Foucault, *Folie et déraison. Histoire de la folie à l'âge classique* (Paris, 1961) pp. 54–96; and above, pp.39–41. For the origins of the movement in Montpellier, see (besides the archives of the Hôpital Général) A.M.M., BB Consulat, BB Reg. and GG unclassified. For the Bon Pasteur, see Chapter 3.

22. For the Miséricorde, see the important holdings in the *Fonds Miséricorde* in the A.D.H.; A.N., S 6171; and see also pp.244ff. See too, for the eighteenth century, Jones, *Charity and 'Bienfaisance',* passim.

23. For reform of the Hôtel-Dieu Saint-Eloi in the second half of the seventeenth century, see the sources cited in note 2.

24. HD I F 13–15. Cf. the 57 beds in the hospital noted by the Bishop of Montpellier in the course of his pastoral visit to the hospital in 1684, A.D.H., Series G. For conditions in the city in the 1680s and 1690s, see pp.242–3.

25. Dulieu, *Essai,* p. 47.

26. Besides the sources cited above, see also HD I E 21.

27. Examples of the *arrêt* in HD I E 1; HD I A 1; and BB Consulat. For details on the financial dealings of successive fourth consuls, cf. BB Reg. and BB Consulat, especially years 1674, 1687, and 1693–4; and GG unclassified.

28. HD I F 34; and GG unclassified.

29. HD I F 34.

30. Of the establishment contracts reviewed on p.172, 79.0 per cent had three sisters or fewer. The census of all the community's

establishments in 1704 revealed that 68.9 per cent had three sisters or fewer, and 85 per cent eight or fewer. A.N., L 1054.

31. As in 1693: HD I E 1.

32. HD I E 1; A.N., S 6171. The Comtesse de Ganges made a similar donation in 1718 (HD I E 4); and in the 1740s Anne Girardot, *veuve* Trinquier, gave the hospital 4,172 *livres*, on condition a further sister was employed (HD I E 9).

33. A.N., S 6171; HD I E 4; and A.N., S 6171.

34. The nature of the relationship between the hospital sisters and medical and surgical staff in the eighteenth century is discussed in Jones, *Charity and 'Bienfaisance'*, pp. 123–30. For the Hôtel-Dieu at nearby Nîmes, see above pp.48–80.

35. HD I E 1.

36. Regulations cited in full in HD I E 3, and reproduced in Dulieu, *Essai*, pp. 333–5. See too the *Recueil de reglemens du Bureau d'administration de l'Hôtel-Dieu Saint Eloy de Montpellier* (Montpellier, 1785) (copy located in HD I E 16); and *Recueil des reglemens de l'Hôtel-Dieu Saint Eloy de Montpellier* (Montpellier, 1754) (in HD I E 19).

37 HD I E 5.

38. HD I E 12.

39. HD I E 4. Decisions on wage levels can be followed in the registers of deliberations for the relevant years.

40. For figures showing the rise of food-prices in the eighteenth century, see F. Braudel and E. Labrousse (eds) *Histoire économique et sociale de la France. II. 1660–1789* (1970) pp. 386–8. The comparison is not terribly fair in that the bulk of the sisters' wages would presumably have been spent on clothes. Unfortunately it is not possible to construct a price series for cloth.

41. Contracts located in A.N., S 6160–80 show wage levels for sisters within hospital foundations in the 1780s as follows: Lodève (1785), 100 *livres*; Avallon (1785), 120 *livres*; Tours (1786), 100 *livres*; Cusset (1787), 120 *livres*; Clermont-Ferrand (1788), 120 *livres*; and Montferrand (1789), 120 *livres*.

42. HD I E 6.

43. HD I E 9.

44. HD I E 11 (1776).

45. HD I F 34 for interesting documents on this dispute.

46. BB Consulat (Contract 13 February 1668).

47. Cf. M. Flinton, *Louise de Marillac. L'aspect social de son oeuvre* (no date or place of publication) pp. 81–2.

48. C 564. All the community's contracts ruled out treatment of *femmes de mauvaise vie.* Cf. p.190.

49. The presence of evidently contagious cases is shown in the clinical record of inmates kept by hospital physician Pierre Fournier, and published by him as 'Observations sur les maladies qui ont regné dans l'Hôtel-Dieu de Montpellier pendant l'année 1763', *Recueil d'observations de médecine des hôpitaux militaires* (i, Paris, 1766).

50. J. Tenon, *Mémoire sur les hôpitaux de Paris* (Paris, 1788) p. 1. Cf. L.S. Greenbaum, '"Measure of civilization": the hospital thought of Jacques Tenon on the eve of the French Revolution', *Bulletin of*

the History of Medicine (1975).

51. HD I E 22. Even the improvements brought complaints, however. Pierre Forestier, former consul of Montpellier and administrator of the hospital, criticized the rebuilding in 1760 on the grounds that it made the building 'more appropriate for a palace than for a hospital' (Archives de l'Hôpital Général de Montpellier [antérieures à 1790] B 47).

52. HD I E 12; A.D.H., C 557 (for Fouquet). For the financial problems of the hospital in the eighteenth century, and their sanitary consequences, cf. Jones, *Charity and 'Bienfaisance'*, passim and esp. pp. 56–61.

53. Between 1695 and 1698 there were 3,213 individuals admitted to the hospital (HD I F 1) and 693 deaths (A.M.M., GG 45) – giving a death-rate of 21.6 per cent. For death-rates later in the century, calculated in a similar way, Jones, *Charity and 'Bienfaisance'*, p. 102 (9.4 per cent in 1741–2, 7.9 in 1763–72, 10.9 in 1785–6, etc).

54. HD I E 1.

55. For sister Reyne, HD I E 13.

56. Table 4.2 shows some information on ages.

57. G. Penot, *Des Clauses restrictives, extensives et religieuses contenues dans les testaments aux XVIIe. et XVIIIe. siècles à Montpellier* (Thesis, Law, Montpellier, 1952) p. 28.

58. M. Reinhard, 'Nostalgie et service militaire pendant la Révolution', *Annales historiques de la Révolution française* (1958).

59. Cf. figures from the hospital in 1816 (Archives de l'Hôtel-Dieu [postérieures à 1790] F 22): of nineteen sisters, two were from the Paris region, two from the north, one from the west, seven from the east, and four (one each from the Gers and the Gironde, two from the Landes) from the south.

60. *VdeP*, VIII, p. 431.

61. *VdeP*, IX, p. 579.

62. Between 1694 and 1720 hospital deliberations record the names of all sisters when referring to payment of wages. As some sisters over this period are called by their surnames, some by their Christian names, and some by both, it is impossible to be exact about figures. Yet it would appear that of the eighty-three sisters who served during this period, seventy-three did so for less than five years. Of the rest, three were *soeurs servantes.* Only one sister who was not a *soeur servante* lasted longer than ten years. For later in the century, cf. the administrators' complaints about the general inexperience of sisters, some of which are recorded below. Evidence from the Hôtel-Dieu of Béziers later in the century is also consonant with this general picture: of thirty-six who served between 1765 and 1789 whose length of service is ascertainable (out of a general total of forty-three sisters), twenty-seven served for less than five years. A.D.H., Archives des hospices de Béziers, II F 1.

63. The *Livre d'or des Filles de la Charité, ou Simple aperçu des plus belles notices des soeurs* (2 vols, Paris, 1938, 1948) contains much information on *soeur* Deleau; ibid. too for *soeur* Durgeilh, who was *soeur servante* in the Montpellier hospitals in the 1790s, and who became *Supérieure*

générale of the community in 1810.

64. HD I E 5. For a similar case in the 1760s, cf. HD I E 10.

65. An example of the rule in A.N., L 1665.

66. HD I E 13.

67. All cases found in the registers of deliberations. Given the apparent frequency of such cases, many others may have slipped detection.

68. HD I E 6. Cf HD I F 34 for similar comments on the behaviour of the board.

69. HD I E 5. Cf. HD I F 34.

70. HD I E 4 for this case.

71. A.D.H., C 508.

72. Dossier on the case in HD I F 34. See too HD I E 5.

73. The long dispute can be followed in HD I E 13, E 19, F 34. Complementary materials are to be found in A.N., F 15 226; and, for the final stages, A.D.H., C 572.

74. Cf. the sampler of cases recorded on pp.85–6, n. 58.

75. Jones, *Charity and 'Bienfaisance'*, pp. 124 ff.

76. HD I E 11. Cf. A.D.H., C 571: 'Nothing affords greater honour to Religion and Humanity than the institute of sisters of charity . . . ' (example from 1780), etc., etc.

77. Jones, *Charity and 'Bienfaisance'*, pp. 196–200; Jones, 'Picking up the pieces: the politics and the personnel of social welfare from the Convention to the Consulate', in G. Lewis and C. Lucas (eds) *Beyond the Terror: Essays in French Regional and Social History, 1794–1815* (Cambridge, 1983) p. 81.

5

The Daughters of Charity in Hospitals from Louis XIII to Louis-Philippe

The Daughters of Charity were originally created by Vincent de Paul as an ancillary organization to support and implement the charitable activities of the numerous confraternities of charity (*confréries*) which had sprung up in the parishes of Paris and throughout the country following their first institution at Châtillon-les-Dombes in 1617.[1] From their very inception, however, the Daughters of Charity manifested the flexibility and the practical orientation which were to distinguish their subsequent development. It was only a matter of years, for example, before they were serving, in different ways, the proud poor (*pauvres honteux*), sick paupers in their homes, prisoners, wounded soldiers, foundlings, schoolchildren, and hospital inmates. In this chapter I will concentrate on only one aspect – albeit an important one – of their multifarious activities: namely the service of the poor in hospitals. Here, faithful to Vincentian precepts and guided from the start by the sagacious counsels of Louise de Marillac, they aimed both to combat ignorance and error, and also, by revitalizing institutions, many of which had fallen into the utmost disorder and distress,[2] to bring spiritual and material consolation to the sick and dying.

Just what did this work of reorganization and remoralization amount to in the centuries following the deaths in 1660 of Vincent de Paul and Louise de Marillac? What contribution did the Daughters of Charity make to the hospitals in which they served? What did their presence entail for the institutions to which they were attached? To what extent did the legacy of the founders prepare them for the times ahead? How well did they adapt to external changes and pressures? In the previous chapters I explored these questions through a case-study approach. Here I want to complement that angle of vision with a more general overview of the way in which the Daughters of Charity worked within hospitals in the first two centuries of their foundation – between the reigns, shall we say, of Louis XIII and Louis-Philippe. My answers will inevitably be only partial and provisional, not least because the research will be based on a single archival collection. When in 1792 the Paris Commune closed down the mother-house of the Daughters of Charity, it confiscated the bulk of the community's archives. These now exist in the Archives Nationales, for the most part under the heading *Corporations supprimées* (series S).[3] This collection of a score or so boxes comprises a source almost entirely neglected by historians. The core of the collection is made up of the establishment contracts, notarial acts for the most part which the officers of the community passed with the different charitable organizations to which the Daughters of Charity were attached. In all, contracts and agreements relating to nearly 400 institutions are to be found here, about 160 of them with hospital administrators,[4] the remainder with individuals and authorities who wished to institute establishments of Daughters of Charity in order to provide home relief to the local needy. Most of the contracts take the form of a lengthy notarial document comprising at least twenty and sometimes up to thirty separate clauses.[5] These were intended to regulate the rights and duties of the Daughters of Charity within the institutions to which they were attached. The researcher may initially find the repetitiveness of these documents, and their bulk, somewhat rebarbative. However, once the standard format of the contract becomes clear, even slight changes and differences are easily detected.[6] Used quantitatively, therefore, the contracts become a serial source which, in its evolution and its variations, allows a certain reflection to be perceived of the nature of the service which the Daughters of Charity provided. It is of course only a partial reflection: lacunae abound. The public nature of the document casts very little light, for example, on the community life of the hospital sisters; its orientation is material and pragmatic rather than spiritual or contemplative; and occasionally it seems to relate to an ideal rather than to the practical realities of hospital life. Nevertheless, despite these biases and partialities, the establishment contracts offer a far more profound insight into the activities of the Daughters of

Charity than has hitherto been provided by historians of the community, or by historians of hospitals.

The Revolution, whose general effects on the community are well known, inevitably changed the format of the contracts in a number of ways. In order to estimate the extent of the change, I have compared these establishment contracts from the seventeenth and eighteenth century with a handful of contracts which I was able to locate from the early decades of the nineteenth century. As we shall see, in practice remarkably little changed after 1789. In the sphere of hospital service – as in many other spheres of social history – the Revolution marked not a clean break with the past but rather a slow continuity and a sluggardly evolution. To a very large extent, therefore, the nature of the hospital service provided by the Daughters of Charity remained the same throughout the two centuries from the early seventeenth to the early nineteenth century.

I

In the early years of the community's history, Daughters of Charity were attached to charitable institutions on a purely informal basis. In the 1630s, for example, many of the parishes of Paris were equipped with Daughters of Charity providing home relief for the poor under the orders of parishional confraternities of Ladies of Charity (*Dames de la Charité*) without the need being felt for any formal contract of service to be drawn up. From the mid-1630s, moreover, as Louise de Marillac began to dispatch her charges further afield – in the Ile-de-France, for example, to Liancourt (1636), Saint-Germain-en-Laye (1638), Montmorency (1638) and even into the Touraine (Richelieu, 1638) – it was very much on the same casual basis.[7] These outposts were sufficiently near for either Vincent de Paul or Louise de Marillac to supervise them in personal visits. Moreover, the authorities under whom the Daughters of Charity served – Ladies of Charity, noblewomen with personal links with Vincent de Paul,[8] the Congregation of the Mission,[9] and so on – could be counted on to respect the personal influence of the founders. Such casual and informal links did continue after the 1630s: down to his death, for example, Vincent de Paul refused to resort to formal contractual agreements with any establishment which the Daughters of Charity had been called to serve by members of the royal family. Thus, no contract was ever passed to regulate the service of the Daughters of Charity in the Hôtel-Dieu of Arras,[10] to which the Queen Mother, Anne of Austria, had called them in 1656; while the establishment at La Fère received a contract only after Anne's death.[11]

Despite such exceptions, it was becoming clear from the late 1630s that a more formal regulation of the relationship between the Daughters of Charity and the administrators of the charitable institutions which they served was needed. A formal contract would be helpful in a number of ways. The hospital administrators at Angers, for example, who in 1639 prevailed upon Vincent de Paul and Louise de Marillac to establish a small community of Daughters of Charity in the city's Hôtel-Dieu were less directly under Vincentian influence than had been the case with most previous bodies. As with the vast majority of hospital administrations with which the Daughters of Charity dealt over the next two centuries, the administrative board of the Angers hospital was not even an ecclesiastical body: most of its members were laymen, including the city's municipal officials. The additional problems of supervision and control which this posed, and the need for a stricter delimitation of powers between Daughters of Charity and hospital administrators, were compounded by the fact that Angers was on the fringes of the area which Vincent de Paul and Louise de Marillac could be expected to visit in person. By the 1640s and 1650s moreover, the two founders were becoming too old and frail to engage in a close personal supervision. By that time, moreover, the Daughters of Charity were establishing themselves ever further and further afield: in Maine and Anjou, in Brittany and Normandy, in Picardy and Artois, in Bourgogne and Lorraine in the east, in Quercy and Languedoc in the south.[12] Close supervision of these establishments was made all the more problematic by the community's lack of a standard rule, to which Vincent de Paul only agreed towards the very end of his life, and which was only generalized among all the outposts of the community in the late 1660s and early 1670s.[13]

When set against this background, the idea of a formal contract was particularly appealing. It provided a means, first, of alerting the authorities under whom the Daughters of

Charity worked of the nature of their requirements and obligations as members of a religious community;[14] second, of delimiting the respective responsibilities and obligations of the administrators and the Daughters of Charity in the actual running of the hospital; and third, of helping to ensure that the Daughters of Charity acted in conformity with the spirit and the precepts of their founders. Vincent de Paul and Louise de Marillac tackled the problem in the case of the Angers Hôtel-Dieu in the following way. First, in a formal but rather uninformative notarial act in Angers on 1 February 1640 in the presence of Louise de Marillac, the administrators agreed to 'admit and receive as sister servants in the government and assistance of the sick poor' eight of the Daughters of Charity; and stipulated that the basis of their service would be the articles which have been drawn up and passed, together with the Rule concerning their function. The latter would in future be read out each year in the presence of the entire administrative board as a reminder of the hospital's undertakings; while the Daughters of Charity in the hospital were also to read out the document on a weekly basis, again as a reminder of their duties, both to the hospital and to the community. In the light of later developments, the 'Articles agreed for the Establishment of women of the Confraternity of Charity and servants of the poor of hospitals and of parish confraternities to serve the sick poor in the hospital of St John the Evangelist of Angers' is something of a hybrid document. On the one hand it contains a great deal of material which later passed into the full rule of the community drawn up by Vincent de Paul and finally codified by his successors as Superior of the Mission, René Alméras and Edme Jolly in the late 1660s: it contains, for example, regulations setting out the daily timetable of the Daughters of Charity attached to the hospital. On the other hand, the 'Articles' also contain material which would pass, more or less modified, into the full-blown establishment contracts of the company: there were clauses relating to their remuneration, the conditions under which they served, and so on.[15] In addition to this document, Vincent de Paul also drew up a specific rule for the sisters which dwelt on the spiritual services they were enjoined to perform.[16] It may be that he also drew up a separate document listing the duties of each post within the hospital to which the Daughters of Charity might be attached.[17] He certainly, in any case, did this in the case of the hospitals at Nantes and Châteaudun, the next large hospitals into whose service the Daughters of Charity passed, in 1646 and 1654 respectively. In the case of Châteaudun, for example, there were *Règles particulières* – which bore illuminating testimony to Vincent de Paul's painstaking attention to detail in all his undertakings – for the 'sister servant' (*soeur servante*), 'she who admits the sick', 'she who gives out bread and wine', 'she who looks after the frail', 'she who prepares the food on fast days', 'she who looks after the effects of the poor', 'the night watch,' 'she who goes to the hospital when the night watch goes to bed', 'the laundress', 'she who looks after the effects of the deceased', and, last but not least, 'the gravedigger'.

Much the same format seems to have remained standard throughout the life of Vincent de Paul and for a decade and a half after his death. The agreed 'Articles' and the 'Reigles' are extant, for example, for the hospitals of Chartres (1664), Alise Sainte Reine (1666), Cahors (1673), Lublé (1679), and Trévoux (1686). The rationale behind such documents was, however, slowly affected by the generalization of the final and official Rule of the community from the late 1660s. From the mid-1670s a formalised establishment contract, virtually identical to that which was to subsist down to the Revolution, was finally emerging. Its clearest early expression were the contracts drawn up in the key years of the late 1660s and early 1670s for the Hôpital Saint Jacques of Cahors (1665), for the Hôtel-Dieu at Chauny (1668), and for the hospital at Montluçon (1671). In these contracts, the separation from the earlier 'Articles' was not always clear: the daily timetable was still precisely itemized, for example, in the contract involving the hospital of Montluçon, just as it was in those relating to the hospitals of Pithiviers (1670) and Nogent-le-Rotrou (1672). Significantly, however, the timetable did not appear in the contracts for the hospitals at Verviers (1672), Evreux (1680), Loudun (1681), Notre-Dame-de-Liesse (1681),[18] or Cahors (1683), and virtually never thereafter. The trend towards standardization was unequivocal.

Another element of the move towards administrative uniformity was the growing tendency for the contract to be drawn up in Paris by the community's official notary. Many of the earliest documents had, like that involving the hospital at Angers in 1640, been drawn up in the actual locality of the charitable institution in question.[19] A number too – such as those regarding the *charités* at Richelieu (1643), Fontenay-aux-Roses (1649), Maintenon (1664), Meudon (1670), and Chasville (1670), as well as the contract regarding the hospital at La Fère (late 1660s?)[20] – were not contracts strictly speaking, but rather donations to the community, in return for which the latter agreed to pay for the upkeep of a certain number of Daughters of Charity in the said localities.[21] From the early 1670s, however, the majority of contracts not only followed the lines of the standard contracts, but also were drawn up in Paris: after 1680, over 95 per cent of establishments took this form.

Down to the 1790s the exact clauses which were used in each contract varied, sometimes considerably. Nevertheless, from the 1670s onwards there is a clear sense of administrative precedent in the workings of the community, and a generally assumed practice of basing new contracts on old ones. The contract eventually drawn up for the hospital of La Fère, for example, was based on those of Angers (1640) and Chauny (1668); that of the Hôpital de la Charité at Langres in 1690 was based on that employed in the case of the Hôtel-Dieu at Chaumont (1672); the revised contract for the Hôtel-Dieu Saint-Eloi of Montpellier in 1693 was based on the contracts of the hospitals of Chartres (1664) and Montluçon (1671); that of the hospital at Tarascon in 1699 was based in turn on the Montpellier contract of 1693; and so on. There was a strong sense of evolution, of learning from experience. When, for example, the administrators of the Hôpital Saint-André of Bordeaux in 1705 complained that the contract which they had been offered by the officers of the community differed in several respects from the contracts regulating the service which the Daughters of Charity were providing in several parishes in the city, the officers replied that they had amended the standard contract in a number of ways in response to suggestions by the bishops of Meaux, Bayeux, and Agen, following the experiences of the Daughters of Charity in the hospitals of Meaux (1700), Bayeux (1704), and Marmande (1705).

By the end of the seventeenth century the Daughters of Charity in Paris were replying to all requests from charitable institutions for their assistance simply by dispatching to them a copy of the basic contract which they felt was appropriate.[22] That relating to hospitals obviously differed in some respects from that concerning parish *charités*, there might be special clauses in regard to certain types of hospitals, and so on. The basic contract offered might well be accepted by the administrators without further hesitation. Otherwise, they might make a number of minor alterations. The deliberation of the administrators of the hospital of Gonesse in 1765, which was appended to the establishment contract probably captures the essence of what often happened:

> reading was given to the draft contract mentioned in the deliberation of last 15 February tending towards the establishment of the sisters of charity for the service and the relief of the sick in the present hospital, together with observations which have been made on the said establishment, and on each article of the said draft by severals of Messrs. the administrators; after which observations and after having maturely examined each article of the said draft, several changes and additions were made, with the result that the said draft is at present drawn up in a form and with dispositions which appear advantageous to the place of the poor; and the said administrators unanimously approved and approve this.[23]

In this particular case, the Daughters of Charity accepted the modifications proposed by the hospital administrators. Yet this was far from always the case. The financial interests of the community had to be protected, so the officers had sometimes to be pretty hard-headed about financial arrangements.[24] There was also the tradition of the community to be upkept, and the proper observance of their rule to be ensured. The negotiations and the haggling which sometimes went on before a contract was finally agreed on by both sides were not always much appreciated by charitable administrators.[25] However, such was the demand for the services of the community that grew up, the community could afford to be very choosy. By 1769 the community's Superior was even commenting that, such was the 'fervour' to have Daughters of Charity in the provinces, that

> one of the greatest predicaments in the administering of this community is to know how it can manage not to agree to the most energetic solicitations that are made nearly every day for new establishments.[26]

The community of the Daughters of Charity, for their part, appears to have recognized the usefulness of having a contract. If nothing else, it made their position legally sounder should anything go amiss with a particular institution. Hence one finds that a number of establishments without formal contracts – especially those created in the early days of the community – had one drawn up, even much later. An establishment had been set up, for example, at Brienne-le-Château as early as 1653; yet it was only in 1731 that a proper establishment contract was drawn up,

> so that the three said Daughters of Charity seem to have been established according to the clauses and stipulations which are observed in the other contracts of similar establishments.[27]

Towards the end of the Ancien Régime, the community appears to have adopted a more stringent policy towards institutions which had no contracts, especially where the Daughters of Charity served only out of a sense of past commitment and where financial arrangements were inadequate.[28] Furthermore, if any institution requested a larger number of sisters, a fresh contract might be drawn up, and the terms even made financially more advantageous for the community. The high cost of drawing up an official contract for such a purpose was, however, resented by charitable administrators who were often extremely hard pressed for cash.[29] Consequently in proposed cases of *augmentations* in numbers, the Daughters of Charity came to agree to accept, in lieu of a notarial act, a deliberation of the hospital administrators to the effect that would pay and treat the additional sister or sisters in the same way as the existing sisters.

II

The establishment contract (*contrat d'établissement*) took the form of an agreement on the number of the Daughters of Charity who were to be attached to a particular charitable institution, and the terms under which they were to serve. The community was represented by its four officers, Superior, Assistant, Treasurer (*Oeconome*), and Bursar (*Dépensière*), and the contract normally stated that they were guided in their counsels by their *Supérieur,* who in most cases was, of course, the *Supérieur* of the Congregation of the Mission. The other contracting party varied. Often he was represented by a *procureur* (proxy), who might be a Parisian bourgeois or cleric, a member of the Congregation of the Mission, or some other individual. In a large proportion of cases, the *procureur* was in fact a member of the administrative board of the hospital to which the Daughters of Charity were to be dispatched. These administrative boards were the contracting partner in over three-quarters of the agreements with hospitals (Table 5.1). In about a sixth of these cases, the hospital administrators included municipal officials acting in that role. The presence of religious notables among the contracting partners in the other contracts is a reminder of the semi-ecclesiastical status of some hospital boards, as well as the role of the local bishop as *père des pauvres.* The nobles who were contracting parties in 14.8 per cent of cases might be, as seigneurs, the nominal head of the local hospital administration; or they might be acting individually by establishing the Daughters of Charity in the locality of their seigneurie as a notable charitable gesture.

Table 5.1: Founders of Daughters of Charity in Hospitals, According to the *Contrats d'établissement*

Founders	%
1. Administrative board[1]	76.3
2. Principal inhabitant(s)	3.7
3. Clergy	3.1
4. Nobles[2]	14.8
5. Unknown	1.9

Notes: 1 In 12.4% of cases the hospital administrators were the municipal officials.
2 Noblemen = 9.2%, noblewomen = 5.6%.

In three-quarters of the establishment contracts, a staff of either two or three Daughters of Charity was initially envisaged. Unlike the *charités,* for which a staff of two or three was thought sufficient, most hospitals took on three or four Daughters of Charity (Table 5.2); while some took on even larger numbers: sixteen sisters were initially earmarked for the Hôpital Saint-André at Bordeaux in 1705, for example, eight for the Hôpital

Général in Laon in 1781, twelve for the Hôpital Général in Tours in 1786, and so on. Even so, it was soon realized that numbers had to grow as hospitals developed over the course of the Ancien Régime. Increasingly, therefore, a clause was inserted into most establishment contracts on the following lines:

> The said sisters, Superior and officers, by the present commit themselves and their successors in their offices to maintain in perpetuity (x) Daughters of Charity in the said hospital, and an even larger number subsequently if needed, and if it is necessary to increase the number of sisters, they shall be admitted according to the same clauses and conditions as the first.

Table 5.2: Number of Daughters of Charity Attached to Institutions, According to the *Contrats d'établissement*

No.	*Hospitals* (%)	*Charités* (%)	*Total* (%)
1	–	1.1	0.6
2	9.7	65.4	39.8
3	51.0	28.0	38.6
4	20.0	5.0	11.9
5	8.4	0.5	4.2
over 5	11.0	–	5.0

Why did these individuals and corporate bodies wish to introduce the Daughters of Charity into hospitals? In the case of the hospital at Angers in 1640, the notarial act stated that the administration's aim was to 'renew and resume with greater firmness the former and primary institution'. Correspondence regarding other establishments evokes the role of the Daughters of Charity in restoring the spiritual atmosphere of the hospital community; combating Protestantism; inculcating the faith; and running the hospital sagely and economically. One or two of the earlier contracts – as that of Corbeil (1672) – mention the desire of the administrators to see the Daughters of Charity 'governing the poor'. The same idea of regulation and the imposition of authority is captured in a rather lengthier preamble to the contract with the Hôtel-Dieu of Montluçon in 1671:

> having a great desire to provide for the good treatment of the sick poor of their hospital, and to this effect to introduce a permanent charitable orderliness, after having sought the most fitting and appropriate means, they had paid particular attention to what they learnt of the zeal, behaviour and experience of the Daughters of Charity, instituted for the relief and assistance of the poor, without any other reward, besides their meagre upkeep, than what they expect from God.

These lengthy preambles were soon, however, being rapidly abbreviated. From the 1670s a more standard form emerged, which evoked the importance of the power of example in the spread of the community:

> to contribute towards the good intention that the said . . . have of assisting the sick poor in their hospital by several of the said Daughters of Charity, following the example which is followed in several places where they have been established to the glory of God and to the relieving of the sick poor.

It was not, however, long before even this formula died out: and virtually no eighteenth-century contract contained a preamble.

The spread of the renown of the Daughters of Charity in the hospitals was partly at least a function of their expansion. On the death of Vincent de Paul in 1660, the community appears to have been serving over a dozen hospitals.[30] Numbers grew thereafter, particularly in the boom years from about 1685 to about 1705, which saw the creation of about a quarter of the total number of establishments down to the Ancien Régime. By the early years of the eighteenth century, there were signs that the community had overstretched itself a little. In a significant proportion of contracts passed in the 1690s and 1700s, the officers stipulated that they would supply the agreed number of sisters to any institution only 'as soon as they are able'. Even greater hesitancy towards taking on new institutions was shown in the 1720s and then again in the 1740s.[31] The motive behind the community's withdrawal from the establishment at Vezins in 1743 was given as the fact that 'they lack suitable candidates to supply and direct a hospital or charitable institution'.[32] In Vichy in 1741, it had been very much the same story, with the officers pleading that

> some time will be necessary, since we have at the moment no suitable candidate in hand, death having taken from us, and continuing to take from us, such a large number that we are often in very great difficulties in providing sisters where they are lacking.[33]

Part of the problem was that as hospitals to which the Daughters of Charity were already attached grew, they requested larger numbers of sisters, thus placing additional strain on what seemed to be dwindling numbers of recruits. From 1750, however, a new round of creations occurred, with the community taking on some fifty-four new hospitals between 1750 and 1790.

The Daughters of Charity served, therefore, in hospitals both great and small. They also served in every conceivable type of hospital (Table 5.3).

Table 5.3: Types of Hospitals Served by the Daughters of Charity

	%
Hôtel-Dieu, Hôpital des malades, etc	43.6
Hôpital Général, Manufacture, Charité, etc.	16.0
Hôpital	40.4

The first hospital with which the Daughters of Charity had passed an establishment contract, that at Angers in 1640, had been an Hôtel-Dieu, and the community continued, down to the Revolution, to proffer its aid to the sick poor, who made up the essential clientele of such institutions. About two-fifths of hospital contracts prior to 1790 were with Hôtels-Dieu.

About one-sixth, on the other hand, were Hôpitaux Généraux. The company seem to have manifested a certain unwillingness to serve in institutions of this sort in the provinces, in the early days of the *grand renfermement des pauvres* following the creation in 1656 of the Hôpital Général.[34] They had long cared for the foundlings of the Enfants-Trouvés in Paris – which after 1676 was incorporated into the Paris Hôpital Général – and certainly extended their care to this type of need in the provinces.[35] However, the community showed itself less willing to accommodate the able-bodied poor (*pauvres valides*) who were one of the prime targets of the *grand renfermement.* Sometimes, this involved making precise stipulations in their establishment contracts. In the case of the Hôpital de la Charité at Langres in 1690, for example, the contract stated that the sisters were only to care for the sick poor,

> without them being expected to have any care of the children of the Manufacture, nor any other persons save when they are ill in the said hospital with the other sick poor.

In the contract with the Hôpital Général of Meaux in 1700, they were even more emphatic in taking up their distance from the whole Hôpital Général movement:

> the said Hôpital of Meaux may expressly not be recognized as a Hôpital Général in regard to the said Daughters of Charity and to their community, nor may it be used as a precedent against them by any Hôpital Général for any reason that may be, without which [the contract] would not have been passed, especially as the principal aim of their institute is the service of the sick poor.

Similarly at Autun in 1705, they were only to care for the aged and for abandoned children, and were not to be called upon to succour 'vagrants and able-bodied beggars', nor indeed any male inmate unless he was adjudged ill.

This distaste for providing care for the able-bodied was a fundamental and long-lasting feature of the work of the Daughters of Charity. In the case of the hospital at Gimont in 1735, for example, the community made it clear that the sisters were not to 'admit vagrant beggars seeing that this is against the institution of the sisters'. None the less, by the end of the seventeenth century the Daughters of Charity were increasingly accepting contracts for the service of Hôpitaux Généraux.[36] Over the course of the eighteenth century, moreover, as the more purely repressive aspect of provincial Hôpitaux Généraux was attenuated, and as the attempts to incarcerate *valides* alongside *invalides* became fewer and less convincing, the Hôpitaux Généraux came to be, in essence, homes for the aged and disabled, and children's homes.[37] There was nothing in such a destination which could upset the susceptibilities of the Daughters of Charity.

Besides the Hôtels-Dieu and the Hôpitaux Généraux, nearly one-half of the establishments with which the community passed establishment contracts were designated only by the term 'Hôpital'. These were often, in practice, small rural or semi-rural establishments which combined as refuges for both the sick and the aged and infirm. A number combined hospitalization with the distribution of home relief.[38] Indeed, such was the tenuous line between some small hospitals and *charités* that certain *charités* to which the Daughters of Charity were attached actually switched their destination to become hospitals.[39] There was thus no hard and fast line which demarcated hospital care from the other kinds of charitable services which the Daughters of Charity rendered to the poor.

III

Much of the main body of the contract between the Daughters of Charity and hospital administrations concerned the types of rewards and remunerations which the sisters could expect from the hospitals which they served. The earliest contracts make no explicit reference to sums of money involved, and left payments on a haphazard basis. In the case of the Hôtel-Dieu of Angers in 1640 – as was indeed to prove the case in all but a handful of hospitals down to the end of the Ancien Régime[40] – it was stated that the sisters would have their food provided at the expense of the hospital. In this they differed from Daughters of Charity attached to *charités*, whose payment normally included a sum to cover the costs of food and drink. It seems to have been expected that the Daughters of Charity would provide for themselves the same kind of fare as they distributed among the sick poor whom they succoured. Contracts which are more precise are rare. But the arrangement with the Hôpital Général of Autun in 1705, which stipulated that the sisters were to receive 'good bread and at least one pound (*livre*) of meat a day each on feast days', may indicate something like what they could expect elsewhere.[41] There would inevitably be a certain amount of variation according to local diet. Thus at Béthune in 1764 it was agreed that the hospital would provide 'a sufficient quantity of beer, so as to make up for the poor quality of the waters'.

The sisters also required other provisions for themselves besides food and drink. Usually this was left on an informal basis, with the sisters being expected to help themselves from the common hospital stocks. There was, however, a clear trend towards more precise definition. Particularly towards the end of the Ancien Régime, a great many contracts specified that the Daughters of Charity

> will have in common with the poor of the said hospital as is ordinarily the practice in their establishments the use of wood, coal, salt, candle, laundering, and also of household linen such as sheets, tablecloths, towels, handcloths, dusters, white and blue aprons.

One important area in which greater clarification was deemed necessary was in regard to the dress which the Daughters of Charity wore. In the first hospital contract with the Angers Hôtel-Dieu in 1640, the *Articles* agreed had stipulated that the hospital would provide '*habits*' for the sisters, 'without them being made to change the colour and the shape of any'. This arrangement perhaps left too much discretion in the hands of the administrators, and the more normal arrangement came to be that the administrators provided the sisters with an annual sum of money to pay for the upkeep of their 'uniforms'. The conventional clause in the standardized contracts in use after the 1670s stated that they

> will be fed at the expense of the said hospital, which will in addition give each one of them (x) *livres* each year for the maintenance of their dress and body linen, without them being obliged to change its colour or its shape.

In order to avoid any unseemly disagreements over the payment of such moneys, it was later stated that these sums would be

> payable in advance every six months, in two equal

> payments, from the day of their arrival of the said sisters in the said hospital, on the invoices of the sister who will be in charge of the others, of which sum they will render account only to their Superior in Paris.

There was a great deal of variation in the amount of money which hospital administrators agreed to pay individual Daughters of Charity for the upkeep of their 'uniforms'. The first contract actually to name a sum – that passed with the administration of the Hôtel-Dieu Saint-Eloi of Montpellier in 1668 – referred to the payment of 40 *livres* per annum to each sister; the second, with the Hôtel-Dieu of Pithiviers in 1670 fixed it at 25 *livres*; and the third, with the hospital of Monluçon in 1671, agreed on a sum of 36 *livres*. The latter sum of 36 *livres* did in fact become pretty standard in the contracts after the 1670s. By the 1690s, however, an increasingly larger proportion of hospital contracts were fixing the sum at 50 or 60 *livres* and these levels became standard from the 1720s. By 1750 anything between 60 and 80 *livres* had become the rule. In the late 1760s 100 *livres* and, on the very eve of the Revolution, 120 *livres* were also registered in the hospital contracts.

There was thus a strong upwards surge in levels of payment down to the end of the eighteenth century. This coexisted, however, with the persistence of wide fluctuations in payments between different institutions at any one time. The reason behind such fluctuations is rarely made explicit. It may be that the officers of the community, in agreeing to a certain sum, took into account the financial capabilities of the hospital in question, or perhaps the general levels of prices in the locality. In addition, it seems that the sum agreed upon could be, in some cases at least, the product of negotiation between the two parties, and could thus represent something of a compromise. Thus for example, in 1763, when the officers sent their standard contract to the administrators of the Hôtel-Dieu at Martel, they were asking for a sum of 80 *livres* to be paid annually to each sister. The hospital administrators, however, felt that this was too much. In the end, the community's officers agreed to compromise: they would drop the sum to 60 *livres*; but in return there were to be slight changes in one or two other clauses of the contracts which slightly improved their financial position.[42]

What other elements of the work situation of the Daughters of Charity were open to collective bargaining of this sort? One possible negotiable facility was the accommodation which the hospitals were expected to provide for their sisters. A separate lodging 'separate and closed-off' as the early contracts stated was usually expected as of right. As the standard contracts of the eighteenth century put it:

> [they] will be lodged and furnished appropriately in a separate apartment in which the domestics will not enter.

Just what the furnishings referred to consisted of might vary from institution to institution. At Béthune in 1764, the contract stipulated that when the Daughters of Charity arrived in the hospital they should find ready for them 'beds furnished with mattresses, pillows and serge bed drapes'. In other cases, the officers could be even more demanding.[43]

There might be a certain margin for negotiation between the two contracting parties in regard to the sums of money which the community expected to be paid prior to dispatching sisters to any particular hospital. Again, this was an element in the contract which became increasingly formalized and standardized. By the last half century of the Ancien Régime, just about every contract contained, as its last or penultimate clause, standard phrases stating sums which needed to be paid as establishment costs: the cost of a first uniform (referred to as *accommodements personnelles*); cash for travelling costs and dispatch of luggage (*frais de voyage, port de ballots*); cash to pay for a certain number (usually three) 'cases of lancets and ligatures', and an additional 'case furnished with surgical instruments'; cash to pay for the books which the Daughters of Charity brought with them, both for their own use (books of piety, as well as medical and cooking manuals) and for the use of poor; cash finally to pay for the notarial act establishing the contract. Taken together, these sums could be substantial. In the case of the hospital of Montauban in 1685, establishment costs for a small community of Daughters of Charity amounted to some 400 *livres*. By 1776 the new creation at Saint Gilles in the diocese of Nîmes required establishment costs of 1,990 *livres*. Needless to say, such sums represented a substantial outlay for institutions, many of which were financially hardpressed.

The often substantial sums needed to pay the travelling costs of sisters who were recalled, transferred, or replaced on account of death or infirmity comprised another negotiable element within contracts. Vincent de Paul had originally intended that the Daughters of Charity should not be maintained in any one location for lengthy periods, but should be constantly moved about.[44] In practice, as the Daughters of Charity's network of institutions came to be organized on a national basis, such a strategy became financially impracticable. Inevitably, however, changes in personnel did take place, and the conditions under which they might occur and regarding who was to be financially liable for them became a standard item in every contract. One or two of the early hospital agreements refer to a sort of probation year, at the end of which either the community or the hospital administrators could request the recall of an individual sister.[45] This kind of arrangement tended ultimately to revolve around the whim of hospital administrators, and the officers of the community soon recognized its disadvantages. In its place, there emerged an agreement under which each side undertook to pay all the travel costs involved in a replacement, transfer, or recall if the change in personnel could be accounted its own responsibility, and to its own benefit. The standard clause in use put it thus:

> If the changes are made for the good of the said hospital or on account of the death of any of the sisters, . . . the travel costs of those recalled and of those who are sent as replacements will be at the hospital's expense. But if the changes are made for the good and at the request of the community of the said Daughters, in this case the travel costs will be at the expense of the said community.

Very occasionally hospital administrators successfully negotiated to pay an annual lump sum to the community (an *abonnement*) to cover all travel costs which might be incurred. Such a practice was, however, far from common.[46]

As a result of this arrangement, hospital administrators were discouraged from requesting the removal of sisters without good cause. The community, for its part, bore the costs of the kind of replacements and transfers of personnel inevitable in an organization of this kind: changes to replace quarrelsome sisters, for example, to put ailing sisters in less physically demanding posts, to discipline the insubordinate, to promote promising sisters to more responsible jobs, and so on. A refinement in the system, very much to the financial advantage of the community, and which helped ensure a certain continuity and stability of service, took the form of a clause which stipulated that if the replacement took place after the sister in question had served the hospital for a given length of time, then the costs involved in her transfer would be borne by the hospital rather than by the community. Such a clause was present in a couple of contracts in the 1680s,[47] and became pretty standard from the 1690s. In virtually all cases, the period of service involved was six years, though there were a number of exceptions.[48] The latter presumably resulted from negotiation between the two sides.

A further, and perhaps more problematic financial burden which hospitals had to bear related to the treatment of sisters who became ill or infirm. Life within hospitals in the early modern period was pretty tough, and dangerous to life and limb. Periodic illnesses of sisters were accordingly not merely possible, they were virtually certain. The very earliest contracts, in recognition of this, stipulated that hospital administrators were duty bound to succour their Daughters of Charity 'both in sickness and in health' and this phrase was much repeated in later contracts. There tended to be little disagreement that if a sister's illness had been contracted in the service of the poor, it was the responsibility of the hospital to ensure the sister was properly nursed back to health. Problems arose, however, when a sister manifested what seemed to be a prior disposition towards sickliness, or when she became totally invalided. In such cases, hospital administrators might complain that they were not getting their money's worth out of the community. A set of conventions consequently evolved to overcome this source of potential friction. The standard clause which passed into most contracts from the late seventeenth century accorded such sisters what were in essence rights to retirement on a pension within the hospital:

> When they become infirm and unable to work, they may not be dismissed on account of their infirmities if the Superior in Paris does not adjudge it convenient to recall them; but they will be lodged in the said hospital and treated with the medicines and food they require; and to make up for those who have become infirm, Messrs. the

> administrators of the said hospital will be obliged to admit other sisters from the same community in the same number and according to the same clauses and conditions as the first.

Doubtless because this clause represented a considerable financial commitment on the part of any institution, it was subject to numerous variations, which were presumably the product both of experience and of negotiation. In many cases, as in the example cited above, the obligation was incurred however long the sister had served the hospital. This was particularly frequently found in contracts passed in the 1690s, the 1700s, the 1720s, and the 1740s. Rather more often, however, a qualification of a specific length of service within the hospital was added as a rider. A period of six years' prior service was the most frequently found stipulation in contracts down to 1720. From about 1730, periods of ten years and then, from the late 1750s, periods of twelve years became the rule. Indeed from the late 1760s the twelve-year rule operated in all but a handful of cases. There were, even so, numerous variations throughout the period. Some hospitals, for example, agreed to pay the travel costs of a replacement; others did not. Some paid the replacement a full wage; others expected her livelihood to be found out of the lump sum the administration traditionally paid the community of sisters in the hospital. A further variation, found in a small number of cases, was that the community agreed not to keep on more than one infirm sister in a hospital, so as not to overburden the finances of the institution, and undertook to bring back any supernumeraries to the mother-house in Paris, where they would be looked after till the end of their days.

The Daughter of Charity who had expended her life and strength in the care of the sick was thus rewarded with due care and attention in her old age, either in the mother-house or else in the hospital to which she had been attached. The contracts also ensured that those who died within the hospital were given the kind of burial which sisters who ended their days in the mother-house could expect. Virtually all contracts had some sort of reference to deceased sisters being buried by their colleagues 'in their customary manner'. Most in fact gave further details, usually on the following lines:

> In the case of the death of any of the said sisters, it will be borne in mind that she died in the service of the poor; it will be permitted to the other sisters to bury the corpse of the deceased in their customary manner, leaving it in their infirmary until it is taken up to be carried to church, and also to follow in convoy the body of the deceased, each one holding a candle in her hand; and after the celebration of one high and two low masses, the body of the deceased will be buried in the church or the cemetery of the said hospital; and there will be placed on the grave a little stone in which will be carved the name, age, and the date of the death of the deceased, all this at the expense of the said hospital, unless M. the curé wishes to do it gratis.

The motivation of the women who became Daughters of Charity was, of course, far from solely materialistic. The send-off to the afterlife which these funeral arrangements embodied would presumably be highly valued by them. So too would the unrestricted ability to live as a full member of the community of the Daughters of Charity, duly observing all their religious regulations and injunctions. In the contracts, hospital administrators undertook not to interfere with the sisters' observance of their community rule:

> the Daughters of Charity will have complete freedom within the hospital to live under the obedience of the said Superior General [of the Congregation of the Mission] and his successors, of their own Superior General in Paris, of the officers of their community and those amongst themselves who direct the others, not as nuns but as sisters of a regular community; they may practise there all the regulations and spiritual exercises of their institute without however prejudicing the care and the relief of the sick poor of the said hospital, whom they will prefer to all other things.

It followed that, in spiritual matters, the authority of the Daughters of Charity's superiors was paramount. These rights were enshrined within the contract in the following way:

> As regards spiritual matters, the said Daughters will be subject to Mgr. the Bishop of (x) and will remain under the direction and dependence of the Superior General of their community and his successors, who may by himself or by some other person he deputes visit them and confess them from time to time with the approval of the ordinaries, designate for them a confessor approved in the diocese, and give the advice necessary for the observance of their rule, recall them when he thinks fit and send others in their place.

All in all, the Daughters of Charity who served within the hospitals could expect standards of rewards for their services which were not unattractive. Materially they were provided with ample food and drink, separate and well-furnished lodgings, care and attention in illness, an assured resting-place and good treatment in old age. Spiritually too, the sense of vocation of the Daughters of Charity was respected first in their being allowed to follow the rule of the community in all its details and second in the decent funeral arrangements which were made for them. These rewards were substantial. What precisely did they give in return?

IV

The basic function of the administrative board of the hospital which was either party to each establishment contract with the Daughters of Charity or else approved its contents, was to supervise the general, and in particular the financial, management of the institution. They sanctioned expenditure, for example, made bulk purchases of supplies, invested donations and benefactions, drew legal contracts, passed leases, conserved the hospital's archives, drew up the annual accounts, introduced hospital rules and regulations, and so on. The board was normally composed of a mixture of secular and ecclesiastical dignitaries, drawn from the local authorities or from the major corporate bodies. The local bishop was often *président d'honneur*, although how much interest he showed in hospital affairs varied. These individuals who formed the hospital boards had far more pressing everyday concerns than hospital management to occupy them. Their supervision of these hospitals under their care was consequently in many cases tenuous and nominal rather than direct and active. Nevertheless, the Daughters of Charity who served in a hospital served under their direct authority, as the establishment contracts made clear. The contracts normally stated that:

> As regards temporal matters and the service of the poor, they will be entirely under the authority of Messrs. the administrators of the said hospital.[49]

Above all, this entailed their being executive agents in the implementation of all regulations relating to the internal life of the hospital which the administrative board saw fit to introduce.

In the early days of the community the orientation of the Daughters of Charity around the care of the sick poor within the hospitals seems to have been total. However, the size and complexity of the hospitals in which they worked, and the tendency for hospital administrators to be negligent in their duties led to the Daughters of Charity expanding their functions beyond the level of care. Administrative and even managerial tasks were taken on. Many seventeenth-century contracts stated, for example, that the sisters should keep admissions registers of the sick who entered the hospital. Thus, at Cahors in 1675, for example, the contract stipulated that:

> they will take care to write the name of the sick who are admitted into the said hospital, the nickname, the age, the place of their birth and residence, the day of their admission and their leaving or the day of their death if they come to die there.

Another frequently encountered clause in contracts at this time stated that the sisters were to hold an annual inventory of all the hospital's possessions on the eve of the feast of Saint John. Probably the most important administrative task which the Daughters of Charity in the hospitals were expected to assume, however, was care of the hospital's daily provisions – or rather, its 'minor provisions' since the 'major provisions' normally were taken to be the responsibility of the administrators. Accounts for the 'minor provisions' were to be presented to the administrative board on a weekly or monthly basis, depending on the terms of the contract. The standard clause covering this part of their responsibilities often associated their duties in this sphere with their purchasing of drugs and medicines for the hospital:

> they will be provided with . . . the money necessary for the purchase of drugs, and they will render accounts of this money as well as of that which will be given them from time to time to buy minor provisions, which account will be audited each month and approved by the duty administrator, under the authority of the administrative board.

Besides organizing much of the hospital's consumption, the Daughters of Charity also on occasion found themselves assuming control of production. At the hospital of Alençon at the turn of the eighteenth century, for example, it was stated that

> in the yard, there will be a sister [who] looks after seven cows, fourteen pigs, and the hens. Sisters will do the milking, make butter and cheese, keep the stables clean, put down bedding straw, bring water twice daily in winter and thrice daily in summer and [word unclear] bran for the feeding and fattening of the pigs.

This picture of a Daughter of Charity acting in much the same way as a peasant's wife was probably not untypical. Indeed, so apparently competent were the Daughters of Charity at this kind of operation that some administrators expressed a fear that the upkeep of livestock might become too major a preoccupation. At Attichy in 1705, for example, the contract specified that

> so that the said . . . sisters give all their time to the care of the said sick poor . . . they may not keep cows or any other livestock, care of which might distract them.

The contract with the Hôpital Général of Meaux in 1700 showed a similar concern, though it was slightly less categorical:

> they will have care of all the household of the hospital, will do the laundry and baking and will keep the accounts of the latter, without concerning themselves with major provisions; nor will they keep a large number of cows to make some money for the said sisters, but they may only keep a few to provide for their needs.[50]

Another aspect of the supervision of production which sometimes fell to the sisters to perform was the control of the work which was organized in the workshops of the Hôpitaux Généraux in which they served. Towards the end of the Ancien Régime, very specific instructions were given in most contracts with Hôpitaux Généraux in regard to this branch of their service. In the case of Abbeville in 1770, for example, the contract stated that

> they will be entrusted with the ultimate responsibility for the children of the said hospital, who will be put into two particular classes, so as to instruct and train them in work. Messrs. the directors will provide a master for the boys' workshop . . . who will keep the sisters carefully informed so that she who has responsibility will have complete freedom to watch over the needs of the children . . . . One of the said Daughters will similarly concern herself with the girls' workshop in the said hospital . . . . If the work of the children in these two workshops produces any profit, the sisters will render an exact account to the administrative board, and will keep a register of expense and income which they will produce whenever Messrs. the administrators judge convenient.

A further function which the Daughters of Charity came to assume was the supervision and control, not only of hospital inmates, but also of ancillary personnel attached to the institutions. In the early days it seems to have been expected that the sisters would perform all menial tasks within the hospitals, and this doubtless continued to be the case in many of the smaller hospitals and in a great many *charités*. Things were rather different, however, in the larger hospitals, and in those hospitals which grew sharply in size over the late seventeenth and eighteenth centuries. The costs involved in sending for and providing for an additional sister was a major disincentive; and the supply of trained Daughters of Charity was far from always sufficient, even at the best of times. Consequently the officers of the community soon showed themselves willing to countenance other servants working in the hospitals, albeit on the strict understanding that these were under the close supervision of their sisters. The contract with the Hôtel-Dieu at Chaumont in 1672, for example, stated that

> they will take great care to watch over the women workers and make sure that the domestics, such as porters, bakers and gardeners use their time well . . . and . . . in the event of disobedience, insubordination, insult, or suspicion of these, the said *soeur servante* may herself dismiss and expel from the said hospital any convalescents, workers, domestics, and officers culpable of such faults.

Although the community admitted the presence of other servants within the hospitals they served, they were adamant that these should not be seen as their equals. In essence, the Daughters of Charity ran a closed shop in the hospitals. The standard contract stated unequivocally

> they will have associated with them no girl or woman or other person for the service of the said poor, so that by the union and harmony there is between them, the poor may be better served.

Over the course of the eighteenth century, this clause was slightly softened to admit the possibility of other servants, a sub-clause added to this clause stipulating that

> they may however have the assistance of some safe and well-known persons in the extraordinary work at the hospital's expense.[51]

This was a choice of words which was not, though, to compromise the sisters' standing in the hospital.

Hospital administrators were not always happy about these clauses: they regretted having to eject from the hospital female servants who, prior to the arrival of the Daughters of Charity, had governed the internal workings of the institution. The community's insistence on the point owed much to unhappy early experiences with surviving servants who saw themselves as the sisters' rivals in the hospitals of Saint-Denis and Nantes in the 1640s.[52] Furthermore, as the wording of the clause suggests, there seems to have been a feeling that the presence of outsiders would disrupt the communal life of the sisters which was the mainspring of the whole service. Consequently the community was quite unmoveable on this point, and was quick to invoke the threat of total withdrawal if hospital administrators showed any signs of backtracking.[53] In addition, a standard clause underlined the closeness and uniqueness of their association with the hospital administrators:

> [they] will render account of their service and of their administration only to the administrators, who must maintain them and support them all the more in that if they had no authorization as regards the officers and the poor, they would not be able to do the good that God demands of them.

The strict segregation which was to be observed towards other hospital personnel extended to the chaplain or chaplains whom most hospitals of any substance would have on their payrolls. A standard clause ran:

> if there is a chaplain he will not be lodged in the said hospital nor have his washing done there, and will have no other access except by the main door; neither will he have rights of inspection over the conduct of the sisters, nor the administration of temporal matters.

In a number of hospitals, implementation of this clause led to the ejection from hospital premises of priests who had in the past doubled as pastors of the sick and as managers of hospital property. One or two early contracts also enjoined the Daughters of Charity to keep their proper distance from doctors and surgeons who might be attached to the hospitals[54] – though such stipulations died out in the early eighteenth century.

The concern of the Daughters of Charity to maintain the limits of a segregation which respected their status as *filles d'une communauté reglée* also involved the exclusion of certain types of potential hospital inmates:

> the sisters will not be obliged to admit or to care for any fee-paying person,

ran one standard clause, echoing the injunction of Vincent de Paul to shun the care of any save the sick poor.[55] Some contracts spelled things out even more clearly, forbidding the sisters to allow entry to any 'rich person' or their servants. Also in line with Vincentian precepts was the exclusion from hospitals of 'girls and women of disordered life, and persons suffering from the illness which proceeds from impurity', and also 'women in childbirth'.[56]

The force of these prohibitions and exclusions was to direct the attention of the Daughters of Charity on what the contracts emphasized was the first and most important function of the sisters: the care of the sick poor within the hospital. Although some hospital administrations permitted the sisters to supervise the provision of home relief in conjunction with their hospital duties, in most hospitals this was not the case, and a specific clause often was included which ruled that

> they will not be obliged to go to serve any sick person in the town, of whatever sex, state or condition.

The spiritual services which the Daughters of Charity performed for their charges within the hospitals were fully itemized in the Rule of the community. The spiritual aspect of their work does, however, also surface in the contracts and in related correspondence. It is clear, for example, that one of the most important tasks of the Daughters of Charity was considered to be their evangelizing function. This was particularly valued in Protestant areas. In the hospital of Gex in the diocese of Annécy, for example, it was stated that

> they take in there all the sick and even by their charitable care Heretics; most of these are converted to our religion along with all their families.[57]

The Daughters of Charity were also drafted into hospitals in the Protestant Cévennes. The administrators of the hospital of Saint-Hippolyte of the diocese of Alès in which they served informed the officers of the community that

> there are many New Converts, whose souls your sisters are saving by having them die good Catholics.

All in all, the evangelizing activities of the sisters were probably exhibited more frequently against religious ignorance than what they conceived of as error. In 1648 two sisters were sent to the hospital at Liancourt. One of them was to provide lessons for local girls. However, it was also noted that

> the sister schoolmistress will take care that all the poor know the principal mysteries of the faith, and will teach them to those who do not know them.

Provisions of this sort are rarely to be found in contracts from the late seventeenth century on. Nevertheless, they do crop up occasionally down to the Revolution – indeed even beyond, for the contract passed with the administrators of the Hôpital Général of Carcassonne in 1790 stipulated that, in regard to all the inmates of the institution, the sisters 'will instruct them in the holy mysteries of religion'.

The most frequently found concrete expression of the evangelizing functions of the community which the contracts contained related to the provision of primary schools (*petites écoles*) in which the local 'poor girls' – boys were always explicitly excluded[58] – were to be taught. The standard clause ran:

> one of the said Daughters will be entrusted with holding school and instructing the poor young girls of the parish in the principal mysteries of our holy religion.

Although such a clause was found most frequently in contracts with *charités*, about one-third of all hospital contracts made some reference to educational provision. It is noticeable that although a number of contracts stated that the sisters should teach how to read and write, the most frequently mentioned service was the provision of religious education. Finally, virtually all contracts made it clear that the schooling which the Daughters of Charity provided was to be adjudged of secondary importance to the care of the sick:

> and when an epidemic (*maladie populaire*) occurs among the sick or the sisters, she will suspend the school if it is necessary that she helps in the care of the sick; and she will resume her task as soon as may be.

V

From the very beginning, there was a medical element implicit in the care which the Daughters of Charity were enjoined to give to the 'sick poor' within the hospitals. In the *Règlement* which Vincent de Paul accorded the sisters sent to the Hôtel-Dieu of Angers in 1640, it was stated that they were to attend to both the spiritual and the bodily welfare of their charges, and that the material aspect of their task was to take the form of 'serving them and administering to them food and medicines'. By 1654 a separate clause had appeared in the contract relating to the sisters sent to the hospital of Châteaudun which stated that the *soeur servante*

> will see that the said poor are visited once daily by the doctor, apothecary, and surgeon, and will inform the said administrators if they do not do their duty towards the said poor.[59]

With one or two minor changes in wording, this clause became a fairly standard item in hospital contracts from the 1650s down to the turn of the century. It reflected Vincent de Paul's respect for the medical profession, and also his feeling that the Daughters of Charity should be fully subordinate to medical personnel. In the 'Advis' which he composed for the sisters bound in 1656 for the military hospital at Arras, for example, he stated that

> they will show great respect . . . for Messrs. the doctors and others who have care of the poor.[60]

Although the standard contract clause referred to medical personnel visiting the hospital on a daily basis, this was almost certainly an ideal to be aspired to rather than an actual reflection of the state of affairs in most hospitals. Even in major Hôtels-Dieu in the seventeenth and early eighteenth century, daily visits were far from the rule. Thus in the case of the important Hôtel-Dieu Saint-Eloi in Montpellier in 1668, the standard clause had to be modified to read, instead of daily, 'every time circumstances require it'. In Clermont in 1672 the sisters were only to ensure that the medical staff 'do their duty'; while the medical staff at the tiny hospital of Bannost in 1692 were only to visit the inmates 'often'. Furthermore, not all hospitals had a doctor, surgeon, and apothecary on their paid staff. The hospital in the city of Tarascon in 1699, for example, made payments only to a doctor. A great many institutions at this time seem not to have kept a surgeon and apothecary on an annual retainer, but rather preferred to pay individual surgeons or apothecaries on a piecework basis for visits made and drugs provided. Even an annual retainer, moreover, did not necessarily imply daily visits. The hospital at Sézanne in 1691, for example, set aside 50 *livres* each year for the local surgeons, 'who sometimes come to take bleedings and to dress some wounds'. The tendency for medical visits to be relatively well spaced out was even more pronounced in the case of those institutions which were Hôpitaux Généraux – the bulk of whose inmates were not strictly speaking ill in any case – and for those in small, out-of-the-way localities in which medical personnel, especially doctors, were few and far between. The phrase used in conjunction with the standard clause in relation to the hospital at Ham in 1716, for example, was 'if there is a doctor'; at Blangy in 1685, the reference was to 'the surgeon, or some other person if it is necessary'.[61]

Besides these deficiencies in the availability of medical care within the hospital, it should also be noted that the duties of doctors and surgeons did not merely involve the care of the sick. They were also there to look after ailing sisters, if need be. Moreover, one of their most important tasks was to vet entrants so as to ensure that individuals carrying diseases normally debarred from the hospital did not accidentally gain admittance. Thus, for example, the contract with the Hôpital Saint-Laurent in Langres stated that the *soeur servante*

> will have the sick who present themselves to be admitted visited by the doctor or the surgeons to see that they do not have a contagious illness.

No mention was made of any other responsibilities of the medical staff. This case was, moreover, probably far from untypical.

It is significant that, to a certain extent at least, the presence in a hospital of a community of Daughters of Charity was felt to obviate the need for the full panoply of medical personnel. This was certainly the case at Pau in 1689, for example, where the administrative board of the hospital recorded that:

> as the said Daughters of Charity know how to make bleedings, to shave and to apply dry leeches and even to scarify and to perform other functions of surgery, this renders the surgeons of the hospital redundant.[62]

The arrival of the sisters did in fact lead to the dismissal of the hospital's surgeons. Developments at Alençon, also in the late seventeenth century, are similarly instructive in this sphere. By the original contract of August 1676, doctor, surgeon, and apothecary were to visit the hospital on a daily basis. However, in the *Règlement* which was drawn up later that year it was observed

> that having decided that there should be made at our expense an apothecary shop, which the said sisters would direct . . . seeing that by this means a considerable saving will be made, it is not at all absolutely necessary that the said decision be executed rigorously; all the more in that the administrators visiting the sick each one in their week in turn will see if it is necessary that the doctors come more or less often.

The existence of a hospital pharmacy run by the Daughters of Charity seems thus to have signally reduced the need for assiduous attendance by medical personnel. How had the pharmaceutical interest of the Daughters of Charity developed? In fact, in the very earliest days, Vincent de Paul and Louise de Marillac had encouraged the Daughters of Charity to provide drugs and medicines and even to administer 'bleedings'.[63] The contract with the hospital at La Fère in the 1660s had referred to the sisters administering bleedings.[64] In general, however, it was the sisters attached to the *charités* who were expected to do most in this respect. The Daughters of Charity in the service of the confraternity of Ladies of Charity at Montluçon in 1667 were urged to administer bleedings and to compose 'syrups, decoctions and tisanes' and other drugs 'following exactly the prescriptions of the doctors, if there are any, as regards their composition'.[65] This became the basis of a standard clause which passed into 85 per cent of all *charités* and institutions for administering home relief. The development of such a clause in hospital contracts was, however, rather slower. It was there, in somewhat embryonic form, in the Lublé hospital contract in 1679, but down to the end of the seventeenth century appeared only very patchily. After about 1710, however, it became relatively standard, appearing in ten out of fourteen hospital contracts in the 1710s, five out of six in the 1720s, then, following a rather barren patch down to mid-century, in four-fifths of contracts passed from 1750 to 1790.

Although a contract clause relating to the provision of a pharmacy was thus rather slow to develop, in fact it is clear that long before 1700 the Daughters of Charity were manifesting a keen interest in the matter. Two sisters had been set up in an *apothiquairerie* in the Hôtel-Dieu of Angers at the request of the hospital's administration, as early as 1668. By 1673 the community was offering to set up a similar institution in the well-established hospital at Nantes. In 1676 it was the turn of the new establishment at Alençon. It seems that the practice of setting up hospital pharmacies, quite independently of the provisions of the establishment contract was already far advanced by the turn of the century. In regard to the hospital at Rethel in 1704, for example, it was confidently stated that

> the apothecary's service will be performed by the said sisters as they are accustomed to do wherever they are established.[66]

An increasing number of contracts came to refer to the Daughters of Charity actually establishing a pharmacy in the hospital in question, and not merely taking over the running of an established hospital pharmacy. In the contract with the hospital of Coulommiers in 1712, for example, it was stated that

> they will practice pharmacy after . . . the said Messrs. administrators establish an apothecary shop and buy the necessary instruments, drugs, and remedies.[67]

In some places at least, the hospital pharmacy became the basis of a dispensary supplying drugs and medicines to the poor of the surrounding countryside, and aiding, with the profits thereby accruing, the hospital's finances.[68] The generalization of the practice of pharmacy in the Daughters of Charity's establishments is seen too in the common practice, from the late seventeenth century onwards, of sending out sisters to a new establishment equipped with a copy of Madame Fouquet's notorious folkloric compilation of remedies, the *Recueil de remèdes charitables*.[69]

There is a clear correlation between the increase in references in hospital contracts in the late seventeenth and early eighteenth centuries to the sisters' pharmaceutical services, and the decline in the use of the clause concerning daily visits from doctor, surgeon, and apothecary. The latter formula was much less utilized in the early years of the eighteenth century, and after 1730 it died out altogether. This seems to indicate that the Daughters of Charity assumed an increased share of responsibility for medical services within the hospital in which they worked. As far as it is possible to judge from the archives of the Daughters of Charity which have survived in the Archives Nationales, the resultant state of affairs did not cause any anxiety on the part of either doctors or hospital administrators. Indeed, both seemed to accept the important medical role which the sisters had assumed.

As the eighteenth century wore on, and as the Revolution approached, however, large numbers of the medical profession became more interested in bedside observation and examination of the sick.[70] There ensued in some localities a certain amount of tension between the sisters on one hand and, on the other, doctors and surgeons anxious to gain greater and freer access to the sick to be found in the hospitals. In some places, tension crystallized over the role of apprentice-surgeons whom clinically minded doctors wished to promote above the sisters in the hospital hierarchy.[71] Elsewhere, it was a question of sisters allegedly not carrying out the strict prescriptions of the doctors regarding treatment.[72] Dissection of corpses was a further cause of conflict in some places.[73] The question of hospital food was also a contentious issue, with the doctors, in the name of a slowly emerging medical dietetics, finding the provision of food by the sisters far too copious and thereby deleterious to the health of inmates.[74] Also at issue in a number of hospitals was the question of control of the hospital pharmacy, which doctors now claimed should be within their rights.[75] A clash in the infirmary of the Hôtel des Invalides in 1772 saw the sisters, who had run the pharmacy here since 1673, protesting to the minister that to submit their pharmacy to the inspection of the Invalides' medical staff was tantamount to casting a slur on the good name of the community. This would, they argued, threaten the autonomy and even the existence of the pharmacies which they maintained in their other establishments throughout the country.[76] On this occasion, their resistance prevailed. But they had learned from their experience. From this time onwards, a slight rewording in the terms of their establishment contracts meant that hospital administrators now had to agree that 'they alone will have the care of the pharmacie, without anyone in the future under any pretext whatever taking it away from them'. This did not, however, put an end to disputes, which bubbled on down to the Revolution.[77]

Opposition to the clinical intentions of the medical profession could easily be presented as sheer obscurantism on the part of the community. In fact, though there is an element of truth in this, it seems indisputable that the sisters were acting in what they perceived to be the best interests of the hospital inmates. And perhaps they were not entirely incorrect in suspecting the doctors of being more interested in the advances of medical science than in the fate of the hospital inmate. The interest of the doctors in the hospitals was, after all, relatively recent; while by 1789 the Daughters of Charity could look back over a century and a half of commitment to the nursing of the sick. The strength of their dedication to the cause of the sick poor in the hospitals was, however, to be rudely tested by the events of the Revolution.

VI

The main threads of the evolution of the central organization of the Daughters of Charity in the Revolutionary decade are fairly well known: the uneasy compromise with the revolutionary authorities in the early years; the dissolution of the order, and the closing down of the mother-house at bayonet-point in 1792; the slow beginnings of the regrouping of the community under the Directory; and finally in 1801, the permission accorded *Soeur* Antoinette Deleau, *Supérieure,* by Chaptal, the Minister of the Interior, to resume the full life of the community.[78] Much has been written of the trials of this period, and in particular, of the fate of the handful of sisters who ended their lives under the guillotine during the Terror.[79] Yet much still remains unknown or uncertain. How did the majority of sisters fare during the revolutionary decade? How serious was the damage done by the revolutionary hiatus?[80] And – the question which will concern us here – how did the Revolution affect the nature of the service which the sisters provided within the hospitals?

From the start, the Ministry of the Interior maintained that the return of the hospital sisters – both the Daughters of Charity and other bodies like them, which were also reconstituted with governmental approval under the Consulate and the First Empire – was motivated purely by the wish to improve the quality of the care available to hospital inmates. It followed, as the minister was to argue in 1802, that their services were to be

> restricted to the care that the service of the sick requires. They may not therefore become involved in any way in what constitutes the administrative part and even less the medical part of the service.[81]

The full implementation of such an injunction would have marked a real and important break in the nature of the service which the Daughters of Charity had long been providing. In both the medical and the administrative spheres, however, the wish of the minister was to remain unfulfilled. The sisters, it is true, showed themselves more willing than before to work with a medical profession whose claims to genuine concern and compassion for the sick seemed – as a consequence of their involvement in the health services of the Revolutionary and Napoleonic era – less pretentious and more well founded than under the Ancien Régime.[82] Disputes between doctors and surgeons on the one hand, and nurses on the other still continued to occur, however, as proof of the persistence of rivalry between them.[83] And well into the middle of the nineteenth century, the sisters continued to run the pharmacy of nearly all hospitals in which they served; indeed nearly half of all French hospitals contained a pharmacy run solely by hospital sisters.[84]

If there was thus a fair degree of continuity at the level of the sisters' involvement in the medical sphere, much the same could be said of administrative matters. This is particularly clear in the contracts which the community signed in the early nineteenth century with hospital administrations. Although it has been possible to locate only a relatively small number of such contracts, it seems quite clear that there is a striking similarity to Ancien Régime contracts.[85] The amount of money awarded annually to each sister had increased relatively sharply from 150 *livres* in 1790 to 200 *livres* for the first decades of the nineteenth century – an increase which probably reflected the strong bargaining position which the community now found itself in.[86] In all other essentials, however – lodgings, provisions, relationships with servants, supervision of accounts, care in illness and infirmity, travel costs for replacements, burial arrangements, etc. – the nineteenth-century contracts reproduced – almost verbatim in some cases, though with a modernization of language in others – the standard clauses of the traditional contracts. Furthermore, it appears that in a great many hospitals it was accepted that the terms of the Ancien Régime contracts should still apply. Government inquiries in the 1820s and 1830s revealed a host of hospitals throughout France where Daughters of Charity served under the provisions of contracts which went way back into the eighteenth and even into the seventeenth century.[87]

Government legislation and ministerial circulars in the 1820s and 1830s did manage to change a number of aspects of the administrative services which the Daughters of Charity had traditionally provided. The power of the *soeur servante* to appoint and dismiss subordinate staff was curtailed, and authority for such matters placed unequivocally in the hands of the hospital commissions.[88] Accounting procedures were streamlined too, and brought more closely under secular authority. After 1830, moreover, hospital authorities were required to obtain the permission of the Minister of the Interior if they wished to increase the number of sisters attached to the hospital. Nevertheless, despite these changes, the core of the old contract continued to be maintained and, with it, the administrative functions of the Daughters of Charity persisted. This state of affairs, moreover, evidently met with the full approval of the Minister of the Interior. In a circular of 9 October 1839 it was stated that every congregation of nursing sisters was to draw up a ministerially approved contract with each hospital commission which they served; and that the contract whose provisions they were to follow was the model-contract of the Daughters of Charity. A concerted effort was made in the early 1840s, and then again in the 1860s to ensure that every hospital served by nursing sisters had a properly endorsed contract on these lines.[89]

In this way, provisions which had grown out of the advice and counsels of Vincent de Paul and Louise de Marillac, and which had been matured and refined under the influence of the Daughters of Charity's hospital experience under the Ancien Régime, came to be the yardstick for all hospital sisters throughout France in the middle of the nineteenth century.

Table 5.4: Location of Establishments of the Daughters of Charity under the Ancien Régime

Source	*Establishment*
S 6160	[All Parisian institutions] Localities: Abbeville – Ax (= Dax)
S 6161A Id.:	Bagnères – Bernay
S 6161B Id.:	Bessé-sur-Braye – Bléré
S 6162 Id.:	Boissy-sous-Saint-Yon – Buzançois
S 6163 Id.:	Caen – Charmont
S 6164 Id.:	Chartres – Choisy-le-Roi
S 6165 Id.:	Cholet – Cusset
S 6166 Id.:	Dammartin – Saint Flour
S 6167 Id.:	Fontainebleau – Guingamp
S 6168 Id.:	Ham – Saint-Julien
S 6169 Id.:	Langres – Lyon
S 6170 Id.:	Mailly – Montpaon
S 6171 Id.:	Montpellier – Mouzon
S 6172 Id.:	Nancy – Orthez
S 6173 Id.:	Pamiers – Puisieux
S 6174 Id.:	Saint Quentin – Rumilly
S 6175 Id.:	Sablé – Senlis
S 6176 Id.:	Serqueux – Surgères
S 6177 Id.:	Taden – Troyes
S 6178 Id.:	Ussel – Verviers
S 6179 Id.:	Vic – Waast
S 6180 Id.:	Yerres – Ivré-l'Evêque

Sources: Archives Nationales Series S 6160–80. See note 3.

Notes

1. For bibliographical guidance on the history of the Daughters of Charity, see Chapter 3, note 6.

2. For the general state of hospitals in the early seventeenth century, see Chapter 1.

3. A typed inventory of all materials relating to the Daughters of Charity – E. Lelong, 'Inventaire numérique et table alphabétique du fonds des Filles de la Charité du Faubourg Saint-Denis' (1891) – is available in the *Salle des Inventaires* at the Archives Nationales. The boxes containing the collection of contracts on which this chapter is based are classified from S 6160 to 6180. In order to reduce the number of note references to this single source, I have given in Table 5.4 a breakdown of the relevant boxes, whose contents are classified alphabetically by locality. A note reference will be given, however, in the case of localities which are out of alphabetical order. Note too that in the case of localities beginning with *Saint(e)*, the classification is not under 'S', but under the patronym.

4. A preliminary breakdown of contracts reveals the presence of contracts with 161 provincial hospitals, and with 4 Parisian hospitals. This chapter is based almost exclusively on the provincial institutions.

5. Examples of the contract are cited *in extenso* in C. Jones, 'The Filles de la Charité in hospitals (1633–circa 1838)', in *Vincent de Paul. Actes du colloque international d'études vincentiennes, Paris (1981)*, (Rome, 1983), an article on which the present chapter is based.

6. In this, the contract resembles certain other notarial acts which are susceptible to serial analysis. For wills, for example, see M. Vovelle, *Piété baroque et déchristianisation en Provence au XVIIIe. siècle. Les attitudes devant la mort d'après les clauses des testaments* (Paris, 1973).

7. P. Coste (ed.) *Saint Vincent de Paul. Correspondance, entretiens, documents* (14 vols, Paris, 1920–5) (henceforth = *VdeP*), I, pp. 363–4 (Liancourt); I, pp. 433, 611–12 (Saint-Germain-en-Laye); I, p. 434 (Montmorency); I, p. 508 (Richelieu).

8. The Duchesse de Liancourt, for example, was responsible for the establishment at Liancourt.

9. Branches of the Lazarists were instrumental in the creation of, among others, Richelieu (1638) and Montpellier (1668).

10. *VdeP*, VI, p. 68; X, pp. 224–8; XIII, p. 377.

11. Archives Nationales (henceforth = A.N.) S 6166.

12. The contracts allow a chronology and geography of the expansion of the community down to the Revolution to be delineated; this will be the subject of further studies.

13. On the community's rules, see Sister B. Delort, 'Du "Règlement" de Châtillon aux "Règles" des Filles de la Charité', in *Vincent de Paul. Actes du colloque international des études vincentiennes, Paris (1981)*, (Rome, 1983).

14. In particular, the secular status of the community required careful explanation to charitable administrators, who often tended to expect the Daughters of Charity to belong to a regular order.

15. Some of the phraseology of the early contracts was to be found,

virtually verbatim, in contracts right down to 1790: notably, for example, the references to sisters being treated 'like daughters of the house, and not as mercenaries'; and the wording relating to the sisters' monopoly of service within the hospital 'so that by the union and harmony which exists amongst them, the poor may be better served'.

16. There were, in addition, the *Avis* which Vincent de Paul gave to sisters leaving Paris for provincial institutions and which are collected in the *Correspondance.* With few examples (e.g. Angers), these are not found in the A.N. collection.

17. In the dossier on Angers (A.N. S 6160), there is a collection of *Règles particulières.* Their date and provenance is uncertain, though they seem clearly to be embryonic versions of the community's Rule.

18. A.N. S 6169.

19. For example, Cahors (1665), Melun (1666), Montpellier (1668), . . .

20. A.N. S 6166.

21. Later examples include Vannes (1682), Choisy (1685), . . .

22. This is made explicit, for example, in contracts and other materials relating to the establishments at Montpaon (1686), the Hôpital Saint-Nicholas in Metz (1687), the Hôtel-Dieu Saint-Eloi in Montpellier (1693); Loudun (1702), Fontenay-le-Comte (1702), Alès (1714), . . .

23. Cf. Montargis (1736).

24. The community's losses in the financial débâcle associated with the System of John Law in the early eighteenth century made its officials even more wary than hitherto of over-committing the community.

25. Good examples of the process of negotiation in the dossiers of Metz (1687), Tarascon (1699), Fontenay-le-Comte (1702, 1705), Rochefort (1741), Orange (1753), . . .

26. N. Gobillon, *La Vie de la vénérable Louise de Marillac, veuve de M. Le Gras, édition corrigée et augmentée par M. Collet* (Paris, 1682) *Appendice,* p. 351.

27. Other examples include Liancourt (foundation, 1636; contract, 1672) and the parish of Saint-Michel of Lyon (foundation, 1682; contract, 1713).

28. See for example correspondence relating to the institution at Varize (1780) and to the parish of Saint-Laurent in Paris (1784): A.N. LL 1665.

29. Cf. Fontenay-le-Comte (1705); Arras (1710); . . .

30. J.C. Martin du Theil, *La Doctrine hospitalière de Saint Vincent de Paul* (medical thesis, Paris, 1939) p. 107.

31. A greater reluctance to accept these new institutions was manifested in the reform endeavours of the Superior Jean Bonnet in the 1700s (A.N. L 1665). For the 1720s cf. the annulment of the contract with the hospital at Tarascon (1722); and the refusal to accept service in the hospital at Mende (A.D. Lozère: archives hospitalières de Mende H 944). For the 1740s cf. the annulments at Belesta (1741) and Liancourt (1743).

32. A.N. L 1054.

33. A.N. S 6179.

34. For the Hôpital Général movement, see p. 39 ff.

35. For example: Cahors (1675), Evreux (1711), . . .

36. See in particular materials relating to the establishments in the Hôpitaux Généraux of Narbonne and Amiens in 1695, and the eventually aborted contract for the Hôpital Général at Lyon in 1698.

37. See pp. 8–9.

38. For example: Pithiviers (1679), Pont-à-Mousson (1690), Aumale (1690), La Ferté-Gaucher (1697: = A.N. S 6166), . . .

39. Cf. Lublé (parish, 1679; hospital, 1683); Boulogne (1687–99), Ardres (1714–circa 1738), . . .

40. Pont-à-Mousson (1690), Aire (1696), Coulommiers (1712), Brienne (1731), Marly (1747), Beaumont (1751), Fronsac (1763), Chateauroux (1769), Coutances (1771), Castres (1776), Avallon (1785), Bagnères (1790), . . .

41. Cf. Alès (1714).

42. Cf. Petit-Saint-Quentin (1682: = A.N. S 6174), Libourne (1720), Nesle (1750), Orange (1753), . . .

43. See for example Commercy (1678), Montrevaux (1716), Gourdon (1725), Auneau (1726).

44. *VdeP*, passim.

45. Montluçon (1667), Chauny (1668), . . .

46. For example: Varennes (1699), Martel (1763), . . .

47. Trévoux (1686), Metz (1687).

48. Three years in the case of Trévoux (1686), Moutiers Saint-Jean (1706), Châtillon-sur-Sèvre (1750); five years in the aborted contract with the Lyon hospital (1698).

49. The articles agreed for the Angers hospital in 1640 went further: 'they will advise them of their shortcomings and will correct them by means of the grace of God'. This phrase was tacked on to the end of the clause in a number of the other early contracts.

50. Cf. Autun (1705), Senlis (1707), Pennautier (1708). Cf. also for the Hôtel-Dieu of Guise, from the 1750s, A.D. Aisne C 665.

51. In the contract with the hospital at Narbonne in 1696, for example, it was stated that the sisters could hire further labour if the number of inmates surpassed fifty.

52. Besides the material in the A.N., *VdeP* contains much reference to these disputes.

53. See in particular the correspondence relating to the Hôpital Saint-André of Bordeaux in 1705.

54. For example: Chauny (1668), . . . ; and *VdeP*, passim.

55. *VdeP*, VII, p. 51; XIII, pp. 649–50, 725, . . .

56. ibid., X, p. 683.

57. Cf. Tougin (A.N. S 6177).

58. *VdeP*, X, pp. 685–6.

59. Similar phraseology was used in regard to the hospital at Nantes in 1646, where reference was made to the 'physician apothecary . . . and also the surgeon'.

60. Cf. *VdeP*, X, pp. 685–6.

61. Cf. Taden (1715).

62. A.D. Pyrénées-Atlantiques: archives hospitalières de Pau E 52. Cf. Bazas (1700), La Réolle (1793: = A.N. S 6174), . . .

63. See for example the *Règles particulières* given to sisters in the early establishments; and cf., for Nantes, *VdeP*, V, p. 529.

64. A.N. S 6166.

65. Cf. Narbonne (1670).

66. A.N. S 6174 (dossier marked 'Mazarin').

67. Cf. Melun (1711), Rambervilliers (1711), Libourne (1720), . . .

68. See for example the case of Nesle, from the 1750s.

69. The earliest example of the use of this manual seems to be the new institution at Colombes in 1681. By the eighteenth century it had become a standard item in the baggage of sisters setting out for every new institution.

70. A brief but classic introduction to this topic in M. Foucault, *The Birth of the Clinic* (English translation, London, 1974).

71. See p. 19.

72. Cf. Marly (1760).

73. For the Montpellier Hôtel-Dieu, see P. Fournier, 'Observations qui ont regné dans l'Hôtel-Dieu de Montpellier pendant l'année 1763, suivi d'observations sur plusieurs maladies particulières', *Recueil d'observations de médecine des hôpitaux militaires* (i, 1766).

74. See ibid.; L.S. Greenbaum, 'Nurses and doctors in conflict: piety and medicine in the Paris Hôtel-Dieu on the eve of the Revolution', *Clio Medica* (1979); and R. Mandrou, 'Un problème de diététique à l'hôtel-dieu de Paris à la veille de la Révolution', *93e. Congrès National des Sociétés Savantes* (Paris, 1971).

75. For Montpellier, A.N. F 15 226; and for the Invalides in Paris, A.N. S 6160, and R. Massy, 'A l'apothicairerie de l'Hôtel Royal des Invalides: le conflit entre l'administration de l'Hôtel et les Filles de la Charité', *Revue d'histoire de la pharmacie* (1954).

76. A.N. S 6160.

77. Yeres (1775); and, for Montpellier (1785–6), see pp. 153–4.

78. Some interesting personalia in *Livre d'or des Filles de la Charité, ou Simple aperçu des plus belles notices des soeurs* (2 vols, Paris, 1938, 1948), esp. i, pp. 69–126.

79. See notably the work of L. Misermont, *Les Vénérables Filles de la Charité d'Arras, dernières victimes de Joseph Lebon à Cambrai* (Paris, 1914); and P. Coste, *Une Victime de la Révolution. Soeur Marguerite Rutan. Fille de la Charité* (Paris and Lille, 1908).

80. A. Dodin (*Dictionnaire d'histoire et de géographie ecclésiastiques*) suggests a fall from 430 institutions in France on the eve of the Revolution to 254 institutions in 1805. Cf. C. Jones, 'The politics and the personnel of social welfare from the Convention to the Consulate', in G. Lewis and C. Lucas (eds) *Beyond the Terror. Essays in French Regional and Social History, 1794–1815* (Cambridge, 1983) p. 80.

81. A.N. F 15 2563. Cf. for 1815 F 15 151.

82. Cf. P. Huard, *Sciences, médecine, pharmacie de la Révolution à l'Empire (1789–1815)* (Paris, 1979).

83. Cf. for Montpellier, A.N. F 15 1422; A.D.H.: archives de l'Hôtel-Dieu Saint-Eloi de Montpellier (postérieures à 1790) E 1; and archives

de l'Hôpital Général de Montpellier (postérieures à 1790) E 1.

84. *Situation administrative et financière des hôpitaux et hospices de l'Empire* (1869) i, p. xxxiii.

85. The following hospital contracts concerning the Daughters of Charity in the early nineteenth century were located in the series F 15 of the A.N.: Moulins (Year X – 1802: F 15 1540); Neuf-Brisasch (1820: F 15 192); Thiers (1829: F 15 192); Bayonne (1829: F 15 1544); Rennes/Saint-Méen (1831: F 15 1542) and Cusset (1839: F 15 193).

86. As early as ventôse Year V (March 1797), the wages of the sisters attached to the Miséricorde and the Hôtel-Dieu Saint-Eloi in Montpellier were recorded as being 200 *livres:* A.D.H.: archives de l'Hôpital Général de Montpellier (postérieures à 1790) E 1. This figure appears to have remained standard at least down to 1839.

87. See in particular the departmental series in the A.N., F 15 192 to 193 and F 15 1535 to 1546.

88. ibid.

89. For efforts in the 1860s to tighten up on the contractual obligations of the hospital sisters, see the departmental series in the A.N., F 15 3651 to 3781.

III

Charity, Repression, and Medicine

6
The Welfare of the French Foot-Soldier from Richelieu to Napoleon

I

Perhaps the most striking feature of the 'Military Revolution' which overtook armed forces from the late sixteenth century onwards was a startling increase in the size of armies.[1] The French army in the sixteenth century, for example, had rarely exceeded 50,000 men and indeed on the death of Henry IV in 1610 stood at fewer than 20,000, a level which was more or less maintained in the following decades. Once France had, in 1635, entered the Thirty Years War, however, the strength of the armed forces quadrupled to 80,000 men or more. This growth was to continue in the early decades of the reign of Louis XIV and for the last quarter of the seventeenth and for most of the eighteenth century the army contained a quarter of a million men and indeed, at the height of the war, occasionally approached the half-million mark.[2] In addition, the composition of the army altered: the mercenary forces of the sixteenth and early seventeenth centuries, many of whom were foreigners and most of whom were disbanded at the end of each summer's campaigning, gave way to a standing army, maintained on a permanent basis and manned largely by volunteers from within France, although never entirely, especially in time of war.

The sudden call for large numbers of volunteers caused Richelieu and his successors a problem of recruitment which was particularly acute also in that campaign losses through death, disease, and desertion could be drastically high.[3] One of the ways in which successive governments attempted to solve their manpower problem was by improving health services and welfare provision within the army, so that men would be less afraid of joining up and that, once recruited, they would remain under arms. This conservationist instinct of government was accentuated by long-term changes in military tactics – in particular by the growing predominance of the infantry over the cavalry and by the move towards battle-formations which demanded a high degree of training and discipline. The good soldier was to be, henceforth, the hardened man-of-war, inured to the rigours of military life, able to carry out orders as unflinchingly on the field of battle as in camp and – necessarily – physically capable of fighting. It thus behoved governments not to squander the lives of their men: quality and experience had the edge over numbers. As Richelieu put it:

> two thousand men leaving a hospital cured and in some sense broken into the profession were far more valuable than even six thousand new recruits.[4]

Moreover, a show of concern for the soldier's welfare bolstered morale as well as strengthening the effective force of the troops. Mazarin, Richelieu's successor in the King's counsels, stated:

> I believe that we must give priority to everything which is necessary for hospitals, for besides the fact that charity requires it, there is nothing which produces a better effect in armies than taking care of the sick and wounded.[5]

The increase in the size of the army under Richelieu's stewardship was thus accompanied by the beginnings of a positive and enduring royal commitment to military welfare policies. If the military hospital established by Henry IV in 1597 during the siege of Amiens is generally held to have been the first of its kind in the history of the French army,[6] it was very much an isolated venture before Richelieu stipulated in the Code Michau of 1629 that every regiment and every military fortress was to be equipped with an infirmary and a surgeon. Even if we regard the strength of government commitment in that dubious document as minimal, from the 1630s onwards there is evidence that regiments were hiring surgeons and spending money on medicines and drugs and that regimental infirmaries and temporary hospitals were being established during the campaigning season.[7]

Nevertheless, the extent of the implementation of the 1629 measures appears *in toto* to have been relatively slight, especially in the early years. It was one of the most critical paradoxes of the early seventeenth century that while the major concern of government was to tighten the fiscal screw on their populations so that they could build up the army, the army's history in the same period is most clearly characterized as one of chronic under-administration and decentralization.[8] The organizational underpinnings of the French army which Richelieu inherited were in any case skeletal and open to abuses: the sheer speed of the build-up forces, which left scant time for a tradition of military administration to develop, led to the continuation of these abuses, only now writ large. With the old system of requisitioning breaking down under the strain of numbers, for example, the government was obliged to have increasing recourse to private contractors to supply the army's food, transport, and equipment. As government checks over contractors were only minimal, these contracts were virtually licences to print money, and were eagerly bid for by cartels of state officials, noblemen, and private businessmen.[9] Profits at the state's expense could also be made by regimental and company commanders – the colonels and captains – on whom the government was obliged to rely for a multiplicity of ancillary services. Under the existing system of venal officership, military command was a speculative enterprise. Colonels purchased their commissions from the government – usually at high prices – and, in order to reimburse themselves, sold to the highest bidders most of the subordinate ranks within their regiment – the most important of which were the captaincies. In return, both colonels and captains were obliged to recruit the total strength of their units. Commanders who were seigneurs, and most were, would count on peasants from their estates, supplemented by individuals whom recruiting officers (*racoleurs*) had persuaded, by fair means or foul, to join up. The commanders received from the government a bounty for each recruit, as well as each man's wages, which they were entrusted with paying. From the wages, the commanders were permitted to deduct sums representing the costs of the food, equipment, and other services which they were also to provide. Given only very rudimentary governmental supervision over transactions between commanders and their men, this system allowed commanders to make two-way profits: they could swindle the government by recruiting and maintaining fewer troops than on paper and by economizing on the services they were supposed to provide for the men; on the other hand, they could also make savings at the expense of their men by withholding part or all of their bounties and wages and by charging excessively for those services which they did provide. Though doubtless many commanders gave consideration to the welfare of their men, the government's practice in the early seventeenth century of disbanding the newer regiments – which formed the majority – before their commanders had had sufficient time to amortize their investment, gave an added incentive to the hunt for profits and made paternalism and reckless financial self-sacrifice cruelly synonymous. In the fevered financial circumstances of the 1630s and 1640s it was foolhardy of a commander not to make money at every opportunity: welfare provision for the men was a luxury which could not be allowed to interfere with a satisfactory return on investment.[10]

The government's welfare policies were thus clearly hostage to the decentralized structure of the army. Fine words and legislative pronouncements were so many pious wishes. All seems to suggest that health provision within the army remained within its sixteenth-century mould. Wealthy officers had long made a habit of including a private barber-surgeon on their retinue when they went on campaign, whose services might be made available to the men – most probably at a fee.[11] Some aid might be forthcoming, alternatively, from the large numbers of camp-followers to be found in the train of most armies. Prostitutes – whom early-seventeenth-century military writers stated should be permitted to follow the troops at the ratio of four per hundred men – along with wives, children, and hangers-on were expected to justify their existence by acting as the army's menials, seamstresses, washerwomen, tobacconists, pedlars and, in time of disease or military action, as unpaid nurses. Finally, an ailing soldier might have recourse to a comrade who claimed some medical or therapeutic powers, or to civilian doctors and surgeons or the monks and quacks of the locality.

All things considered, the medical and sanitary infrastructure of the army could not inspire confidence. Health conditions appear to have been primitive in the extreme, especially in military camps, deaths in which always far exceeded deaths in battle. One early-seventeenth-century report stated

> A body of troops which camps cannot for long remain in the same place, without an extreme infection occurring as a consequence of the dirtiness of the soldiers, the horses which die there and the entrails of the beasts slaughtered.[12]

Disease was thus a frequent visitor to the camps of the army and there combined with the effects of exposure to climatic extremes and the hunger and even starvation to which the soldier was prey when, as so often, supplies or wages failed to materialize; as well as the flies, mosquitoes, bedbugs, fleas, and lice who were his most steadfast companions. Armies were in fact important vectors of infectious disease: most critically of plague,[13] most frequently perhaps of syphilis, as well as of typhus ('camp fever'), typhoid fever, and dysentery. Scurvy also caused its ravages – testimony to the poor diet of the troops – while pulmonary and respiratory diseases, skin disease, rheumatism, gout, hernias, and premature senility also took their toll,[14] to say nothing of mental disorientation associated with homesickness, which medical writers of the eighteenth century were to classify under the heading of 'nostalgia'.[15] Hospitals were likely to be of little avail in such a context of disease and lack of sanitation. Moreover, even when they were established, the sick appear to have been dumped unceremoniously into what were really only hastily converted churches or barns, with very little clothing, bedlinen, or dressings, and in often appalling sanitary conditions.[16]

It may seem surprising that France was able to build up the size of its army so successfully in the middle decades of the seventeenth century. Besides the above litany of misery and woe, chances of promotion appear to have been slim. Wages were not high and were invariably late or even non-existent: the government appears to have treated the soldiers' wages as a sort of luxury which they could afford to dispense with. Though the fact that civilian life too at this time could be stark and miserable and might offer fewer employment opportunities than the army – particularly a standing army – it would appear that the greatest incentive to recruitment was the opportunity for plunder which warfare offered.[17] Pillage – 'Mademoiselle Picorée'[18] – constituted, along with drunkenness and rape, 'the unofficial wages of war':[19] it was, in Richelieu's own words, 'an encouragement for the men to do better'.[20] Not only was plunder a right and a custom, but also it might often be an unavoidable necessity: Vauban could remember in his youth going three weeks on campaign without a single convoy of food supplies getting through to his detachment.[21] It constituted a field of private enterprise in which both men and, when they could take their minds of swindling the government and the troops, the officers too could engage. Captains and colonels traditionally took the largest share of any pooled booty and they, rather than the government, would pocket the sums with which villages and towns purchased exemption from plunder under the so-called 'contribution system'. The men were great plunderers too and indeed were encouraged to be so: for plunder had the simultaneous effect of harming the enemy and also maintaining French armies at his expense. So ingrained was the habit, however, that French as well as enemy territory was prey to the rapacious soldiery, particularly out of the campaigning season when disbanded troops might be instructed by their commanders to 'winter' in a district – in other words, to live off the land. There was a market in booty too: treasures, foodstuff, livestock, enemy equipment, even civilians and prisoners held to ransom, all was grist to the booty mill and, transmuted into cash, allowed the formation of private capital which, provided the soldier was provident and that he survived, could do something to compensate for the rigours of military life. The promise of plunder kept armies together, particularly during the long sieges with which the wars of the period were replete. It was, significantly, when the mirage of plunder had disappeared, that desertion rates were liable to rise: banditry in the hills, theft and petty crime in the towns might then seem to offer the soldier alternative forms of subsistence and enrichment in which he could deploy his martial arts in much the same way as under the royal banner.

II

The general and unthinking acceptance of virtually indiscriminate plunder in the early and mid-seventeenth century was a telling indication of the decentralization of the military machine which Richelieu had inherited.[22] Moreover, given the feebleness of supporting military institutions and the growth in the scale of warfare, it seems quite plausible that the spirit of plunder prospered as never before. As time wore on, however, the state came to combat the administrative decentralization on which the spirit of plunder was premissed. The process was a protracted one, and indeed was far from complete even in 1789. Nevertheless, by that time the state had greatly circumscribed the extent and the effects of decentralization by building up a powerful civilian administration controlling military affairs. There were two stages in this process, both sketched out in Richelieu's time, though developed extensively only after his death. First, the state interposed more rigorous and exacting supervision over different spheres of military administration. The War Department, under the dynamic and often brutal control of first Michel Le Tellier in the 1640s and 1650s and then down to 1691 of his son Louvois, savagely repressed anything which smacked of malversation of funds. Through the generalization and strengthening of the powers of high civilian officials appointed to the army (the *intendants des armées*) they gradually extended civilian control over almost every aspect of military life except fighting. A much closer eye was also kept on government contractors – 'those colossal cheats', in Richelieu's phrase. By Louvois's death in 1691 the administration was firmly in place, the abuses of the contractors were less glaring and, helped by a number of other important reforms, the anarchic, bloody-minded, and entrepreneurial army officer of Richelieu's day had given way to the altogether sleeker, better trained, and highly obedient officers of Louis XIV's last campaigns.[23]

The second aspect of the centralization of authority within the army was the extension of state control over areas of administration formerly in the hands of the captains, the colonels, and the contractors: not content with supervising the activities of its servants, in other words, the state set out to supplant or circumscribe them. This process, begun by Richelieu, carried on by Le Tellier and Louvois, made the most marked advances in the eighteenth century. Arms – previously charged for out of wages or on the accounts of commanders – after 1727 came to be provided gratis by the state.[24] They were consequently increasingly standardized. Uniforms, which had not existed strictly speaking before Louis XIV's personal rule, were now generalized at the state's expense.[25] In addition, rather than encourage the troops to plunder and forage for their subsistence, and rather than allow commanders to make private contracts for the provision of food and other supplies, the state now organized a proficiently run system of magazines from which supplies could be drawn.[26] The state took a larger part in recruitment too: indeed, with the plunder incentive being whittled away and with traditional seigneurial forms of recruitment proving increasingly unreliable, it was obliged to. In 1688 a conscript militia was formed, whose members could be drafted to the front when the wars were at their height.[27] In addition, the state periodically made administrative arrangements to facilitate the entry into the army of various sorts of social undesirables, such as beggars, vagrants, prisoners, and orphans.[28]

The motives behind the state's gradual assumption of close control over the army, and in particular the reduction of opportunities for plunder, were many and overlapping. Any state, and *a fortiori* an absolutist one, requires its orders to be obeyed and, so, to the extent that many of the reforms were simply the correction of abuses, there was an in-built bias towards centralization once the over-arching authority of the state was better established, as was the case from the personal reign of Louis XIV onwards. There was a political dimension to the problem too: the rebellions of the first half of the century, culminating in the Fronde, had revealed the dangers of the armed retinues of the king's over-mighty subjects. For governments increasingly receptive to mercantilist thinking, moreover, there was also an economic motive: if the fighting power of the state really did depend on its economic infrastructure, then the marauding and destruction of the military on home soil had to be stopped, the goose that laid the golden egg had to be protected. It could not escape the government's attention that, under the old scheme of things, the pockets of colonels, captains, and contractors were being lined at the direct expense of the state treasury. It was symbolic of the general direction of change that the 'contribution system' for the purchase of exemption from the effects of warfare was not done away with, but now tended to benefit the government rather than the generals. Governments were not against fleecing enemy populations, but wanted the fleecing performed rationally and economically and to their own benefit. Military thinkers from the late seventeenth century supported this view when they contended that indiscriminate pillaging, especially by the huge new armies, risked exhausting localities economically and turning the indigenous population against the invader. Purely military factors also counted for something in this: plunder had shown itself – most notoriously in the indiscipline of the troops in the invasion of the Palatinate in 1689 – as a solvent rather than as a cement within the war-machine. In a period where, above all, discipline on the field of battle seemed the passport to military success, pillaging was, though not yet a crime, certainly a blunder.[29]

As the restrictions upon private indulgence in plunder suggest, the period inaugurated in the late seventeenth century was to be one in which painstaking efforts were made to restrict the incidence and the effects of warfare on civilian populations, strengthening the state's control over its fighting men. This new concern was further exemplified in government attempts to solve the social problems of ex-soldiers. Since the twelfth century sovereigns had offered pensions and *oblates* to retired soldiers and this practice continued well into the seventeenth century.[30] Great strain was placed on the system, however, by the growth in the size of armies, and efforts were made from the late sixteenth century to increase it in some way. Large-scale projects devised by both Henri IV and Richelieu to establish a retreat for retired soldiers proved abortive, however, and it was not to be until 1670 that Louis XIV created the Hôtel des Invalides.[31]

If the establishment of an institution of this kind seems to fit neatly within a centuries-old tradition of royal grace and favour, this should not blind us to the fact that it was conceived primarily as a police operation. Demobilized soldiers, war veterans, and deserters proved potentially a greater threat to law and order in this era of mass armies than they had in the England of the Wars of the Roses or in the France of the Hundred Years' War or the Wars of Religion. The destitution which frequently faced the disbanded soldier who had been unable to cash in on the spoils of war drove him into the ranks of tax rioters and under the banners of the king's rebellious grandees. Disbanded troops were also a source of crime: indeed Richelieu's plans in the 1630s for a retreat on the lines of the Invalides had foundered precisely because it was feared that such a large community of desperadoes would certainly end by terrorizing the whole district round their new home.[32] After the disorders of the Fronde, however, and under the influence of a new vogue in social thinking in favour of the exclusion of alleged deviants from society within specialized institutions, the tide eventually turned. Just as, after 1656, the pauper and the vagrant could find themselves confined within the Hôpital Général, just as gypsies in 1682 and prostitutes in 1684 were also to be shut away, just as the children of Protestants were to be institutionalized in monasteries after 1685, so the retired soldier – able-bodied or disabled – would after 1674 find himself offered a place within the Invalides.[33]

While the Invalides served to insulate the retired soldier from civil society, the barracks came to perform a similar function in regard to the serving soldier. For most of the seventeenth century soldiers had lived in billets in the homes of the civilian population. This was a particularly convenient arrangement from the point of view of the state, in that billeting effectively represented a form of taxation in kind over which there seemed few problems of imposition; in addition, the billeted troops could act as a police force, ensuring law and order in turbulent or rebellious areas.[34] Significantly it was a government report in 1691 which claimed that the depredations wrought by billeted troops in the Maine and Orléanais were causing such economic destruction that the local population could not afford to pay their regular taxes, which led the government, ever responsive to its financial interests, to place the crack troops of the French army in barracks.[35] The movement towards barracks got under way over the next decades and was accelerated by a royal decree of 1719 which stipulated that barracks were to be constructed in towns on all major roads over which troops would be likely to travel. By 1742 over 300 towns had barracks, and if the movement was never wholly complete, by 1775 it was claimed that some 200,000 men were in barracks.[36] The process was eased by the reform in 1720 of the *maréchaussée*, the mounted and paramilitary police force, which made most of the army's policing duties obsolete.[37]

Tactical changes on the field of battle on the one hand, which placed a premium on training and experience, and the evolution of state policy in the direction of protecting the civilian population on the other, combined to make discipline a major priority of every European army. The barracks was a discipline-factory: at its most efficient, as with industrial production, greater concentration allowed a much higher degree of control, co-ordination and an inbuilt commitment to technical improvements;[38] at the very least, it helped to keep in check the desertion which afflicted every eighteenth-century army.[39] The enormous volume of military regulations which the state poured out indefatigably over the eighteenth century, which aimed to produce within the troops 'the perfections of the cloister',[40] made of military discipline not merely a way of life but even a mode of bodily comportment: the head was to be held high, the chest out, the moustache was to be trimmed and shaped, the pace brisk, and so on. The progress of discipline was testimony to the greater bureaucratic control over the military life of the soldier and also the degree of loyalty and obedience the state could now rely on from the officer corps which instilled these disciplinary values. It was a development which was generally popular with the civilian population. Where in the seventeenth century the very mention of troops passing was sufficient to provoke a rush for the protection of the woods or of the local château, with much locking up of wives and daughters, in the eighteenth century, in contrast, the civilians were more likely to turn up to cheer as the gallant soldiery marched by, with their bright uniforms, to the regular beat of the drum and the sound of military music. This greater acceptance of the soldier by civilian society owed much to the fact that, unlike the previous century, warfare in the eighteenth century was rarely waged on French soil. This, along with the barracks, the Invalides, and the imposition of discipline, distanced the army from society.

III

If, as a result of these changes, the army was much more professional than hitherto, and if it was less feared and hated by the civilian population, the soldiers themselves did not necessarily experience an improvement in their general living conditions. True, they were now safe from being swindled by their captains and colonels, while the very worst excesses of the contractors had also been checked and wages were now paid with greater exactitude and regularity. Nevertheless, all was far from rosy.[41] Inefficiency and corruption could still reappear in the contracting service, especially when the whole system was strained by war-time conditions. Moreover, if wages rose over the course of the century, prices rose faster.[42] With the higher echelons of command fiercely competed for by nobles and bourgeois, chances of promotion must still have remained slim. In addition, though more officers were found urging humane treatment for their men, the aura attaching to the Prussian army meant that the imported codes of discipline were spartan at best, draconian at worst.[43] Finally, the new restrictions on plunder severely reduced a component of the soldier's income which had allowed his seventeenth-century forebear a chance of emerging from his army days with money in his pocket. Denied the opportunity of engaging in the petty entrepreneurial activities of the appropriation and disposal of loot, and more completely dependent on his wages, the soldier was all the more likely to end his soldiering career destitute. The economy found it difficult to absorb ex-soldiers, especially after mass demobilizations, when up to 100,000 men could be suddenly thrown on to the labour market. It was symbolic of the problem for social order which the ex-soldier still caused that the main legislation against criminal vagrancy occurred in the years following the end of a major war: 1719 and 1720 (and later 1724), 1750, 1764.[44] Given these conditions, the state, influenced partly too by the vogue for philanthropy late in the century, increased its welfare provision for retiring soldiers: the Order of Saint Louis, established in 1693, provided pensions for valorous retired officers; the Invalides was expanded so that by the second half of the century its numbers had swollen to 30,000; and soldiers with very long terms of service were accorded a pension as of right from the 1760s.[45]

Besides plunder, another of military life's compensations which military regulations now frowned upon was sex. The camp-follower-cum-prostitute was an accepted part of the baggage train of every European army in the early seventeenth century. By the end of the century, however, in France as elsewhere, to use the clipped Germanic English of historian Fritz Redlich, 'we find everywhere a policy of restricting soldiers' copulations'.[46] A series of laws passed between 1684 and 1687, aimed apparently both to arrest the spread of syphilis among the troops and to make them more willing to risk death in battle by giving them less to live for, stipulated that any prostitute found within two leagues of a military camp was to have her nose and ears split. Military regulations at about the same time also actively discouraged the marriage of the troops.[47] More populationist governments towards the end of the eighteenth century slightly relaxed the constraints on marriage, and indeed even encouraged the enrolment of soldiers' children from the age of 6. Prostitution was still frowned on, however – by the authorities at least. If the laws of 1684 and 1687 were no longer executed in all their grisly detail, new regulations in 1768 stated that any prostitute found consorting with the troops should be either handed over to the civilian authorities for punishment or imprisoned. Finally, in 1781, any soldier who had caught venereal disease more than three times was obliged to spend an extra two years' service within the army.[48]

Evidence concerning the living conditions of the troops also suggests that greater state paternalism was far from synonymous with amelioration of the soldier's lot. If uniforms were now issued free of charge, it was widely acknowledged that they were more suited to the parade-ground than to the battlefield or the military camp. Moreover, in wartime, or under a niggardly commander they were often in short supply.[49] The old military diseases – bar plague – were still as prevalent as ever. Indeed, there is a strong case for maintaining that the trend towards barracks made the troops more susceptible to 'crowd diseases' such as typhus, typhoid fever, and dysentery. Certainly conditions in barracks could be most insanitary: the constructions were often jerry-built, and were insufficiently heated and ventilated; overcrowding was a problem too – even at the best of times the men slept two to a bed.[50] Life on campaign was still one of privation and misery too, as Marshal Saxe commented:

> Long hair is an unseemly appendage to a soldier. Once the rainy season has arrived, his head is seldom dry. . . . As for his feet, it is not to be doubted that his stockings, shoes and feet all rot together.[51]

Little wonder, given such living conditions, that the state was obliged to intervene to help recruitment, that 'nostalgia' was often rife, that desertion was frequent. Although there were attempts towards the end of the Ancien Régime positively to improve the lot of the soldier, whose human and moral qualities were increasingly appreciated, the comment of the military writer Guibert was eloquent: the misery of the poor soldier was 'the greatest of all vices of our present constitution'.[52]

IV

If neglect, maladministration, and financial shortages combined to make the eighteenth-century soldier's lot an unenviable one, it none the less remained true that governments retained a strong conservationist instinct towards their troops: trained and battle-hardened soldiers remained a much sought-after item of military hardware. As in the seventeenth century, this emerged also in copious welfare legislation: in 1708, 1709, 1716, 1717, 1718, 1719, 1729, 1747, 1772, 1774, 1777, 1780, 1781, and 1788 there were important welfare measures introduced, and there were many minor laws in addition.[53] As the preamble to the 1708 law stated:

> the important services that our troops render engage us to provide for their conservation and their relief when they fall sick or wounded.[54]

One of the main concerns of this military welfare legislation was the improvement in the network of military hospitals. Many frontier fortresses had come to possess their own infirmaries and hospitals in the latter decades of the seventeenth century.[55] In 1708 fifty royal military hospitals were established, and the number grew over the rest of the century. These military hospitals were complemented, in particular in the interior, by civilian hospitals which were reimbursed by the Ministry of War for the cost of each day spent by soldiers within them. Even civilian hospitals now had to conform to military health regulations, however: in return for their reimbursement, the hospitals were obliged to accept the periodic inspections of the Ministry's official inspectorate, and to implement various regulations concerning health and hygiene. In addition to these, specialized military hospitals were established: syphilitic hospitals at Montpellier[56] and Besançon, mineral water spas at Bourbonne, Barèges, Saint Armand, Balaruc, and elsewhere.

The government also displayed a wish to improve the quality of medical care within its military hospitals. The establishment of an inspectorate helped to standardize levels of care. From 1747 doctors in every military hospital were to provide annual anatomy courses, where aspiring military doctors and surgeons could learn their art at first hand. In 1775 clinical teaching methods were introduced in three hospitals, in Lille, Metz, and Strasbourg, followed by Brest and Toulon in 1782.[57] An emphasis on the medical aspects of hospital care was evinced too by the government's sponsorship of two medical newspapers bearing reports from the military hospitals: the short-lived *Recueil d'observations des hôpitaux militaires* in 1766 and 1767, and the *Journal de médecine, chirurgie et pharmacie militaires* from 1782.

Royal legislation did much to improve the quality of military medical personnel. In 1708 venal offices for military surgeons and doctors were created, and although the motive behind this law appears to have been largely financial – they were in fact abolished in 1716 – further legislation multiplied the numbers of doctors and surgeons attached to both regiments and hospitals. Their training within the hospitals was practically biassed, and was probably more medically orientated than the training that was available in most faculties of medicine or colleges of surgery, which normally found it hard to pierce the walls of the charitably inspired civilian hospitals.[58] The practical experience which service in the army provided, as well as the chance of benefiting from patronage within the royal administration, made these posts useful stepping-stones in the careers of ambitious medical men, and in particular, surgeons. In civilian life surgeons tended to be looked down upon by the doctors, but their practical skills made them if anything even more useful than doctors in the army. Many of the great names of eighteenth-century surgery – Lapeyronie not least[59] – had, like their sixteenth-century forebear Ambroise Paré, spent a period of service in the military medical services. The increased esteem in which military surgeons came to be held as the century advanced is evident in the fact that their salaries rose from 180 *livres* in 1718 to 500 *livres* in 1762 to 2,000 *livres* in 1788, at which time they were given parity in wages and prestige with military doctors.

Despite the growing sophistication of hospital and health services within the army over the eighteenth century, grave deficiencies continued to exist. Part of the increased prestige of doctors and surgeons derived from the fact that the state used them as stalking horses in its secular struggle to limit the abuses and corruption of government contractors: thus, after 1718, doctors were to report to the government's local agents (*commissaires des guerres*) any negligence or abuses on the part of the contractors.[60] Moreover, the state's perennial shortage of cash often led it into taking financial expedients which were not in the best interests of the health services. Thus, for example, the state sold the franchise for the treatment of venereal disease within military hospitals to an individual called Keyser, whose patented pills, besides causing some apparent cures, also produced, military doctors claimed, stomach pains, trembling, spasms, diarrhoea, and fevers of various kinds.[61] Cash shortages on the part of the state also reduced the potential effectiveness of the army's health services, particularly in time of war when, by the admission of one Minister of War, 'the administration of the hospitals is where disorder enters most easily'.[62]

The Marquis de Feuquières commented following the War of Austrian Succession:

> the roguery committed in the hospitals is unlimited. Greed for profit induces the entrepreneurs to act in a way outside all consideration of humanity,[63]

while the Comte de Clermont remarked during the Seven Years' War:

> the hospitals are in a state pitiable enough to touch the hardest heart. There exists within them a filth and stench which by themselves would cause the healthiest man to perish.[64]

Perhaps the best indictment of the military hospital system, however, was the emergence, late in the eighteenth century, of a strong movement urging their total suppression. One of the most crucial figures in this movement was Jean Colombier, sometime inspector of military hospitals and after 1780 the first Royal Inspector of (civilian) Hospitals and Prisons.[65] For Colombier, experience demonstrated that large hospitals, military and civilian, were disease- and death-traps, and that accustomed and affectionate surroundings – the regiment in the case of the soldier, the home and family in the case of the sick pauper – provided a more suitable environment for care and cure. Colombier's brand of social medicine which gave primacy to hygiene over purely medical considerations had its first success in 1788 when the vast majority of military hospitals were closed down, to be replaced with regimental infirmaries. It was testimony to the strength of the intellectual current which Colombier represented that the revolutionaries of 1789 were to follow his lead and to attempt to 'dehospitalize' society just as he had done the army.[66]

V

In the event, things were to turn out quite differently. If 'war revolutionized the Revolution', it certainly also reversed the general direction of government policy towards both civilian and military hospitals. Sheer lack of funds and the pressure of events severely limited the extent of the reorganization of the hospital system in the civilian sphere.[67] In the case of the army, the closure of military hospitals in 1788, and the closure of medical faculties and surgeons' colleges in 1793, left the troops desperately vulnerable to disease and wanton mortality once war had broken out. Under the pressure of circumstances, military hospitals began to proliferate throughout the country in 1792; and in 1794 three special medical schools were established at Paris, Montpellier, and Strasbourg, to give crash courses in medicine to students who were rushed off to the front. By 1795 there were literally hundreds of military hospitals in France and over 10,000 medical men on active service.[68]

The new wave of military welfare measures which were inaugurated from 1792 onwards owed much to the nature of the Revolution, the nature of the war, and the resultant change in the image of the soldier in the eyes of civil society. If the well-disciplined and trained professional soldier of the eighteenth-century Ancien Régime was no longer the semi-criminal desperado and pillager of the early seventeenth century, his isolation in barracks and the discipline he was obliged to endure showed that he was not accepted on equal terms within society, that he was at best a second-class citizen.

In 1792, however, the image of the soldier was transformed: he was now the super-patriot, the revolutionary *par excellence*, fighting courageously against tyranny at home and abroad. Formerly, with the standing army, the main function of welfare measures had been to conserve valuable military manpower. Now, to cater for the needs of the soldier-patriot and to reward him for his efforts was a first-ranking social and political priority. 'Rallier le peuple', in Robespierre's phrase,[69] meant not simply passing a battery of radical social legislation – the final abolition of feudalism, the Maximum, the Laws of Ventôse, the introduction of the *Grand Livre de Bienfaisance Nationale*, and the rest; it also meant a heavy investment of government time and attention into improving the living conditions of the massed hordes of the 'nation in arms'.

In the critical circumstances of the mobilization for war, military welfare became a popular enthusiasm as well as a governmental priority. The health and medical infrastructure which emerged behind the front-line armies testified to this, with welfare measures introduced not merely as a result of government decree but arising out of the varied initiatives of *représentants en mission*, of departmental, district, and municipal authorities, of local *sociétés populaires* or *comités de surveillance*. Behind the Army of the Eastern Pyrenees, for example,[70] a dense network of military hospitals developed, stretching way beyond Perpignan and Narbonne to Béziers and Montpellier. In a matter of months, sequestrated church property had been turned over and converted into makeshift hospitals, and the homes of suspects and *émigrés* ransacked to provide the necessary equipment to allow them to function properly – bed-frames, mattresses, linen, clothing, pots, and pans. By September 1794 there were over 4,000 hospital beds available for sick and wounded soldiers in the department of the Hérault alone – which was nearly three times the number of civilian and military hospital beds available in the area prior to 1789. The internal service was revolutionized too: local doctors were press-ganged into lending a hand; frequent inspections ensured that standards of hygiene were being kept up; workmen were requisitioned into making improvements to the buildings; efforts were made to segregate the convalescents; specialized hospitals were created too – some for soldiers suffering from the ever-recurrent scabies and other skin diseases, others for what the administrators of a military syphilis hospital in Montpellier grandiloquently called 'les enfants de Mars et de Vénus'(!) A host of other measures aimed to bring the soldiers' conditions into conformity with those of the civilian population as a whole or else to give them the priority to which it was thought that their heroic efforts gave them a right: the wealthier members of the community were forced to pay for the upkeep of the families of *défenseurs de la patrie* in those cases where government pensions were lacking; special local health committees were established to watch over hygiene and hospital conditions; the food rations of the hospitalized soldiers were improved; the men were to receive the same treatment as their officers; soldiers were not to be buried in sackcloth but in sturdy pinewood coffins; civilian transport was requisitioned to act as ambulances for the war-wounded. These earnest efforts to make the army's welfare a system fitting for an army of *braves républicains* were not always crowned with success. A government report in mid-1795 found the hospital network in the rear of the Army of the Eastern Pyrenees both irregular and improvised.[71] Certainly the makeshift and emergency nature of the whole operation played havoc with the good intentions of local patriots: many hospitals were over-crowded, the buildings humid and lacking in ventilation, the diseases insufficiently segregated, and epidemics – dysentery and typhus along with gangrene – swept through several hospitals, sending death-rates soaring.

This period of intense military welfare provision – which roughly corresponds to the most radical stages of the Revolution from 1792 to 1794 – was also marked by a rise in the prestige and influence enjoyed by military medical personnel. The zeal with which young doctors and surgeons answered the call-up in 1793 of all medical personnel between the ages of 18 and 40, and the devotion to duty which many of them displayed, won them numerous plaudits. A typical expression of their new-found position was the development by the military surgeon Larrey of the system of flying ambulances, which brought prompt aid on the field of battle to the wounded. Never had the star of the military doctors and surgeons stood higher: their numbers were larger than ever before; their ranks were given some sort of equivalence with fighting officers for the first time; their wages were high. By the middle of the 1790s all seemed set for the establishment of an autonomous medical corps within the army to continue the achievements of the period of the Terror.

VI

The 'golden age of military medicine'[72] was, however, to prove short-lived. As the Revolution moved to the Right after Thermidor, so the state commitment to military welfare policies – as indeed to far-ranging social welfare policies – faded away. Many doctors and surgeons were summarily dismissed in 1795 and although their numbers grew again with the campaigns of the late 1790s, a further and more brutal round of reductions occurred after 1800 at the hands of First Consul Napoleon Bonaparte. The number of medical personnel attached to the armies – doctors, surgeons, and pharmacists – fell by half between 1800 and 1802 and indeed reached the levels of 1800 only in 1809, by which time the size of the army had more than doubled.[73] Napoleon's motives in making these dismissals appear to have been largely financial: the steady subordination of doctors to the penny-pinching war-commissaries from the late 1790s showed where his priorities lay. In 1803 he closed down military teaching hospitals and reduced the number of military hospitals in France to a mere thirty – a measure which in practice placed an extremely heavy burden on civilian hospitals near to the war-zones. Finally, he refused to countenance requests from military doctors that their commissions should be permanent – thus denying them the security of tenure enjoyed by fighting officers – and that they should be formed into a properly constituted medical corps.

These reforms reduced not only the numbers but also the quality and the prestige of medical men attached to the armies, and standards of care suffered considerably thereby. The troops of Napoleon's armies often preferred to turn to those of their comrades who claimed some knowledge of healing rather than risk consulting military doctors and surgeons whose training, following the closing of the teaching hospitals, was often almost non-existent.[74] The *officier de santé* was now treated with contempt by officers and men, where in the early 1790s his advice had been listened to with respect. So skeletal was the medical infrastructure now, moreover, that Napoleon's men would often have to wait days lying wounded on the field of battle before aid was forthcoming; while their commander-in-chief was not averse to leaving the diseased and wounded to the often far from tender mercies of Spanish, Portuguese, Polish, German, or Russian doctors, as the army advanced.[75]

Napoleon did not neglect all military welfare measures. Indeed there was a sort of bureaucratic humanitarianism at which his government was very skilled: schemes for the vaccination of all troops against smallpox, for example, or the free distribution to needy veterans of herniary trusses or wooden legs.[76] Such measures also had publicity value – and Napoleon had a flair for publicity. The portraits of Napoleon riding over the battlefield to survey and salute the dead and the wounded, his visits to battlefield infirmaries, his apparent concern for his men's sufferings, his protection of the Invalides, the numerous bonuses, rewards, and *légions d'honneur* which he showered upon his troops, are far better known than the savage cuts he instituted in the army's medical services. Partly, it is true, Napoleon felt that hygiene and nourishment were more crucial to his troops' well-being than doctors or hospitals; 'good food and exercise', he claimed, 'are the best antidotes against illness'.[77] Nevertheless, the fact that for the pampered Imperial Guard he did organize a properly run battle surgery unit under the guidance of Surgeon General Larrey showed that he did not underestimate the positive value of medical care when it suited him.

It may appear at first sight somewhat surprising that Napoleon effectively neglected the welfare of his troops in these ways: after all, the armed forces had experienced in the 1790s a new 'quantum leap', comparable in scale with the one which France had experienced in the second and third quarters of the seventeenth century, when the size of the army had increased from less than 20,000 men to something approaching a quarter of a million. In the 1790s in the war of national defence, the size of the army leapt from a quarter of a million in 1789 to perhaps a million or more in 1794, most of whom were under arms.[78] Just as the mercenary army had been succeeded by the standing army, so this now made way for the 'nation in arms'. Increases in size of this order posed acute recruitment problems. Richelieu had boosted recruitment by giving the spirit of pillage and plunder its head and by legislating for the welfare of the troops along lines which his successors would amplify once a fairly centralized administration had been developed; this administration would set limits to the extent and incidence of plunder while still ensuring a steady flow of volunteers. The revolutionaries, in contrast, and then Napoleon, solved the recruitment problem in three main, interrelated ways.

First, the social legislation of the Revolution gave Frenchmen something to fight for and ensured that, for most of the time at least, a war to make safe these gains enjoyed a substantial degree of popularity. It was far from coincidental that the most radical social legislation of the revolutionary period had occurred under the Terror, when the build-up of military manpower was at its most critical phase. If many of the reforms of the period of the Terror were subsequently dismantled, to the very end there were important reforms – the abolition of feudalism, fiscal equality, the land settlement, the 'career open to the talents' (not least in the army), etc. – which were at stake in the war.

In 1798 the Jourdan Law introduced the principle of universal obligation for military service in France. The fact that conscription was accepted – it would never have been countenanced under Ancien Régime conditions – was testimony to the changed social and political context of the late 1790s. Conscription constituted the second main method by which France manned its armies. It was all the more crucial in that from the late 1790s there began to emerge a fact which the social and political radicalism of the Terror had temporarily obscured: namely that with the 'nation in arms', life on the battlefield was cheap. The sharp increase in the size of the armies in the 1790s had been accompanied – as had been the case with the 'Military Revolution' of the seventeenth century – by significant changes in the manner in which war was waged.[79] Whereas the strategy and tactics of the standing army of the seventeenth and eighteenth centuries had set a high premium on trained and disciplined troops, the French in the 1790s owed their successes to mass rather than cohesion, quantity rather than quality, numbers rather than experience. This superiority found its expression on the field of battle in the inability of the linear tactics of the Ancien Régime standing armies to withstand the massed column onslaught of the French forces. This change, taken together with the introduction of conscription, effectively brought to an end the theoretical commitment which the rulers of Ancien Régime France had displayed towards the conservation of their troops – a commitment manifested in their military welfare policies. If no sane commander threw the lives of his men away, manpower-preservation was no longer the military priority it once had been. Conscription made life cheap, and welfare policies dispensable. Napoleon could now boast that he could afford to 'spend' 30,000 men a month on the battlefield.[80]

The third factor which helps to explain the capacity of France to find sufficient manpower to fill out her armies was the revival of plunder. With large numbers of new recruits, and with the officer corps more than decimated by the emigration, it had been very soon proved impossible to maintain the high degree of discipline and restraint which the Ancien Régime soldier had displayed as an everyday virtue. This was all the more so in that the growth of the size of armies and the new warfare of high mobility which the revolutionary armies developed made it virtually impossible to ensure supplies through the old magazine system: necessity more than intention thus obliged a return to an atavistic 'living off the land' policy which harked back to before the 'Military Revolution' of the seventeenth century. Political radicalism had to some extent inhibited the full development of this trend: military regulations in 1793, for example, made indiscriminate looting an individual offence punishable by death. Nevertheless, with the attenuation of this radicalism after Thermidor, and with the armies of the late 1790s having to face terrible privations as a result of the insufficient build-up in military administration and the dispersal of the war zones, the way was soon open for a more complete return to the practices of plunder. The manner in which the generals of the Directory period were concentrating, under their leadership, armies more loyal to themselves than to the Republic, only accelerated the process.

Plunder was once again a military cement. When, with the build-up of military administration under the Empire, many of the pickings which the generals of the Directorial and Consular period had enjoyed came to an end – in particular the chances of making huge illicit profits from corruption in the government contracting services – Napoleon, who understood only too well the value of material rewards, rained pensions, honours, and power upon his trusted subordinates. The common soldier benefited too. If, under the 'contribution system', the state and the generals took the lion's share of the available plunder, this nevertheless allowed the soldier to be paid his wages and fed more regularly than ever before. The private pickings were not negligible either; the treasure-laden baggage-train of the Grand Army on leaving Moscow in 1812 bore eloquent testimony to that. The appeal of plunder reinforced and perhaps even outweighed the incentive which easier promotion constituted: if the legend has it that every foot-soldier carried a marshal's baton in his knapsack, he would surely also have reserved a little space as well for his choicest spoils. The soldier was also allowed, under the revolutionary and Napoleonic period, greater access to the other traditional object of his predatoriness: women. Camp-followers were now freely admitted, and were only periodically purged when their numbers threatened to bog down military administration.[81] The French soldier held that his sexual allure to the women of occupied territories was irresistible: and indeed the very high incidence of syphilis among the troops suggests that in fact it was. A French sergeant boasted:

> Making conquests: such is the character of the French soldier: *du combat à l'amour et de l'amour au combat.*[82]

Napoleon made of plunder not only a means and an end of warfare but also a primary article of governmental policy. At some time during the late 1790s the line between a war of national defence and a war of plunder, and then of conquest, had been crossed. If Napoleon's reign saw the attempted extension of direct or indirect control over the greater part of Europe, the preliminary act of conquest – from the sack of Rome in 1798 to the sack of Moscow in 1812 – was one of naked plunder. Plunder not only financed war and fed the troops, but also helped the régime become firmly established and popular in France. The army was, in Mathiez's phrase, 'a prosperous industry which did not suffer unemployment',[83] and one which by relieving pressure on jobs in France helped to keep unemployment there very low. The booty returning from the front, and the measures of political and economic control which Napoleon was able to enforce upon subject territories were also a tonic to French industry and agriculture: bread, like jobs, was plentiful, prices were not high, taxes were lower than pre-revolutionary levels.[84] In sum, Napoleonic France was truly a society geared for war and, like all such societies, stood a grave risk of self-ruination once the plunder frontier had been reached, and once plunder had to be converted more single-mindedly into political and economic exploitation. If these problems were clearly becoming insoluble in the latter years of Napoleon's reign, it is none the less true that for the most part, plunder oiled the wheels of Napoleon's state as efficiently as it ensured a plentiful supply of willing recruits for his army. Only when plunder faltered significantly would desertion reappear on a massive scale.

VII

From the point of view of the soldier who survived the Napoleonic Wars then – and this is of course a very false perspective in that nearly a million Frenchmen died in them – it would appear that, in the early nineteenth century as in the early seventeenth, plunder provided a more effective incentive to join up and to remain within the army than welfare services or career prospects. In what was still a pre-antiseptic, pre-anaesthetic and proto-scientific age, military hospitals, it is true, were unlikely to offer a sufficient guarantee against disease, let alone suffering or death: thus Larrey, Napoleon's Surgeon General, won his master's approval and the respect of the men by being first and foremost an amputationist, on the well-grounded assumption that one limb less was preferable to a prolonged convalescence in a military hospital.[85] Nevertheless, it must still be admitted that, by running down the military health services and by starving them of funds, Napoleon only added to their impotence and disarray. Military medical personnel, with one or two brilliant exceptions such as Larrey and Percy, would emerge from the Napoleonic period with a low reputation and would have to wait until the second half of the nineteenth century to be formed into an autonomous medical corps and their activities given some priority in military administration.

The renewed importance of the spoils of war in the Napoleonic period had partly offset the miseries of the military life and obscured Napoleon's neglect of welfare provision for his troops. It had brought about a perceived improvement in the prestige of the army within society as a whole and in the condition of the common soldier who had entrepreneurial flair enough to benefit from plunder and promotion – and sufficient luck to survive. The attraction of the gains to be had in Napoleon's armies highlighted the failure of the state centralization and centrally administered welfare policies of the Ancien Régime monarchy to make the soldier more than a second-class citizen. It was also to throw into dismal relief military life in the suffocating social atmosphere of France under the Restoration and July Monarchy. The heads of Stendhal's heroes, for example, were only too easily turned by the glory and advancement the capable soldier might win in Napoleon's armies: to Lucien Leuwen, for instance, there was something faintly obscene about an army which had seemingly abandoned aggressive international involvements for ignoble internal policing operations and 'the boredom and pettiness of a garrison'.[86] It was little wonder that an army, poorly paid, generally disparaged, and called on to wage 'a war of chamberpots and boiled potatoes', 'a war of cabbage-peelings against dirty workers dying of hunger', should nurture nostalgic memories of the Napoleonic period and thereby foster the emergent Napoleonic myth.[87]

Notes

1. M. Roberts, *The Military Revolution, 1560–1660* (Belfast, 1956); G. Parker, 'The "Military Revolution", 1560–1660 – a myth?', *Journal of Modern History* (1976) esp. p. 206; and, for the broader view, Parker, *The Military Revolution: Military Innovation and the Rise of the West, 1500–1800* (Cambridge, 1988).

2. I am grateful to Dr David Parrott for figures for the 1630s (personal communication); see too his Oxford D.Phil. thesis (1985), 'The administration of the French army during the ministry of Cardinal Richelieu', p. 142. The other figures seem to accord with the general consensus among recent syntheses on early modern warfare: see, for example, A. Corvisier, *Armies and Societies in Europe, 1494–1789* (Indiana, 1979); M. Howard, *War in European History* (Oxford, 1976); J. Childs, *Armies and Warfare in Europe, 1648–1789* (Manchester, 1982); J. Gooch, *Armies in Europe* (London, 1980); W.H. McNeill, *The Pursuit of Power: Technology, Armed Force and Society since AD 1000* (Chicago, Ill., 1982). Military welfare policies which are the subject of the present study receive in all these at best scant attention. Cf., though, Parker, *Military Revolution*, pp. 72–5; and the nicely illustrated J. Guillermaud (ed.) *Histoire de la Médecine aux armées. I. De l'Antiquité à la Révolution* (Paris, 1982).

3. G. d'Avenel, *Richelieu et la monarchie absolue* (4 vols, Paris, 1884–90) iii, p. 17. Cf. Richelieu, *Testament politique* (Paris, 1947 edn)

p. 478; Maurice de Saxe, *Rêveries, or Memoirs upon the Art of War* (English translation, London, 1757) p. 92.

4. Cited in A. Cabanès, *Chirurgiens et blessés à travers l'histoire: des origines à la Croix-Rouge* (Paris, 1912) p. 167n. Cf., for a similar quotation by Mazarin, J. Des Cilleuls, 'Le service de santé en campagne aux armées de l'Ancien Régime', *Revue historique de l'Armée* (henceforth = *Rev. hist. Armée*) (1950) p. 7.

5. Des Cilleuls, 'Le service de santé en campagne', p. 7.

6. J.J. Mayonade, *La 'Maison des blessés' de Longpré-les-Amiens (1597): premier hôpital d'armée en France* (Paris, 1953).

7. Archives de la Guerre, A1 24–32, passim, and Archives des affaires étrangères: mémoires et documents, 819, 826, 832, passim, for such hospitals, which were often staffed by the Brothers of Charity (references supplied by Dr David Parrott). Cf. Guillermaud, *La Médecine aux armées*, pp. 349–60; d'Avenel, *Richelieu*, iii, p. 148; Cabanès, *Chirurgiens et blessés*, p. 187; A. Babeau, *La Vie militaire sous l'Ancien Régime* (2 vols, 1889–90) p. 212; L. André, *Michel Le Tellier et l'organisation de l'armée monarchique* (Paris, 1906) pp. 473, 478 ff.

8. For military institutions generally in the early seventeenth century, see (in addition to the works cited in notes 2, 3, and 5) L. Susane, *Histoire de l'ancienne Infanterie française* (8 vols, Paris, 1849–53), especially Book I, chs 8 and 9; and G. Hanotaux and the duc de la Force, *Histoire du Cardinal Richelieu* (5 vols, Paris, 1932–44). X. Audouin, *Histoire de l'administration de la guerre* (4 vols, Paris, 1811) is still worth consulting. Among more recent work, D.C. Baxter, *Servants of the Sword: French Intendants of the Army, 1630–70* (Urbana and Chicago, Ill., 1976) is useful, but has been severely criticized on a number of particulars by Parrott, 'The administration of the French army'. For comparison with central Europe, see the outstanding work of F. Redlich, *The German Military Enterpriser and his Work-Force: A Study in European Social and Economic History* (2 vols, Wiesbaden, 1964).

9. The shady world of the state's financial transactions is brilliantly dissected in D. Dessert, *Argent, pouvoir et société au grand siècle* (Paris, 1984). See too J. Bergin, *Cardinal Richelieu: Power and the Pursuit of Wealth* (London, 1985).

10. D. Parrott, 'Strategy and tactics in the Thirty Years War: the "Military Revolution"', *Militärgeschichtliche Mitteilungen* (1985) p. 16.

11. For the situation in the sixteenth century, see the *Works* of Ambroise Paré (English translation, London, 1634) passim. Cf. Mayonade, *'Maison des blessés'*, p. 24 n. 2, and d'Avenel, *Richelieu*, iii, p. 148. For comparison with the Spanish army in the Netherlands in the late sixteenth and early seventeenth centuries, see G. Parker, *The Army of Flanders and the Spanish Road, 1567–1659: The Logistics of Spanish Victory and Defeat in the Low Countries' Wars* (Cambridge, 1972) p. 176.

12. D'Avenel, *Richelieu*, iii, p. 148.

13. J.N. Biraben, *Les Hommes et la peste en France et dans les pays européens et méditerranéens* (Paris, 1975) pp. 139–46.

14. For sanitary conditions, besides the general works cited above, see the writings in the eighteenth century of Jean Colombier, especially his *Médecine militaire, ou Traité des maladies tant internes*

qu'externes auxquelles les militaires sont exposés dans leurs positions de paix et de guerre (Paris, 1778).

15. M. Reinhard, 'Nostalgie et service militaire pendant la Révolution', *Annales historiques de la Révolution française* (1958).

16. Cabanès, *Chirurgiens et blessés*, pp. 187, 192 ff.

17. For much of what follows, see the classic work of F. Redlich, *De Praeda Militari: Looting and Booty, 1500–1815* (Wiesbaden, 1956), a work which has been freely pillaged (usually with acknowledgement) by most writers on the subject since. See too Parker, *Military Revolution*, pp. 58 ff.

18. *Encyclopédie*, xii (1765), article 'Picorée'.

19. G. Lewis, *Life in Revolutionary France* (London, 1972) p. 158.

20. D'Avenel, *Richelieu*, iii, p. 99.

21. C. Rousset, *Histoire de Louvois, et de son administration politique et militaire* (4 vols, Paris, 1862–3) p. 248.

22. M. Van Creveld, *Supplying War: Logistics from Wallenstein to Patton* (Cambridge, 1977) pp. 17 ff. For the wider perspective, cf. Baxter, *Servants of the Sword*; Parrott, 'The administration of the French army'; and R. Bonney, *Political Change in France under Richelieu and Mazarin, 1624–61* (Oxford, 1978).

23. See in particular Rousset, *Histoire de Louvois*, and A. Corvisier, *Louvois* (Paris, 1984) esp. pp. 331–43. For the poor quality of the officer corps during the Thirty Years War, see Parrott, 'Strategy and tactics', passim; and for the officer corps in the eighteenth century, see Babeau, *La Vie militaire;* E.G. Léonard, *L'Armée et ses problèmes au XVIIIe. siècle* (Paris, 1958); and the superb doctoral thesis of A. Corvisier, *L'Armée française de la fin du XVIIe. siècle au ministère de Choiseul: le soldat* (2 vols, Paris, 1964).

24. Susane, *L'ancienne Infanterie*, i, p. 240.

25. ibid., p. 242. Cf. Parker, *Military Revolution*, p. 71.

26. C. Rousset, *Histoire de Louvois*, especially vol. i, chapter 3; and Van Creveld, *Supplying War*, pp. 17 ff.

27. For the formation of the militia and its history down to the Revolution, see Corvisier, *L'Armée française*, esp. pp. 248 ff.

28. ibid., pp. 120 ff., 281 f.

29. Redlich, *De Praeda militari*, passim, for a shrewd discussion of these points.

30. M. Prévost, 'L'assistance aux invalides de guerre avant 1670', *Revue des questions historiques* (1914); R. Chaboche, 'Le clergé de France et l'assistance aux invalides de guerre au XVIIe. siècle', *97e. Congrès National des Sociétés Savantes (Nantes)* (1972) i, pp. 31–47; and A. Corvisier, 'Anciens soldats oblats, mortes-payes et mendiants dans la première moitié du XVIIe. siècle', ibid., pp. 7–29.

31. A. Solard, *Histoire de l'Hôtel royal des Invalides depuis sa fondation jusqu'à nos jours* (Paris, 1845).

32. D'Avenel, *Richelieu*, iii, p. 151.

33. For the general movement of social thinking in this period, see pp. 39–41. For gypsies, see M. de Vaux de Foletier, *Les Tsigannes dans l'ancienne France* (Paris, 1961); for prostitutes, see Chapter 7.

34. Most notably against tax rebels in the early seventeenth century,

and against Protestants in the infamous *dragonnades* which accompanied the Revocation of the Edict of Nantes in 1685.

35. M. Marion, *Dictionnaire des institutions de la France aux XVIIe. et XVIIIe. siècles* (Paris, 1923), article 'casernement'.

36. M. Foucault, *Discipline and Punish: The Birth of the Prison* (English translation, London, 1975) p. 142.

37. For the maréchaussée, see I. Cameron, *Crime and Repression in the Auvergne and the Guyenne, 1720–90* (Cambridge, 1981); Corvisier, *L'Armée française*, pp. 924 ff.; G. Larrieu, *Histoire de la gendarmerie* (Paris, 1933); and M. Le Clère, *Histoire de la police* (Paris, 1957).

38. Foucault, *Discipline and Punish*, pp. 143 ff. and passim for the progress of discipline in the army. Cf. for the factory, D. Landes, *The Unbound Prometheus: Technological Change and Industrial Development in Western Europe from 1750 to the Present* (Cambridge, 1969) pp. 121 f.

39. Corvisier, *L'Armée française*, pp. 693 ff.

40. Foucault, *Discipline and Punish*, p. 150 (citing Boussannelle).

41. This point, clear in Corvisier, *L'Armée française*, and Léonard, *L'Armée et ses problèmes*, is underlined by the recent treatment by J. Chagniot, *Paris et l'armée au XVIIIe. siècle: étude politique et sociale* (1985). For the soldier's lot generally in the eighteenth century, see these works, plus A. Corvisier, *Les Hommes, la guerre et la mort* (Paris, 1985) pp. 377–82; M. Spival, 'L'hygiène des troupes à la fin de l'Ancien Régime', *Dix-huitième siècle* (1977); S.F. Scott, *The Response of the Royal Army to the French Revolution: The Role and Development of the Line Army, 1787–93* (Oxford, 1978) pp. 39–40, 43; J.P. Goubert, *Malades et médecins en Bretagne, 1770–90* (Paris, 1974) pp. 197 f., 332, 337, 348–64; Babeau, *La Vie militaire;* Colombier, *Médecine militaire*; and the four volumes of the *Encyclopédie méthodique* (Paris, 1784–97) devoted to 'Art militaire'.

42. The problem of military living standards is, on present evidence, insoluble. Matters were made complicated by the fact that over the eighteenth century more goods and services were provided separate from wages; and that many soldiers appeared to have worked part-time in civilian occupations. Cf. Corvisier, *L'Armée française*, p. 828.

43. For the Prussian influence on discipline, see Susane, *L'ancienne Infanterie*, pp. 286–7; and J. Egret, *The French Pre-Revolution, 1787–9*, (Chicago, Ill. and London, 1977) pp. 50, 53.

44. For legislation against begging and vagrancy, the best guide is still C. Paultre, *De la Répression de la mendicité et du vagabondage en France sous l'Ancien Régime* (Paris, 1906). See too J. Depauw, 'Pauvres, pauvres mendiants, mendiants valides ou vagabonds? Les hésitations de la législation royale', *R.H.M.C.* (1974).

45. Corvisier, *L'Armée française*, p. 793.

46. Redlich, *The German Military Enterpriser*, p. 208.

47. Cf. Corvisier. *L'Armée française*, pp. 757 ff., 886 f. For sexual matters, see below pp. 242–3.

48. Marion, *Dictionnaire*, article 'hôpitaux militaires'.

49. Redlich, *The German Military Enterpriser*, p. 195; Cabanès, *Chirurgiens et blessés*, p. 280; A. Latreille, *L'Oeuvre militaire de la*

Révolution: l'armée et la nation à la fin de l'Ancien Régime. Les derniers ministres de la guerre de la monarchie (Paris, 1914) p. 222.

50. For life in barracks, *Encyclopédie méthodique*, article 'casernes'; Marion, *Dictionnaire*, article 'casernement'; Goubert, *Malades et médecins*, p. 66.

51. Cited in Redlich, *The German Military Enterpriser*, p. 226.

52. Cited in Egret, *The French Pre-Revolution*, p. 49.

53. For health legislation and medical personnel in the army during the eighteenth century, see principally the articles by A. Des Cilleuls in *Rev. hist. Armée*: 'Le service de santé en campagne aux armées de l'Ancient Régime' (1950); 'Les médecins aux armées de l'Ancien Régime' (1950); and 'Le service de santé à l'intérieur sous l'Ancien Régime' (1955). See also L.R.M. Brice and M. Bottet, *Le Corps de santé militaire en France: son évolution, ses campagnes, 1708–1882* (Paris, 1882); X. Audouin, *Histoire de l'administration de la guerre*, esp. vol. 3; Spivak, 'L'Hygiène des troupes'; Corvisier, *L'Armée française*, esp. pp. 655 ff.; Guillermaud, *La Médecine aux armées*, pp. 424 ff.; and Cabanès, *Chirurgiens et blessés*, esp. chs 14–23.

54. Cited in Cabanès, *Chirurgiens et blessés*, p. 195.

55. L. André, *Michel Le Tellier*, p. 484. Cf. S. Graux, H. Beylard, and Reboul, 'L'Hôpital des armées Scrive de Lille', *R. hist. Armée* (1972); Chagniot, *Paris et l'armée*, pp. 393, 579, 612, etc.

56. Cf. L. Dulieu, 'L'Hôpital royal et militaire de Montpellier', *Monspeliensis Hippocrates* (1966).

57. P. Huard, 'L'enseignement médico-chirurgical', in R. Taton (ed.) *Enseignement et diffusion des sciences en France au XVIIIe. siècle* (Paris, 1964). Cf. Guillermaud, *La Médecine aux armées*, pp. 455–6; J.C. White, 'Un exemple des réformes humanitaires dans la marine française: l'Hôpital maritime de Toulon (1782–7)', *Annales du Midi* (1977).

58. C. Jones, *Charity and 'Bienfaisance': The Treatment of the Poor in the Montpellier Region, 1740–1815* (Cambridge, 1982) esp. pp. 123–30.

59. Others include Tenon, de la Martinière, Ravaton. Cf. T. Gelfand, *Professionalizing Modern Medicine: Paris Surgeons and Medical Science and Institutions in the Eighteenth Century* (Greenwood, Conn., 1980) pp. 43–4.

60. Brice and Bottet, *Le Corps de santé militaire*, p. 5.

61. J. Colombier, *Médecine militaire*, p. 381. Cf. the dispute with the medical faculty of Montpellier over these pills in Archives départementales de l'Hérault (henceforth = A.D.H.) C 555.

62. Babeau, *La Vie militaire*, p. 218.

63. Cabanès, *Chirurgiens et blessés*, p. 256.

64. Marion, *Dictionnaire*, article 'hôpitaux militaires'. Cf. L. Kennett, *The French Armies in the Seven Years War: A Study in Military Organization and Administration* (Durham, NC, 1967) esp. pp. 131–3.

65. For Colombier's career, see P.L.M.J. Gallot-Lavallée, *Un Hygiéniste au XVIIIe. siècle. Jean Colombier* (medical thesis, Paris, 1913). On the civilian applications of military medicine, see Colombier, *Médecine militaire*, 'avertissement', p. v. For the anti-hospital bias of pre-Revolutionary social thought, see C. Bloch, *L'Assistance et l'état à la*

veille de la Révolution, 1750–1789 (Paris, 1908) pp. 154, 434; M. Foucault, *Birth of the Clinic* (London, 1973) pp. 16 f.; Jones, *Charity and 'Bienfaisance'*, pp. 131–3; and Guillermaud, *La Médecine aux armées*, pp. 471–3.

66. For the Constituent Assembly, see C. Bloch and A. Tuetey (eds) *Procès-verbaux et rapports du Comité de Mendicité de la Constituante (1790–1)* (Paris, 1911); and, for the decade as a whole, C. Jones, "Picking up the pieces: the politics and the personnel of social welfare from the Convention to the Consulate', in G. Lewis and C. Lucas (eds) *Beyond the Terror: Essays in French Regional and Social History, 1794–1815* (Cambridge, 1983) pp. 54–7.

67. J. Imbert, *Le Droit hospitalier de la Révolution et de l'Empire* (Paris, 1954) provides the best account of hospital policy in the 1790s.

68. For the medical changes inaugurated in the Revolutionary and Napoleonic periods, see P. Huard, *Sciences, médecine, pharmacie de la Révolution à l'Empire, 1789–1815* (Paris, 1970); Brice and Bottet, *Le Corps de santé militaire*, D.M. Vess, *Medical Revolution in France, 1789–96* (Gainesville, Fla, 1975); and D.B. Weiner, 'French doctors face the war, 1789–1815', in C.K. Warner (ed.) *From the Ancien Régime to the Popular Front: Essays in the History of Modern France in Honor of S.B. Clough* (New York and London, 1969).

69. For the soldier as super-patriot, see especially J.P. Bertaud, *La Révolution armée* (Paris, 1979) and S.F. Scott, *Response of the Royal Army*, passim; J. Lynn, *The Bayonets of the Republic: Motivation and Tactics in the Army of the French Revolution, 1791–4* (Chicago and Urbana, Ill., 1984) pp. 63 ff. For the impact of this change on another area of welfare legislation, see I. Woloch, *The French Veteran from the Revolution to the Restoration* (Chapel Hill, NC, 1979). The Jacobin strategy as regards radical social legislation is outlined in A. Soboul, 'Robespierre and the popular movement, 1793–4', *Past and Present* (1954) esp. p. 56.

70. Details from the following paragraph are drawn largely from the copious holdings in A.D.H., series L, relating to military welfare. Cf. Jones, *Charity and 'Bienfaisance'*, esp. pp. 172–4; and C. Alberge, 'Vie et mort des soldats de l'An II à l'hôpital de l'Egalité de Pézenas', *Etudes sur Pézenas et sa région* (1971).

71. Brice and Bottet, *Le Corps de santé militaire*, p. 79. Cf. the general remarks on military hospitals in Bertaud, *La Révolution armée*, pp. 249–51.

72. Weiner, 'French doctors face the war', p. 60.

73. Brice and Bottet, *Le Corps de santé militaire*, p. 171, for full statistics.

74. Huard, *Sciences, médecine, pharmacie*, p. 51.

75. Cabanès, *Chirurgiens et blessés*, chs 28–31.

76. A.D.H., Archives de l'Hôtel-Dieu Saint-Eloi de Montpellier (Archives postérieures à 1790), E 72.

77. Cited in Cabanès, *Chirurgiens et blessés*, p. 502.

78. For estimates, compare J. Godechot, *Les Institutions de la France sous la Révolution et l'Empire* (Paris, 1968) p. 362, with the more up-to-date Bertaud, *La Révolution armée*, p. 137.

79. Cf. G. Best, *War and Society* (London, 1982) pp. 82–92; Howard,

War in European History, pp. 79–80.

80. Cited by J.F.C. Fuller, *The Conduct of War, 1789–1961* (London, 1961) p. 35. Cf. Napoleon's arguably vainglorious remark to Metternich in 1813, 'a man like me troubles little about the lives of a million men', cited in I. Woloch, 'Napoleon and conscription: state power and civil society', *Past and Present* (1986) p. 101.

81. Cf. A. Forrest, *Society and Politics in Revolutionary Bordeaux* (Oxford, 1975) p. 184; and P. Wetzler, *War and Subsistence: The Sambre and Meuse Army in 1794* (New York, 1985) pp. 81, 155, 211.

82. Cited in Cabanès, *Chirurgiens et blessés*, p. 325.

83. Cited in M. Bouloiseau, *La République jacobine (1792–4)* (Paris, 1972) p. 170.

84. The most judicious reviews of the internal state of Napoleonic France are G. Lefebvre, *Napoleon* (English translation, London, 1969), and L. Bergeron, *France under Napoleon* (English translation, Princeton, NJ, 1981).

85. Cf. Brice and Bottet, *Le Corps de santé militaire*, p. 243; and Huard, *Sciences, médecine, pharmacie*, p. 59.

86. Stendhal, *Lucien Leuwen* (Geneva: Edition Cercle du Bibliophile, no date) I, p. 156.

87. ibid., I, p. 20; III, p. 73. Cf. D. Porch, *Army and Revolution: France, 1815–48* (1974).

7

The Montpellier Bon Pasteur and the Repression of Prostitution in the Ancien Régime

I

Sexual life was always much freer in the towns of Ancien Régime France than in the villages, but Montpellier was a particularly thriving centre of prostitution.[1] The city was in the process of becoming – with Toulouse – one of Languedoc's two capitals; it was a strategically crucial garrison town to the south of the turbulent Protestant Cévennes; it was a university city; it was a commercial and manufacturing centre; and it was situated on one of the major roads into Spain. The city's floating population was very large. Although the municipal officials claimed in 1745 that the inhabitants numbered some 24,835, the Intendant of Languedoc, the royal agent in the province, was convinced that the true figure was nearer 35,000, once soldiers, students, and other outsiders were taken into account.[2] The city always gave the impression, as one local worthy put it, of being full to the brim with 'strangers, adventurers and a great many riffraff'.[3] Assured as it was of more than its fair share of single and unaccompanied men – soldiers, students, servants, itinerant artisans, immigrant workers, travellers, vagrants, and beggars – Montpellier was a bachelor town, whose demographic climate ideally suited prostitution.[4] Not only was there a strong demand for sexual companionship, but also the supply of prostitutes was probably more plentiful than in most other similar cities. Montpellier prided itself upon being the premier medical city of provincial France and its numerous doctors, surgeons, apothecaries, students, and quacks made it a notoriously easy place in which to obtain treatment for the prostitute's blight, venereal disease. The city was to gain a reputation in the eighteenth century as a mecca for all the prostitutes of southern France.[5]

In the last two decades of the seventeenth century, prostitution, normally endemic within the city, was approaching epidemic proportions.

> Over the last few years [the municipal officials lamented in 1691], the number of girls and women leading a debauched and scandalous life has greatly increased and it continues to grow every day.[6]

The roots of this sudden increase in the scale of prostitution were evidently social. There had been an acute economic depression in the 1680s.[7] In addition, the period witnessed a concerted campaign, culminating in the Revocation of the Edict of Nantes in 1685, in which the degree of religious toleration which non-Catholics had enjoyed was completely eroded. The brutal attacks which Basville, the Intendant of Languedoc, launched on the numerous Protestant communities in the Cévennes flushed out a huge refugee population into the towns of Bas Languedoc. Montpellier's population grew dramatically by 10 per cent in the two years between the censuses of 1689 and 1691, and the city was crammed to overflowing with a rootless and drifting population which the slumbering urban economy was unable to absorb.[8] Matters were made worse by the fact that the Revocation had involved the systematic dismantling of the Protestant church's poor-relief institutions, which had formerly supplied assistance to the third of the city's population who were Protestants. Existing poor-relief institutions were overwhelmed by the scale of the social crisis and found themselves turning away from their doors droves of needy Catholics and newly converted Protestants.[9] They were quite incapable of concerning themselves with the repression of prostitution, a task which government legislation had assigned them in the 1680s.

The government measures of the 1680s, which were to remain the basis of legislation relating to prostitution down to the end of the Ancien Régime, comprised a three-pronged attack on female sexual deviancy. First, a series of laws between 1684 and 1687 attempted to eradicate the problem of prostitutes following the army.[10] These laws stated that any prostitute found within two leagues of either Versailles or any military camp was to have her nose and ears split. Although these barbaric laws do not appear to have been enforced for long in all their grisly detail, military authorities were henceforth permitted to take punitive action against camp-followers. New military regulations in 1768 confirmed this right and stipulated that any prostitute found consorting with the troops should either be handed over to the civilian authorities or else imprisoned under the orders of the Intendants.[11]

The second aspect of government measures in the 1680s was concerned with the honour of families. Two royal ordinances in 1684 aimed to preserve well-born families from the disgrace or dishonour which was felt to attach to reckless or immoral behaviour on the part of their children.[12] In practice, the errant child was often a prodigal daughter, an unfaithful wife, or an indulgent widow. Heads of families were now permitted to imprison their children for correctional training either – if they were rich enough – in convents, or else in Hôpitaux Généraux.

Hôpitaux Généraux had been created at royal request in most major towns and cities in France in the last half of the seventeenth century. Keystone of the government's reformulation of the nation's poor laws, they were not hospitals in the medical sense, but rather social institutions which aimed simultaneously at the relief of the poor and the repression of the crimes of poverty.[13] The diffusion of these institutions throughout France owed much to the unofficial and clandestine support given to the government by the ultra-secretive Company of the Holy Sacrament, the well-connected confraternity of laymen and clerics who sought a general reformation of manners and morals within the tradition of post-Tridentine spirituality. In the Hôpitaux Généraux the motley elements of the worlds of poverty and vice – paupers, beggars, vagrants, gypsies, lunatics, the aged, foundlings, orphans, and prostitutes – were subjected to a régime of intense religious indoctrination and were also, within their capacities, set to work. As a result of this general movement, from mid-century the public prostitute was becoming the object of more assiduous policing, and in particular was being threatened with forcible confinement. Another measure, again in 1684, went further. In the interests of public order and relief, separate buildings within the grounds of the Hôpitaux Généraux were to be specially reserved for the detention and correction of public prostitutes. This was the third aspect of the reformulation in government policy towards female sexual deviancy in the 1680s. Slightly modified in 1713, this law as to remain fundamental to the repression of public prostitution until the Revolution.[14]

There was no lack of support among Montpellier's ruling class for the confinement of social problem groups within special institutions on the lines advocated by the Company of the Holy Sacrament and generally accepted by the government. Religious orthodoxy here had received a great fillip in the anti-Protestant campaign which had accompanied the Revocation of the Edict of Nantes.[15] Religious militants from the wealthiest and most prestigious local families were among the architects of the establishment of an Hôpital Général in the city in 1678.[16] This institution was, however, too fully preoccupied with relieving the distress caused by the social crisis of the last two decades of the seventeenth century to contemplate assuming the responsibility for the repression of prostitution which the laws of the 1680s had assigned it.

The initiative behind the creation of institutions for the confinement of female sexual deviants was to come from the wives and daughters of the ruling class, many of whom were grouped into the highly exclusive *Dames de la Miséricorde* (Ladies of Mercy).[17] This lay association of hyper-devout and charitably minded women from the cream of local high society moulded their activities on the pattern set by Saint Vincent de Paul's *Dames de la Charité* (Ladies of Charity).[18] Since the 1650s the Miséricorde had been meeting together to concern themselves with a wide variety of social problems. Their initial aim, the provision of food and care for sick paupers, diversified in their enthusiasm to include charity schools, sewing classes, a dispensary, aid to prisoners in the town gaol, and subsidized funerals for paupers. Even before the laws of 1684, they had been instrumental in the establishment in Montpellier of a convent, the Refuge, for repentant prostitutes. After 1684 this came to serve as the institution where the city's middle-class parents, anxious to preserve the purity of the family name, sent their errant wives and daughters for correction under the provisions of the 1684 law on families.[19]

On 25 September 1691 the Miséricorde took the first step towards the imprisonment of Montpellier's public prostitutes. On that day it undertook, with the support of the municipality, to build within the grounds of the Hôpital Général, 'cells, commonly called galleys, for the confinement of girls and women of scandalous and notoriously debauched life'. The buildings were ready to receive their first inmates by the winter of 1692.[20] The worsening social and economic conditions of the 1690s and the continuing wave of public prostitution underlined the inadequacy of the eight places in the 'galleys'. In addition the new bishop after 1696, the austere Jansenist Colbert, stern moralist and the scourge of 'public sinners' and pregnant brides, seems to have placed his support behind the new institution.[21] On 30 April 1698 the municipality agreed to put 4,000 *livres* towards the purchase of a large house within the city walls which the Miséricorde was to prepare for immediate use as a reformatory for public prostitutes.[22] The institution was known henceforth as the 'Bon Pasteur' ('Good Shepherd').

Figure 7.1: Montpellier Bon Pasteur: Admissions, 1694–1793.

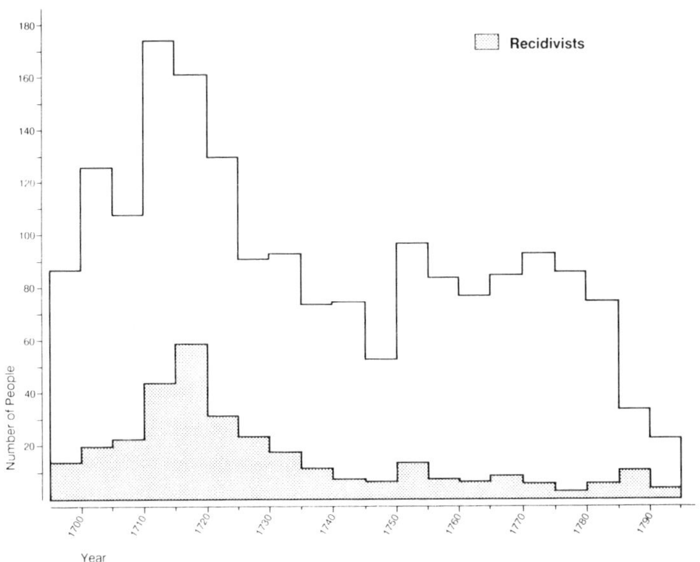

Montpellier's Bon Pasteur was to serve as the house of correction for the city's prostitutes until the Revolution.[23] At most times during the eighteenth century it contained between 40 and 45 inmates, and in all over 1,500 women passed through it (Figure 7.1). It was, however, to pass away, unappreciated and unlamented, in 1793. Its fall from grace and eventual disappearance reflect important changes in legal, religious, charitable, and sexual attitudes and practices in eighteenth century Montpellier and – it seems likely – in urban France as a whole.

II

Although the prime mover in the establishment of the Bon Pasteur was the Miséricorde, the new establishment received the full approbation and support of the local dynasties who dominated municipal government. During the 1690s municipal justice was reorganized and concentrated in the hands of a *Bureau de police*, which met twice weekly under the direction of the municipal officials, the *maire*, and *consuls*.[24] Most members of the *Bureau* were drawn from the major corporate bodies within the city, including the prestigious legal and administrative elite who sat in the *Cour des Aides* and *Présidial*, the wealthy tax officials who staffed the *Bureau des Finances*, and the great mercantile interests who dominated the local chamber of commerce, the *Bourse des Marchands*. Alongside these delegates sat a varying number of *bourgeois*, that is wealthy and untitled residents living off private income. The variegated membership of the *Bureau de police* constituted something approaching a microcosm of the legal, financial, and economic elites who composed the local ruling class. Their competence ranged beyond the repression of public prostitution to include matters as diverse as market regulation, wage-fixing, the standardization of weights and measures, street lighting, Sunday observance, the supervision of strangers and travellers, and much else besides.[25]

The very range of matters which the part-time members of the *Bureau de police* were expected to control meant that their efforts were bound to be superficial in many areas. This was all the more so in that they could count on a police force of only a score of *valets de ville* (town servants) to assist them in the policing of a city whose population grew during the eighteenth century from 20,000 to well over 30,000.[26] These *valets* were normally drawn from the Lyonnais, Dauphiné, and Savoy, areas far beyond the main recruiting-grounds of the indigenous population. They were in addition often of a similar social origin to the many beggars and vagrants with whom they were expected to deal. Their thankless task of enforcing the rarely popular measures of the *Bureau de police* was performed with neither skill nor conscientiousness, and the force's rate of turnover was high. Even municipal officials admitted that, to be at all effective, the *valets* would have to be 'better chosen, better turned out, less dirty, less contemptible and more suited to fulfil functions that at present they perform mechanically and without any intelligence'.[27] Although in the course of their duties – during evening patrols, for example, or in investigations into rowdy and disorderly lodging-houses – the *valets de ville* might well come across prostitutes plying their trade, it was by no means certain that arrest would ensue. First, they would have to face the resistance of by-standers. Beating up the town's police was a favourite popular recreation, which combined an elemental dislike of outsiders with hatred of class renegades.[28] Second, as their wages were low, the *valets* were notoriously easy to bribe.

It is not surprising, then, given the wide range of their activities and the inferior quality of the forces at their disposal, that the *Bureau de police* averaged only a half dozen or so cases of prostitution each year.[29] At least some of these, moreover, came to their attention by means other than their own police forces. Some lower-middle-class families who could not afford the fees charged by the Refuge might be compelled to request the *Bureau's* permission to have their deviant daughters shut away in the Bon Pasteur. Members of the *Bureau* themselves also acted on complaints concerning unruly sexual behaviour from neighbours, priests, and charitable persons. Particularly in the early years of the century, the *Bureau* also relied heavily upon the female members of the Miséricorde in the policing of morals.

The Miséricorde directed the Bon Pasteur until the Revolution. It appointed from among its most illustrious members a Mother (*mère*) of the Bon Pasteur who supervised the institution and usually had a seat on the board of the

Miséricorde itself.[30] The administrative skills these ladies exercised on the Bon Pasteur's behalf were most beneficial. Their high social status ensured it a constant income from private charity, which in the early years normally accounted for at least half of the institution's annual revenue. More important than this in the early years, however, was the constant stream of inmates whom the members of the Miséricorde supplied. Besides denouncing prostitutes to the *Bureau*, they were also themselves responsible, unofficially and often pre-emptively, for a large number of detentions. On their rounds to the poor and the sick, they kept their ears and eyes open for young women and girls in their neighbourhood of dubious reputation – women who had been seen walking out with soldiers and students, for example, or who seemed on the point of seduction by a boyfriend or employer.[31] They appear also to have run vigilante patrols, scouring the streets after dark and seizing wretched and harassed women out of the hands of carousing soldiers and lackeys, then carting them off to the Bon Pasteur. Once within the walls of the institution, these women would receive spiritual instruction, and Protestants who could be made to abjure their faith might be prepared for first communion. The charitable lady 'sponsoring' an inmate might also provide a dowry for the woman if a potential husband could be found. However repressive this policing of morals might appear, by the primacy it accorded confinement, by the link it posited between poverty and vice, and by its emphasis upon spiritual welfare, it clearly lay in the main-stream of Counter-Reformation thinking about charity. For the ladies of the Miséricorde, confinement in the Bon Pasteur was less a legal punishment than a favour bestowed upon a needy and corrupt pauper;[32] the spirit of charity dispensed it from following legal procedures. The preservation, defence, and rehabilitation of female honour must have struck a chord among both men and women from a ruling elite in which family and lineage – and therefore female fidelity – were absolute values. The *Bureau*, for its part, connived in 'charitable detentions', if only because the problem of prostitution was beyond a solution with the forces it had at its disposal. Although the foundation agreement accorded the *Bureau* a monopoly of detentions in the Bon Pasteur, in practice charitable detentions accounted for a large proportion of confinements in the early years. In the period from 1694 to 1729 the *Bureau* was responsible for the admission of only about half of those cases where the authorizing body is known. Ladies of the Miséricorde, acting either on their own authority, by soliciting the authorization of ecclesiastical personages, or by prevailing upon women to enter the Bon Pasteur voluntarily, were responsible for nearly as many admissions as the *Bureau* (Table 7.1).

Table 7.1: Admissions to the Montpellier Bon Pasteur: Authorizing Bodies and Individuals

	1694–1729		*1730–59*		*1760–93*		*Total*	
	No.	*%*	*No.*	*%*	*No.*	*%*	*No.*	*%*
1. Municipality and municipal authorities	325	37.1	255	53.4	188	39.8	768	42.1
2. Hôpital général	66	7.6	16	3.3	–	–	82	4.5
3. Ladies of Miséricorde and Bon Pasteur	106	12.1	8	1.7	–	–	114	6.2
4. Voluntary entries	23	2.6	13	2.7	1	0.2	37	2.0
5. Ecclesiastical authorities and personages	80	9.1	61	12.8	7	1.5	148	8.1
6. Intendant of Languedoc	12	1.4	–	–	15	3.2	27	1.5
7. Military authorities	13	1.5	18	3.8	142	30.0	173	9.5
8. Judicial authorities	5	0.6	3	0.6	21	4.4	29	1.6
9. Administrative orders	–	–	5	1.0	28	5.9	33	1.8
Total known cases	630	72.0	379	79.3	402	85.0	1,411	77.3
Unknown	245	28.0	99	20.7	71	15.0	415	22.7
Total	875	100.0	478	100.0	473	100.0	1,826	100.0

Source: *A.D.H. Fonds Bon Pasteur:* registers of admissions.
Note: The total of 1,826 orders authorizing admission concern 1,520 women.

It was only from the second quarter of the eighteenth century that the *Bureau* began to tighten its grip over the Bon Pasteur, and to attempt to exert its rightful monopoly over admissions.[33] Charitable detentions dwindled from at least one-quarter of total admissions at the turn of the century to less than 2 per cent in the last decades of the Ancien Régime (Table 7.1). This decline sprang partly from a reaction against arbitrary imprisonments: the government began to insist after about the 1740s on the proper observance of legal forms in the local policing of prostitutes and of those imprisoned for correctional training, and became more sparing even in its own use of administrative orders (*lettres de cachet*).[34] Although from the institution of the Bon Pasteur, the majority of its inmates had been notorious public prostitutes, the solicitude of anxious parents or zealous ladies of the Miséricorde had led to the entry of women who were guilty of little more than sexual peccadilloes, and who had not been legally convicted of offences against public morality. Such cases now became fewer, as a result of closer administrative supervision.

A further cause of the startling drop in the number of charitable detentions lay in an important change in the attitude of the ladies of the Miséricorde themselves. Even before the government and the municipality had begun to tighten up on admissions, the number of charitable detentions had fallen. By the 1720s and 1730s and increasingly as the century wore on, the old vigilante spirit of the Miséricorde was being lost. A greater degree of perfunctoriness now came to characterize members' self-assigned duties towards the poor and needy. At the turn of the century they had patrolled the streets hunting out prostitutes, they had supervised admissions in person, they had been frequent visitors of the prostitutes in the Bon Pasteur, the prisoners in the gaols, the poor in their homes. Now apparently anxious to widen the social distance between themselves and their charges, they increasingly entrusted the day-to-day running of their institutions to quasi-professional bodies brought in from outside Montpellier: the Daughters of Charity, *Filles de la Charité*, Saint Vincent de Paul's congregation of nursing sisters, were allowed to assume responsibility for the running of the Miséricorde, and similar 'charitable professionals' from other nursing orders came to take charge of the Bon Pasteur.[35]

The obligations of the ladies of the Miséricorde were shrinking from duties of service to duties of cash payment. Though the attachment of their prestigious names to the Bon Pasteur still attracted some charity to it, here too their contribution was in decline. Private charity was proving incapable of keeping pace with the rising institutional costs inevitable in an age of inflation.[36] Whereas at the turn of the century charity had accounted for over a half of annual revenue, in the decade 1779 to 1788 active charity made up only 3 per cent of total income (Table 7.2).[37] True, past legacies had helped build up the returns on investment (*rentes*) which comprised over a quarter of revenue; yet here too there was evidence of decline towards the end of the Ancien Régime. In

1740 and 1741 for example, of all those private individuals who made a will before a Montpellier notary, three had made benefactions to the Bon Pasteur, totalling 2,200 *livres*. In the years 1785 and 1786, however, not one such benefaction was made in any Montpellier will.[38]

Table 7.2: The Montpellier Bon Pasteur: Average Annual Income, 1779–88

	Livres	%
1. *Rentes* (= return on investment)	3,686	26.8
2. Fees and pensions for inmates	2,947	21.4
3. Work of inmates	6,020	43.7
4. Charity	488	3.5
5. Other	633	4.6
Total	13,774	100.0

Source: *A.D.H. Fonds Bon Pasteur:* account-books.

With charity increasingly unable to pay its way, the Bon Pasteur's administrators were obliged to look elsewhere for sources of revenue. By the 1780s wage labour in the textile trades brought in nearly half of the institution's annual income. Fees extracted from the Ministry of War in return for the detention of camp-followers under the provisions of the military regulations of 1768 were a further valuable source of income: such women were either interned on the orders of the military authorities or else transferred from the local *depôt de mendicité* (workhouse) on the orders of the Intendant.

III

The waning interest of the ladies of Montpellier's social elite in the city's prostitutes reflected changes in attitudes towards poverty and charity which the whole of France was experiencing.[39] Social conditions in the period after the 1730s were far removed from those at the turn of the century: economic depression and population stagnation had given way to industrial expansion, economic growth, and unprecedented population increase.[40] The intellectual climate had changed accordingly. The religious militants of the Counter-Reformation had been only too quick to see in the poverty and distress which threatened to engulf them signs of man's intrinsic viciousness. The 'enlightened' elites of eighteenth-century France, in contrast, were at once less theological and less pessimistic. For them, poverty was susceptible of amelioration in that it derived not from Original Sin but from deficient social and economic organization. The undifferentiated charity of the seventeenth century, with its emphasis on confinement as a means of providing both material assistance and spiritual and moral correction, was now rejected. It was increasingly thought that a proper distinction should be made between the honest poor who should receive relief, preferably in their homes and through the provision of work, and the criminal or wilfully idle poor who should be punished and, if possible, reformed.

An important shift in the role and the functioning of the Bon Pasteur mirrored these changes within Montpellier. The greater control of the municipality and the government over admissions and the decline in charitable detentions increasingly transformed the inmate population from an immoral set of individuals to a criminal group. So, too, religious concern for the salvation of the sinner gave way to a more temporal concern with the punishment and reform of the criminal. The prime aim of the institution changed from catering for the spiritual needs of the prostitute to punishing her and preparing her for reintegration within society.

This change was evident, first of all, in sentencing policy. At the turn of the century, the *Bureau de police* rarely set limits to the period of time prostitutes were to spend in the Bon Pasteur, and normally merely appended to the sentence a phrase such as 'at the discretion of the Bon Pasteur', or 'until she shows true signs of repentance'. The length of time the prostitute came to spend in the Bon Pasteur was not a function of the gravity of her offence in the world outside, but rather of the degree of her repentance once inside the Bon Pasteur. The procuress and the recidivist would probably spend no longer in the Bon Pasteur than the first offender – probably a matter of months in both cases (Table 7.3). More serious cases would be punished by combining confinement with some other penalty, often banishment or exemplary punishment (Table 7.4).[41] By the middle of the eighteenth century – and even more clearly by the last decade of the Ancien Régime – this pattern of punishment had completely changed. After the 1740s and

Table 7.3: Length of Detention in the Montpellier Bon Pasteur

	Less than 3 months	*3 months to 1 year*	*1 year to 5 years*	*Over 5 years*	*Unknown*	*% known*	*Total*
1695–99	28	22	35	–	–	100.0	85
1720–29	87	40	73	3	18	91.9	221
1735–44	22	26	80	7	14	90.6	149
1775–89	10	17	144	6	18	90.8	195

Source: *A.D.H. Fonds Bon Pasteur:* registers of admissions.
Note: Only those five-year periods where information is available for over 80 per cent of entrants are shown.

Table 7.4: Punishment of Prostitutes in Eighteenth-century Montpellier

	1700–9	*1750–9*	*1780–9*
1. Banishment from the city	16	9	61
1a. Combined punishment including banishment	11	1	–
2. Exemplary punishment	1	–	–
2a. Combined punishment including exemplary punishment	10	5	1
3. Confinement in the Bon Pasteur	27	36	30
3a. Combined punishment including confinement	11	5	1
4. Other forms of punishment	12	–	1
5. Unknown	6	3	5

Source: A.M.M. FF Reg.
Note: Between 1700 and 1709 the *Bureau de police* sentenced 72 women; between 1750 and 1759, 53; and between 1780 and 1789, 93.

1750s the Bureau gave time-limits to its sentence, and in years rather than months. The prostitute could expect to be detained between three and five years, the hardened recidivist and the procuress between five and ten years (Table 7.3). Getting out of the Bon Pasteur was thus no longer a question of repenting and promising to be a true Christian, but rather of having to pay in time and in the loss of freedom for the offence committed outside. Moreover, imprisonment, along with banishment, was the dominant form of punishment by the 1750s: the variety and the combinations of punishments characteristic of the turn of the century had disappeared (Table 7.4).

The internal organization of the Bon Pasteur changed over

the course of the century too. The life of the institution was still as immersed as ever in religion – the nuns who now ran it made sure of that. However, the values of the prison and the reformatory were coming to supplant those of the convent. In the early years spiritual concerns had completely outweighed temporal ones: the Miséricorde appears to have been more anxious to have a chapel built inside the Bon Pasteur, and to obtain the bishop's permission to employ a full-time chaplain to supervise the religious life of the inmates, than to concern itself with the proper provision of work, or even of the most elementary comforts.[42] The institution was run on a shoe-string, and the life was one of convent-like privations and shortages. After the 1740s, however – perhaps slightly earlier – the menial chores were taken out of the hands of the inmates and given over to the staff; the inmates were thereupon set to work in the textiles trade, working under contract for outside cotton, wool, and silk merchants.[43] Religious life now appeared to take second place to work: 'all the exercises of piety', remarked an advocate of the new régime, 'are performed while working'.[44] The emphasis was not on work as a means of subduing the flesh and assuring a deeply felt repentance, but of inuring the women to an industrial work-discipline, and of apprenticing them to a craft with which they could earn their living outside.

Crucial to the success of the enterprise was the awakening of a spirit of self-reliance and self-interest in the inmates by means of a system of incentives and deterrents. First, the women were given a material incentive to work hard in that they were allowed to retain a small fraction of the value of what they produced over and above a daily quota. Second, lax observation of the work-routine was deterred by the enforcement of a strict system of discipline. For the inmate who toed the line, life in the Bon Pasteur was no longer one of material privations. Within fairly Spartan limits, life was even comfortable. Medical care was now available for the ailing, the syphilitic, and the pregnant; food was very good, and the diet varied; their grey linen uniforms at least ensured that the women were warmly dressed; their sleeping conditions were probably unequalled among all institutionalized individuals in the city, for whereas the prisoners in the gaol had to make do with straw, and the poor and the dying in the adjacent hospital were often piled up more than three to a bed, each inmate in the Bon Pasteur had her own bed, mattress, two or three woollen blankets – and even a hot-water bottle![45] These comforts, however, were conditional upon good behaviour. The incentive to conform was all the stronger in that each inmate, on her entry, was subjected to a dose of house discipline. All the erstwhile prostitute's possessions were confiscated, her head shaven, her former clothes removed. For a fortnight she lived in solitary confinement in the dungeons, during which period her only human contact would be with the sister who brought her a daily ration of bread and water and who periodically chastised her with a whip. This rite of passage typified the terroristic discipline which the women could expect in the institution if they misbehaved or harked back to their former preoccupation: a combination of isolation, mortification, and loss of privileges. Disobedience and insubordination towards the staff were always punished by public whipping. If more than one person was involved, then a spell in the dungeons might be insisted upon as well: for feelings of solidarity among the inmates endangered the whole basis of the institution's appeal to the individual self-interest. 'Great care must be taken', the regulations insisted, 'to prevent the women from forming personal relationships between themselves'. This was of course why women were privileged to have a bed each: sleeping together not only would be sinful in itself, but also necessarily involved more than one person! Each inmate was to be as cut off from the others as she was from her own past. A rule of silence was invariably observed, and whispering was severely punished. To retain the full set of privileges, the inmate must be as pure in thought – day-dreaming was a punishable offence – as she was industrious in deed. All combined to give the former prostitute an incentive to work hard and to exercise a strong self-discipline.

If, as the *maire* of Montpellier was later to contend, the Bon Pasteur, had been 'originally a charitable institution (*maison de charité*) rather than a repressive one (*maison de force*)', this was increasingly less the case.[46] From the mid-century onwards, the Bon Pasteur was clearly pre-figuring the model prisons of the late eighteenth and nineteenth centuries.[47]

IV

What can be learnt of these prostitutes who over the course of the century paraded before the *Bureau de police* before being shut away in the Bon Pasteur, delivered up to public scorn or banished from the city? Who were they? Where did they come from? How was their profession organized? How did they come to enter it? What sort of career could they expect from it?[48]

The *Bureau de police* was convinced that the typical prostitute was an outsider, a stranger to the community. The calendar of their repression of prostitution reflected this fact, for they timed their major arrest months to occur when the city was most full of passers-through, during the Carnival in Spring, at the peak of the influx of seasonal immigrants in the summer, and preceding and following the meeting of the Estates of Languedoc during the winter. Moreover, police regulations pertaining to prostitutes were closely linked to the control of strangers and travellers in the city.[49] Landlords were forbidden to rent rooms to beggars, vagrants, or to prostitutes and other women of ill-repute, on pain of being fined, or having their beds and mattresses destroyed. Any person wishing to take up residence in the city had to present his or her credentials to the consuls. Servant girls – normally country girls working in the city prior to marriage – were subject to additional regulations: no one was permitted to rent a room to a woman who had been dismissed from service, and she was to return to her home village within a week. This battery of measures, largely inherited from the seventeenth century, was added to periodically throughout the eighteenth, as the *Bureau* strove to eradicate loose morals and prostitution by an even more thorough control over lodgings: after 1755, in particular, all landlords, inn-keepers, and hotel proprietors were obliged to make up daily lists of their overnight guests – in triplicate! – and send these lists to the *Bureau*, to the Intendant, and to the garrison commander.

The *Bureau de police*'s picture of the prostitute as an outsider is largely confirmed by statistical evidence relating to the origins of prostitutes. Of the 1,520 women who entered the Bon Pasteur between 1694 and 1793, the place of origin of nearly 70 per cent is known. About three-quarters of these originated outside the city, most of them coming from dioceses within a radius of about fifty miles of Montpellier. After the diocese of Montpellier, which provided 20 per cent of these outsiders, the biggest contingents were from the dioceses of the Bas Languedoc plain (Nîmes 7.4 per cent, Agde 5.8 per cent, Béziers 4.2 per cent) and the Cévennes and the foothills of the Massif Central (Alès just under 10 per cent, Lodève 5.8 per cent, Uzès 3.7 per cent) (Map 7.1).

Map 7.1: Women from Outside the City of Montpellier Admitted to the Hôtel-Dieu Saint-Eloi in the Eighteenth Century.

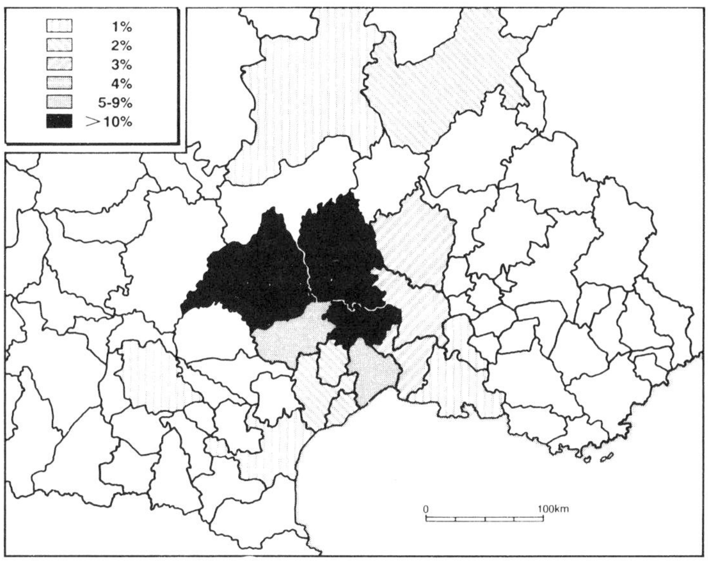

Of those dioceses beyond the 50 miles radius, only the great human reservoirs in the Massif Central, the Gévaudan (Mende 6.6 per cent) and the Rouergue (Rodez 5.3 per cent, Vabres 1.5 per cent) provided significant numbers. This was very much the pattern of all female immigration into the city, with the exception that the more urbanized dioceses of the coastal plain provided a rather higher proportion of prostitutes than of normal female immigrants (Map 7.2).[50] An urban pedigree may thus have denoted a somewhat easier virtue than a rural one.[51]

Whether they came from town or village, Montpellier's prostitutes came overwhelmingly from lowly social background. Of those who gave details of their family circumstances to the *Bureau*, about one-third were the daughters, widows, or wives of artisans, one-third of peasants, and one-third of other, mainly menial, social groups. Of

Map 7.2: Women Outside the City of Montpellier Admitted to the Bon Pasteur, 1694–1793.

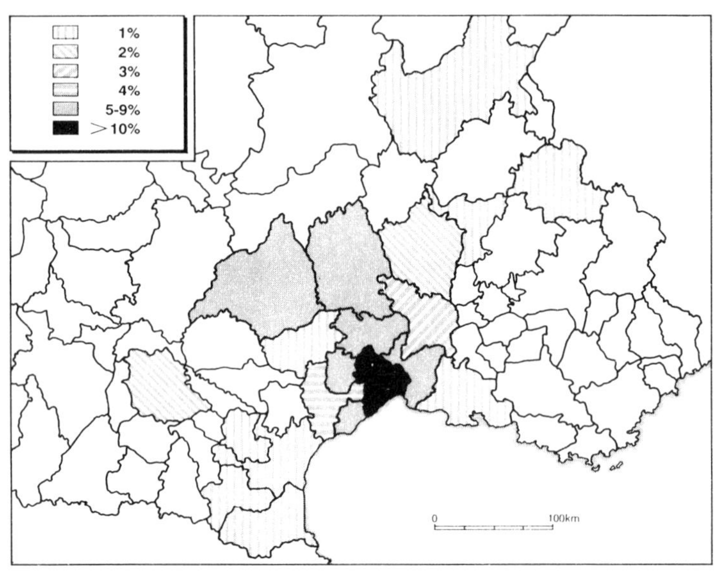

prostitutes claiming to exercise a profession, about 40 per cent were in domestic service, and 40 per cent worked in the clothes and textiles trades as seamstresses, spinners, silk-workers, laundresses, and the like. Certainly the *Bureau* was convinced that domestic service and the textiles trade – the major sources of female employment in the city – constituted prostitution's 'dangerous classes':

> Women and girls arrive from every region. Some to serve as chambermaids, others as servants. Following an event it is easy to imagine, they soon leave the households into which they were originally admitted, and establish themselves in rented rooms (*chambres garnies*). Busying themselves with sewing or some other handiwork, they are soon leading a licentious and dissolute life.[52]

What the textiles trade and domestic service had in common,

from the point of view of the single woman, was chronic economic uncertainty and low wages, and it was these factors which impelled many of them to try the rewards of mercenary sex. Although some married women are found on the files of the *Bureau* – for the marital economy too was fragile, particularly through the sudden loss of the earning power of one of the marriage partners – the vast majority of prostitutes appear to have been single women between the ages of 15 and 24. There was a high turnover rate among servants, especially of the more menial sort, who might be employed only on a seasonal basis. So too women attracted to the city by boom conditions in the textiles trade would often be the first to be laid off in times of economic uncertainty. How ironical that the Bon Pasteur should be training its inmates in the rudiments of this trade, unemployment in which was frequently the occasion for women resorting to prostitution! If the single woman could not be sure of a roof over her head, or a daily wage which would buy her enough food to live, and if, as was usually the case with these outsiders, she had no family to fall back upon, then mercenary sex could appear an ephemerally attractive bread-ticket. Though more women would be tempted in this way in periods of chronic unemployment and high prices – such as the 1690s – whatever the general state of the economy, the fragility of the economic position of the immigrant serving girl and seamstress was always likely to throw up a fair number for whom the stark choice between sex and hunger presented itself.[53] Contrary to what her name suggests, then, the *fille de joie* rarely embarked upon a career of prostitution out of her own *joie de vivre.*

There was in theory at least a great difference between part-time and freelance mercenary sex on one hand and a career in prostitution on the other.[54] Certainly a great many women would indulge in mercenary sex without wishing to end up as full-time *filles de joie.* Some may even have been tempted to use their bodies as a means of saving towards their dowries.[55] Certainly the economic rewards of the game for the young and pretty woman were not to be sneered at. A virginity, real or simulated, could always fetch a good price – probably more than most women could earn in a week. Some women were set up as the kept mistresses of students and the better-off members of the city: if they could manage to keep hold of at least some of the money that passed through their hands, they might in this way use sex as a means of social ascent, even if their boyfriends came to tire of them. In general, however, the occupational hazards of mercenary sex for kept woman, public prostitute and part-timer alike, were such that it was more typically the beginning of a long downhill road.[56]

Besides the fear of imprisonment in the Bon Pasteur, disease, pregnancy, and loss of employment and of reputation threatened the sexually promiscuous single woman. Syphilis was an ever-recurrent problem: the existence in the city of one of the army's few VD hospitals,[57] as well as the flow of diseased prostitutes from outside availing themselves of Montpellier's resources as a medical centre, probably made the dangers of infection higher than in other cities. Treatment with ointment of mercury, or with mercury-based tablets, was rarely completely effective, and normally did little more than temporarily suppress some of the external symptoms of the infection.[58] Venereal disease could induce further physical and mental afflictions: scabs and sores, the risks of neurosyphilis from the disease, the dangers of mercury poisoning from its treatment. Pregnancy too was a disaster for the single woman who could not persuade the father, if she knew who he was, to marry her. Although abortionists did exist in the city, the close supervision of morals in this sphere by the clergy made it unlikely that it was anything more than a rare and emergency operation, and one fraught with dangers. Even if the woman was able to abandon her baby to the Hôpital Général, her subsequent chances of finding a husband or even, given the bad reputation which she would have acquired, an employer were much reduced. Virginity – or its appearance – was the capital resource of the single woman, and loss of reputation was one of the great hazards for a woman wishing to indulge in extramarital or mercenary sex.[59] Sexual impropriety inevitably meant loss of job, and this would point her even more clearly towards greater reliance upon prostitution as a livelihood. For those women teetering on the brink of the trade, moreover, the final pull might be given by procurers or procuresses.

V

The history of the organization of prostitution is even less well known than that of prostitutes themselves, if only because the law directed its attentions more against the 'sinful' woman herself than upon the individuals who were often found arranging her rendezvous, fixing her accommodation, offering her protection and, inevitably, taking a share of her earnings.[60] The little evidence concerning the organization of prostitution which it is possible to adduce from the Montpellier archives concerns, significantly, only procuresses: the enforcement of morals in which the all-male *Bureau de police* and the exclusively female Miséricorde engaged was directed solely at women.

The procuress was normally a middle-aged woman beyond the menopause. Probably the majority were former prostitutes who had managed to survive the occupational hazards of imprisonment, disease, and early death. The procuress could not normally count on buyers for her own body, though she might oblige if group sex was required. Typically she was a single woman, normally a widow, though some were married and benefited from the physical protection that a husband could offer. The ideal procuress possessed a potent mixture of persuasiveness, discretion, and contacts. She knew the best places in town for prostitutes to ply their trade, the spots to avoid, the times of police patrols. Although she would probably live in rented rooms, she would not overuse her facilities there, for fear of arousing the irritation of her neighbours or her parish priest. She was very rarely, then, a brothel-keeper in the accepted sense of the term. Rather, she relied on contacts who could allow her 'girls' entry, without questions asked, into rooms at the back of a bar, or a shop, or into shaded gardens on the outskirts of town. For the most casual encounters, she would be able to recommend a host of nooks and crannies – down back-alleys, under certain bridges – where the sex act could be performed without fuss and distraction. Contacts in other towns were valuable too: each July there was a regular exodus of procuresses and their charges to the international trade fair at nearby Beaucaire, where business was always brisk.[61]

To supplement her income, and to enable her to ride out periods of police zealousness, the procuress would often keep up another line of business. The best sort of occupation was one which gave continuing scope for making useful contacts, and which could double as a 'front' for her procuring. In the early years of the century there appear to have been links with the occult arts: Marie Bisonde from Gascony was said to be 'a woman of scandalous life who was involved in making horoscopes and selling love-potions to young men and women, and who under this pretext performed the role of a pimp'.[62] Others were part-time abortionists: Madame Dystande told one of her nervous young charges in 1700, 'not to be afraid, for if she became pregnant, she [Dystande] would make her drink a potion which would cause the child to leave her body'.[63] More conventional – and less dangerous – trades were followed by most other procuresses. Many rented out rooms to strangers and travellers, an accepted way for poor widows to supplement their incomes: a great many comings and goings could be disguised behind this front. Renting rooms was also a means of recruiting prostitutes. The procuress Marie Nibourel, for example, operating in the 1750s, would pick up young girls just arrived from the countryside, and would offer them free board and lodging while they waited for a job to turn up. When a sizeable bill had been run up, Madame Nibourel would oblige the poor girl to make repayments in an instalment plan she can barely have suspected beforehand.[64] An even better bet as lodgers were women in the final stages of pregnancy, or who were being treated for syphilis: such women had sexual experience, a bad reputation, were totally dependent, and could therefore be fairly easily bullied into eventually paying off their debts in sexual assignations. Other trades followed by procuresses included putting out socks and stockings for darning, the fabrication of verdigris, and taking in laundry. These trades not only brought the procuress into contact with young girls, but also gave unremarked entry into many homes and residences. Madame Toulouse, for example, kept an apparently respectable shop where she ironed the sheets and linen brought to her from homes of the wealthy; at the back of the shop, however, behind a curtain, was a bed on which sexual rendezvous were discreetly kept while she kept a look-out to the front.[65]

There was little love lost between a procuress and her prostitutes. Some of the latter harboured residual resentment against the procuress for the way they had been brought into the trade: it was common practice, for example, for a procuress to attract a pretty woman on some pretext – seeing someone about a job, eating a meal together – to a room or to a garden where she could be delivered up to a man or a group of men and raped. The ageing prostitute who was getting desperate for

Map 7.3: Residence of Prostitutes Sentenced by the Montpellier *Bureau de police* in the Eighteenth Century.

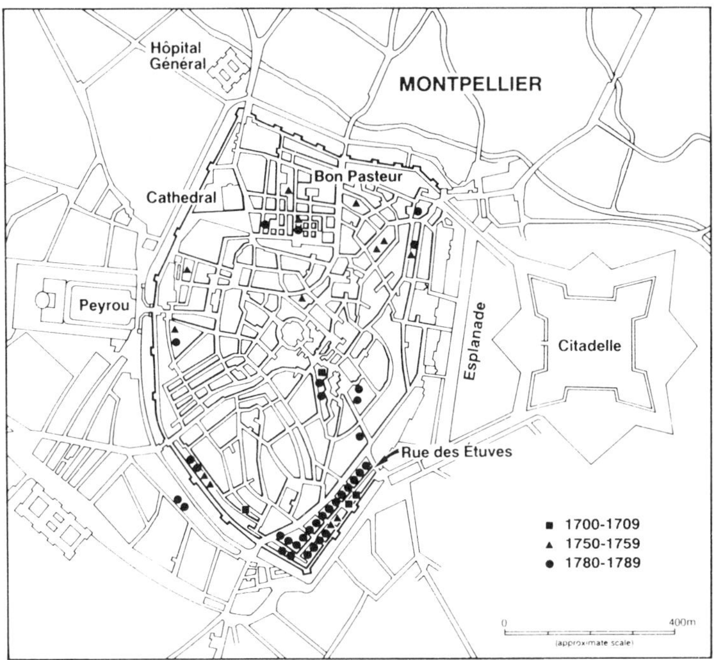

clients, the young woman paying off some sort of debt for rent, were hardly likely to have a very affectionate view of their 'employer'. The economic relationship between the two sides tended to favour the procuress more than her charges. The latter ran the greater risks of punishment, disease, and unwanted pregnancy. Yet their 'employers' took as much for arranging the encounter as the prostitute earned, and often a great deal more.[66] Only when an angry ex-virgin threatened to take the matter to the police would a procuress ever agree to give her more than half the fee.

A greater degree of orchestration in the world of Montpellier's organized prostitution became evident towards the end of the Ancien Régime. Whereas in the early part of the century those prostitutes who appeared before the *Bureau* either lived or were in lodgings fairly evenly scattered throughout the poorer quarters of the city, by the 1780s the majority of cases coming before the *Bureau* involved women living in one particular part of town, and in particular in one street, the Rue des Etuves (Map 7.3). A 'red light district' thus came to be centred on what one indignant father, ruing the loss of his daughter's virtue, called 'the shady houses of the Rue des Etuves where vice seems to seek out a refuge which hides it from the public's gaze'.[67] The specialized leisure institutions of the eighteenth century often provided 'fronts' for houses of debauch; coffee-houses, of which there were over a dozen in 1768 whereas none had existed forty years previously,[68] and billiard-halls, the haunt of gamblers and out-of-hours drinkers, would have a few rented rooms on the upper floors where obliging women were only too willing to receive paying guests. Closer links may well have resulted with the world of organized crime. Prostitutes in the last fifty years of the Ancien Régime are found picking the pockets of their distracted clients; they encourage their friends in domestic service to steal from their masters, and pass on the stolen goods to receivers; procuresses dabble in the sale of smuggled tobacco and cotton fabrics; a slave trade in babies develops, prostitutes selling their children to soldiers who receive a bonus from the army for signing on new recruits;[69] vice rings specializing in child prostitution emerge. Much prostitution now has an atmosphere of gang violence to it: neighbours who complain of being kept awake at night, or being insulted and harassed by queueing clients, are terrorized into silence or beaten up by thugs. It may be that organized prostitution was finding its protectors among the city's notables. Certainly many of the procuresses included members of the upper classes among their patrons, and a couple were even related to noblemen.[70] Many of the scions of the highest families took their pleasures on the Rue des Etuves and it is quite possible that their worthy fathers may have benefited from the high rents which it was possible to charge for a place in the street. With this greater degree of organization of prostitution went a great openness about the trade. Unbridled street soliciting was upsetting the *Bureau* from the 1760s onwards: women walked about the Rue des Etuves clad only in the flimsiest of nightdresses, and encouraged clients in the most brazen way.[71]

VI

Flagrant and uninhibited street soliciting and the changing quality of urban life in the last decades of the Ancien Régime were sufficient to persuade contemporaries that Montpellier was veritably awash in sexual licence.

> Not forty years ago [lamented one well-informed source in 1768] a young woman who took tobacco and wore silk stockings would have been assumed to be a prostitute. Today, all women, even down to serving-girls wear silk stockings, take tobacco and drink coffee every day. Young women earn four or five *sols* daily by sewing; yet they spend ten *sols*, dress themselves neatly and pay for their own food and lodgings. Where does the extra money come from? There is no need to explain.[72]

There was doubtless a degree of sensationalizing in all this. Nevertheless, the author of these lines was quite correct in thinking that changes were taking place in young people's sexual behaviour – in Montpellier as in France as a whole. The illegitimacy rate in the city, for example, rose by over 40 per cent between the beginning of the century and the end of the Ancien Régime.[73] Abandoned children were becoming a social problem which sorely taxed the already heavily burdened Hôpital Général.[74] The problem would have been even worse had not methods of controlling births become more commonplace: doubtless coitus interruptus, but also abortions were apparently becoming more frequent:

> There is perhaps no other city [commented the experienced Intendant of Languedoc in 1767] in which more young babies are destroyed than in this city of Montpellier. There exist wretched women who possess the barbarous art of killing them within the bodies of their mothers, whom they wound in the process.[75]

Cohabiting before marriage appeared to be on the increase too and, complain as the *Bureau* did, it was to little avail. Indeed, single women hauled before the *Bureau* as prostitutes gave as evidence of good behaviour a long-standing sexual relationship with one man outside marriage. At the turn of the century, women had been interned in the Bon Pasteur for far less! Attitudes had changed and sexual exploits seemed to rouse little shame in the younger generation. After all, protested one *ingénue* before the *Bureau*, by engaging in extramarital liaisons 'she was only doing what a lot of other young women do'.[76]

Such candour could only disarm the *Bureau*: it was subversive of the seriousness with which it viewed the problem of prostitution and the efforts it had made over the century to repress it. Increasingly the members of the *Bureau* had taken the policing of morals out of the hands of the Miséricorde; they had co-operated with the military authorities in the execution of the 1768 regulations against camp-followers; they had passed an arsenal of regulations relating to lodgings in their efforts to track down the prostitute; they had stepped up their supervision of the Bon Pasteur and acted to orientate it more around the punishment and the reform of the prostitute than her spiritual salvation. They had also been among the keenest advocates of the re-implementation of laws against infanticide and concealing pregnancies.[77] Yet the Bureau's failure to arrest the development of either organized prostitution or greater sexual licence was plain for all to see by the last decades of the Ancien Régime. There was something almost doleful in the *Bureau*'s complaint in 1782 that

> the disorders caused by licentiousness are increasing all the time within the town and suburbs and, either by negligence or by some other motive, no one wishes to denounce it to us. People content themselves with speaking openly about it and even go so far as to complain about the city's police.[78]

The *maire* for his part was convinced that Montpellier had become 'the most dissolute city in the world' and, in somewhat misogynist vein, characterized it as a spot 'where licentiousness knows no limit and where women brazenly use every means of satisfying their passions'.[79]

Such statements contrasted strikingly with the situation at the turn of the century: sexual licence had become a subject for gossip and indulgence where once it had been a spur to 'charitable' action. Although part of the city's wealthier citizens were still influenced by rigid Jansenist codes of sexual morality, most of the local ruling class appear to have considerably relaxed their views. The works of scientists and philosophers – the latter term often synonymous with pornographers and satirists of the church's precepts on sexual matters[80] – now replaced the Augustinian and Jansenist classics which had hitherto dominated the private libraries of the rich. The city which at the end of the seventeenth century had been a staunch bastion of Catholic orthodoxy had, by the eve of the Revolution, undergone a subtle metamorphosis into a centre of tolerated pleasures and conspicuous leisure.

The growing indifference of Montpellier's ruling class towards direct action against prostitution, together with the more liberal attitude of the young population towards premarital sex, made futile a policing of morals which was in any case undermined by the growth of the city and by the acknowledged deficiencies of the local police force. Even before 1789, in the face of greater sexual licence, the Bon Pasteur was appearing obsolete. In 1776 both the Intendant of Languedoc and the *maire* of the city, struck by the fall in admissions, proposed its closure.[81]

VII

In the event, the Montpellier Bon Pasteur staggered along until 1789 and beyond. After 1790, however, fewer prostitutes were detained within it, and only a dwindling number of petty criminals kept it about half full. Finally in 1793 it was closed down altogether and the empty building converted into an annexe of the adjoining hospital.[82]

By this time, government legislation had effectively made the Bon Pasteur redundant. When in July 1791 the National Assembly had come to institute a new set of municipal regulations for the country as a whole, it had not only ended all existing laws relating to the repression of prostitution but also put nothing in their place. The new regulations which, although making procuring a punishable offence, turned a blind eye to the existence of prostitution and of brothels, were eventually incorporated into Napoleon's Penal Code of 1810.[83] Henceforth the use of the law by private individuals and religious pressure groups – such as Montpellier's Miséricorde – to police the morals of lower-class women was entirely discredited. Yet the *laissez-faire* rationale implicit in allowing the single woman legal freedom to dispose of her body as she saw fit was not necessarily to her ultimate advantage – any more than industrial workers benefited from their new-found economic 'freedom'.[84] Significantly the reports of Villermé in the 1830s on the wretchedness of working-class conditions in industrial towns also threw light on a mass prostitution of destitution and desperation which was grounded in the economic vulnerability of – in particular single – women.[85] Nor was the situation of such women in early-nineteenth-century Montpellier – largely by-passed by extensive industrialization – much improved. The police commissioner dispatched to the city by the Restoration government of Louis XVIII in 1818 was to express shock at the 'unbridled licentiousness' which characterized post-revolutionary Montpellier: numerous extramarital sexual liaisons, hordes of kept women, prostitution extensive and unregulated, venereal diseases rife, with the male inhabitants of the city displaying a brutality and an 'absence of care and concern towards women which astonishes civilized outsiders'.[86] Against this background, the unmarried Montpellier serving girl or seamstress might have to admit that, if she did not regret the passing of the Bon Pasteur, the freedom which the revolutionaries of the 1790s had granted her to prostitute herself to all-comers had turned out in practice to represent one of the fundamental Rights of Man.

Notes

1. The best guide to the history of prostitution in the Ancien Régime is E.M. Bénabou's *La Prostitution et la police des moeurs au XVIIIe. siècle* (Paris, 1987). Unfortunately this work deals only with Paris, in which the situation of prostitution was in many respects different from that which obtained in the provinces. The same applies with much other writing on the subject, starting with N. de La Mare, *Traité de police* (4 vols, Paris, 1705–38) and N.T. Le Moyne des Essarts, *Dictionnaire universel de police* (8 vols, Paris, 1786–90). See also Sabatier, *Histoire de la législation sur les femmes publiques et les lieux de débauche* (Paris, 1828); P. Dufour, *Histoire de la prostitution* (8 vols, Brussels, 1861); and W.W. Sanger, *The History of Prostitution* (New York, 1859). Although ostensibly concerned with a later period, of considerable value are A. Parent-Duchâtelet, *De la prostitution dans la ville de Paris* (3rd edn, 2 vols, Paris, 1857); J. Harsin, *The Policing of Prostitution in Nineteenth-century France* (Princeton, NJ, 1985); and A. Corbin, *Les Filles de noce: misère sexuelle et prostitution aux XIXe. et XX. siècles* (Paris, 1978).

2. Archives départementales de l'Hérault (henceforth = A.D.H.). On Montpellier in the seventeenth and eighteenth centuries, see 'Montpellier en 1768', in J. Berthelé (ed.) *Archives de la ville de*

Montpellier. Inventaires et documents. Vol. IV (Montpellier, 1895); Amoreux, 'Mémoire sur la topographie médicale de Montpellier et de son territoire', Bibliothèque municipale de Montpellier; C. d'Aigrefeuille, *Histoire de la ville de Montpellier* (new edn, M. de la Pijardière ed., Montpellier, 1885); G. Cholvy (ed.) *Histoire de Montpellier* (Paris, 1985); L.J. Thomas, *Montpellier, ville marchande. Histoire économique et sociale de Montpellier des origines à 1870* (Montpellier, 1936); A. Blanchard, 'De Pézenas à Montpellier: transfert d'une ville de souveraineté', *R.H.M.C.* (1965).

3. 'Montpellier en 1768', p. 86.

4. In his *Introduction à la démographie historique des villes d'Europe du XIVe. au XVIIIe. siècle* (Louvain, 2 vols, 1954, i, p. 198), R. Mols notes that of all Ancien Régime towns, only garrison and university towns would normally contain a higher number of men than women. Montpellier fell into both categories. The phrase 'batchelor town' was suggested to me by Richard Cobb.

5. A.D.H., C 568, 131 M 1.

6. Archives municipales de Montpellier (henceforth = A.M.M.), BB, *Registres des délibérations du conseil de ville* (henceforth = BB Reg), 8.viii.1691. These municipal registers contain much of relevance to the history of prostitution in the city. The registers of the municipality's *Bureau de police* in the series FF at the municipal archives (henceforth = FF Reg.), plus other police materials in the same location, in particular a collection of bundles labelled *'FF. Filles et femmes de mauvaise vie'* and containing trial materials, comprise one of the major sources of the present article. The other major source is the archive of the Montpellier Bon Pasteur. The latter forms an unclassified series located in the Archives départementales de l'Hérault, and includes a virtually unbroken series of admissions registers as well as account-books, sets of regulations, etc.

7. E. Le Roy Ladurie, *Les Paysans de Languedoc* (Paris, 1966) p. 612.

8. D'Aigrefeuille, *Histoire de Montpellier*, iv, pp. 208, 212.

9. A.D.H., Hôpital Général de Montpellier (archives antérieures à 1790) (henceforth = HG I) E 388.

10. A. Corvisier, *L'Armée française de la fin du XVIIe. siècle au ministère de Choiseul: le soldat* (1964) pp. 757 ff., 886 ff.

11. A.D.H., C 141.

12. For the 1684 legislation, see Bénabou, *La Prostitution*, pp. 22–5, and M.G. Badir, 'Législation et définition de la prostitution au XVIIIe. siècle', *Studies on Voltaire and the 18th Century*, 249, 1987.

13. See p. 39 ff.

14. Bénabou, *La Prostitution*, pp. 23–5; Harsin, *Policing of Prostitution*, pp. 56 ff.; Badir, 'Législation', pp. 451–2; Parent-Duchâtelet, *De la prostitution*, pp. 287–9.

15. L. Guiraud, 'La Réforme à Montpellier', *Mémoires de la Société archéologique de Montpellier* (vols XIV, XV, 1918); P. Gachon, *Quelques préliminaires de la révocation de l'Edit de Nantes en Languedoc (1661–85)* (Toulouse, 1899); Le Roy Ladurie, *Paysans de Languedoc*, Annexe 44, p. 889.

16. A.D.H., HG I A 1; P. Béral, *Histoire de l'Hôpital de la Charité de*

Montpellier (1646–82). Berceau de l'Hôpital Général (Montpellier, 1899).

17. A.D.H., Fonds Miséricorde (unclassified) (henceforth = Mis.). *Documents historiques sur l'Oeuvre de la Miséricorde de la ville de Montpellier* (Montpellier, 1840), and A. Leenhardt, *La Miséricorde et le bureau de bienfaisance* (Montpellier, 1840) have references to documents from this collection which have since been lost.

18. P. Coste, *Monsieur Vincent. Le grand saint du Grand Siècle* (3 vols, Paris, 1931) i, pp. 323–84. See also above pp. 92–4.

19. D'Aigrefeuille, *Histoire de Montpellier*, p. 475; A.D.H., G 1295.

20. A.M.M., *Continuation du Grand Thalamus*, no. 1,701, no. 1,704.

21. V. Durand, *Le Jansénisme au XVIIIe. siècle et Joachim Colbert, évêque de Montpellier* (Toulouse, 1907).

22. A.M.M., BB Reg., 30.iv.1698.

23. A.D.H., Fonds Bon Pasteur (unclassified) (henceforth = BP). See also d'Aigrefeuille, *Histoire de Montpellier*, p. 477; 'Montpellier en 1768'.

17. Strictly speaking of course, not all women 'of scandalous life' or 'of ill repute' were prostitutes. Nevertheless, the overwhelming majority of women admitted to the Bon Pasteur appear to have been women whose public prostitution was acknowledged. Cf. Badir, 'Législation', passim.

24. Reboul, *Sommaire des règlements faits par le Bureau de police de la ville de Montpellier* (Montpellier, 1760); A. Arnauld, 'Fonctions et jurisdiction consulaires à Montpellier aux XVIIe. et XVIIIe. siècles', *Annales du Midi* (1919–20).

25. A.M.M., BB Reg., passim.

26. Population figures in L. Dermigny, 'De la Révocation à la Révolution', in P. Wolff (ed.) *Histoire du Languedoc* (Toulouse, 1967). For the *valets de ville*, see A.D.H., HG I E17–32 registers of deliberations, passim), E 289, E 388, G 13.

27. A.M.M., BB Reg., 30.xi.1778.

28. A.D.H., HG I, G 13. For the situation in Paris, A. Farge, 'Le mendiant, un marginal?', *Les Marginaux et les exclus dans l'histoire* (Paris, 1979); Bénabou, *La Prostitution*, pp. 480–1.

29. Cases noted in A.M.M., FF Reg., and for which trial materials were located in the 'FF. Filles et femmes de mauvaise vie' bundles. Sampling on the first, sixth, and ninth decades of the eighteenth century produced the following statistics: between 1700 and 1709, sixty-six cases involving eighty women; between 1750 and 1759, fifty cases involving fifty-six women; and between 1780 and 1789, sixty-one cases involving ninety-eight women.

30. A.D.H., Mis; BP. The *Mères* of the Bon Pasteur from 1720 onwards were the wife of the millionnaire *Trésorier de la Bourse du Languedoc*, Bonnier de la Mosson (1720–6); the wife of Cambacérès, *conseiller* in the *Cour des Aides* (1726–32); the wife of the *Premier Président* in the *Cour des Aides*, Mme. Pujol de Bon (1732–55); the wife of a member of the *Cour des Aides*, Mme. Vassal de Mogé (1755–71); and then finally the two Ramond sisters, wives, then widows of *conseillers* in the *Cour des Aides*, Mmes Ramond de Roux (1771–85) and Ramond de Reclot (1795–93).

31. Cf. L. Cahen, 'Les idées charitables à Paris au XVIIe. et XVIIIe. siècles', *R.H.M.C.* (1900). For students, see C. Jones, 'Montpellier medical students and the medicalization of eighteenth-century France', in R. Porter and A. Wear (eds) *Problems and Methods in the History of Medicine* (London, 1986) p. 61.

32. Thus for example the charitable practice of bequeathing a place in a hospital for a pauper of one's heir choosing had its counterpart in respect to places in the Bon Pasteur. Cf. for example the will of Philippe de Boudon, *Trésorier de France*, 29.iv.1707. A.D.H., BP. For the importance of female honour, see the works relating to illegitimacy and unmarried mothers, notably M.C. Phan, *Les Amours illégitimes: histoires de séduction en Languedoc (1676–1786)* (Paris, 1988) (esp. pp. 156–7) and A. Molinier, 'Enfants trouvés, enfants abandonnés et enfants illégitimes en Languedoc aux XVIIe. et XVIIIe. siècles', *Hommage à Marcel Reinhard sur la population française aux XVIIe. et XVIIIe. siècles* (Paris, 1973); A. Lottin, 'Naissances illégitimes et filles mères à Lille au XVIIIe. siècle', *R.H.M.C.* (1970); and J. Depauw, 'Amour illégitime et société à Nantes au XVIIIe. siècle', *Ann. E.S.C.* (1972). See though J. Solé, 'Passion charnelle et société urbaine d'Ancien Régime', *Annales de la Faculté de Lettres et Sciences de Nice* (1969). Prostitutes appear less in the archives relating to illegitimacy and foundlings than one would expect, perhaps because they already employed contraceptive practices which reduced their child-bearing chances. Cf. F. Lebrun, *La Vie conjugale sous l'Ancien Régime* (Paris, 1975) p. 99.

33. See in particular A.M.M., FF Reg., 23.vi.1742 and 26.vi.1742.

34. For the reform of *lettres de cachet* in 1784, A.D.H., C 141; and see too F.X. Emmanuelli, '"Ordres du Roi" et lettres de cachet en Provence à la fin de l'Ancien Régime', *Revue historique* (1974) esp. pp. 369–70. For administrative precautions relating to their use in the 1740s and 1750s, A.D.H., C 111, 115. Cf. A. M.M., FF Reg., 19.x.1776, 17.viii.1782; and Bibliothèque Nationale. Manuscrits français (henceforth = B.N. Ms. Fçs.) 7513.

35.Archives Nationales (henceforth = A.N.), S 6171, F 15 226; A.D.H., C 141; and above, Chapter 5.

36. Witness the case of the city's other charitable institutions: C. Jones, *Charity and 'Bienfaisance': The Treatment of the Poor in the Montpellier Region, 1740–1815* (Cambridge, 1982) esp. Chs 3 and 4.

37. Unfortunately the fragmentary nature of the Bon Pasteur's accounts precludes any more detailed analysis and comparison with the structure of the institution's income earlier in the century.

38. For fuller details of charitable benefactions, see C. Jones, 'Poverty, vagrancy and society in the Montpellier region, 1740–1815', Oxford D.Phil. thesis (1978).

39. Besides Jones, *Charity and 'Bienfaisance'*, see, for example, M. Vovelle, *Piété baroque et déchristianisation en Provence au XVIIIe. siècle* (Paris, 1973); and K. Norberg, *Rich and Poor in Grenoble, 1600–1815* (London and Berkeley, Calif., 1985).

40. For economic trends in eighteenth-century France, see F. Braudel and C.E. Labrousse (eds) *Histoire économique et sociale de la*

France.II. 1660–1789 (Paris, 1970).

41. The normal form of exemplary punishment was exposure to public scorn on the *chevalet de bois* (stocks) for three hours. In particularly serious cases, the offender was likely to be whipped and beaten about the town, 'with a straw hat covered with feathers on her head'.

42. A.D.H., G 1144.

43. A.D.H., BP: account-books from the 1750s onwards.

44. A.D.H., BP: *'Règlement pour les filles pénitentes de la maison du Bon Pasteur'* (no date, but seemingly dating from the 1750s).

45. A.D.H., BP; Hôpital Général (archives postérieures à 1790) (henceforth = HG II) G 9; and A.N., F 15 226.

46. B.N., Ms. Fçs., 7513.

47. M. Foucault, *Discipline and Punish: The Birth of the Prison* (London, 1977); P. O'Brien, *The Promise of Punishment: Prisons in Nineteenth-Century France* (Princeton, NJ, 1981).

48. The social profile of Montpellier's *filles et femmes de mauvaise vie* may be compared with that of Parisian prostitutes (Bénabou, *La Prostitution*, pp. 267 ff., and that of unmarried mothers in Lille, Nantes, and Carcassonne (works by Lottin, Depauw, and Phan, cited in n. 32).

49. Reboul, *Sommaire*, A.M.M., FF Reg., passim.

50. The comments on female migration are based on admission registers into the female wards of the local hospital, the Hôtel-Dieu Saint-Eloi. A.D.H. Hôtel-Dieu Saint-Eloi (archives antérieures à 1790) F 2–3 (admissions in 1740 and 1741) and F 11 (admissions in 1777 and 1778).

51. Cf. the comments of O. Hufton, *The Poor of Eighteenth-Century France, 1750–89* (Oxford, 1970) p. 311; R. Cobb, *The Police and the People: French popular protest, 1789–1820* (Oxford, 1970) p. 237; and J.P. Gutton, *La Société et les pauvres: l'exemple de la généralité de Lyon, 1534–1789* (Paris, 1971) p. 103.

52. A.M.M., FF Reg., 18.viii.778.53.

53. This, the change in the functions of the Bon Pasteur, the gradual lengthening of sentences in an institution with a relatively static capacity, and variations in the zeal and effectiveness of the *Bureau de police* preclude any evident correlation between bread prices on the one hand, and entries to the Bon Pasteur or cases coming before the *Bureau de police* on the other. Indeed, in the disaster years of 1709 and 1710, one is struck by the rareness of prosecutions and entries to the Bon Pasteur, even though prostitution was clearly rife: the resources of the Bon Pasteur and the *Bureau de police* were inadequate to cope with the scale of the problem. A.D.H., G 1144.

54. Hufton, *The Poor of Eighteenth-Century France*, p. 308.

55. Although the evidence is highly fragmentary and deals with a great range of circumstances, it would appear that the basic rate for a casual sexual encounter in the last fifty years of the Ancien Régime was 12 sous. This compared favourably with a day's wage. Much larger sums were often involved – 5, 10, 20 *livres* and even more. Normally a virginity would be worth at least double the basic rate. Contrast

Hufton, *The Poor of Eighteenth-Century France*, p. 315, where much lower rates are suggested, on the basis of evidence from Rodez. Montpellier, however, had a reputation as a town where everything was expensive.

56. Hufton, *The Poor of Eighteenth-Century France*, p. 317.

57. A.D.H., C 559; L. Dulieu, 'L'Hôpital royal et militaire de Montpellier', *Monspeliensis Hippocrates* (1966). After 1769 the local *dépôt de mendicité*, or beggars' workhouse, gave treatment to camp-followers suffering from venereal disease.

58. Dulieu, 'L'Hôpital royal et militaire', p. 8. Cf. Bénabou, *La Prostitution*, pp. 407 ff.; and C. Quétel, *Le Mal de Naples: histoire de la syphilis* (Paris, 1986) pp. 102 ff.

59. For the importance of loss of reputation for single women, cf. M.C. Phan, *Les Amours illégitimes*, pp. 155–7, 178. The crucial role of reputation for single women is analogous to that of respectability for men analysed by Y. Castan, *Honnêteté et relations sociales en Languedoc, 1715–90* (Paris, 1974).

60. In most cases in Montpellier, procuresses are treated as *femmes de mauvaise vie*, and only closer investigation in the case-histories in A.M.M., FF reveals the nature of the offence.

61. A.M.M., FF Reg., 12.ix.1703 and 23.viii.1709. Cf. Sabatier, *Histoire de la législation*, p. 165.

62. A.M.M., FF Reg., 25.viii.1709.

63. A.M.M., FF Reg., 29.v.1700.

64. A.M.M., FF Reg., 19.iv.1755.

65. A.M.M., FF Reg., 29.v.1704.

66. Marie Fabantine, *dite* Pastourelle was alleged to have received 200 *livres* for procuring an 8-year-old girl. A.M.M., FF Reg., 7.v.1761.

67. A.M.M., FF Reg., 20.viii.1785.

68. 'Montpellier en 1768', cited in n. 2.

69. A.M.M., FF Reg., 19.ii.1784. Cf. Corvisier, *L'Armée française*, pp. 761 ff.

70. A.M.M., FF Reg., 17.xi.1756; Honorée Hautier 'veuve de Noble Guillaume Miallet', 14.ix.1784; Magdelaine Devèze, *Veuve* Rousseau claimed that she was the illegitimate daughter of a nobleman.

71. See esp. A.M.M., FF Reg., 2.viii.1763. When challenged by the police, the nearly naked prostitutes disingenuously claimed that they had just sent all their clothes to the laundry, or else that they were finding the weather oppressively hot.

72. 'Montpellier en 1768', p. 99.

73. Dermigny, 'De la Révocation'. p. 428. For illegitimacy in France as a whole, see Y. Blayo, 'Illegitimate births in France from 1740 to 1819 and in the 1960s', P. Laslett *et al.* (eds) *Bastardy and its Comparative History* (London, 1980) pp. 281–2. It seems important to reject E. Shorter's conclusion that higher illegitimacy suggests a 'sexual liberation' for females in this period – see his *The Making of the Modern Family* (London, 1975) and the heavy damage inflicted on his thesis by L. Tilly, J.W. Scott, and M. Cohen, 'Women's work and European fertility patterns', *Journal of Interdisciplinary History* (1976) – while nevertheless registering a change in the emotional ambience and the possibility of growing female initiative in sexual liaisons. Cf.

Phan, *Les Amours illégitimes*, pp. 218 ff.; Norberg, *Rich and Poor*, pp. 210–11.

74. The Hôpital Général was on the verge of bankruptcy by the 1770s. Jones, *Charity and 'Bienfaisance'*, passim.

75. A.D.H., C 568.

76. A.M.M., FF Reg., 29.i.1788. For the change in the emotional climate, see esp. Phan, *Les Amours illégitimes*, pp. 193 f., 218 ff.

77. A.M.M., FF Reg., passim; A.D.H., G 1298

78. A.M.M., FF Reg., 22.vii.1782.

79. B.N., Ms. fçs., 7513.

80. R. Darnton, 'Le livre français à la fin de l'Ancien Régime', *Annales E.S.C.* (1973); D. Mornet, *Les Origines intellectuelles de la Révolution française, 1715–87* (Paris, 1947) p. 155.

81. B.N., Ms. fçs., 7513. See also Figure 7.1.

82. A.D.H., BP; L 3962; L 397; 2 X 102; and A.D.H., Hôtel-Dieu Saint-Eloi (archives postérieures à 1790), E. 2.

83. Sabatier, *Histoire de la législation*, p. 108; Harsin, *Policing of Prostitution*, p. 83.

84. In both cases, moreover, government intervention came to circumscribe the degree of freedom. For workers, see J. Godechot, *Les Institutions de la France sous la Révolution et l'Empire* (Paris, 1968); and for prostitutes, from the Consulate onwards operating under an increasingly suffocating system of regulation, M. Alletz, *Dictionnaire de police moderne pour toute la France* (2nd edn, 4 vols, Paris, 1823); and the works of Sabatier, Parent-Duchâtelet, Harsin, and Corbin cited in note 1.

85. Villermé, *Tableau de l'état physique et morale des ouvriers employés dans les manufactures de coton, de laine et de soie* (2 vols, Paris, 1840).

86. A.N., F 7 9663.

8

The Prehistory of the Lunatic Asylum in Provincial France: The Treatment of the Insane in Eighteenth- and Early Nineteenth-Century Montpellier

The law of 30 June 1838 which created a nationwide network of departmental lunatic asylums throughout France fixed the legal and institutional framework within which the insane were to be treated for the remainder of the nineteenth and well into the twentieth centuries, and marked a watershed in the emergence of the French psychiatric profession.[1] The law was a victory for the campaign of public opinion and pressure on government which interested parties, especially in the medical profession, had been waging since the Restoration for the improvement of the conditions in which the insane were treated. One of the key symbols in the campaign had been the mythopoeic gesture by which in 1793 Philippe Pinel, founding father of French psychiatry, had – allegedly – ordered the release of insane inmates of the Paris Hôpital Général from the chains customarily used to restrain them, thus ushering in a mode of treatment which, in its emphasis upon humane conditions under medical supervision, prefigured the regime to be favoured in the post-1838 lunatic asylums. Moreover, the foundation in 1797 of the *Maison Nationale de l'Aliénation mentale* in the Parisian suburb of Charenton permitted a further centre for the scientific study and treatment of insanity to develop in the capital.[2] Paris, however, was not France: and the conditions in which the insane were kept in the provinces were sufficiently scandalous to fuel a significant reform campaign. In 1818, for example, Esquirol, one of Pinel's foremost disciples, published a semi-official report on conditions for the insane in hospitals, prisons, *dépôts de mendicité*, and similar institutions throughout France, which helped fan the righteous indignation of middle-class opinion.

If in Paris the insane were no longer treated like animals or wild beasts, Esquirol noted, everywhere in provincial France 'the insane are covered in chains'.[3] Invoking his own very extensive knowledge of conditions, Esquirol painted a graphic and shocking picture of generalized misery:

> I have seen them covered in rags, having only straw to protect themselves from the cold humidity of the stones on which they lay. I have seen them rudely fed, deprived of air to breathe, of water to quench their thirst and of the prime needs of life. I have seen them delivered over to veritable gaolers, abandoned to their brutal surveillance. I have seen them in caves in which one would fear to shut away wild beasts.[4]

Horror stories of this kind adduced by reformers prior to the 1838 law, for all their merits and arguably because of the evident truth behind them, have tended to obscure from the historian's gaze the detailed history of the treatment of insanity in the eighteenth and early nineteenth centuries. This constitutes a lacuna which the extremely fragmentary nature and relatively sparse quantity of relevant source material have made all the more difficult to fill.[5] We know from historians of ideas and of science that insanity was becoming the subject of growing interest over the eighteenth century even before Pinel's work.[6] Pinel, for his part, has received extensive treatment especially at the hands of medical hagiographers.[7] Yet apart from the worthy expostulations of the pre-1838 reformers, little is known of the institutional framework for the treatment of the insane which had emerged in the eighteenth century in many provincial cities,[8] and which in some places endured through the Revolutionary era into the post-Napoleonic period. It is upon the institutional treatment of the insane in one such city, Montpellier, in this 'prehistoric' period of the provincial lunatic asylum that this chapter will focus. Montpellier – a little over 30,000 strong for most of the period under consideration – was even under the Ancien Régime a profoundly medical city, with a Faculty of Medicine second in prestige and intellectual renown only to Paris. In fact, as will be seen, the medical profession was to have remarkably little to do with the treatment of the insane for most of the period; and from the beginning to the end of the period the motives behind the institutionalization of the insane tended to be social rather than medical – a fact that was not without bearing on the history of the lunatic asylum after 1838.

I

Public concern for the insane in eighteenth-century Montpellier was prompted initially by considerations of public safety and security. In 1707 the long-serving Intendant of Languedoc, Lamoignon de Basville, had expressed concern to the city's municipal authorities over 'individuals who drift about the town and commit disorders while in a state devoid of reason and commonsense.[9] Basville – 'Intendant, or rather king of Languedoc', in Saint-Simon's acidulous phrase[10] – was something of a reformer in the field of social welfare, although his conception of social welfare was typical of the late seventeenth century and early eighteenth century in placing a premium on confinement of all the needy and deviant poor in specialized institutions. In the last decades of the seventeenth century, for example, he had been instrumental in the creation in Montpellier of an Hôpital Général, the prototype of the workhouse-like institutions for the so-called *grand renfermement des pauvres* which simultaneously harboured the destitute and punished the deviant and workshy within its walls.[11] Basville had also had a hand in the establishment of special institutions for Protestant children and for public prostitutes.[12] By 1707, however, the Intendant was growing old, and was inclined to place his trust in the energy and goodwill of 'devout and charitable persons' coming forward to provide the seemingly increasingly recognized need for a place of confinement for the insane.

In the event it was not local philanthropists but the Montpellier municipality which, instigated by an incident in 1713 in which an alleged madman had stabbed his wife to death before proceeding to burn down his own and his neighbours' houses, was eventually stirred into action.[13] Municipal officials at that time were quite alive to questions of public order and hygiene: they had made special provisions for the vagrant and diseased masses during the famines of 1693 and 1709, they had helped reorganize the police services in the 1690s, and had joined in a full-scale campaign against public prostitution, which was alleged to be dishonouring local families almost as fast as it was spreading venereal disease.[14] Now, accepting the need to protect citizens against the excesses of the insane, the municipality arranged with the administrative board of the local hospital, the Hôtel-Dieu Saint-Eloi, for the building of twelve cells, or *loges*, in the hospital's premises for the confinement of the city's insane.[15]

The municipality financed six of the twelve *loges* which the hospital proceeded to build. In addition, it undertook to make an annual payment of 1,200 *livres* for the upkeep of the *loges*' inmates. The city's *maire* and consuls or its *Bureau de police* were to have sole right to confine the insane and it was agreed that the latter should normally be from the city or its immediate environs. The other six *loges* were to be filled with candidates approved by the hospital board, usually in return for an annual sum of at least 200 *livres* each to cover the costs of upkeep.[16] The number of places in that part of the Hôtel-Dieu Saint-Eloi which, in reference to the notorious Paris madhouse, came to be known as the *petites maisons*, grew over the course of the century. What had originated as a municipal policing measure expanded its scope somewhat from the 1730s, when the hospital agreed to build four *loges* for individuals from the diocese of Montpellier chosen by the bishop, who was to reimburse the hospital for their upkeep.[17] During the hospital's major building programme in the 1760s and 1770s, extra *loges* were constructed for the city, the diocese, and for the hospital's own use. By the time of the Revolution, the Hôtel-Dieu contained twenty-five *loges* – six for the diocese, nine for the municipality, and ten for the hospital's use.[18] The average number of inmates in the *loges* had by then grown from just over ten in the early years of the century to over twenty (see Figure 8.1).[19] The turnover of inmates was not high, however: on average only four persons were admitted each year in the 1780s.[20]

These numbers are small enough to suggest that the Hôtel-Dieu never managed to get to grips with the overall contours of the world of insanity. Twenty-odd inmates out of a city population of more than 30,000 means that, even allowing for uncertainty of definition and diagnosis, only a small proportion of the number of those who might be accounted insane were received in this hospital. This fact is not substantially altered by the existence of mentally disordered

Figure 8.1: Average Number of Insane Inmates and Average Total Population in the Hôtel-Dieu Saint-Eloi of Montpellier in the Eighteenth Century.

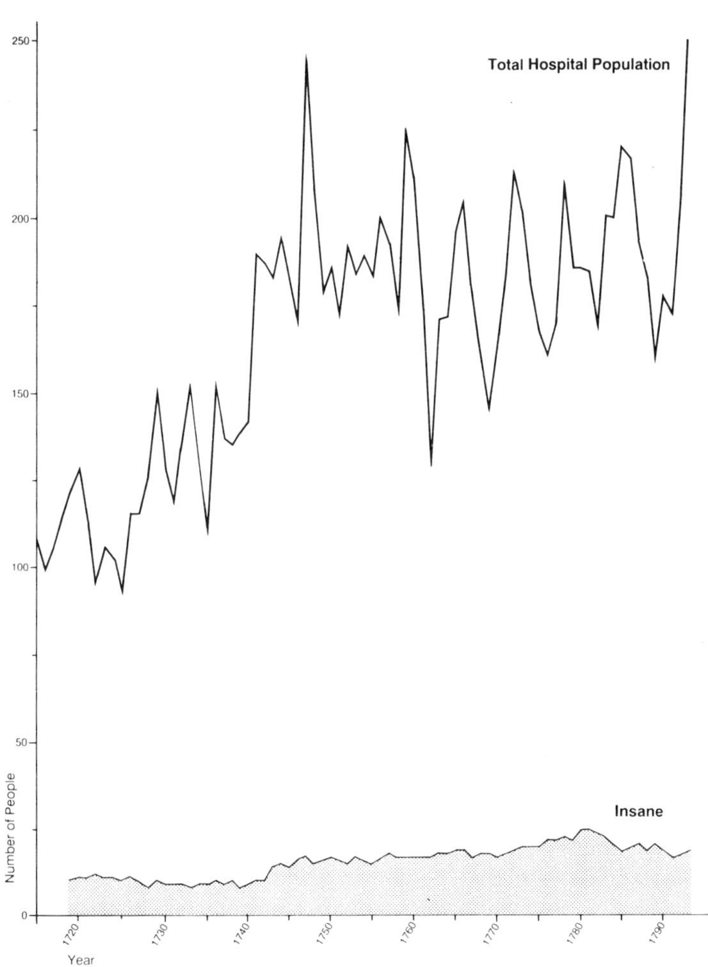

persons in other institutions in the city. Well-off families might have their disturbed or deviant members put away in a convent or monastery. The Hôpital Général, for its part, had its fair share of the senile and feeble-minded. The same was probably true of the *dépôt de mendicité*, the poor-house established in the 1760s to institutionalize the begging and vagrant poor. The numbers of recognizably insane individuals in all these places was not however great and it seems certain that the institutionalized world of insanity was never more than a fraction of the total number of mentally disturbed: in this sphere at least, *grand renfermement* is something of a grandiloquent misnomer.[21]

II

The initial aim behind the introduction of the Hôtel-Dieu Saint-Eloi's *loges* – the ensuring of 'public security' within city walls – remained potent throughout the eighteenth century. A large proportion of detainees were individuals whose insanity for one reason or another was adjudged a menace to public order. In 1769, for example, a certain Robert, an agricultural labourer from the workers' suburbs, was arrested for 'running round the streets day and night, and having almost set on fire the whole of one neighbourhood'.[22] In 1753 a certain Bouissonnade was arrested 'after having wounded several inhabitants', and was carted off to the *loges*.[23] Even when there was not a strong case to be brought against an individual but where the individual seemed dangerously eccentric or psychologically disturbed, the consuls or the *Bureau de police* could still sentence pre-emptively. If the municipality's own *loges* in the Hôtel-Dieu were full, then the consuls negotiated with the hospital administrators to pay for the use of one of the other *loges* until a municipally-financed one became available.[24]

The perceived danger to the public which the insane constituted was sometimes moral rather than physical. Louis Dorel, for example, 'claiming to be from the chateau of Escuve, two leagues from Albi', entered one of Montpellier's parish churches one August morning in 1753, leapt on to an altar, and began smashing religious images and ornaments to right and left.[25] Whether the man was a religious maniac, an iconoclastic Protestant, a precocious dechristianizer, or a juvenile delinquent, he was hauled off by soldiers to the garrison prisons to cool his heels before passing into the Hôtel-Dieu's *loges*. Moral cases frequently involved the honour of families as well as – sometimes more than – public order. In 1739, for example, the consuls of the nearby village of Montbazin prevailed upon the bishop of Montpellier to support the petition of François Donnadieu, father of four children, to have confined in the *loges* his wife who, it was alleged, had long since lost her reason and

> commits extraordinary extravagances, even running around from village to village in a radius of four or five leagues and seeking to argue with everyone, insulting people in all kinds of malicious language and even placing her hands on them.[26]

Such detentions were sometimes viewed as charitable acts. Certainly they saved many families from the embarrassment and dishonour perceived to be attendant on having a lunatic in the family, and from the manifold inconveniences which sprang from having to care for or protect oneself from a deranged relative in the confines of the home. A growing concern to prevent arbitrary or repressive imprisonment – even by *lettre de cachet* – made such charitable detentions look somewhat obsolete. In 1776, for example, the central government admonished the *maire* over the allegedly 'charitable' confinements of dissolute young women from honest families in the Bon Pasteur, a sort of prostitutes' prison and reformatory.[27] About the same time, the hospital's administrators, evidently afraid of losing the charitable status on which they depended to tap the benefactions and liberalities of the townspeople, reacted vigorously against abuses in this sphere. They made it clear that, although they confined the insane, 'our hospital cannot be regarded as a prison (*maison de force*) designed to punish the guilty'.[28] A recent case in which a jealous husband had unjustly had his wife shut away in the *loges* on the grounds of her supposed insanity had, in the administrators' eyes, highlighted

> the danger of the consequences, since in seeking merely to fall in with the wishes of fellow-citizens and the circumstances of families, the administration risks being

taken unawares, and might find itself compromised and charged either with connivance with unjust parents or with setting itself up as a judge of the need to shut away a fellow-citizen.[29]

From this time on, the hospital's regulations insisted that each candidate for confinement should be presented along with a valid police order or with a court judgement (*interdiction*), a covering letter from his or her family, and a medical certificate of insanity.

The dossiers on inmates which the administrators of the hospital came to compile have unfortunately not survived, and it is difficult from the sparse and incomplete documentation still remaining to analyse in any detail how closely regulations on admissions were observed.[30] What little has survived suggests a fair degree of laxness, both before and after the supposed tightening up of admissions in 1776. This was especially the case with diocesan confinements. Bishops had little sense of legal niceties in such matters – and yet the hospital administrators well realized the need to keep on good terms with such an influential dignitary. A lunatic's family who turned up on the doorstep of the hospital armed only with a letter of recommendation from the bishop was unlikely therefore to be turned away. The municipality was, in contrast, more particular. By the last decades of the Ancien Régime, cases which came before the consuls seem normally to have been accompanied by the required documentation: the order of the *Bureau de police*, where this was relevant, a copy of the judicial *interdiction*, letters from the individual's family, a certificate of insanity from his or her neighbours, and a medical certificate as well. The medical certificate did not act as an independent check on the insanity of the person to be confined, however. Usually it merely purported to show that all attempts at cure had failed and that there was little chance of a speedy return to reason. Furthermore, the exiguity of the professional knowledge of many rural practitioners in the Midi – where it was sometimes said that a man's capacity to wield a razor entitled him to call himself a surgeon – does not inspire confidence in their diagnostic and therapeutic capacities.[31]

III

Could those admitted to the Hôtel-Dieu Saint-Eloi's *loges* expect proficient medical treatment at the hands of the more high-flying medical personnel who clustered together in this centre of academic medicine? It would seem not. Despite the medical profession's increasing bent towards clinical methods over the course of the eighteenth century, the most celebrated writers on insanity prior to Pinel were remarkably little interested in treating the institutionalized lunatic. In addition, in Montpellier at least, the structure of the hospital had the effect of shielding the insane from the medical profession (see Figure 8.2). Clinical medicine seemingly stopped short at the gates of the *loges*: and there is no hard evidence to suggest that local doctors approached inmates with anything more than indifference.

The nursing sisters who presided over the internal running of the hospital insulated the inmates of the *loges* from direct medical concern. The regulations introduced for the newly created *loges* in 1716 had stipulated that the hospital's administrators were to provide servants 'to provide remedies and other foodstuffs necessary'.[32] To this end, in 1718 the hospital board passed a contract with Saint Vincent de Paul's Daughters of Charity for a tenth sister to join the congregation of nursing sisters who supervised the internal life of the hospital.[33] The additional sister was to be specially assigned to the treatment of the *pauvres incensez* – though she was to double up by looking after the hospital's extensive wine-cellar as well. The medical knowledge of the Daughters of Charity was not negligible: they were renowned blood-letters and some possessed profound pharmaceutical knowledge. However, it may be doubted whether they could give as full rein to these skills in such a well-organized hospital as the Hôtel-Dieu Saint-Eloi, where they were constantly under the eye of both the medical profession and the hospital administrators, as they would in a smaller more rural hospital. The silence of hospital deliberations on this score suggests that the care the sisters accorded the insane was longer on compassion than on medical pretensions.

How assiduously the inmates of the *loges* were treated by the medical staff attached to the hospital also remains something

Figure 8.2: Plan of the Ground Floor of the Hôtel-Dieu Saint-Eloi of Montpellier, 1785.

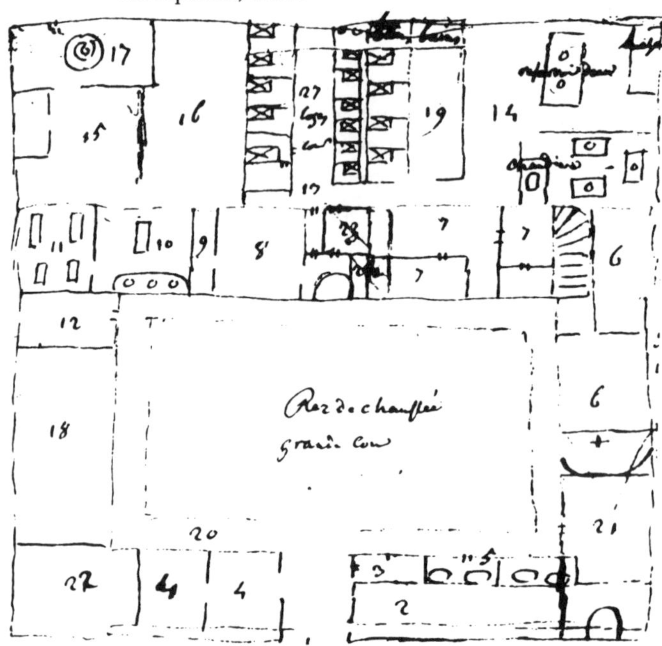

Source: Untitled pen drawing discovered among printed materials relating to Montpellier hospitals in A.N., AD XIV 3.
Notes: Internal evidence suggests that the drawing was done by (or possibly for) Jean Colombier, Royal Inspector of Hospitals and Prisons, who visited the hospitals in October 1785. His report on the institution is located in A.N., F 15 226.
Not shown: drawings of the first and second floors of the hospital (where most of the rooms containing beds were situated).
The entry to the hospital is shown in the middle of the bottom of the photograph. At the opposite end of the courtyard is the *département des fous* (number 13). Number 19 is the *cour des fous*. Drawn on the plan are the *loges* (marked '27 *loges*'), another smaller courtyard (*cour*) and a couple of baths (*bains*).
Colombier's key to the rest of the plan is as follows:

(2) *bibliothèque*
(3) *salle de visite des malades*
(4) *portier*
(5) *salles de bain*
(6) *lingerie*
(7) *pharmacie et laboratoire*
(8) *bureau de l'administration*
(9) *bureau des commis*
(10) *cuisine*
(11) *réfectoir des soeurs*
(12) *lavoir*
(14) *buanderie*
(15) *basse-cour*
(16) *bucher*
(17) *puits à roues*
(18) *greniers*
(20) *galeries*
(21) *église*
(22) *panneterie*
(23) *salle des soeurs*
(24) *cabinet de la Supérieure*

of a mystery. Pierre Fournier, who served as doctor in the hospital from 1755 to 1766, and who published an account of his dealings with inmates in the course of 1763, included among his list of cures a young man who had fallen into 'mania' after being victim in a highway robbery, and whom Fournier restored to health by using the traditional medical techniques of blood-letting, purgatives, emetics, and narcotic drugs.[34] Just how typical this case is – of methods of care, levels of attention, or rates of success – is unknown, although it is probably significant that the individual was treated within the main part of the hospital and not within the *loges.* The administrators, for their part, were not averse to boasting of the cures performed by their doctors in the *loges.*[35] They were flattered by the complimentary remarks on the service in this department accorded them by Jean Colombier, the Royal Inspector of Hospitals and Prisons, who made an inspection of the hospital in 1785. They even disdained use of the government-sponsored pamphlet, the *Manière de traiter les insensés,* penned by Colombier in conjunction with François Doublet, which Colombier attempted to foist on them, replying in their defence that they had nothing to learn from the moral methods, hydrotherapy, and pharmaceutical advice preached there.[36]

Despite the bravura of their public pronouncements, however, the off-guard remarks of the administrators revealed a far more pessimistic attitude towards the therapeutic value of a stay in the *loges.* In 1780, for example in the case of one Caulet, the hospital board was commenting that 'we cannot dissimulate . . . that Sr Caulet does not have possession of all his reason, but it is also true to say that his detention can only help to make him lose it altogether'(!)[37] If a cure was effected, the board maintained in a similar case, it was best for the party involved to leave the *loges* as swiftly as possible since 'a longer detention could effectively make him relapse into the sorry state he was in originally'.[38]

A further dubious note in the medical record of the hospital's medical service towards the insane is the inefficiency of its release policy. One individual spent three years in the *loges* without showing at any time the slightest sign of insanity before it was adjudged appropriate to release him.[39] The frequently recurring motif in medical certificates prior to admission that all efforts at cure had failed was probably taken as a sign of the hopelessness of cases who ended up in the *loges*. If medication did seem to hold out some hopes for cure, then the individual would be released provisionally from the *loges* to undergo treatment in the world outside.[40]

Living conditions within the *loges* were in any case far from conducive to cure. Inmates might be shut away in solitary confinement for lengthy periods in their small – eight feet square – stone-walled and bar-windowed cells, with only, for the non-violent and non-dangerous, the occasional relief of a stroll in the courtyard or through the main wards.[41] Such conditions were, it is true, superior to those pertaining in the other institutions in the city in which the insane might find themselves confined. In the Hôpital Général or the *dépôt de mendicité* for example, the feeble-minded and senile would find themselves rubbing shoulders – such was the overcrowding, often literally! – with the destitute and the down-and-out, the criminal and the vagrant, in an atmosphere of stark austerity and privation.[42] In the two prisons, overcrowding, high humidity levels, and an almost total absence of daylight made life unbearably unhealthy and uncomfortable.[43] Even this, however, was often preferable to the situation in which the insane might be placed in private homes. The labouring and artisan classes who provided the majority of cases of insanity in the city rarely had the room or facilities to provide a comfortable environment for the members of their families they adjudged insane, and the latter could well end up ignominiously chained up in a cellar or shut away in a tiny cubby-hole or airless cupboard under the stairs.[44]

The Hôtel-Dieu Saint-Eloi could certainly offer more than all this. Yet the sympathy of the hospital administrators was more with those who had to endure the anti-social or asocial behaviour of the insane than with the insane themselves. Nor did they feel duty-bound to offer medical aid to the inmates of the *loges* as they did to the other inmates of the hospital. Before the beginning of the eighteenth century, the insane had always been specifically excluded from the hospital, and even after the building of the *loges*, the administrative board viewed care of the insane as essentially extraneous to their *oeuvre*.[45] If they had expanded the number of *loges* over the course of the century, and increased the proportion of places for the insane vis-à-vis the other inmates, this was above all in response to demand from outside.[46] In addition, the hospital found the pensions which private individuals, the municipality, and the diocese paid for the inmates of the *loges* a valuable financial adjunct in a period in which demographic expansion, inflation, and a decline in charitable giving all placed great pressure on the traditional precepts of hospital budgeting. By the 1780s income from such pensions represented 6.3 per cent of the hospital's annual income.[47]

Like all those who came into contact with them, therefore – families, neighbours, municipal officials, ecclesiastical dignitaries, nursing sisters, etc. – hospital administrators regarded the insane as a social rather than a medical concern. Protection of the community from damage at the hands of the unruly or pyromaniac lunatic, the maintenance of family honour and name in the face of the insanity of a close relative, the upholding of traditional codes of conduct which risked subversion by the social deviant, along with the real financial benefits to be reaped from caring for the insane: all these factors bulked larger than a care for the well-being of the individual lunatic or a desire to fit him out for reintegration into the wider society.

IV

The French Revolution – which in Paris was to lead to the 'humanization' of the treatment of the insane at the hands of Pinel and his followers – brought considerable strains and pressures to the institutional treatment of the insane in the provinces. The sometimes politically reactionary *aliénistes* of the early nineteenth century maintained, as a result of clinical observation of the havoc which political passions could wreak on the human mind, that the Revolution had considerably increased the incidence of insanity among the population at large.[48] In Montpellier a greater number of individuals passed through the *loges* of the Hôtel-Dieu Saint-Eloi than before – though the number of places remained relatively constant (see Figure 8.3).[49] Estimates of the numbers of the insane at large were of course likely to be wildly impressionistic, but it was the opinion too of both the *maire* of Montpellier and the hospital board that the numbers of the insane in the region had grown markedly.[50]

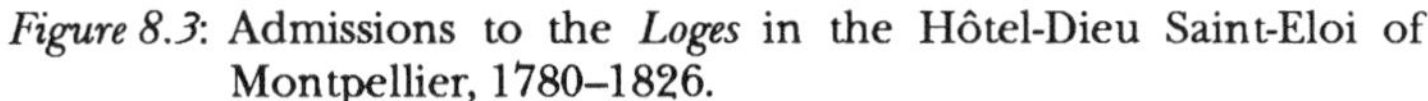

Figure 8.3: Admissions to the *Loges* in the Hôtel-Dieu Saint-Eloi of Montpellier, 1780–1826.

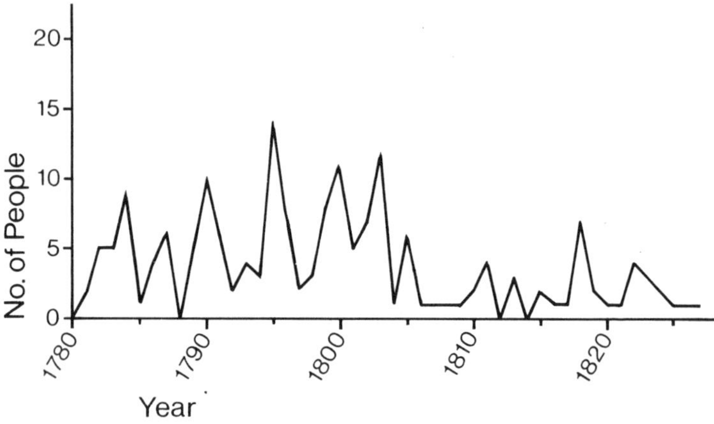

Besides possibly increasing the numbers of those adjudged insane, the Revolution also changed some of the modes of procedure by which the insane could be committed to confinement in the *loges*. However, the sparse documentation which survives suggests that it was not appreciably more difficult to have someone put away for the loss of his or her reason than under the Ancien Régime.[51] Legislation framed in the light of the political campaign against *lettres de cachet*, to protect individuals against arbitrary arrest and administrative detention, cut little ice where the fate of the insane was concerned.[52] The board of the hospital continued to receive as fee-payers those individuals forwarded as insane by their families – especially where the families had managed to secure a judicial *interdiction*. The new law on municipal police of 16/24 August 1790 confirmed the rights of municipalities in this sphere, according them powers to clear the streets of *furieux* and *bêtes féroces* (*sic*).[53] The *loges* of the former diocese were now placed at the disposal of the new district authorities.[54]

The effective scope for detention of the insane seemed in practice to have been as wide as ever, despite the alteration of the political climate. Several inmates of the *loges* despairingly petitioned the public authorities in the atmosphere of political freedom of the early 1790s, contending that they had been unjustly imprisoned for various nefarious reasons.[55] They were all, however, unsuccessful in their pleas. At the height of the

Terror in the city, moreover, the municipal authorities were able to dispatch to the *loges* as insane *citoyenne* Mathieu, *épouse* Robert, simply for uttering 'remarks in favour of the re-establishment of the monarchy'.[56] Despite the eclipse of the Catholic church in the 1790s, there was still much the same concern for 'moral cases' – perhaps partly because of the running down of the old Bon Pasteur which had acted as a detention-centre for women of loose morals. Stonemason Pierre Vincent, for example, anxious to protect the honour of his 'honest family', urged the confinement for insanity of his niece who, he claimed,

> by frequenting bad company, by a taste for luxury and by the excessive freedom she has acquired for herself, had departed from the feelings of puberty and practices vice almost without question.[57]

The continuing slipshod facility of gaining admission into the *loges* and the apparently larger numbers of persons adjudged suitable cases for treatment during the Revolutionary decade threw a heavy burden on the Hôtel-Dieu Saint-Eloi. It was a burden, moreover, which the hospital was ill-equipped to bear. The finances of a great many hospitals in France had been fragile in the last years of the Ancien Régime; but it was to be the Revolution which brought them financial catastrophe – or at very least major financial dislocation.[58] Much of this was due to the steep depreciation over the course of the 1790s of the paper money – the assignats – which the revolutionaries introduced in 1790. Both private individuals and the public authorities – where they could be made to carry on bearing their responsibilities – paid the pensions of inmates of the hospital's *loges* in devalued assignats. Even the raising of the size of the average pension from 400 to 500 *livres* a year could not keep abreast of the scale of depreciation – nor indeed of the rate of inflation either.[59] In fact, the fee-payers were only the tip of the iceberg. The backbone of the hospital's Ancien Régime finances had been its *rentes constituées* (returns on investment). In the course of the 1790s the hospital found itself being paid – or even reimbursed the capital sum – in assignats. This would have been catastrophic for the hospital even without the losses caused by revolutionary reforms which struck at various privileged forms of income such as tithes, seigneurial dues, and municipal tolls from which the hospital had benefited under the Ancien Régime. In the early 1790s the government was prepared to make extraordinary grants of aid to hospitals which suffered in these ways. These funds progressively dried up after 1792, however. First, the Revolutionary Government in 1793 and 1794 gave financial priority to pensions schemes for the home-bound poor rather than hospital subsidies – and even went so far, by the notorious, if short-lived law of 23 Messidor Year II (11 July 1794), as to expropriate all hospital property. Thereafter the Thermidorian and Directorial regimes down to the end of the 1790s espoused a *laissez-faire* policy towards all forms of poor relief, which came close to inhumane negligence. For most of the 1790s, therefore, Montpellier's Hôtel-Dieu Saint-Eloi, like most French hospitals, lived a dependent and at times desperately hand-to-mouth existence in which the hospital board not infrequently found it impossible to make ends meet. Those hospital inmates who remained within the institution – and the discharge rate tended to be high as a result of the forced reduction in commitments or alternatively through a high death-rate – suffered a deterioration in their living standards and in the levels of care which the staff could provide. In 1799 it was reckoned that the cost of a day's care in the hospital was only two-thirds of the cost of 1789 – a reduction which owed almost everything to worsened conditions.[60]

In order to keep afloat financially, the hospital's administrators began to place greater reliance on the care of sick and wounded soldiers, a branch of treatment for which they were reimbursed by the Ministry of War. A hospital which offered soldiers medical care, the logic was, would not be left to fall into financial ruin by governments which were, especially in the mid-1790s, more committed to ensuring the welfare of the *défenseur de la patrie*.[61] In the tactical sphere, too, the aid which the hospital received from the Ministry of War came as a precious adjunct to its tattered finances. The existence of large numbers of military men within the hospital – nearly 40,000 soldiers, over 80 per cent of admissions, entered the hospital between 1807 and 1815[62] – reduced the space available to civilian inmates and also contributed to the general deterioration in conditions. Recuperating soldiers ruled the roost and unmercifully submitted the other inmates to their bad temper, rough tricks, and callous sense of humour.[63] They were also the source of the outbreaks of typhus, typhoid fever, dysentery, and the other epidemics which periodically decimated the inmate population.[64]

The insane were among the worst affected by the changes wrought in the Revolutionary decade. Although the quasi-militarization of the hospital may have contributed towards improvement in general levels of care – for doctors and surgeons always enjoyed a far greater degree of latitude in military than in civilian hospitals – this does not appear to have percolated down to the inmates of the *loges*. About half of those who entered the *loges* died there – a figure far higher than was the case for other entries.[65] Improvements doubtless occurred as hospital finances were re-established in the Napoleonic period. Nevertheless, by 1807, the hospital's administrators were regretfully confessing that:

> we have long been saddened by the restricted limits within which service of the insane at the civilian hospital of this town has been circumscribed as a result of the shortage of space available to us, which is so bad that it obliges us daily to refuse asylum to a limitless number of individuals suffering from this illness.[66]

A plan to increase the number of *loges* and to improve conditions for the insane by annexing the former Providence convent which adjoined the hospital had been mooted as early as 1801. Funds were lacking, however, and the project was still being talked about nearly two decades later.[67] In these circumstances, and in the general context of financial shortage, the best that could be hoped for by the insane was that they might be fed and looked after as well as their fellow inmates. There was no question of medical aid. Early in the Restoration, an independent observer, reviewing the regime inside the *loges*, commented favourably on the foodstuffs the insane were given; but as for therapy, he concluded, 'it all seems to me to be restricted to a concern for cleanliness and supervision'.[68]

In their desire to squeeze funds out of mean and parsimonious governments, hard-pressed hospital administrators in the 1790s had affected an emotive rhetoric of harassed compassion and pity for their charges. It was significant of the move in attitudes towards a desire for greater segregation of the insane, however, that they often jerked the consciences of government by portraying the sick poor harassed and their condition worsened by the propinquity of the insane. This was as true of other institutions in Montpellier as of the hospital. Requesting the transfer of a woman inmate allegedly suffering from 'complete mania' and 'melancholic delerium', the administrators of Montpellier's Hôpital Général, for example, affirmed that 'such an individual can only trouble the order of the room in which he has been placed and the peace of the aged who have there found refuge'.[69] For similar reasons, the administrators of the hospital at nearby Sette requested that Montpellier's *loges* receive a deranged sailor who 'has managed to secure admission, who cannot be made to leave and who mistreats the sick as well as the persons who attend to them'.[70] Compassionate concern for the feelings and conditions of the normal inmate was also behind the decision of the administrators of the Hôtel-Dieu Saint-Eloi in 1801 that henceforth the insane would always be kept under lock and key and not allowed to wander round the wards: to allow the latter was tantamount to 'neglecting the security of inmates' and might occasion 'acts of insanity' which could 'disrupt the peace of the sick'.[71] The limitations in the capacity and facilities of the Hôtel-Dieu Saint-Eloi in the aftermath of the Revolution eventually made an impression on the Prefect of the Hérault. After 1810, at his behest, the regenerated departmental *dépôt de mendicité* in Montpellier relieved the pressure on places in the Hôtel-Dieu Saint-Eloi's *loges* by making special provision for the insane within its own buildings, situated in the grounds of the Hôpital Général.[72] In the course of 1813, for example, while the Hôtel-Dieu's *loges* admitted only six new entrants, the *dépôt de mendicité* admitted a dozen lunatics, most of them drifters, down-and-outs, and paupers whose families were too poor to pay a pension for their upkeep in the Hôtel-Dieu.[73] By the time of the Restoration, while the Hôtel-Dieu contained some eighteen *loges* still in use, nearly forty persons categorized as insane were to be found in the *dépôt de mendicité*.[74] The Restoration authorities were to preside over the running down of the Hôtel-Dieu's *loges*, now decayed and discredited, and the erection of a separate building for the insane adjoining the *dépôt*, which furthered the segregation of the insane from the world of institutionalized poverty.

V

A new stage in the treatment of the insane in Montpellier began under the Restoration with the opening of what soon acquired the title of the Clinique des Aliénés. In August 1817 the Minister of the Interior informed the Prefect of the Hérault that he desired a *maison centrale d'aliénés* to be established within the department. At first, the city's hospital commission turned its attention to the old plan of converting the Providence buildings.[75] The reduction in the scale of the operations of the *dépôt de mendicité* after 1819, however, released buildings and potential building space whose conversion for the care of the insane was likely to prove less expensive than the work necessary on the Providence. In 1821 the hospital commission undertook a building plan to establish a proper *maison d'aliénés* in the grounds of the *dépôt*. Further expenditure of just under 200,000 *livres* in the years down to 1827 increased the number and improved the conditions of the new buildings. The new institution started receiving the insane into its sixty-four *loges* from 1823 – at first the men and later the women. At the same time, provision within the Hôtel-Dieu's *loges* was run down, with the last inmate being received there in 1826.[76]

At first glance, the new establishment was nothing more than the consecration of the desire for segregating the institutionalized poor from the vagaries of the insane which had been increasingly making itself felt. A new significance was injected into the institution, however, by the decision of the hospital commission in 1821 to appoint a pupil of the celebrated Esquirol, Hippolyte Rech, as 'physician specially entrusted with the service of the insane'. It was under his influence that what had originally been conceived of simply as a holding-place and quarantine centre for the insane was converted into a testing-ground for the new theories of mental alienation preached in Paris by Pinel and Esquirol.

Hippolyte Rech came to his new job with all the bright-eyed enthusiasm of a man who felt himself to be a part of a general movement of science and philanthropy which promised to be enormously beneficial to mankind. A native of Montpellier, Rech had, during a three-year stay in Paris, come into close contact with the teaching and works of Pinel and had trained under Esquirol.[77] In the preliminary report on his *Clinique des*

Aliénés published in 1826, he cited Esquirol's famous comments on the appalling conditions in which the insane were kept in provincial France as representing, *grosso modo*, the state of the insane in Montpellier in the aftermath of the hospital crisis of the Revolutionary period. By the early 1820s, however, Rech noted, special measures had been introduced in Rouen, Bordeaux, Lyons, and Toulouse to care for the insane using the methods preached by Pinel and Esquirol. Now it was Montpellier's turn to take its place in a general development which, in Rech's eyes, 'seems to presage a general revolution.'[78]

Crucial to Rech's sense of mission was his firm conviction that it was the doctor's role to preside over the treatment of the insane. In Montpellier this was new, as the seeming lack of medical treatment on the inmates of the *loges* in the Hôtel-Dieu Saint-Eloi in the eighteenth and early nineteenth centuries suggested. It had been Pinel's achievement to show that the clinical methods which the medical profession had embraced over the late seventeenth and eighteenth centuries could be extended to the study of insanity – rechristened mental alienation and classified according to medically recorded symptoms. Rech cited the therapeutic successes and the intellectual prowess of his predecessors to pour scorn on those who held the ancient prejudice that medical care was of no avail against insanity. The figure of the doctor was, according to Rech, pivotal: in the internal regime of the *Clinique des Aliénés*, 'It is to him that everything connects'.[79] The Montpellier hospital commission, eager to indulge the theories of their bright young man, gave him a carte blanche in the internal running of the new establishment.

It was a significant paradox of the new treatment of the insane which Rech espoused that the unparallelled standing and powers of the doctor over inmates was not based on his specifically medical prowess. The doctor had gained admittance to the asylum not because of the power of his drugs but because of the strength of his personality in applying the so-called 'moral treatment' held in awe by the disciples of Pinel. The doctor was a 'moral entrepreneur' within the new institution rather than a dispenser of medical therapy.[80] Rech was scathing, for example, about the ineffectiveness of the blood-letting, purgatives, and standby drugs which were traditionally used in the treatment of the insane. In contrast, he maintained, 'moral treatment seems to me so far to deserve the greatest confidence, and it is to putting it effectively into action that I am devoting my attention'.[81] He proudly confessed that in the *Clinique des Aliénés*, 'I prescribe only few medicines'.[82] If occasionally he did have recourse to drugs, it was for their tranquillizing rather than curative effects: rather, he noted, 'with the intention of calming their virulence and habituating them to passive obedience than with a mind to bringing them back to reason'.[83]

The establishment of appropriate environmental conditions within the establishment was a *sine qua non* of the effectiveness of moral methods. Rech highlighted the importance of 'hygienic relief [which] is much superior in its effectiveness than remedies whether internal or external which are often lauded with ridiculous grandiloquence'.[84] First and foremost, Rech set about creating living conditions which were not an affront to the humanity of the insane. The hospital commission, he acknowledged, had endeavoured to improve conditions for the insane even prior to his own arrival in Montpellier. Most of the improvements were introduced in the years following Rech's arrival and under his direct supervision. By the mid-1820s each of the approximately fifty inmates was housed in a *loge* approximately three metres by two. A door which unfortunately opened inwards – an obvious design fault which Rech hoped to remedy – and a small window provided light and ventilation. Initially the staff experimented with having latrines inside each *loge*. This was a generally acknowledged hygienic disaster, however, and was replaced by a community latrine some way distant from the *loges*. The furnishings within each *loge* varied according to the state of the inmate – an attempt at classification and differentiation which appears to have been quite new in Montpellier. If the inmate were adjudged *furieux* and broke and smashed things, then he might be accorded only straw and blanket. Those who periodically had fits of frenzy were allowed iron beds which were firmly fixed to the floor, sheets, and a couple of blankets. The inmates who were calm for most of the time were allowed a table and chair as well.

The days of the insane were moulded into a similarly austere but basically practical routine which was thought to provide a suitable framework for care. Order and regularity were among the moral methods preached by the new school. The doors of the *loges* were opened from 5 a.m. until dusk, and the insane spent the day working in the gardens and vineyards of the Hôpital. On rising, the *loges* were cleaned out. Meals began at 10 a.m. with a bread dole and there followed further breaks for meals at 3 p.m. and 5 p.m. (6 p.m. in the summer). The rations were identical to those distributed at the adjacent Hôpital Général: bread, vegetables, and alternately vegetable soup or a meat bouillon. The other main occasion in the day of the inmate was the visit of the doctor. He, or in his absence the surgeon attached to the establishment, made a morning visit in which he checked up on the physical state of the insane and perhaps prescribed baths for them. The afternoon visit was a lengthier, more constructive, and selective affair in which the doctor endeavoured to converse with a number of the inmates 'to try to produce an effect on their morale'.

The way in which the doctor could 'produce an effect on the morale of the sick' was varied. Rech observed of the methods which he, following the examples of Pinel and Esquirol, utilized, that 'One utilizes in turn pleas and threats, gentleness and violence, rewards and punishments'.[85] A preliminary was always the strict segregation of the insane from other inmates; and the absolute separation of the sexes. Among punishments, cold baths, as Pinel had found, were especially good, notably for 'individuals weakened by masturbation'.[86] Yet punishment did not go much further than this: for a vital ingredient of the moral method was the deliberate exclusion of gratuitous violence from the treatment of the insane.

The symbol of the appalling conditions to which the insane had been subjected before Pinel had been the violence of the staff towards the insane, and the chains used to restrain them. The new moral treatment turned its back on such methods of intimidation and restraint. Rech acted swiftly in this sphere. Realizing that beatings and ill-treatment were partly the consequence of weakness on the part of the staff, he immediately on arrival dismissed 'two aged orderlies who had the habits of former days'. They were replaced with more numerous domestics. The emphasis was that these should be 'young and robust' and should with the occasional help of the porter and the other guards

> present an imposing forcefulness, maintain the recalcitrants' respect and subject them without difficulty.

> The greatest gentleness is expressly enjoined to them. They must shut the insane away when they disturb good order, but may never punish them and still less strike them.[87]

The removal of violence was the watchword of the moral treatment, and what gave it much of its public renown and *éclat*. The pivotal figure of the doctor was to act as moral censor of possible violence towards the insane. It was Rech's proud boast that 'since the new building started to contain the insane, we have never had recourse either to chains or to blows of any kind'.[88] Yet the removal of chains did not get rid of violence entirely from the emergent asylum. Rather than highlighting an absence of care for the humanity of the insane, violence was harnessed, confined, canalized into a positive form of treatment: chains gave way to the *camisole de force*, the strait-jacket, whose appearance in the hospitals of France coincided with the disappearance of more punitive forms of restraint.[89] The element of violence in the use of such restraining devices is clearly apparent, despite Rech's emphasis on 'freedom':

> With the strait-jacket, all lunatics may be restrained; if one of them is too strong or too nimble, we reinforce the strait-jacket by means of a wide strap which fixes his arms against his body without in any way obstructing him; if one of them threatens to kick out, we have put on him two garters which, connected together by a strong piece of cloth, allow the lunatic to walk but do not allow him the freedom to open his legs widely apart. We use these methods only when the insane are in the courtyard; when they are in their cells we leave them perfectly free. If however it is to be feared that this freedom might become harmful to themselves, we leave the strait-jacket on. In some circumstances we have been obliged to attach the lunatic on his bed by means of two wide straps attached to the bed by both ends: one around the body allows him to turn over either way, the other linked to two wide rings in manipulable hide and in which the lower legs are trapped. The lunatic can thus turn and turn around to either side, he can stay lying down on his back without feeling any evident discomfort by the means which are restraining him and without these means, even in his most violent exertions, being harmful to him.[90]

VI

Despite the high hopes of Hippolyte Rech, the embryonic lunatic asylum of Montpellier was not a conspicuous success. Rech amassed the sort of statistical information on inmates which the post-Pinel students of mental disorder recommended as essential to the progress of medical science. But in the event they did not amount to much. Part of the problem was that local people profoundly distrusted the new institution: as Rech bewailed, people with lunatics on their hands, 'only decide to send us them when they have become too much of a burden or when badly administered remedies have made the illness totally incurable'.[91] With the flow of inmates through the institution silting up in this manner, it failed to achieve the high cure rate that had been hoped for. By 1833 Rech was sadly admitting to the Prefect of the Hérault that

> we only have incurables remaining. This is what happens in all the institutions for the insane which are not very large. As the number of cures is only one out of every three entries, those who are not cured remain and end up by occupying all the places.[92]

The logic of the situation was such that matters could only get worse. By 1838 the cure rate had fallen from a third to approximately 5 per cent. The therapeutic pretensions of the institutions seemed unfounded.[93]

When the law of 1838 stipulated the creation of a lunatic asylum in each of France's departments, the departmental authorities of the Hérault used the facilities and buildings embodied in Rech's *Clinique des Aliénés.* Although the Prefect insisted upon the continuing obligations of local charity in ensuring the upkeep of the harmless and indigent insane – there was never thus any question of the asylum containing all the mentally disordered of the whole department – it was clear that a large proportion of the inmates of the new institution would continue to be, in the Prefect's words, 'lunatics whose mental state . . . compromised . . . public order and the security of prisoners', and for whom there could frequently be little hope of cure.[94] The asylum's stated obligations thus disabled any pretensions that Rech might have that the new institution could fulfil the therapeutic and scientific functions which he had formerly ascribed to the *Clinique des Aliénés*. Indeed Rech, seeing which way the wind was blowing, withdrew to set up a small privately run madhouse under his direction in which he continued to treat the insane according to the precepts of the new science of 'mental alienation'. By the kind of carefully restrictive admissions policy which was denied him at the departmental lunatic asylum and its pre-1838 predecessor, he was again able to achieve cure rates of 25 per cent or more in the 1840s.[95]

Rech's experiences in the treatment of the insane in early-nineteenth century Montpellier highlight the fact that – if the city is at all representative – the new lunatic asylum instituted by the law of 1838 was still above all a holding and restraining place rather than a therapeutic establishment. Since the middle of the eighteenth century, the medical profession had managed to carve out for themselves – nationally as well as locally – an important niche at the heart of the institutions for the care of the insane, a niche which a century before they had not even desired, let alone achieved. Medical ideas about insanity had evolved too. In the writings of Pinel, Esquirol, and their pupils – who collectively dominated the French psychiatric scene down to the last quarter of the nineteenth century – the treatment of the institutionalized insane had become a central rather than a marginal or non-existent object of interest and research. The insane were now 'mental patients' rather than offenders or criminals and the treatment proposed for them embodied all the main leitmotivs of the ongoing 'Medical Revolution': the importance accorded physical examination and observation, the use of statistics, the location of care in specialized institutions. Yet despite all this, the new lunatic asylum over which the medical profession presided was certainly not a 'mental hospital'. Public safety, the convenience of families and, since the turn of the eighteenth century, pity for the lot of the sick poor who hitherto had had to share their hospital lodgings with the insane, all made of the institution for the care of the insane a dumping-ground rather than a place where entrants could be fitted out to return into the wider community as a result of the healing powers of the medical profession. All this, moreover, in the premier medical city of provincial France. In this sense, the 'prehistory' of the provincial lunatic asylum loomed large over the form and the functions of the post-1838 institutions.[96]

Notes

1. The recent work by J. Goldstein, *Console and Classify: The French Psychiatric Profession in the Nineteenth Century* (Cambridge, 1987) provides an excellent and informed overview, supplanting on many important particulars the classic work of M. Foucault, *Folie et déraison. Histoire de la folie à l'âge classique* (Paris, 1961), which ends in the early nineteenth century, as well as a number of works more focused on the early nineteenth century: notably R. Castel, *L'Ordre psychiatrique: l'âge d'or de l'aliénisme* (Paris, 1976); G. Swain, *Le Sujet de la folie: naissance de la psychiatrie* (Toulouse, 1977); and M. Gaucher and G. Swain, *La Pratique de l'esprit humain: l'institution asilaire et la révolution démocratique* (Paris, 1980); as well as the general overviews provided in C. Quétel, *Les Fous et leurs médecines: de la Renaissance au XXe. siècle* (Paris, 1979); and C. Quétel and J. Postel, *Nouvelle histoire de la psychiatrie* (Toulouse, 1983).

2. For a cursory overview, see C. Jones, 'The "New Treatment" of the insane in Revolutionary Paris', *History Today* (October 1980). For Pinel, see his authoritative *Traité médico-philosophique sur l'aliénation mentale* (Year IX = 1801). Was the story of Pinel and the 'liberation of the insane' a myth? A growing body of literature advises caution. See in particular G. Swain, *Le Sujet de la folie: naissance de la psychiatrie* (Toulouse, 1977), and D.B. Weiner, 'The origins of psychiatry: Pinel or the Zeitgeist?', in O. Baur and O. Glandieu (eds) *Zusammenhang. Festschrift für Marielene Putscher* (2 vols, Cologne, 1984).

3. J. Esquirol, *Des Etablissements des aliénés en France et des moyens d'améliorer le sort de ces infortunés* (Paris, 1819) p. 7.

4. ibid., pp. 3 f.

5. In spite of the work cited in note 2, the study of the institutional treatment of the insane in a local context and over the eighteenth and the early nineteenth century which is attempted in this chapter remains much neglected. See, for comparisons, J.B. Lautard, *La Maison des fous de Marseille. Essai sur cet établissement depuis sa fondation en 1699 jusqu'à 1837* (Marseille, 1840); J.P. Huber, J.P. Macher, and J. Alliez, 'L'hospitalisation "forcée" des insensés à Avignon au XVIIIe. siècle', *Information psychiatrique* (1980); C. Quétel, 'Garder les fous dans un asile de province au XIXe. siècle', *Annales de Normandie* (1979); and, for later in the nineteenth century, G. Bléandonu and G. Le Gaufey, 'The creation of the insane asylums of Paris and Auxerre', in R. Forster and O. Ranum (eds) *Deviants and the Abandoned in French Society. Selections from the 'Annales'* (Baltimore, Md and London, 1978), an article which appeared in French in *Annales. Economies. Sociétés. Civilisations* (1975). The main source utilized here are the archives of the charitable institutions in which the insane were kept, notably, in this case, the archives of the Hôtel-Dieu Saint-Eloi of Montpellier. These are divided into two chronological series: archives preceding 1790 (henceforth = HD I); and archives posterior to 1790 (henceforth = HD II). Both series are located in the Archives départementales de l'Hérault (henceforth = A.D.H.). For the early nineteenth century the Hôtel-Dieu's archives may be complemented by the records of the

city's Hôpital Général (henceforth = HG I, for archives prior to 1790, and HG II, for those after that date). The archives of the municipality of Montpellier (henceforth = A.M.M.) also contain much relevant data, especially the registers of deliberations of the *Conseil de ville* (henceforth = BB Reg.).

6. Foucault, *Histoire de la folie*, passim.

7. R. Semelaigne, *Phillippe Pinel et son oeuvre* (Paris, 1927) is a good example of the genre.

8. Some by now rather dated works take the story up to the Revolution: for example, P. Sérieux and L. Libert, *Le Régime des aliénés au XVIIIe. siècle* (Paris, 1914); Sérieux and Libert, 'L'assistance et le traitement des maladies mentales au temps de Louis XVI', *Revue historique de droit français et étranger* (1931); and P. Sérieux, 'Le Parlement de Paris et la surveillance des maisons d'aliénés et de correctionnaires aux XVIIe. et XVIIIe. siècles', ibid. (1938). See too Quétel and Postel, *Nouvelle histoire*, pp. 105 ff., 171 ff.; Castel, *L'Ordre psychiatrique*, pp. 24 ff.; and A. Bigorre, 'L'Administration des malades mentaux dans les établissements de soins de 1789 à 1838', medical thesis (Paris, 1967).

9. A.M.M., BB Reg. (14 December 1707).

10. C.H. de Saint-Simon, *Mémoires* ('Grands Ecrivains de France' edition, 36 vols, 1923–4), xiii, p. 132.

11. See p. 243 ff.

12. C. d'Aigrefeuille, *Histoire de la ville de Montpellier* (new edition published by M. de la Pijardière, Montpellier, 1885) provides an interesting municipal chronicle of the late seventeenth and early eighteenth centuries.

13. A.D.H., HD I F 35. HD I E 3 (2 November 1715).

14. For police and prostitutes, see Chapter 7.

15. A.D.H., HD I F 35.

16. ibid.

17. A.D.H., HD I E 5.

18. For rebuilding, see A.D.H., HD I F 35 (16 August 1766) and E 11 (23 May 1772). For the Revolution, A.D.H., L 3970.

19. Figure 8.1: A.D.H., HD I F 15 to 33. A figure for each year was arrived at by averaging twenty-four readings, one at the beginning and one in the middle of each month. Changes in the methods of recording inmates prevent us from knowing the size of the insane population in the hospital after 1793. A.D.H., HD II F 14.

20. A.D.H., HD I F 36.

21. Monasteries and convents normally admitted lunatics interned by royal *lettre de cachet.* An examination of the use of this administrative procedure in Languedoc suggests that there were only small numbers of the insane amongst the moral offenders, disobedient family members, and occasional political dissidents also interned in this way (A.D.H., C 111 to 144). In an analysis of *lettres de cachet* in neighbouring Provence, F.X. Emmanuelli reckons about 15 per cent of cases were attributable to insanity: '"Ordres du Roi" et lettres de cachet en Provence à la fin de l'Ancien Régime', *Revue historique* (1974); while for the généralité of Caen, C. Quétel comes up with a

figure of 20 per cent: *De par le Roi: essai sur les lettres de cachet* (Toulouse, 1981). Similarly at the Hôpital Général, most adult inmates were aged, disabled, or infirm rather than insane. Moreover the number of adult inmates was dwindling over the last decades of the Ancien Régime as a result of the institution's grave financial problems: C. Jones, *Charity and 'Bienfaisance': The Treatment of the Poor in the Montpellier Region, 1740–1815* (Cambridge, 1982) pp. 67–70, 262. As for the *dépôt de mendicité*, the fact that the Intendant of Languedoc did not feel it necessary to build special cells for the insane as the government urged in 1769 suggests that the number of lunatics there was insignificant: A.D.H., C 569.

22. A.M.M., BB Reg. (17 April 1769).

23. ibid. (21 August 1753).

24. References concerning the insane are extremely numerous in the registers of municipal deliberations (A.M.M., BB Reg.) throughout the century.

25. A.M.M., GG (unclassified documents).

26. A.D.H., HD I F 35.

27. Bibliothèque Nationale, Manuscrits français, 7513.

28. A.D.H., HD I F 35.

29. A.D.H., HD I E 11 (13 July 1776). Cf. ibid. (27 May 1775).

30. A.D.H., HD I F 35, for a handful of surviving dossiers on individuals detained on the orders of the bishop.

31. See in particular the sometimes barely literate medical certificates to be found in A.D.H., HD I F 35, HD II G 8. Cf. A. Babeau, *Le Village sous l'Ancien Régime* (Paris, 1882) p. 332; L. Dermigny, 'De la Révocation à la Révolution', in P. Wolff (ed.) *Histoire du Languedoc* (Toulouse, 1967) p. 390; and A. Molinier, *Une Paroisse du Bas Languedoc: Sérignan, 1650–1792* (Montpellier, 1968) p. 170.

32. A.D.H., HD I F 35.

33. Archives Nationales (henceforth = A.N.) S 6171. For the Daughters of Charity, see above, chapters 3–5.

34. P. Fournier, 'Observations sur les maladies qui ont regné dans l'Hôtel-Dieu de Montpellier pendant l'année 1763, suivi d'observations sur plusieurs maladies particulières', in Richard de Hautesierck (ed.) *Recueil d'observations de médecine des hôpitaux militaires* (i, 1766).

35. A.N., F 15 226.

36. ibid. For Colombier, cf. Goldstein, *Console and Classify*, pp. 44 f.

37. A.D.H., HD I F 35.

38. A.D.H., C 570.

39. A.D.H., HD I F 36.

40. ibid.

41. A.D.H., HD I F 35. Cf. HD I E 12 (27 September 1783). See Fig. 8.2.

42. For the institutional context of eighteenth-century Montpellier, see Jones, *Charity and 'Bienfaisance'*, passim.

43. A.N., F 15 226.

44. A.D.H., HD I F 35 and F 36. Cf. frequent indications of this sort in A.M.M., BB Reg.

45. A.D.H., HD I E 1 (18 August 1696: 'the insane must not be admitted'). Cf. HD I E F 35.

46. The proportion of places within the hospital occupied by the insane grew from 10.7 per cent in the 1720s to 12.9 per cent in the 1780s. Jones, *Charity and 'Bienfaisance'*, pp. 58–9, 262.

47. A.D.H., HD I E 119 to E 128 (annual accounts of the hospital).

48. See discussion of this point in G. Rosen, *Madness in Society* (London, 1968), p. 178. Cf. Goldstein, *Console and Classify*, p. 101.

49. A.D.H., HD I F 36, HD II G 9.

50. A.D.H., HD II E 90, F 2.

51. See in particular the handful of dossiers in HD II G 8, and also those in A.D.H., L 3968. For a discussion of the legal position of the insane in post-Revolutionary Montpellier: A.N., BB 18 366.

52. Foucault, *Histoire de la folie*, pp. 508 ff.

53. ibid., p. 511.

54. A.D.H., L 3968; HD II E 1 (23 October 1790, 15 January 1791).

55. A.D.H. HD II G 8; L 3968.

56. A.D.H., HD II G 8.

57. A.D.H., L 2972.

58. For the financial problems of hospitals in the 1790s, see the overview presented by J. Imbert, *Le Droit hospitalier de la Révolution et de l'Empire* (Paris, 1954).

59. A.D.H., L 3968.

60. A.D.H., HG II F 53.

61. See Chapter 6.

62. A.N., F 15 1423.

63. A.D.H., HD II E 127; HD II E 1 and E 2.

64. A.D.H., 1 X 2; HG II E 1, E 2.

65. Average death-rate in the hospital between 1807 and 1814 was 6.2 per cent (1 X 2). For the insane, the figure between 1790 and 1815 was 47.3 per cent: HD II G 9.

66. A.D.H., HD II E 90.

67. ibid.; and A.D.H., 1 X 2.

68. A.D.H., 1 X 2.

69. A.D.H., HG II G 8.

70. A.D.H., L 3774.

71. A.D.H., HG II E 12. For similar sentiments, cf. HG II E 2 (20 October 1807); L 3774; HD II G 8.

72. A.D.H., HG II G 96.

73. A.D.H., HD II G 9; and for the *dépôt de mendicité*, HG II G 13, G 20.

74. A.N., F 15 751.

75. A.D.H., HD II E 90. Cf. 1 X 2.

76. For the creation of the new establishment, see especially A.D.H., HG II G 94, G 95; H II E 111; and the works of Rech cited in note 77.

77. for a cursory summary of his life and works, see L. Dulieu, 'Le Professeur Rech', *Monspeliensis Hippocrates* (1966). The pattern of life in the new establishment is made clear in A.D.H., HG II G 96 and in H. Rech, 'Clinique de la Maison des Aliénés', *Ephémérides médicales de*

Montpellier (Montpellier, ii, 1826); Rech, *Clinique de la Maison des Aliénés de Montpellier (depuis le premier janvier jusqu'au 31 décembre)* (Montpellier, 1828) (henceforth = *Clinique I, Clinique II*).

78. *Clinique I*, p. 12.

79. ibid., p. 121.

80. Cf. Foucault, *Histoire de la folie*, pp. 604–12. The phrase 'moral entrepreneurs' is from A.T. Scull, *Museums of Madness: The Social Organization of Insanity in Nineteenth-Century England* (London, 1979) pp. 125 ff. Scull's work is influenced by Foucault, and brings out the similar position of the medical profession vis-à-vis the insane in early-nineteenth-century England.

81. *Clinique I*, p. 122.

82. ibid. For corroborating evidence on this point, see R. de Vilback, *Voyages dans les départements formés de l'ancienne province de Languedoc* (Paris, 1825) p. 291.

83. A.D.H., HG II G 96.

84. *Clinique II*, pp. 2 f.

85. A.D.H., HG II G 96.

86. *Clinique I*, p. 122.

87. ibid.

88. A.D.H., HG II G 96.

89. The first mention of a *gilet de force* in Montpellier occurs in 1804: A.D.H., HD II G 8.

90. A.D.H., HG II G 96.

91. *Clinique I*, p. 129.

92. A.D.H., HG II G 96.

93. ibid.

94. A.N., F 15 3904.

95. ibid.

96. See the social control arguments mounted in Goldstein, *Console and Classify*, passim, and notably p. 284: the new treatment of the insane aimed 'to control and contain as well as to heal and improve'.

Index

about their own faith, including their doubts. Deacon's mom asked me to offer a prayer.

After most of the kids left, I phoned Jackie. She had asked me to call her sometime during the night, saying she didn't mind if I woke her. I knew it was because she was worried about my safety. I decided to tell her about using my car to try to draw out Harley and Dirk. I hated to worry her but wasn't willing to keep it from her.

"Were you asleep?" I asked.

"No. I was watching TV. So what's up, cowboy? Not getting shot at tonight, I hope."

I filled her in on our gathering at Deacon's mother's place. Then I told her about our plan to park Night Watch on South Division, emphasizing Johnson's approval of the plan. I was surprised at her reaction.

"It makes sense to me," she said. "As long as you won't leave town, you're at risk whatever you do or don't do. Just be very careful."

After I called Johnson and told him we were ready to place my car, Lydia and I headed to the Souls' pad. Lawton, Mad Dog and Red Feather were sitting on the front steps when we got there. I noticed an unmarked police car parked across the street and smiled at the thought of the gang and the cops cooperating on this gig.

Lawton approached my rental car. "How about I ride with you and Lydia to your place to pick up your wheels," he proposed.

"Sounds good to me," I said, and he climbed into the back seat.

Red Feather and Mad Dog followed us to my house, the unmarked a few cars behind. When Lawton and I got out, Lydia slid over to the driver's seat. Lawton and I made our way to the alley behind my house so I could retrieve my car from the garage.

"You're not even limping anymore," I said to Lawton. I was surprised, then, to notice he was holding a gun at his side.

"Just a minute," he whispered. He checked out the alley. After peering through the window of the small door into the garage, he opened that door carefully. He scoped out the interior of the garage and signaled me to raise the main door.

As we got into Night Watch, I said, "Didn't the police keep your gun for evidence after you shot Van Boven?"

"Yeah, they did."

"So what's that, and where did you get it?"

"It's a twenty-two pistol," he said tucking it behind his belt under his colors. "That's all you need to know."

I backed into the alley and drove to where Mad Dog and Red Feather waited with Lydia. I didn't see the unmarked. We made it uneventfully to South Division, where I parked the car near Swinging Doors. I hoped Harley and Dirk would take the bait. I imagined them parking nearby, waiting for me to return to my car. Then instead of them nabbing me, the police would arrest them.

Lydia slid back to the passenger side of my rental and I got behind the wheel. Lawton checked something with Mad Dog, then came back. "I'll stick with you till you drop Lydia at her place. Then you can take me home. Okay?"

My own security guard. I wasn't complaining.

As we crossed the Grand River, I looked in my rearview mirror. "Looks like Red Feather and Mad Dog are still with us."

"Figured it wouldn't hurt," said Lawton.

After I dropped Lydia off, I said, "I'll bring you to your pad, and then I'm going to stop back at my house before I go to Nathan's. I need to pick up a sermon I've been working on."

Lawton shook his head. "Bad idea. If it's real important to get that sermon now, how about I go with you?"

about their own faith, including their doubts. Deacon's mom asked me to offer a prayer.

After most of the kids left, I phoned Jackie. She had asked me to call her sometime during the night, saying she didn't mind if I woke her. I knew it was because she was worried about my safety. I decided to tell her about using my car to try to draw out Harley and Dirk. I hated to worry her but wasn't willing to keep it from her.

"Were you asleep?" I asked.

"No. I was watching TV. So what's up, cowboy? Not getting shot at tonight, I hope."

I filled her in on our gathering at Deacon's mother's place. Then I told her about our plan to park Night Watch on South Division, emphasizing Johnson's approval of the plan. I was surprised at her reaction.

"It makes sense to me," she said. "As long as you won't leave town, you're at risk whatever you do or don't do. Just be very careful."

After I called Johnson and told him we were ready to place my car, Lydia and I headed to the Souls' pad. Lawton, Mad Dog and Red Feather were sitting on the front steps when we got there. I noticed an unmarked police car parked across the street and smiled at the thought of the gang and the cops cooperating on this gig.

Lawton approached my rental car. "How about I ride with you and Lydia to your place to pick up your wheels," he proposed.

"Sounds good to me," I said, and he climbed into the back seat.

Red Feather and Mad Dog followed us to my house, the unmarked a few cars behind. When Lawton and I got out, Lydia slid over to the driver's seat. Lawton and I made our way to the alley behind my house so I could retrieve my car from the garage.

"You're not even limping anymore," I said to Lawton. I was surprised, then, to notice he was holding a gun at his side.

"Just a minute," he whispered. He checked out the alley. After peering through the window of the small door into the garage, he opened that door carefully. He scoped out the interior of the garage and signaled me to raise the main door.

As we got into Night Watch, I said, "Didn't the police keep your gun for evidence after you shot Van Boven?"

"Yeah, they did."

"So what's that, and where did you get it?"

"It's a twenty-two pistol," he said tucking it behind his belt under his colors. "That's all you need to know."

I backed into the alley and drove to where Mad Dog and Red Feather waited with Lydia. I didn't see the unmarked. We made it uneventfully to South Division, where I parked the car near Swinging Doors. I hoped Harley and Dirk would take the bait. I imagined them parking nearby, waiting for me to return to my car. Then instead of them nabbing me, the police would arrest them.

Lydia slid back to the passenger side of my rental and I got behind the wheel. Lawton checked something with Mad Dog, then came back. "I'll stick with you till you drop Lydia at her place. Then you can take me home. Okay?"

My own security guard. I wasn't complaining.

As we crossed the Grand River, I looked in my rearview mirror. "Looks like Red Feather and Mad Dog are still with us."

"Figured it wouldn't hurt," said Lawton.

After I dropped Lydia off, I said, "I'll bring you to your pad, and then I'm going to stop back at my house before I go to Nathan's. I need to pick up a sermon I've been working on."

Lawton shook his head. "Bad idea. If it's real important to get that sermon now, how about I go with you?"

"Boy, I just can't shake you," I said. But, in fact, I was relieved. Since the electricity at my house was still turned off, going upstairs in the dark, alone, to get the sermon would probably feel a tad spooky.

When I stopped for a traffic light, Red Feather pulled up alongside. "You might as well take off," I called. "I want to pick up something from my house, and then I'll drop Lawton off."

Red Feather looked past me to Lawton. "Yeah, go ahead," said Lawton. "See you back at the pad."

A short time later, I parked in front of my house. We walked around back, and I unlocked the door. Lawton and I climbed to the study upstairs. There was just enough light coming in the one unbroken study window so that I could find the sermon folder in the file drawer.

I held the file up and was about to say, "Got it," when I heard a noise downstairs, like someone bumping into a piece of furniture. Then, a quiet, "Shit!"

CHAPTER 24

Lawton threw me a startled look. I put a finger to my lips. If we went down the stairs, we'd bump into the intruder or intruders. Even though Lawton had a gun, I wanted to avoid another shootout. Was it Harley and Dirk? It could be kids from the neighborhood wanting to see what they could loot.

Motioning Lawton to follow, I tiptoed to the end of the hall, away from the stairs. I sometimes used the window here at night to go out onto the flat roof over the back entry to think or pray. I unlocked the window and opened it quietly.

We slipped through, and I eased it closed. I stepped cautiously to the far corner of the roof and surveyed the back yard. I saw no one. My garage blocked my view of the alley behind it. The intruder could have a car in the alley and somebody could be staying with the car. I listened but heard nothing. I quickly dismissed the idea of waking my neighbor Jerry to call the police. We'd be too exposed while waiting for him to answer his door. Better to try a neighbor a few doors away.

I shoved the sermon folder into the back of my jeans. Getting down on my hands and knees, I slid over the side of the roof and dropped to the ground, moving quickly to make way for Lawton.

I glanced toward the back door. It was standing wide open. I was sure I'd closed it. Lawton and I raced across the neighboring backyard and pushed our way through the hedge into the next yard and around to the front of the house.

I rang the bell and waited. Lights came on. The curtain parted. The door stayed closed.

"Call the police," I said. "I'm your neighbor from a few doors down. My house was the one that burned the other night. There's an intruder in my house."

* * *

The police searched the house. Once again, neighbors stood around in bathrobes talking with each other, the night lit by flashers on a squad car. A cop escorted me through the house with a flashlight so I could tell him if anything was missing. Nothing obvious had been taken, but it was hard to tell because of the mess from the fire.

As we came back out to the street, Red Feather and Mad Dog arrived, concerned that Lawton hadn't gotten back to the pad. To top things off, my rental car wouldn't start, so Red Feather dropped me off at Nathan's.

Tired as I was, I couldn't sleep. My mind buzzed with questions and speculation. Were Dirk and Harley the intruders at my house? If they'd read the newspaper article about the fire damage being minor, they might think that I was still living there. Why didn't they just get out of town while they could? It might have been anyone at my house looking for something to steal, but I couldn't shake the feeling that it was Dirk and Harley.

I began to reevaluate the motive for the murders? To clean up the city like the note on Deacon's body suggested? I didn't buy it any more. Why single out two female gang

members and a head? Suppose Dirk was also guilty of the murder of that young woman in Detroit. If he was into killing young women, why kill Deacon? Deacon must have known something that could tie Dirk to Star and Cat's deaths. Had Deacon gotten into that upstairs room at the station and discovered something incriminating like photos of naked girls? Perhaps that's why the room had been cleaned out by the time Sam went up there.

Harley probably had a history of protecting his nephew. I'd thought that might be the extent of his involvement, but he was the driver during the chase through downtown, even if Dirk was the shooter. Harley had to be in on the whole thing up to his eyeballs.

I was so frustrated I wanted to scream.

* * *

The sound of the phone jolted me awake. My insurance adjuster told me they were backed up and he wasn't sure when their contractor could get to our house. He'd keep me posted.

I called the car rental company, and they said they'd be at my house in an hour to fix or replace the car. I told them I'd left the key under the driver's side floor mat.

Nathan drove us to the Ministry in his VW van. Stacy was working the front desk, so we met with Lydia in my office for our staff meeting. We speculated fruitlessly as to the whereabouts of Dirk and Harley. Then Stacy buzzed and announced that Detectives Johnson and Kincaid were waiting to see Lydia and me.

Nathan left the room as the detectives entered. Johnson glared at me. "Going to your house last night at that hour was just plain dumb. Do you have a death wish?"

I was beginning to like that glare. "Nice to see you, too, Sid."

"Anyways, wanted to tell you there's no sign of Dirk or Harley. I think the idea of spotting your car on South Division was a good one. It just didn't work. How about if I have one of the guys bring it to the station and then get it back on the street tonight?"

I tossed him my keys.

A few minutes after the detectives left, I got a call from the car rental company. They had another vehicle waiting for me at my house. I buzzed Nathan on the intercom. "Can you drop me off at my place so I can get my new rental car?"

"No problem."

"Okay. I want to make a call first."

Jackie answered before the second ring. "So what's up? Another night of high drama? Nobody called me to report anything, so I guess I'll have to get it from you."

The lightness in her voice told me she was joking, but when I reported about the intruder at our house the previous night, I could sense her mood change.

"I think you'd better come out here so we can talk," she said.

"How about we meet at the restaurant so we can talk privately?"

"You know there's no privacy in Borculo. But that's fine. See you there."

Was I ready for another round with Jackie?

On the drive to Borculo, I obsessed about the murders. I still had little besides questions, assumptions and suspicions. I prayed that Dirk and Harley would be caught soon, before anyone else got hurt or killed. I was grateful Andy and Jackie were staying with her parents where they were safe.

Or *were* they safe? Dirk and Harley might be following me now. I checked my rearview mirror, then turned off the highway in Jenison to see if I was being tailed. I detoured

a short distance and then returned to the highway. No one seemed to be following me.

As I turned off onto the road that would take me to Borculo, I realized I was getting paranoid. But, hey, it was probably a good idea to be paranoid till Dirk and Harley were locked up.

Entering the restaurant in Borculo a short time later, I saw Jackie seated at a table by the front window. She was the only customer, so maybe we would have some privacy after all. I sat opposite her, wishing I could just feast my eyes on her. Instead, my paranoia made me look out the window so I could watch the traffic for any sign of Dirk and Harley.

The waitress came with a pot of coffee. "Hi, Reverend Vander Laan. Coffee?"

I ordered a pop, too preoccupied to remind her to call me Rob.

"So, you think it was Harley and Dirk at the house last night?" asked Jackie.

"Yes, I do."

"It's really dangerous for you in town. I don't want to lose you to those two assholes."

I glanced at Jackie, then turned back to look out the window. A black Chevy pickup went by. Had I seen one like it when I detoured through Jenison? Pickups were common in the rural community of Borculo.

"Rob, I'm talking to you!"

My attention jerked back to Jackie. "I'm sorry, Jacks. It's just that I'm so paranoid. I'm watching the traffic to make sure I wasn't followed out here." I looked out the window again as a car drove by.

"Sorry I jumped on you, hon. You need to be paranoid."

"At least it's safer for you and Andy here than in town," I said.

"You could stay out here, too. Maybe take a little vacation from work. They have to catch Dirk and Harley soon."

I looked at her, not really seeing her, and then returned my gaze to the occasional vehicle passing on the street. The black pickup was going by again. "Jackie, do you recognize that pickup?"

Jackie turned to look and identified the truck as belonging to a local farmer.

My shoulders dropped and I let out a whoosh of air. Jackie reached across the table, took my hand and squeezed it. We drank our pops and held hands for a few minutes without speaking.

Suddenly what Jackie had said before registered. "Jacks, did you say that you don't want to lose me and that I could stay out here with you and Andy? Are you in a different place about our relationship?"

She looked at me with that soft-eyed gaze that always made me melt. "For better or worse. I'd say these last few weeks have been the worst. Anyway, big guy, I'm definitely hanging around."

I glanced up to see the waitress turning away and wiping her eyes. So much for privacy in Borculo.

"Let's go," I said, getting to my feet and tossing a buck on the table. "I want to see Andy." I practically danced out of the restaurant with my wife.

At the farm I played catch with my little guy in the back yard and then helped him net a couple of butterflies.

Later, Jackie and I went behind the barn to shoot clay pigeons. The activity always helped Jackie work out tension. Her horse, Winston, galloped to the far end of the pasture when he saw the guns. I loaded skeet into the thrower for Jackie and let it fly. I kept trying to throw in an unexpected direction at the last second. Jackie missed two out of a couple dozen. Then she threw for me, and I hit about half of them. Jackie's dad stood with Andy by the fence and watched.

"Mama's a way better gun shooter than you, Daddy," pronounced Andy. No one questioned his verdict.

After we cleaned the guns and put them away, I phoned Nathan to let him know I wouldn't be there for supper.

When we finished eating, I said, "Jackie, since I'm going back to town to do street ministry with Lydia, I might as well stay at Nathan's." It was my answer to her suggestion at the restaurant that I stay with her at the farm till Harley and Dirk were caught.

She gave me a soulful look that almost made me change my mind.

I took her hand and grinned. "Friday and Saturday nights are when most of my congregation convenes, and you know how I hate to skip church," I said, trying to lighten her mood. This time it worked. Jackie smiled back.

After I called Lydia and told her when I'd pick her up, I gave Jackie a hug. Andy, as usual, wiggled his way between us. "Time for an Andy sandwich," I said. I picked him up, and Jackie and I squeezed him between us. Andy gave me a kiss, then turned to give Jackie one. He rapidly showered each of us with kisses. When Jackie and I began to dodge him and kiss each other, Andy wanted none of that. He giggled as he tried to keep his head between us.

When he started to wheeze a little, I sat down on a kitchen chair and held him on my lap, talking quietly. Sometimes his asthma started acting up when he got too excited or laughed a lot. I helped him calm down until his breathing returned to normal and then headed back to Grand Rapids.

On the drive into town, I debated about the safety of Lydia's going with me on night ministry while Dirk and Harley were on the loose. When Lydia came out her front door, one look told me she wasn't likely to be talked out of going. Her cheeks had the flush of a schoolgirl. She tossed a light jacket into the back seat.

"Lydia," I said, as she got into the car, "I've been thinking maybe you shouldn't do night ministry with me till Dirk and Harley are caught. I just don't think—"

"Don't be silly. Now let's go. Wild Bill is doing another gig at Koinonia. Why don't we start there?"

Well, I thought, *that went pretty much like I expected.*

As we headed downtown, a police car followed me. Nothing like being shot at to make me appreciate being tailed by the GRPD. Driving through downtown, I observed that the circuit wasn't as congested as usual, probably because of the news about the murders.

Our evening, however, was a busy one. Our clergy/granny duo continued to draw people at the coffee house, Swinging Doors and Amigos Bar.

It was midnight when Lydia and I pulled into the parking lot downtown. There were only a dozen cars in the lot and not many kids. We saw Lawton and a handful of Souls coming up the street toward us. They'd probably come from Drop-in, which had just closed. They walked into the lot and greeted us.

"Hey, Chaplain," said Lawton. "I applied for a job as cook at Windmill Cafe." He reached into his pocket and handed me a piece of paper with the manager's name and phone number. "I was wonderin' if you'd let him know what a great guy I am."

"No problem," I said. "Shall I tell him that for an additional fee, you'll provide security for the place?"

"I didn't know you could cook," said Lydia.

"He can't," chorused several gang members, laughing.

A short time later, Lydia and I moved on to River City where Sam's boss looked tense. "Sam didn't show for work tonight," he said. "She was supposed to be here at six-thirty, I've been calling her place, but I don't get an answer."

Lydia's face blanched. "When did you talk to her last?"

"Middle of the afternoon. I called her about next week's schedule, so she was okay then."

I used the phone at the bar to call Johnson. Neither he nor Kincaid was available. I left an urgent message for them

with the officer at the desk and added that Lydia and I were heading over to Sam's place. I asked the bartender for her address and gave it to the officer, requesting that he send someone to check it out.

Lydia and I rushed out of the bar. We rode in silence to Sam's building. A cruiser was parked in front, lights flashing. Behind the cruiser was Sam's car. I raced up the covered outside stairway to Sam's second floor apartment with Lydia at my heels. I dreaded what we'd find.

Chapter 25

Lights were on in Sam's apartment, and the cop whose cruiser I'd bumped at the police station, stood at the top of the stairs in a little entry porch.

"Miss Fairchild is not here and the door was left open," he said.

Thank God we weren't finding another body. "That's her car parked behind your cruiser," I said. Looking into the kitchen, I saw another officer. A half-eaten sandwich on a plate and a bottle of pop were on the table. A chair lay tipped over on the floor.

I turned around at the sound of footsteps hurrying up the stairs. Johnson stepped onto the crowded porch, a little short of breath, Kincaid right behind him.

After getting the report from the uniformed officers, Johnson instructed them to check the downstairs apartment to see if anybody witnessed anything and to interview the neighbors. Johnson turned to me as the two cops squeezed by us. "So what's the story?"

"We went to River City Lounge," I said, "and the bartender told us that Sam never showed up for work. We called the station to report it and then came here."

"Sam's shift was supposed to start at six-thirty," added Lydia.

I took a deep breath and tried to let go of my anxiety. "The bartender told us he talked with Sam on the phone the middle of the afternoon and she seemed fine."

"We'll finish checking the apartment," said Johnson, "and then go talk to the bartender."

I tried to hide the panic I felt as Lydia and I hurried to my car. "Let's get back to River City," I said, "so we can tell Sam's boss what we've found here and see if she's contacted him yet. I mean, let's not jump to conclusions. Maybe she had a family emergency or something." I was trying to calm myself as much as Lydia.

"A family emergency? She leaves a chair tipped over, the door open and doesn't take her car, doesn't call her boss? Don't forget that someone may have seen her snooping upstairs at the station."

All the things I'd been thinking.

"After we go to River City, I'd like to go home," said Lydia, "just in case Sam tries to call me. I don't know, maybe that's silly, but I did give her my number."

When we got to River City, we told Sam's boss what we had found at her apartment.

"Shit. I was afraid of something like that." He leaned with both hands on the bar.

"Detectives Johnson and Kincaid will be in soon to talk with you," I said.

"You think the cops will care enough about a cocktail waitress to do any good?"

"Yes, I do. Johnson knows Sam, and I trust him. Kincaid seems solid too."

"I guess all we can do is hope and pray."

I drove to Lydia's, walked her to the door and gave her a long hug. It was understood we'd call if either of us heard anything.

I sat in the car, drumming my fingers on the steering wheel. I hated feeling so helpless, but I couldn't think of

anything to do. I pounded the steering wheel in frustration. Sam must be terrified. If she was still alive.

I drove mindlessly for half an hour until I realized I was in the neighborhood of Lookout Park. I turned into the park and shut off the engine. I looked over the city, the lights, the traffic moving below, people going about their business, getting drunk, loving, dying. Sam was out there somewhere.

I prayed for her safety and that she would be found soon. The knot in my stomach was, if anything, worse. "Cast your cares upon Him," went through my mind. The knot in my stomach made it clear that I was still hanging on to my cares. I thought of the adage: "Pray like it's all up to God and work like it's all up to you." I liked that sentiment. But if I was going to work like it was up to me, what the heck should I do?

I decided to go to the Windmill Cafe for coffee. If the manager was in, I'd talk to him about Lawton. It was something to do. At the restaurant I slid onto a stool at the counter, and the waitress came over with the coffee pot.

"Coffee, Father?"

I made myself smile. "Yes. Thanks." As she poured the coffee, I read the note Lawton had given me and asked her if the manager was in.

"Yes, he is. You want to talk to him?"

"If he's not busy."

"I'll check with him."

The manager came over a moment later and extended his hand."

I introduced myself and said that Lawton had given my name as a reference for his job application.

Twenty minutes later, I walked quickly from the restaurant in a light rain and dropping temperature. As I got into my car, I spotted Lydia's jacket in the back seat. I was only five or ten minutes from her house and decided to swing by to see if her lights were on. They were. I parked at the curb and grabbed her jacket.

When I rang the doorbell, Lydia appeared wearing a light housecoat, her knitting in her hand. "What?" Then she noticed I had her jacket. "Oh, I left it in your back seat. You want to come in for coffee? I'm too worried about Sam to sleep. How come you're still out?"

I handed her the jacket as I stepped inside. She tossed her knitting on a chair, hung the jacket in the closet and headed for the kitchen. I followed, pausing to notice a record album on a table—the soundtrack from *Easy Rider.* "Did Nathan let you borrow that?" I pointed to the album.

"I bought it after I saw the movie," she said, looking back. "I love that new actor, Jack Nicholson. I hope we see a lot more of him."

I sat down at the kitchen table as Lydia poured coffee into two mugs, and I told her about my stop at the Windmill Cafe to talk to the manager about Lawton.

"What's your guess as to why Dirk and Harley would take Sam, if they did?" I asked.

Lydia paced the kitchen. "Maybe Dirk wanted to finish what he started upstairs at the station. Or, if someone was in the room behind the mirror, Sam may be a liability they want to get rid of."

"But they would know that Sam didn't find anything, so would they risk staying in town for that? We know they're after me, so maybe they took Sam to get at me. Still doesn't make any sense though—"

The phone startled us. Lydia rushed into the dining room. I stood and watched from the doorway. She went white as a ghost. When she hung up, she dropped into a chair by the phone.

I crossed the room to her, leaned down and grasped her shoulders firmly. "What is it?"

"They've got Sam. The guy said, 'Tell Rob if he wants to see Sam alive, come to eight ninety five Tuttle Street and come alone.' My goodness, Rob, that address is just a block over."

"How would they know your phone number?"

My name's been in the paper with those newspaper articles on the Ministry, and I'm in the phone book."

"Then they know where you live. They would know I'm here."

"Not necessarily. My address isn't listed with my phone number, and the guy said to find you and get you over there."

I stood up straight. "I am not going over there alone." I lifted the receiver, called the police station, and quickly filled Johnson in. I gave him Lydia's address as well.

"Stay put!" he said.

I relayed his order to stay where we were.

"We can't wait," Lydia said, jumping up from the chair.

I shook my head, trying to clear my brain. "Hold it. We have to think like they would. What would keep you or me from notifying the police, which I just did? If I were the one who snatched Sam, I'd give an address on the opposite side of the street or maybe next door so I could split if the cops showed up."

"You're right. There's an alley behind my place and the next street is Tuttle. Let's start with the house opposite eight ninety-five Tuttle. We can check it from the alley. I know all the houses in the block. Just a minute." She disappeared quickly into another room and returned, wearing slacks and a sweater, her purse slung over her shoulder.

She led the way out the back door, and we crossed her back yard to the alley. As we passed the second garage, I saw a small pile of bricks. I picked up two of them. We passed the third garage. There wasn't much light in the alley. The rain was now a drenching downpour. Good. That would cover any noise we made.

Lydia stopped behind the fourth garage and pointed at it. The dilapidated garage door was partially open. It looked like the track the door slid on was broken. I looked inside

and saw a black Chevy pickup, probably a few years old. It had been backed in so that it faced the alley. Lydia was peering around the corner of the garage toward the house. She pointed. “The people who live there are in Europe for the summer,” she whispered.

I looked toward the back stoop of the house and saw a light on in what was probably the kitchen. I mimed to Lydia that I was going to sneak up and peek in the window.

I slid along the side of the garage, a brick in each hand, and then ran in a low crouch to the back of the house. Cautiously, I inched my head up and peered inside through the window. Sam, alive and well, thank God, sat at the kitchen table. Dirk stood at the counter, a gun in his hand, pouring a cup of coffee as he kept his eyes on her.

I heard a muffled voice coming from another room in the house. As Dirk turned to answer, Sam glanced toward the window. Not daring to breathe, I stood up so I could be seen. Sam’s face showed a quick expression of surprise. Then she looked down so as not to give me away. I did my crouch–run back to Lydia.

I whispered my report to her.

“I’m going around to the front to create a distraction while you get Sam out,” she whispered.

I put the bricks down and held up a finger to indicate she should wait a moment. Then I slipped into the garage and opened the driver’s door of the pickup as quietly as I could. I felt around for the hood release and pulled it. I froze at the sound. In a few seconds, Lydia appeared. She held up her hand, making the okay circle with thumb and forefinger. She disappeared again, and I stepped to the front of the truck, raised the hood, and moved my fingers over the engine until I found the distributor cap. I popped loose the two snaps and yanked the cap free of the plug wires. Closing the hood, I walked out to Lydia and showed her the cap. Then I tossed it into the bushes on the other side of the alley.

Lydia picked up the two bricks. I watched her turn into the back yard next door. I waited a moment, then crouch–ran back to the window, inching my head up again to look into the kitchen. Sam was sitting in the same place, with Dirk sitting across from her and drinking his coffee, gun still in his hand. Harley, standing in the kitchen doorway, said something and then moved away toward the front of the house. As Dirk's gaze followed him, Sam stole a glance at me.

The sound of glass shattering broke the silence. Dirk practically flew off his chair and charged toward the source of the sound. In the kitchen doorway he suddenly swung back, pointed the gun at Sam, who was halfway out of her chair, and yelled something I couldn't make out.

At the second sound of breaking glass, Dirk turned away from Sam again. She was on her feet in a flash. She snatched the coffee pot off the counter. As Dirk whipped his attention back to her, she threw the hot coffee at him. He screamed and covered his face with his hands, dropping the gun.

Sam was out the back door before I reached it. I heard gunshots. I grabbed her hand, and we fled across the alley, cutting through the neighbor's yard. We raced down Lydia's street, ran up the front steps of her house and through the front door, and fell onto the couch.

Sam was in my arms, laughing and crying. We held each other tightly for a few minutes as our breathing returned to normal. Then I got up and closed the door.

A moment later the back door exploded open, and Lydia rushed in, panting heavily. Dropping her purse on the dining room table, she went into the bedroom and returned with blankets. Wet and chilled, we all wrapped ourselves in the blankets and huddled in the living room.

Sam told us how Dirk and Harley had surprised her at her apartment and abducted her at gunpoint. I didn't want to think about the mess we might have been in if the police had arrived while we were freeing her.

The doorbell sounded. I inched back the curtain by the couch and peered out. Two uniformed cops stood on the porch. Still wrapped in a blanket, I opened the door. The officers were young, one tall and skinny, the other shorter and with the upper body of a man who worked out with weights.

"Detective Kincaid sent us over to make sure you're okay," said Muscle Guy.

I told them Sam was with us and that we were all safe. The taller officer returned to the cruiser to radio the news to Johnson and Kincaid. Muscle Guy came in to take our statements. After a moment, the other officer joined us.

As the two cops finished with us, the detective duo entered. A boozy smell clung to Johnson. The tension between the two detectives was palpable, as if the air around the two men were electrified. The uniformed officers felt it, too, and seemed to shrink into themselves.

CHAPTER 26

Johnson glared at us without saying anything, then turned to the uniforms. "So what you got?" he growled.

Muscle Guy repeated the gist of what we'd told him.

Johnson turned to Lydia and me, his face and neck red as a ripe tomato. "Do you have any idea what might have happened if we'd arrived while you two were playing God's rescue squad? All three of you could have been killed. Of all the dumb, amateurish … Jesus, Joseph and Mary!"

Silence seemed the wisest course.

Johnson continued to glare, breathing heavily. Finally, he shook his head. "The guy at the address you gave me came out when he saw the cruisers pull up. Told us he heard glass breaking and gunshots across the street. He said that, while he was calling it in, he saw a dark blue, late-model Chrysler sedan squealing away from the curb. Just when we get a handle on the vehicle Boyle and Scanlon are driving, they've stolen a different one. Neighbor guy also told us the couple that lives in the house across the street is in Europe for the summer. He mentioned seeing someone, a woman he thought, running down the sidewalk before the Chrysler took off."

"Dirk and Harley escaped?" I knew the answer, just didn't want it to be true.

"Yeah," Johnson said in a quieter voice. "The evidence crew will go through the house with a fine-tooth comb. Found a pickup in the garage. Lady in the house on the other side of the alley said she saw a couple of people prowling back there, and one of them threw something in her yard. Said she called it in. We found a distributor cap from the pickup in the bushes. I assume one of you knuckleheads did that."

I nodded.

"We've got uniforms all over the city looking for Boyle and Scanlon, but nothing so far. Damn! Sorry, Lydia. We should have picked these jokers up by now."

Kincaid stood to the side, arms folded across his chest, a hard look on his face I'd not seen before. His gaze never left Johnson.

My mind went to the black pickup I'd disabled. I wasn't sure if it was like the one I'd seen in Jenison. Jackie thought the one we'd seen from the restaurant in Borculo belonged to a farmer she knew. But had she actually seen the farmer driving it, or just assumed it was his? I shivered.

"Sam," said Johnson, "did Boyle or Scanlon hurt you physically or try to rape you or anything?"

"Dirk touched my breasts and slapped me when I pushed his hand away. When I screamed, Harley came in and made Dirk quit. He told Dirk to keep a gun on me all the time, and keep his hands off me. Dirk hung his head like a little kid when Harley chewed him out. It was weird."

Johnson ran a finger under his collar. "Maybe Harley Scanlon plays a bigger role in this thing than I thought. Anything else that you saw or heard that you think we should know?"

Kincaid's scowl grew darker, but he took his notebook and pen from his pocket.

Sam cast a quick glance at me and said, "Dirk said Rob was a sucker, so he was sure Reverend Pervert—that's what he called Rob—would turn up to try to save me."

Why would Dirk call me Reverend Pervert? I shook my head and squinted as if that could help me see something I couldn't quite make out. I thought of the public displays of affection the kids sometimes showed. Harley had said the girls were all whores, and Dirk probably felt the same. Was I perverted, then, in Dirk's mind, by association? Or maybe he thought all clergy were perverts. Then a thought hit me. Could a priest or minister have molested Dirk when he was a kid? I wished I knew more about adults molesting children and the effects on the children. I wondered if it happened a lot. Maybe people didn't want to talk about it. That way society could pretend it wasn't a problem.

I came out of my reverie, knowing I'd missed some of Sam's answers to Johnson's questions. At a pause I said, "I wonder if Dirk could have been molested by a clergyman."

Johnson flashed me a look, bushy eyebrows shooting up. "Yeah, I've looked into that. We'll come back to the molestation angle in a minute."

Kincaid closed his eyes and shook his head, then resumed jotting notes.

Johnson shifted his attention back to Sam. "Anything else?"

Sam pulled her fingers through her damp hair. "Dirk said he was going to make a movie with me. That was when he started copping a feel and I threw a fit. He was still talking about the movie when Harley came storming in. Harley was really mad. He slapped Dirk on the back of the head and ordered him to keep his mouth shut."

Johnson glanced at Kincaid who was studying his notes, then turned back to us. "Get a hold of me, Sam, if you think of anything else, no matter how unimportant it may seem. Now, Rob, just so I'm clear. You were in back of the Tuttle house the whole time, and you got Sam out?"

"Sam got herself out. All I did was get her back here."

"And, Lydia, you were out front, causing the commotion with the bricks we found in the living room and bathroom?"

"That's right." Lydia smiled broadly.

"In the report you gave these two officers here, there is no mention of a gun. But a couple of shots were fired from outside the house into the living room, and the neighbor reported hearing gunshots. Do you own a gun, Lydia?"

"Yes, sir. I surely do. I must have forgotten to mention it in all the excitement. I fired two shots into the living room so that Harley or Dirk wouldn't come storming out the front door and chase me or shoot me. I'm not as fast as I used to be, and it seemed only fair to better the odds of my getting away. You can understand that." She gave Johnson another smile.

"May I see your gun, Lydia?"

She got her purse off the dining room table, opened it, retrieved the gun, and handed it to Johnson. He broke it open, smelled it, emptied it, closed it again.

"Sorry, Lydia, but I'm going have to keep this for a little while."

Lydia gave him her shit-list look.

"Was Dirk molested by a clergyman?" I asked again.

Kincaid looked at me, back at Johnson, and sighed. It was clear that Kincaid didn't approve of Johnson letting us in on so much related to the case. It made sense to me that it might not be good cop procedure, but Johnson had been doing it ever since he'd told me about losing his son. I made a mental note to see what else I could find out about his son. Even so, there seemed to be more to the tension between the two detectives than Kincaid's irritation with Johnson about sharing information.

"Cousin of mine on the Chicago force interviewed Dirk Boyle's mother," Johnson said. "When Boyle was a teenager he tried to join a gang of hoodlums in the neighborhood. The

gang beat him up and sent him home with a broken arm and a bunch of cuts and bruises."

"That could explain Dirk's having it in for the gang kids."

"Boyle's mom also said that the minister from their church is in prison for statutory rape. A number of similar allegations against the minister came up in the investigation, but only two were proved. Nothing about the minister molesting Boyle, but it's a possibility."

I nodded, wondering how difficult it might be to prove molestation cases if no one wanted to talk about it.

"Then there's this," Johnson continued. "We already knew that Dirk Boyle's old man is doing time for murder. The Chicago cops figure Harley Scanlon was in on the murder, but it couldn't be proved. If Scanlon was in on it, but his brother took the rap and didn't rat Scanlon out … See where I'm going with this?"

"Yes, Harley could feel obligated to take care of Dirk."

"Yeah, and he takes care of Boyle's mother, too. She says that Scanlon is a saint. He sends her money sometimes. She gets a new car every few years and my contact says she recently had the house redecorated. Scanlon and Boyle ran a gas station in Detroit before they came here. I don't see how they could make enough to support themselves and give that much to Boyle's mother. That's about it."

It was a lot to digest.

I turned to Sam. "You probably don't want to go back to your apartment."

Lydia took Sam's hand. "She's staying with me tonight."

Belatedly, I remembered my promise to Sam's boss. "Sam, I told your boss I'd call him as soon as I learned anything. You want to give him a buzz, instead?"

While Sam was on the phone, Johnson turned to the uniforms. "I want you guys to drive by this place a buncha times the rest of the night. Now let's get out of here."

I stood, took off the blanket and handed it to Lydia. Sam, who'd finished her phone call, gave me a hug.

I left with the cops and drove to Nathan's. Johnson and Kincaid followed me, Kincaid driving for a change. I saw in my mirror that the left front fender of the cruiser was buckled. I thought of the alcohol smell on Johnson and the charged atmosphere between the detectives. Had Johnson had too much to drink and been in a fender bender?

Back at Nathan's, I dreamed of Lydia wearing a western hat and cowgirl boots, two six-guns in holsters on her belt.

* * *

"Hey, Rob," said Nathan. "What's with the wet clothes hanging in the bathroom? Get caught in the rain?"

I'd awakened as the guys were gathering for breakfast. I joined them at the table and poured myself a cup of coffee. Nathan had made a heaping plate of pancakes. Between bites, I told the guys the story of Sam's abduction and rescue. When I came to Sam's report about Dirk referring to me as "Reverend Pervert," Nathan said, "Well, Reverend, "there's some truth to that. You are a little perverted. Of course, you can't help it, seeing as how you're totally depraved. Did you know that only Calvinists are totally depraved? It says so in Calvin's Institutes."

"This is serious, man," I said.

"Lighten up, Rob."

I held both hands up in surrender. "Okay. Guilty on both counts—taking myself too seriously and being a little perverted."

When the conversation moved to the guys' lawn jobs, I left the table to call Jackie and tell her about the previous

night. Before I reached the phone, it started ringing. “I’ll get it,” I yelled.

It was Jackie. “Any word on Sam?”

“What? How’d you hear about Sam?”

“You have to ask? I gather that the cop you plowed into at the police station met you at Sam’s apartment. I assume that was Lydia with you?”

“Sam’s okay,” I said, and told her the rest of the story.

“I’m glad Sam’s okay, babe. You and Lydia, too. By the way, do you realize that you forgot to get your stitches out yesterday? So please get your butt over to the doctor’s office.”

“I’ll do that. There’s something else. Something I thought of last night. What was it? Oh, that black pickup we saw from the restaurant. Did you actually see the driver, or did you just assume you knew who it was?”

“I just assumed … Oh, my gosh. Were Harley or Dirk driving a pickup like that?”

“Yes. It was parked in the garage behind the house where they took Sam. I’d feel a lot better if you and Andy and your folks left the farm. It’s possible Harley or Dirk followed me to Borculo, maybe even followed us to the farm. Maybe it was that farmer driving the pickup we saw, but just to be safe—”

“I’ll talk to the folks about getting away from here and let you know what we decide. How soon are you going to get the stitches out?”

“I’ll take a quick shower and then go over there.”

“I’ll call to let you know what we’re going to do. If you haven’t heard from me when you’re finished at the doctor’s, call me.”

I hung up the phone and dialed my parents.

“We’ve been calling and calling,” Mother said, “but your line there has been busy. You never tell us anything. You think ministry is rescuing a cocktail waitress from guys with

guns? And your ministry partner is an old lady who carries a gun?"

Mother was in her usual form.

After my shower, I hurried downstairs as the phone rang again.

"I got a search warrant for the house Scanlon and Boyle rented," said Johnson. "We didn't turn up anything. Seems like they're ready to clear out of town, but their actions point to the fact they're bound and determined to get you first. It still makes no sense to me why you're so important to them. Anything you're not telling me?"

"I'm not holding anything back unless it's something I don't know that I know."

Johnson grunted. "You sure you don't want to take Kincaid's suggestions and go on a vacation?"

"I'm sticking around, Sid."

At the doctor's office later, after getting my stitches removed, I used the phone to call Jackie.

"I called the guy I thought was driving that black pickup," she said. "He told me he was working at his farm all afternoon, and nobody borrowed his truck. The folks and I decided getting away from here is a good idea. We're just about packed and ready to go."

"That's great," I said, feeling relieved.

"Andy is excited. He thinks it's a vacation. I guess it would be if I weren't so worried. We're going to the motel where you and I stayed in Grand Haven. How about joining us? Maybe Andy could sleep in the folks' room, and we could have a room to ourselves. Does that get your *klompen* stompin'?" *Klompen* are Dutch wooden shoes.

"Does it ever! Problem is I should be in town for night ministry, but I can join you for the afternoon."

"You might want to skip night ministry. We just heard the weatherman on the radio predicting severe storms for late this afternoon and tonight."

"Let's see what happens with the weather this afternoon. I'll stop at my office when I leave here to call Lydia and talk it over with her. I should be at the motel by one thirty. How's Andy doing?"

"His asthma started up a bit this morning, and I just gave him his med. See you at the motel."

I hung up, thinking how much I needed to spend time with my family. Lying on the Lake Michigan beach, playing with Andy in the sand, out for dinner. Maybe even time alone with Jackie. It sounded wonderful.

Until I started thinking about Dirk and Harley. The cops were bound to catch them soon, weren't they? I thought about Sam's description of Dirk's reaction when reprimanded by Harley. I'd thought Dirk seemed pretty evil, but now it looked like he was under Harley's control.

What about the movie thing Sam had mentioned? Perhaps Dirk wasn't only into pornographic photos of girls, but movies too. Had he made porno movies with other girls? What about the murdered girl in Detroit? Did he make a movie of her before killing her?

The sky was overcast, but the day was warming quickly after the cool temperatures of the night. I parked the car in front of the deserted Ministry and called Lydia from my office.

She told me that she and Sam were fine. "Sam's going to stay with me for the next few days," she added. "And she's not going to work tonight."

"Sounds good."

"Another thing," said Lydia. "Sam and I went to the library this morning to look at old *Times* articles on Detective Johnson's son's death. The interesting thing is that Johnson's boy was close to your age and actually looked a bit like you. That may explain why Johnson tells us so much about the case. Drives Detective Kincaid up the wall."

"You noticed that, too, huh? Different subject. Harley and Dirk may have followed me to Borculo yesterday. Jackie's

going with Andy and her folks to the motel in Grand Haven, which should be safer than staying at the farm. I'm going to join them there for the afternoon. I'm not sure if I'll come back in for night ministry because they're predicting severe weather. I'll call you about that later."

I heard Lydia relaying the information to Sam.

"Borculo!" I heard the exclamation in the background.

Lydia said, "Wait, here's Sam."

Sam came on. "Rob, I just remembered. When Dirk and Harley had me in the house on Tuttle, Dirk was complaining that you might not come after all. Harley said, 'Then we'll just have to go to plan B.' And Dirk said, 'Yeah, B for Borculo.'"

CHAPTER 27

A vise clamped down on my gut as Lydia got back on the line. "I'll make sure that the family has left the farm," I said, "and I'll let Johnson know what Sam just told me."

I hung up and dialed the farm. No answer. That meant they had left for Grand Haven. Had to mean that.

I forced myself to focus. I called the police station and left a message for Johnson. I reported what Sam had told me and that I might be staying the night at the motel, depending on the weather.

I was desperate to be certain my family was safe. And to put the murders behind me, at least for the afternoon. On the ride to Grand Haven, I kept looking into my rearview mirror.

At the motel, the desk clerk told me that my family had checked in. Thank God. The room was on the second floor and overlooked a small marina on Spring Lake, like the room Jackie and I had stayed in two weeks earlier. I opened the door and was greeted with a yell. "Daddy!" Andy jumped off the bed and ran to me. "We're on vacation, Daddy! Will you build a sand castle at the beach with me?"

I gave him a squeeze. "You bet, Andy." I turned to Jackie and she came into my arms. We had two whole seconds before Andy squirmed between us. I greeted Jackie's parents. "Everybody okay?"

Jackie's mom hugged herself nervously, then quickly dropped her arms and smiled. "Yes, we're all fine. A vacation is just what we need."

"I brought your swim suit and some clothes for you," said Jackie.

I hadn't even thought about packing. I knew the stress was making it hard for me to remember things. "Anybody hungry for lunch?" I asked.

"How about if we get burgers at the drive-in by the beach," proposed Jackie.

Andy was jumping on the bed. "I want French fries. I want French fries. I want French fries."

I dove onto the bed, tackled him, and began tickling him with my face on his tummy and sides. "You're a Dutch fry and I'm going to eat you.

I turned to Jackie. "*Moeder*," I said, using the Dutch for mother, "get me some catsup. Mmm. *Smakelijk eten*!" Tasty eating.

We put our swimming suits on so we'd be ready to go in the water as soon as we got to the beach. Jackie said, "Come on. Let's blow this pop stand."

"Yeah, let's blow this pop stand," yelled Andy.

After a quick lunch at the drive-in, we moved up the street to the park on Lake Michigan. The sun was breaking through the overcast sky as we trudged through the sand to a vacant spot on the crowded beach. Before I could sit down, Andy pulled me by the hand toward the water.

The afternoon was a kaleidoscope of sensation—the smell of suntan lotion, the warmth of sun and sand, the sounds of children yelling and laughing, parents scolding, and waves lapping at the shore. While Andy walked down the beach with his grandpa and grandma, Jackie and I lay side by side on our towels, holding hands. It was one of those endless, lazy summer afternoons, like when I was a kid. And like those long-ago days, it whizzed by all too soon.

I woke from a short nap as Jackie's hand left mine. "Look at that sky," she said. "We'd better get going."

The dark clouds rolled in off Lake Michigan and the wind increased. People scrambled to pick up their beach gear and gather their kids.

Andy didn't want to stop making wet piles of sand with his pail, so I went over and scooped him up while the others gathered the towels and beach chairs. "We've got to go, Andy. A storm is coming."

He cried as if his heart would break. "Let's stay, Daddy. We can watch the storm. I don't want to go, Daddy."

"The weatherman said this could be a bad storm. It's the kind you have to watch from indoors."

Back at the motel, we showered and changed for dinner. By then, the storm had blown in and the rain poured down in sheets. Andy and I watched through the window as boats rocked in the marina.

After dinner, we returned to our rooms. Andy got his pajamas on. I grabbed some books, and we went to Jackie's parents' adjoining room.

"I want one story from Mama and one from Daddy."

We arranged ourselves on a bed as Jackie's parents looked on from their chairs where they'd been reading.

"Mama first."

Jackie read *Bread and Jam for Frances*, and I read *I Will Go To the Moon*. After Andy said his prayers, the adults kissed him goodnight and went into the other room.

"Leave the door open a little, Mama."

"I will. 'Night, Andy."

"'Night, Mama."

I flicked the TV on with the sound turned low. There was a severe weather watch with a possibility of tornadoes. Jackie's parents resumed reading. The rain stopped, though the sky still looked threatening. I called Lydia and said I wouldn't come in for night ministry.

"Want to walk down by the boat docks?" I asked Jackie.

As we headed toward the door, I paused for a minute to listen to Andy who was singing about going to the moon. I wondered if I heard him wheezing slightly.

Out by the lake, the air smelled freshly washed. Thunder rumbled in the distance. Jackie and I strolled along the walkway, holding hands, listening to the choppy waters lapping at the boats and dock pilings. When we reached the end of the walkway, we looked at the lights across Spring Lake.

Jackie leaned her head against my shoulder. I felt a stirring in my groin.

"Wherever this Street Ministry gig takes you, babe," she said, "I'm sticking with you. I don't think either of us would be happy in a typical church. We're changing too much."

I put my hands on her shoulders, turned her toward me and kissed her deeply. The stirring increased. "I love you, Jacks."

"I love you, too, babe."

She pushed up against me and moved provocatively. "Think Andy is asleep yet?"

I dropped my hands to her butt and squeezed gently. "Let's go find out."

We returned to our room to find Jackie's dad sitting in the chair, still reading. Her mom was in the other room with Andy, who was wheezing moderately now. "Did Mom give Andy some more medication?" Jackie asked her dad.

"She didn't know where you put it."

Jackie looked quickly through her toiletries kit and her suitcase. "I remember putting it on the counter by the back door after giving some to Andy at the farm. I put it there so I wouldn't forget it. Dad, you put the bags in the car. That's when you called me, Rob. Shoot! I'm sure I left his medicine on the kitchen counter."

I said, "Don't sweat it, babe. I'll run back to the farm and pick it up. Shouldn't take longer than forty-five minutes."

"Wait," said Jackie. "I'm going with you." She grabbed her purse from the top of the armoire.

Her dad stood up and took her arm firmly. "You'd better stay with Andy, honey. I'll go with Rob. There's a tornado watch."

She jerked her arm away. "I'm going." She looked at me. "When I said I'm sticking with you, I meant it." She turned back to her father. "If anything should delay us and Andy gets worse, you and Mom take him to the ER in Muskegon. We could just plan to take Andy there, but you know how long it usually takes to get seen. It'll be faster to pick up his medicine from the farm. Let's go. Andy will be fine."

Jackie always handled Andy's asthma attacks with great calm, which helped the rest of us learn to do the same. But I saw fear in my father-in-law's eyes, and it wasn't about the weather or Andy's asthma. Suddenly, what was not being said hit me—Dirk and Harley, the reason for the sudden decision to leave the farm. I'd been lulled by the sweetness of the day into forgetting.

As I drove to Borculo in the growing darkness, Jackie turned in her seat to look out the rear window. "That sky looks really ugly," she said. "Turn on the radio."

I turned it on. No longer just a watch. A tornado *warning* was in effect and funnel clouds had been sighted over Lake Michigan. Counties in the path of the front should expect severe thunderstorms with hail and possible tornadoes.

Jackie was still looking back. "The sky is really weird, sort of yellowish-blackish. I've never seen it look like that before."

I white-knuckled the steering wheel as I raced east. Lightning and thunder were all around us. My heart leaped to my throat at one brilliant flash followed by a thunderous crash.

It was fully dark by the time we reached Borculo. The wind continued to buffet the car, and the lightning crackled

around us. The thunder was almost continuous. As we neared the farm, the storm diminished, moving off to the east. I slowed and pulled cautiously into the drive, peering forward as my headlights swept the garage, shed and barn. By the time I parked near the back door, the wind had stopped.

"I'll run in and get it," said Jackie. "You stay here."

"What if Harley and Dirk are inside?"

"You really are paranoid, aren't you?"

"Yes."

We got out of the car into an eerie stillness, the only sound a distant rumble of thunder.

Jackie came around the car and stood next to me. "Just to be on the safe side," she whispered. The click of her purse opening and closing sounded loud in the stillness. I felt comforted knowing a gun was in her hand, even as I prayed she wouldn't have to use it. I heard another click as she released the safety. Then all was quiet again.

There were none of the usual night sounds of cicadas, bullfrogs in the pond or the rustle of leaves in the oak trees. Nothing but an eerie silence.

I looked toward all the places someone might hide. The safe, familiar farm now felt ominous. I sensed Jackie's apprehension, too. The oppressive humidity combined with raw fear soaked the back of my tee shirt with sweat.

I nudged Jackie with my elbow. We moved toward the back door and stood under the small roof over the rear entrance. We waited, listened. I tried the door. Locked.

"Did you lock the door before you left?" I whispered.

"Yes." She retrieved her keys from her purse.

"What happened to the yard light?"

"Power's probably gone out with the storm."

That made sense. I took the key from her, unlocked the door. I slowly turned the knob and opened the door a crack. I waited a moment, then pushed it open all the way. Stop, look and listen—the childhood adage for crossing the

street—flitted through my mind. I strained my eyes but it was too dark to see anything beyond the door. No sounds either.

A muffled noise came from the direction of the barn, or was it my imagination? Jackie must have heard it too because we both turned around. It might have been Jackie's horse, snorting softly.

"Probably Winston," she whispered.

I turned again and stepped through the open door. I tried the light. Nothing. So Jackie was right. The storm had caused a power outage.

Unless the fuses had been removed by someone.

"There's a flashlight here someplace," whispered Jackie, pushing past me. "I'm not sure if the batteries are still good." She opened a cupboard. Suddenly the entry room was filled with light as she turned on the flashlight. We gasped simultaneously, too shocked by the sudden dispelling of darkness to check the area out. Jackie switched the light off and handed it to me.

I turned it on again, and we looked around, seeing nothing out of the ordinary. We went up the steps to the kitchen door. I opened it, sweeping the light through the kitchen. I felt too exposed with the light on, so I flicked it off again. Stepping inside I tried the switch to the right of the door, checking one more time with the same result.

I turned the flashlight back on, swung it once more around the kitchen. I leaned close to Jackie and whispered, "Might as well keep it on. We probably don't have to whisper."

"Okay," Jackie said in a quiet voice. "Here it is." She picked up Andy's medication and put it in her purse.

I tensed as a vehicle drove slowly past the front of the house, sounding loud in the stillness. Jackie and I looked at each other, our eyes reflecting the same question: *Harley and Dirk*?

CHAPTER 28

I ran into the living room, inched back the curtain, and peered out the window "The car has its lights off." I saw brake lights. "Now it's pulling into the farmyard across the road." That house and outbuildings were less than a quarter of a mile up the road and had been abandoned for years.

"Nobody ever goes in there," said Jackie.

Without waiting to see whether they were parking there or just turning around in the drive, I rushed back to the kitchen.

"Let's get out of here," said Jackie.

"If they pulled in there to turn around and come back here, we won't make it."

"Quick! Down the basement."

I locked the back door and raced down the basement steps after Jackie. She laid the flashlight on the workbench, unlocked the cabinet and handed me the 12-gauge.

Now I had my preferred weapon. I wasn't sure how I felt about that.

She opened the drawer at the bottom of the cabinet. I grabbed some slugs. I loaded the gun, and laid it on the workbench. I stuffed some extra slugs and buckshot in my pockets. Jackie locked the cabinet.

I'd been vaguely aware of a low rumbling increasing in intensity for the past minute. As I reached my hand toward the shotgun, the volume increased to a roar. Jackie and I looked at each other with apprehension. Then, letting out a sudden exhalation of air, I said, "It's only a train."

Jackie grabbed my arm fiercely. "There are no train tracks near here. That's a tornado."

"Quick, under the workbench," I said. I pushed Jackie down and under the bench, following her immediately and putting my arms around her.

Now the sound was deafening and there was no mistaking it. The whole house seemed to tremble.

Then the roar diminished. After a moment, we came out from under the bench and stood up. The flashlight lying on the workbench was still turned on.

At the sound of a loud bang we jumped.

Jackie grabbed the flashlight and turned it off, before handing it back to me. Her lips went to my ear. "That was the back door. Grab the shotgun."

Muffled noises from upstairs, moving into the kitchen. Then a voice that sounded like Dirk's. "Jesus Christ! That was close. I told you we should have parked—"

"Shut up! Let's find 'em."

I slipped the flashlight through my belt and picked up the shotgun. Extending my hand in front of me I found Jackie's shoulder. She made her way across the darkened basement, but not toward the steps we'd come down. I didn't understand what she had in mind. She stopped and we listened to the floor creaking overhead, the hum of voices.

I saw a bright flash through the basement windows as lightning struck close to the house. I heard an explosion of thunder. My heart raced.

"What are we doing, babe?" I whispered.

"We'll use the old basement steps and come out by the driveway. Flash the light."

I did and she began moving again. I slipped the light back under my belt and placed my left hand on her shoulder.

I felt her move up a step, then another. She fumbled with the latch. There was another flash of lightning close by, followed by a deafening crash of thunder. I felt, rather than saw, the old half door open as the rain and wind slapped my face. I kept my hand pressed against Jackie's shoulder. We moved as one up into the night. I closed the old basement door as silently as I could, and we set off toward the car.

Suddenly I froze, clamping down on Jackie's shoulder. "What?" she whispered impatiently.

"We can't take a chance on the car. They've probably disabled it."

As lightning flashed again, she pointed toward the road. A large tree limb, taken down by the storm, blocked the driveway. We couldn't get out with the car even if they hadn't disabled it. She turned and moved rapidly in the darkness toward the barn with me at her heels, my hand on her shoulder.

We froze again as a flash of lightning illuminated us. I felt the anticipatory tightening of Jackie's muscles and bolted with her, my hand now gripping her firmly. She slowed a moment later, and we moved forward cautiously. Dirk and Harley were still busy inside the house, but for how long? Jackie moved us to the left, then stopped.

A flash of lightning showed we were in front of the barn door. We ducked inside as the back door of the house slammed.

A yell. "They went into the barn!" Sounded like Dirk.

From the doorway, I aimed the twelve-gauge toward the house. I could see nothing. A second person emerged from the house holding a flashlight and the back door slammed again.

I aimed several feet to the right of the light so I'd miss them and the house, pumped a shell into the chamber and fired. I pumped another shell and fired again.

A loud, "Jesus Christ!" and the light went out.

I closed the door and followed Jackie swiftly across the barn toward the rear door that opened into the pasture. She bumped into something and I bumped into her. The flashlight clattered to the floor. I swore under my breath, but we kept moving.

We reached the rear door of the barn and stepped outside. Now what? I was sure Jackie had a plan, but, once again, I didn't know what it was. I heard a low whistle, and then I knew. In a moment, I heard the sound of galloping hooves and then a soft snorting. A flash of lightning revealed Winston nuzzling Jackie's shoulder as she stroked the horse's neck.

She grabbed a handful of mane and swung up to sit astride the big horse. Jackie often rode bareback. I had ridden Winston several times but always with a saddle. I worried whether the horse would be too nervous for Jackie to control, given the storm and the gunshots.

"Grab my hand and swing up, cowboy," she said.

I couldn't do it holding the shotgun. I'd probably pull her off the horse.

She read my mind. "The old stump, to your left. Quick!" It was the way she'd mounted Winston when she was young.

I moved through the soggy barnyard and stepped onto the stump as Jackie moved the horse alongside.

"Take the shotgun," I said. Somehow, I managed to drag myself up behind her. Winston was surprisingly still. Jackie passed the shotgun to me and urged Winston forward. I held the gun in my right hand and wrapped my left arm around Jackie's waist. We moved off in the darkness. I feared the next flash of lightning would expose us.

I didn't have to wait long before there was a bright flash followed by Jackie's yell, "Hang on!" I longed to drop the shotgun and wrap my other arm around her, but didn't dare. I held on for dear life. Another flash, thunder and gun shots.

I heard someone yell as we zigzagged right and left, Jackie guiding Winston with the pressure of her knees. Then darkness again, and Winston galloped straight across the pasture. I expected to slide off at any moment.

When Winston slowed to a trot, I took a ragged breath. The trot slowed to a walk. It was too dark to see. Looking back toward the barn, I hoped they would give up, but I knew better.

I saw headlights. They were moving. They stopped by the gate to the pasture. Someone, illuminated by the lights, was trying to open the padlocked gate. I reported this to Jackie.

"We're almost to the woods," she said. "Keep an eye back toward the barn."

I saw the headlights of the car backing up. Then I heard the engine revving. The headlights lurched forward. "They're crashing the gate," I said.

To my surprise, Jackie laughed. "We'll see how the car does following us."

As Jackie urged Winston to the right and then back to the left, I realized she was skirting the low spot at the far end of the pasture that tended to be muddy even in the driest of times. The sound of Winston's splashing walk made it clear that the low spot was now a small pond.

Soon we were near the fence. I slid off, hanging on to the shotgun, splashing as my feet hit the ground. Jackie slid off after me. She slapped Winston on the rump, and he galloped off.

As the headlights moved toward us, bouncing over the uneven ground, Jackie and I hurried forward. When we reached the fence, I stretched the barbed wire strands apart with a foot and a hand. Jackie climbed through, then did the same for me. Soaked and chilled, I followed her into the woods. She had often played here as a kid. Once we'd come with a blanket and made love under the oaks and maples.

Jackie stopped, then pulled me around a tree trunk. I thought I knew this spot. The moon found a way through the clouds for a couple of seconds, confirming my hunch. Two large oak trees stood five feet apart with boards nailed between, all that remained of a "cabin" Jackie had built when she was twelve. We dropped to our knees and peered over the boards as headlights bounced toward us.

I heard the snap of Jackie's purse closing.

They were close now. Another flash of lightning revealed my rental car, up to the floorboards in water, stopped not more than a dozen feet from us. The keys were in my pocket, so they must have hotwired it. I remembered Harley bragging once that he could hotwire most cars in less than three minutes. I heard the sound of the transmission thrown into reverse, wheels spinning, gears changing again, wheels spinning again as the car became more mired. The car idled, lights shining on our hiding place.

"We need to get away from the light," Jackie whispered.

I leaned toward her. "Not enough cover, and they have guns."

The sound of cursing came from the car. "I've got the headlight on our left," Jackie whispered. "You take the one on the right. And don't miss. If they fire at us, you take the driver."

Were these words really coming from the woman I loved?

The headlight, yes, but could I shoot at the driver? Whenever I'd hunted small game or deer with Jackie and her dad, I'd never been able to bring myself to kill anything. Of course, I wasn't that great a shot either.

"Jackie," I whispered, "I don't think—"

"Andy's not growing up without his parents!" she hissed.

I heard voices from the car, this time more hushed. Somebody killed the engine. The doors opened. The doors slammed shut.

"Now," whispered Jackie.

We both fired, my shot ringing out a second after Jackie's. Both headlights went out.

They returned fire. The top board between us disintegrated.

I dropped my aim slightly, and we both fired, only this time our shots sounded as one. Like a rookie, however, I failed to press the stock to my shoulder. The kick knocked me back on my butt as someone cried out. Or was it two cries? I scrambled to my knees and hid behind the tree. We waited.

A groan. Sounded like it was from the driver's side and it sounded like Dirk. "I'm hit. Goddamn. It's my leg. You guys okay?"

Guys?

"Harley? Bran?" Dirk's voice again.

Then, "Hush."

A volley of shots sprayed around us.

CHAPTER 29

We held our fire and listened. We heard the sound of splashing, probably someone moving quickly through the water. I risked a look around the tree, hoping for a flash of lightning. Seeing nothing, I jerked my head back. I popped more shells into my gun.

We crouched behind the two trees anchoring the remains of the "cabin" wall. More splashing sounds. No lightning or moonlight.

We waited, thoroughly soaked. When I moved to my left and reached toward Jackie to touch her shoulder, she was shivering.

The wind died and so did the rain. No more lightning. When the moon emerged from the clouds, we peeked out and saw the car in the pond.

"See anybody?" I asked Jackie.

"Looks like something by the front passenger side tire, but it's not moving.

I peered around the tree and stiffened at a muffled snort, then relaxed. If Winston had returned, it was probably safe.

"Hey, Winnie." Jackie spoke quietly.

We walked forward cautiously, keeping a careful eye on the car. Winston stood at the fence. After holding the wires for each other again and ducking through, we moved to the

driver's side of the car, looked inside and found it empty. We stepped around to the other side where we found Harley slumped against the front tire, hands in his lap, head on his chest as if he were napping. No gun in sight.

Jackie placed her hand on Harley's neck to check for a pulse. She looked up at me, shaking her head.

I touched her arm. "You okay, babe?"

"I don't know. I don't feel anything."

"Let's go," I said. "We've got to stop Dirk before he gets away."

As we raced back across the pasture with Winston trailing us, some things fell into place for me. "Jackie," I panted, "there was a third person in the car. After we fired at them, I heard Dirk say 'you guys.'"

"I wondered about that, too. Someone named Bran?"

"The third person must be Brandon Sharp from the camera store."

"But he's on your board of directors."

"Yes," I said. I made another connection about Cat's murder, then, that I didn't want to admit to myself, much less say out loud.

Back by the barn, we moved cautiously through the shattered gate with our guns ready. In the farmyard only Dirk was in view, wearing his baseball cap, leaning heavily on a pole as he limped toward the road. Must have been the pole used to prop open the back door of the barn. Was I wrong about Brandon? No, I was sure he'd been there.

I was trying to determine our next move when a familiar voice said, "Stand where you are, Dirk, and drop it."

Lawton stood, mostly protected by a tree, gun aimed at Dirk. No more than eight or ten feet separated the two men. What the heck was Lawton doing at the farm?

Dirk's weapon came up and two shots were fired. Lawton staggered back, but he remained upright, holding his

shoulder, his gun slipping to the ground. Dirk dropped to his knees. He still held his gun.

Jackie and I stood with our weapons aimed at Dirk. "Put your gun down, Dirk," I said.

Dirk kept his gun on Lawton, even though he was no threat now.

All thoughts of Brandon Sharpe fled. Before Jackie could stop me, I laid the shotgun down and moved quickly between Dirk and Lawton. I decided to play a long shot. Doing that had paid off with Sam's sister.

"Dirk," I said, trying to ignore the gun now pointed at my chest, "shooting me won't fix the wrongs your minister did to you."

His eyes widened and looked into mine for the first time. "How'd you know?" he said.

"It doesn't matter how I know. What happened with your minister was not your fault. You were a kid."

"Uncle Harley always said it was my fault."

"Harley was wrong. It was your minister's fault. Give me the gun."

I held my breath, then tried another tack. "My wife's here and she's a nurse. She can't help you until you hand over your gun."

The weapon dropped to the ground, and another familiar voice said, "I've got it." It was Lydia. I glanced up and saw Sam standing next to her. I gave them a look of disbelief, as Lydia picked up Dirk's gun.

Dirk shivered and fell to his side, his cap falling off. I helped him lie on his back and knelt above him, my hand on his shoulder. "I ain't gonna make it," he said.

Jackie moved to his other side and pulled up his shirt to check the wound in his abdomen. "Sam," she said, "run into the house and grab some towels from the rack in the kitchen." She pulled up his left pant leg to see the wound in his leg.

I flashed on my unfinished sermon: "The truth will set you free."

"Dirk," I said, "get it out while you can. Did you murder Star and Cat and Deacon?"

"I was takin' pictures of Star upstairs at the station. I had to leave for a minute. Killed her because I caught her snooping."

The piece I hadn't wanted to admit to myself now lodged clearly in my mind. I'd read a mystery about a serial killer who made stag films in which he murdered girls after raping them, all while the camera was rolling. I was so repulsed I hadn't finished the book.

Since the long shot had paid off, I tried again. "How about Cat?" I said. "You strangled her as part of a movie?"

"Uncle Harley made me. Like the other girls. Movies for special customers. Paid big bucks."

He coughed weakly and closed his eyes. I was afraid I was going to lose him, and I had too many questions. "Dirk." I squeezed his shoulder. His eyes fluttered open.

Jackie applied pressure to Dirk's abdominal wound, using a towel that Sam had brought. Jackie asked Lydia to wrap the wound on his leg.

"Why did you torch my house and come after me?"

"Bran's orders. First wanted to scare you off. In case you heard something in the bathroom. Then Bran said your racing away from me and Harley through downtown and getting Sam to snoop upstairs proved you were on to us."

"Was Brandon behind the mirror when Sam was up there?"

"Yeah. Brandon and Harley."

"Still, why didn't you and Harley just take off?"

"Can't tell you. Uncle Harley made me swear."

I wanted to shake him. "Your Uncle Harley is dead. Tell me, Dirk."

He looked into my eyes again, then his eyelids closed. I squeezed his hand and felt a weak attempt to respond.

"Dirk," Jackie said, "can you hear me?"

No answer.

Suddenly I wondered where Brandon was. He had probably cut through the pasture, crossed the road to the abandoned farmhouse, and was coming back with their car for Dirk. I desperately wanted it to be over. Let the police deal with Brandon. I'd done enough, taken enough risks.

I pictured Brandon sitting at board meetings, a caring member of the community. I saw him in my office, giving me advice, offering support, wanting all the details of whatever I'd gone through. I understood now that he was trying to determine what I knew about the murders and that hearing the details excited him. I visualized him behind the mirror watching young women being murdered. "Bran's orders," Dirk had said. Brandon, not Harley, had to be running the porno business. My jaw was clenched so tight it hurt.

I grabbed Dirk's cap and came to my feet. I saw Lawton sitting on the ground, his back supported by the tree. Sam was wrapping his shoulder with a towel. "Everybody stay put," I said. "I've got an idea for how to keep Brandon from getting away."

Before anyone could object or ask questions, I slapped Dirk's cap on my head. I grabbed the pole Dirk had used and raced down the driveway to the road, skirting the blown-down tree limb and Lydia's Chevy, parked at the end of the drive. A car approached, no lights on. I lowered my head and limped slowly forward, leaning much of my weight on the pole. I hoped the darkness and Brandon's anxiety to get away would be enough to fool him into believing I was Dirk.

Brandon's Cadillac stopped. He reached across and opened the passenger door. "Get in, quick. My wife will take care of you. What were the shots I heard?"

I kept my head turned away as I lowered myself carefully into the car, tossing the pole away.

"Listen," said Brandon. "Sirens."

He was just starting to accelerate when I leaned across the middle of the seat as if I were struggling to get all the way into the car. I reached over, rammed the gearshift into park. I turned the key off and yanked it from the ignition. I tossed it out the door as the car bucked to a grinding halt.

"It's over, Brandon," I said.

"Rob? What are you doing? Are you okay? I came out here to try to stop Harley and Dirk."

"Enough of your bullshit. Dirk told me all about you. You were the brains behind the mirror. You gave the orders. You got off on watching, didn't you? Always behind the scenes."

Brandon pulled out a gun and aimed it at me. I was surprised that I didn't feel afraid. I felt cold. I did not want the son-of-a-bitch to get away. I seemed to have used up all my compassion on Dirk.

"You had to keep sticking your nose into my business, Rob. I tried to warn you about that. I liked you at first but you didn't show me respect. You made me look bad at your board meetings and at the meeting with the businessmen. I couldn't let that go."

A sheriff's car pulled up behind us, flasher on, siren dying. A State police car rolled past, angling in front of us to cut off escape. Brandon gave up without a struggle.

The next couple of hours were a flurry of activity. Dirk and Lawton were taken away by ambulance. Brandon sat handcuffed in one of the cruisers. Lydia, Sam, Jackie and I were all questioned at length. Winston wandered into the farmyard just as Johnson and Kincaid arrived, causing a bit of commotion until Jackie put her horse in the barn.

Jackie called her parents at the motel to let them know we were okay. They had taken Andy to the hospital for treatment and now he was sleeping.

At last Lydia, Sam, Jackie and I collapsed in the living room of the farmhouse. Lydia reported how, earlier in the evening, Lawton had come over and told them his suspicions that Dirk and Harley had a stag movie business and sometimes killed the girl in the movie. Snuff flicks, he called them. He thought that was how Cat died.

"Lawton was kind of frantic," Lydia continued. "He believed you were a loose end and that Harley and Dirk would come after you if they found out where you were staying. I called the motel so Lawton could talk with you. When I learned from Jackie's dad that you and Jackie had gone back to the farm for Andy's medication, all I could think of was 'B for Borculo.' I called Johnson and then tore out here with Lawton and Sam."

We learned that county and State law officers, contacted by Johnson, had been delayed by the storm. Johnson and Kincaid had been held up by a road closure due to a downed tree. Because Lydia had taken a different route from Johnson's, she had avoided the delay.

After officers removed the limb from the driveway, Lydia and Sam headed back to Grand Rapids. Jackie and I used her mother's car to return to the motel. Mom came through the adjoining door into our room. She gave Jackie a hug, then held her at arm's length and gave her a long, searching look. "You okay, honey?"

Jackie's eyes glistened and the tears began streaming down her cheeks. She collapsed into her mother's arms. "I killed a man, Mama. I killed a man. Oh, Mama." She sobbed quietly as her mother held her till her sobbing ceased.

Then Jackie turned to me. "I guess I'm feeling something now." I put my arms around her and her crying resumed.

The adjoining door opened again and Jackie's dad slipped in, closing the door behind him. Jackie turned at the sound and went into his arms.

When Jackie stopped crying, she turned to me. Her smile was tentative as she looked at me through tear-bright eyes. "It's over, babe. With the help of your amateur detective team, we did it."

"I think I'd better call my folks," I said with a smile. "Just once I'm going to beat that dang Dutch grapevine."

"You'd better hurry then," said Jackie's mom, laughing through her tears. "But, frankly, I don't think you've got a chance."

Dad picked up on the first ring. "Hi, Dad, it's me."

"It's Rob," he called, not bothering to cover the mouthpiece. "Are you okay?"

Before I could answer, Mother's voice came on the extension. "Robbie, you actually shot and killed those three guys who were after you? What kind of ministry is that?"

The Dutch grapevine—what it lacks in accuracy, it makes up for in speed.

Epilogue

Lydia resigned from her position as secretary at the Ministry and became my permanent night ministry partner. Lawton recovered from his shoulder wound and was hired as a cook at Windmill Cafe. Red Feather moved back to Oklahoma.

As I'd suspected, Detective Sid Johnson, after having too much to drink, had been in an accident with his cruiser on the way to the house where Harley and Dirk were holding Sam. The chief had threatened him with early retirement unless he got counseling. He confided to me that the counseling was a waste of time.

Warren Van Boven was convicted and sentenced to ten years in prison for assault with intent to commit murder.

Contrary to his expectation Dirk Boyle recovered. I learned more about the murder/porno business at the trials of Dirk and Brandon, and Johnson later filled me in on the rest.

When Dirk realized Brandon was trying to pin everything on him and his uncle Harley, he decided to come clean. He killed Star after catching her snooping, as he'd confessed to me. Since she was too drunk to see straight, he took her to the Soul's apartment after she assured him no one would be there. He killed her there. He strangled Cat and other girls in Detroit and Chicago as part of the porno movie business. Cat had posed for the nude photos willingly, but she had resisted doing a movie until Dirk offered her a thousand dollars and promised to take her with them to L. A. and make her a famous movie star. Harley cut Deacon's throat after finding him snooping in the upstairs room at the station and ordered Dirk to stab him to make it look similar to Star's murder. It

had been Brandon's idea to pin the note to the body, hoping to mislead the investigation. Dirk said that Brandon and his wife ran the business. Dirk and Harley were ready to cut and run to L.A. to continue their operation there, but Brandon ordered them to kill me first. His leverage over Harley had been a movie he possessed of Dirk's father strangling a girl while Harley held her. Dirk was sentenced to life in prison.

Movies, photos and newspaper clippings of Cat, as well as murdered girls in Detroit and Chicago, were found in a safe in the basement of the camera store. Brandon finally confessed to their stag movie business but not the murders. He was nonetheless convicted of conspiracy to commit murder and sentenced to life in prison.

Brandon's wife got three months for her part as bookkeeper for the porno business. She also turned out to be the legal owner of the three businesses that Brandon had claimed to own and the gas stations Harley had managed. I wondered if her role in the whole thing had been fully revealed. Dirk, as well as Brandon and his wife, were still to be tried in Detroit and Chicago.

So far, the Reverend John Vanden Berg, my nemesis on the Urban Mission Committee, had not made good on his threat to have me brought up for an ecclesiastical examination of my theology. I wondered if he was biding his time.

My family life was good. Jackie wondered sometimes whether killing Harley had been necessary, but she didn't dwell on it. We eventually moved back into our house.

Sam continued to work at the bar and attend Junior College. I still had the occasional Samantha fantasy. I could live with that.

The End

F
HAG

10133888

Hager, Terry.
Death on the night watch : a
Reverend Rob Vander Laan
mystery.

WITHDRAWN

Sioux Center Public Library
102 South Main Avenue
Sioux Center, IA 51250

Made in the USA
Lexington, KY
21 March 2011